El Camino de Santiago

A Pictorial Pilgrimage

A Pictorial Pilgrimage

SANTIAGO

ISBN: 978-0-9799628-1-3

Published by
James Clem
P.O. Box 598
Alpine, Ca. 91903
619-820-2395
Sore Feet Publishing

El Camino de Santiago

A Pictorial Pilgrimage

By

Jim and Eleanor Clem

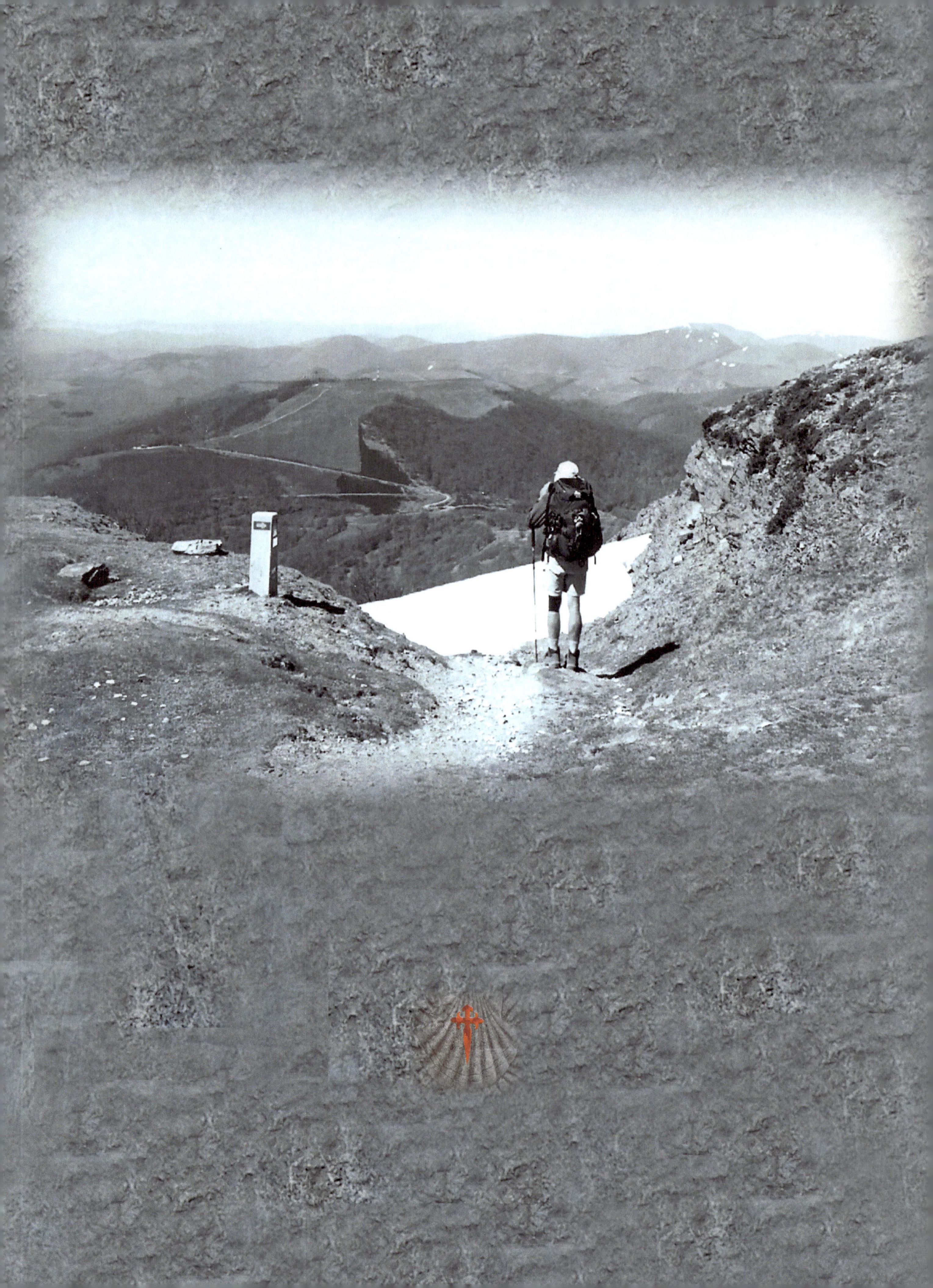

Dedication

To

Deborah and Jamie
Dave and Dave
and of course
Big Jake

To our family and friends

To everyone who puts on their boots and hits the trail

To everyone who keeps going when the going gets tough

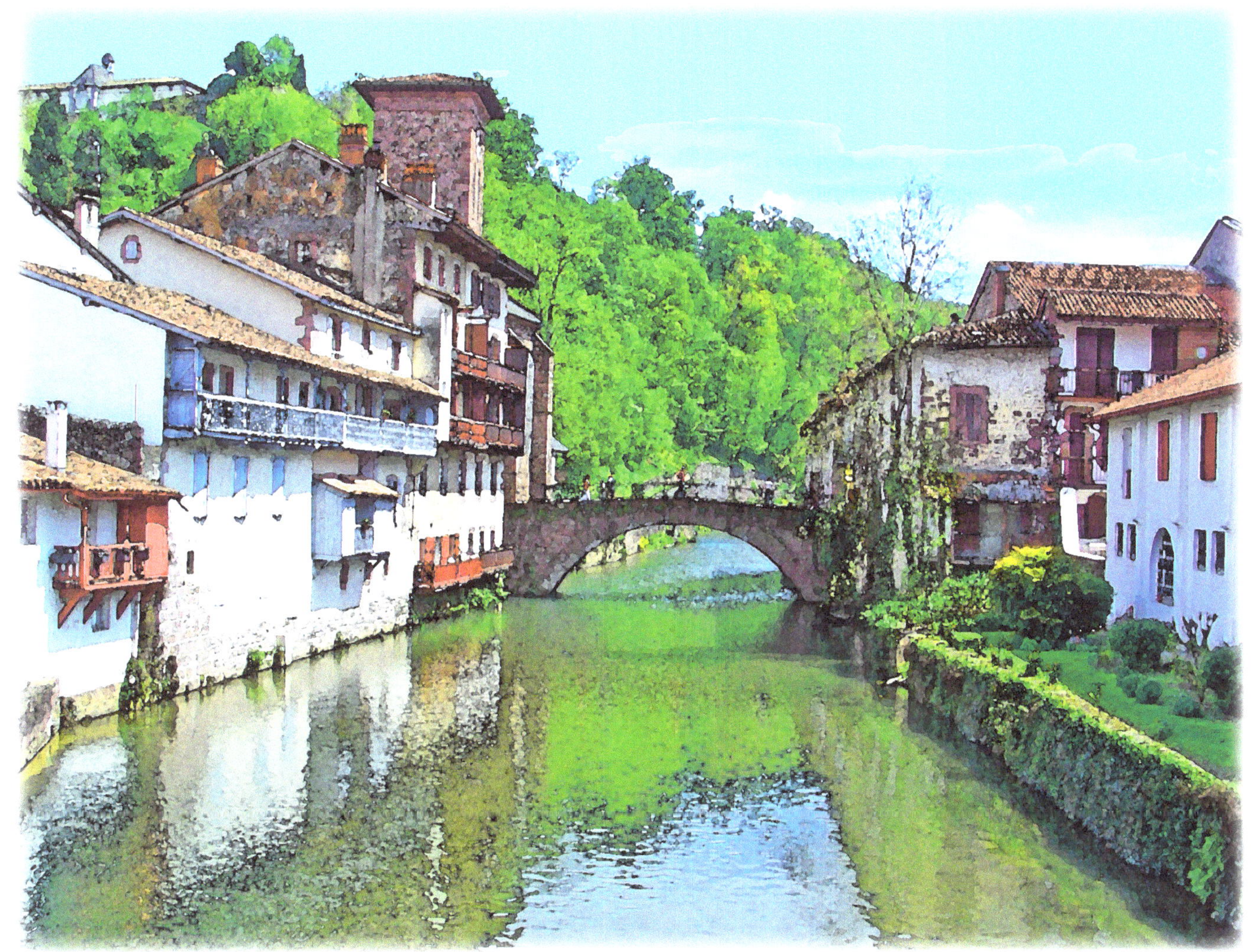

Located just a few miles from the Spanish border in the Basque region of France, Saint Jean Pied de Port is the traditional starting point for the Camino de Santiago-Camino Frances.
Over 500 miles in length, the Camino is not only a walk across the hard-packed rocky soil of Spain, but a journey through history, religion, and western culture.
For hundreds of years, this path has been used by the faithful making the holy pilgrimage to Santiago de Compostela. It was also the route used by Roman Legions, Moor and Saracen invaders, the Knights Templar, and the armies of Charlemagne and Napoleon.

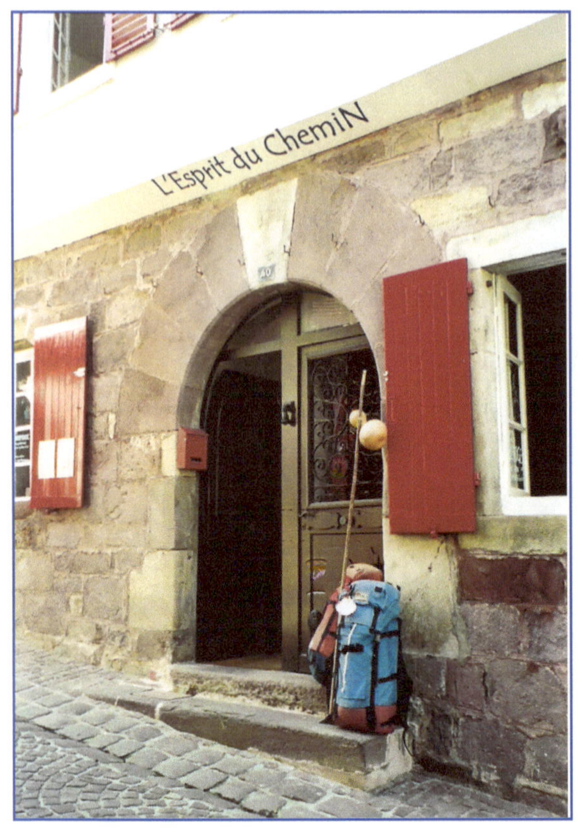

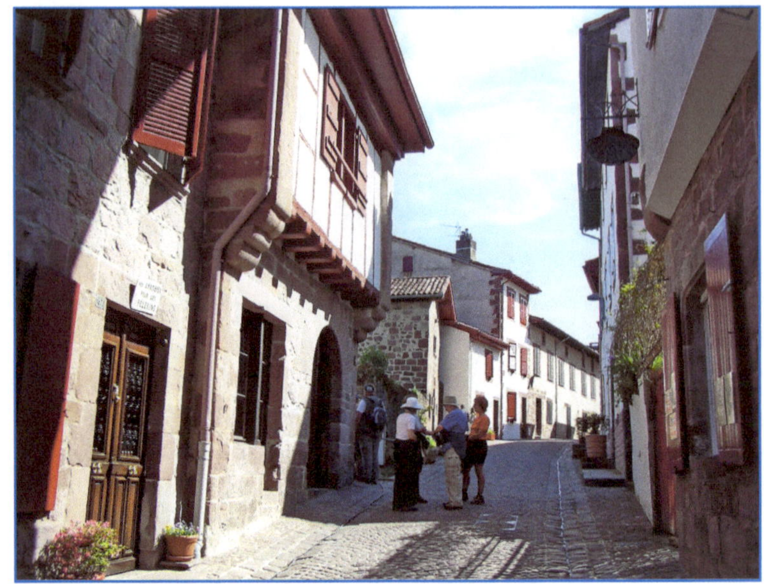

Pilgrim's Office

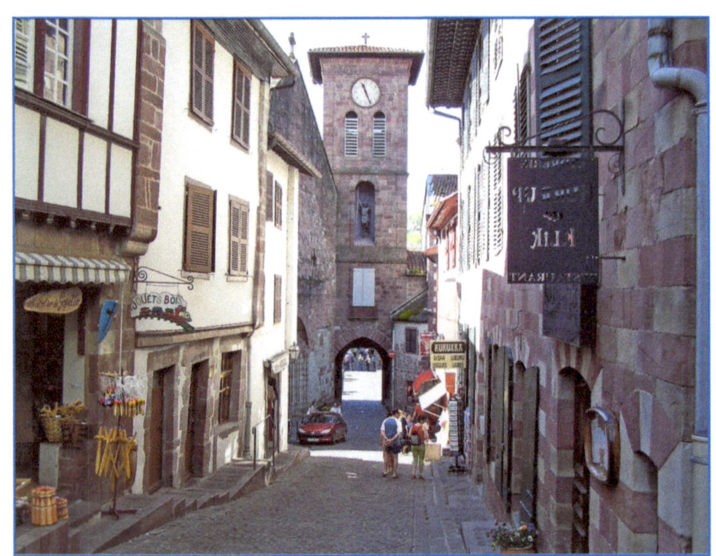

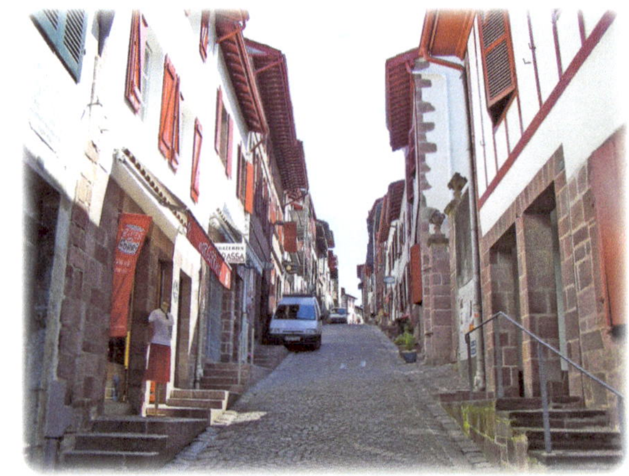

Rue de Citadelle

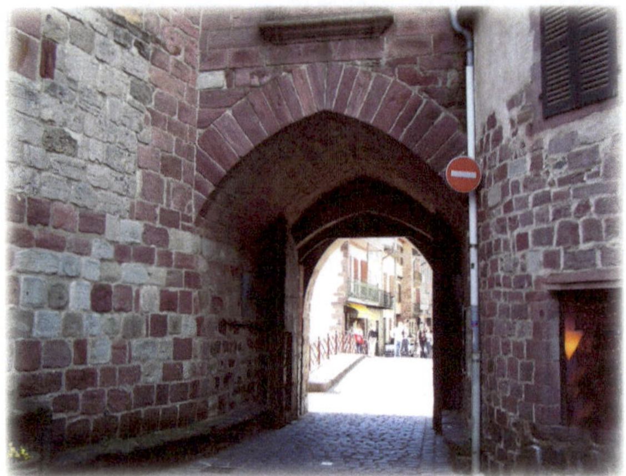

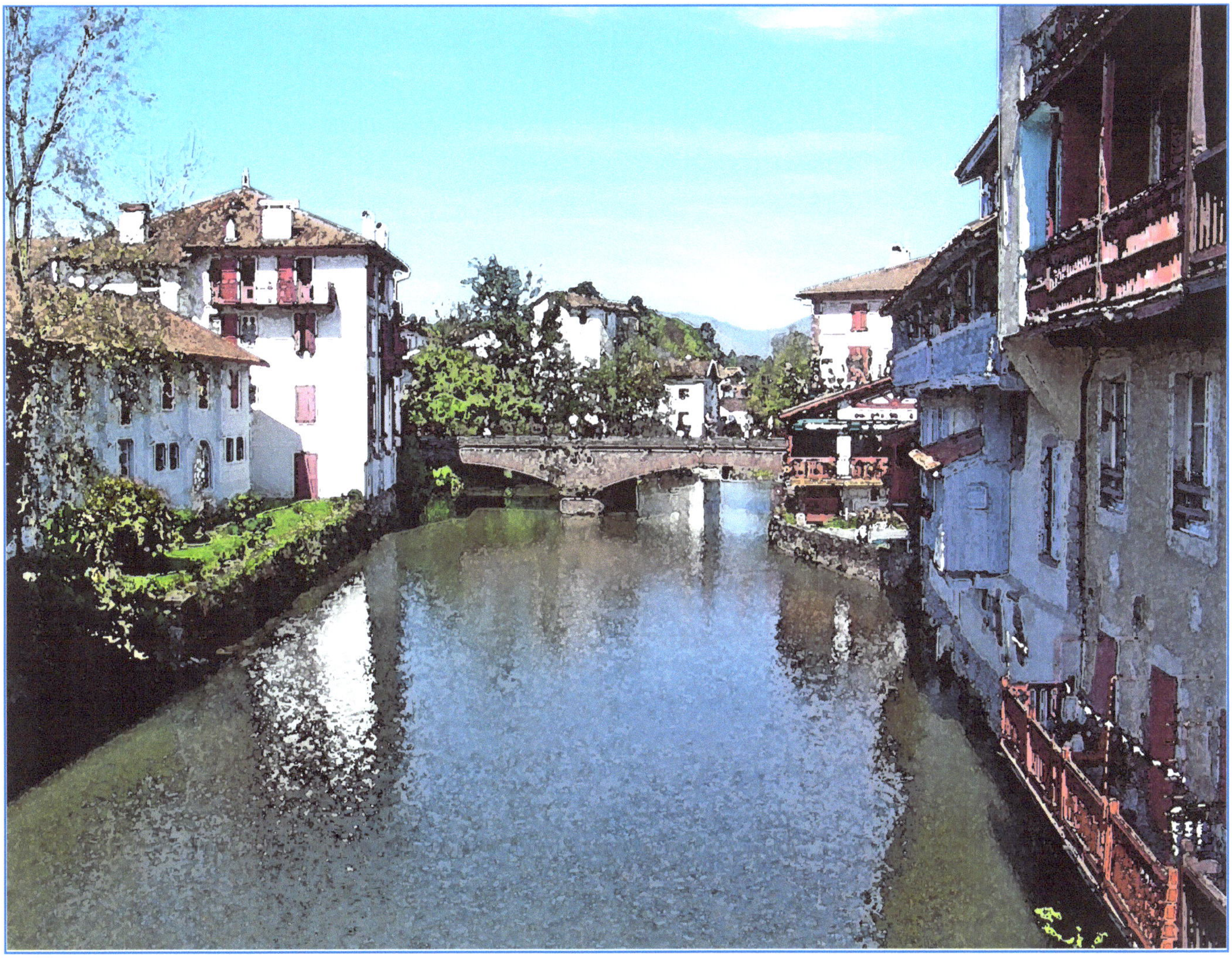

View from Rue D'Espagne

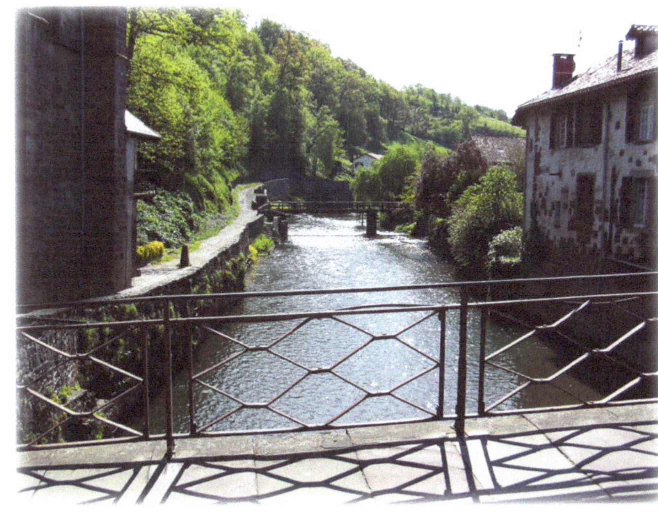

Riverside Pathway

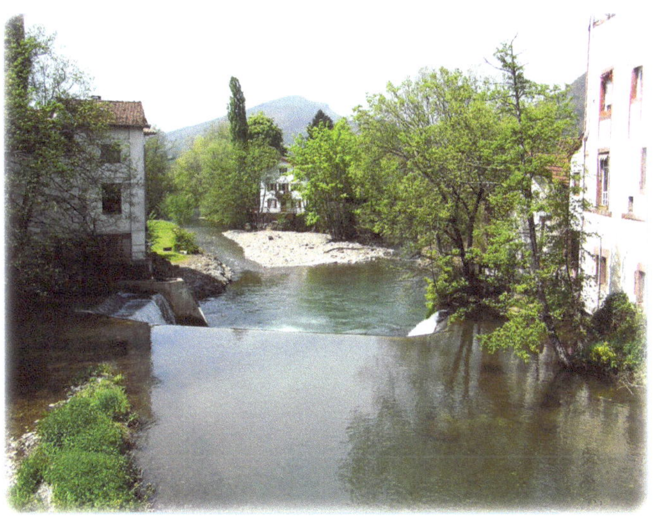

River Nive

All roads lead to Santiago

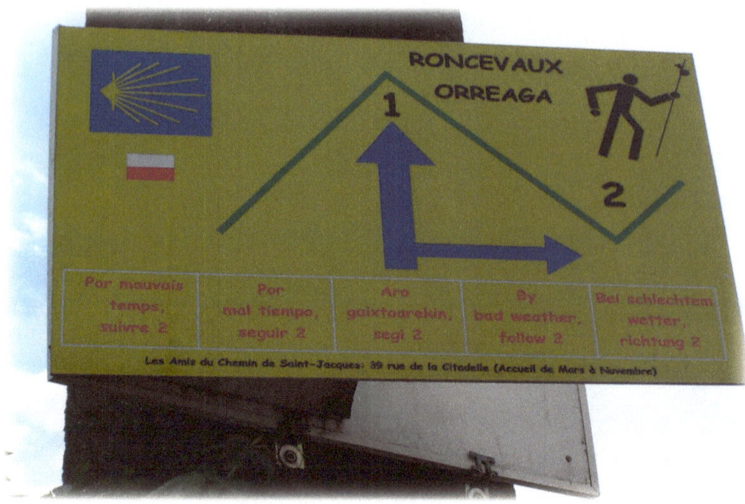

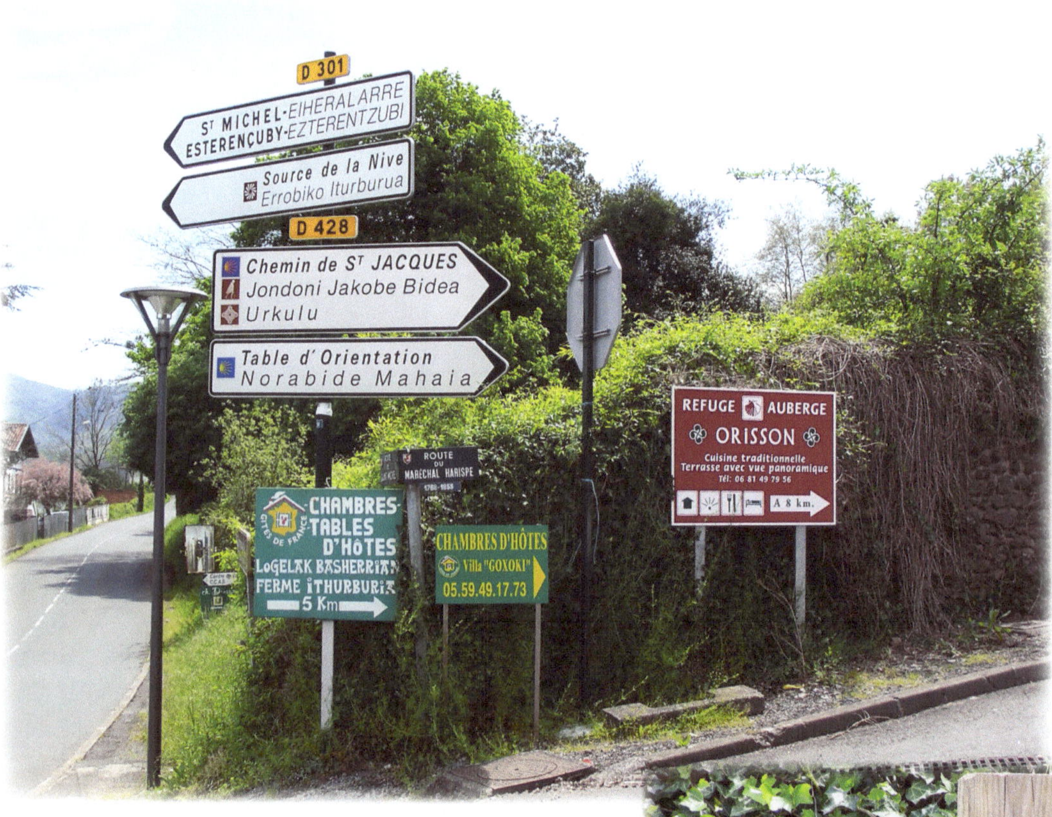

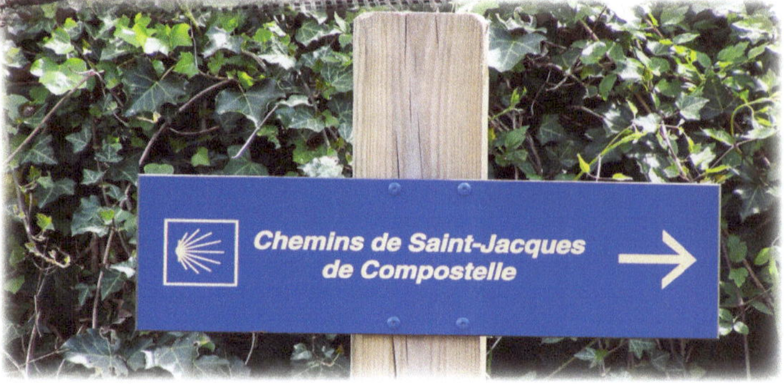

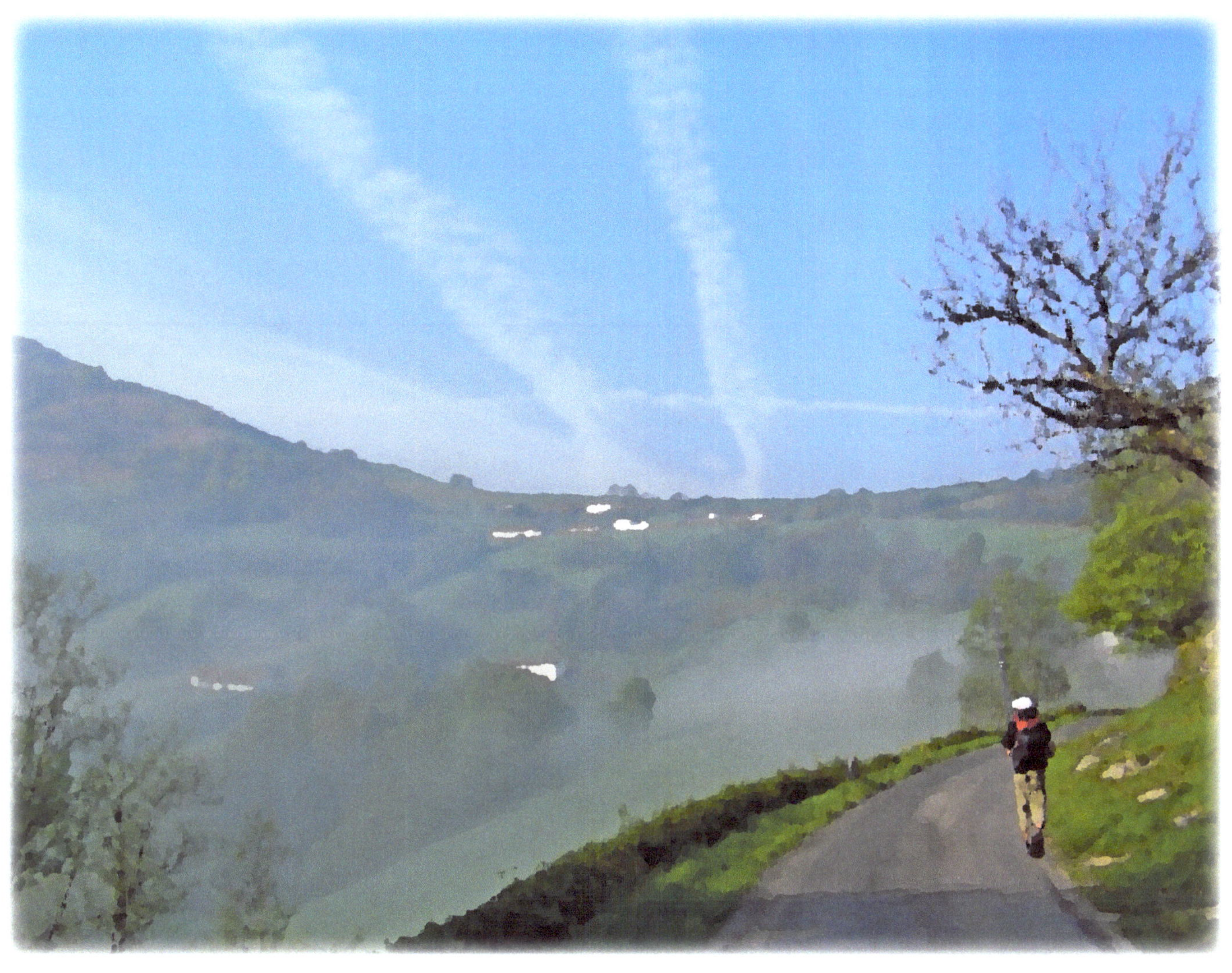

The Route Napoleon. A hard climb better done in two days that rewards the pilgrim with beautiful views and vistas.

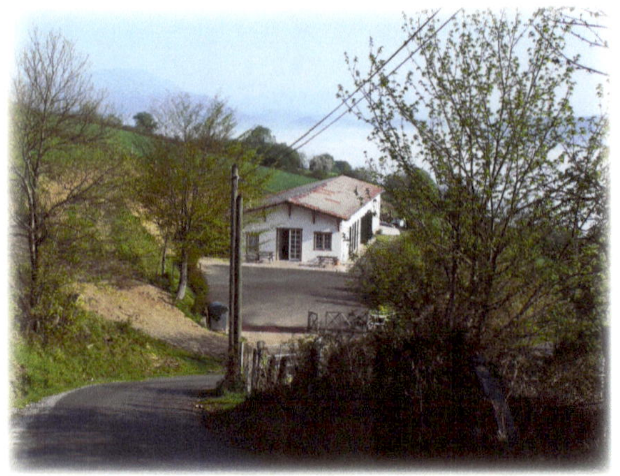

Huntto

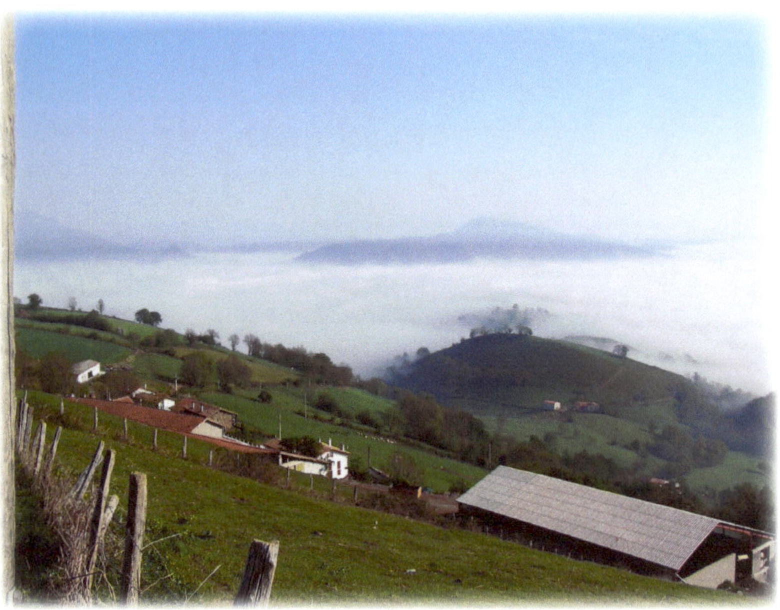

View to St. Jean Pied de Port

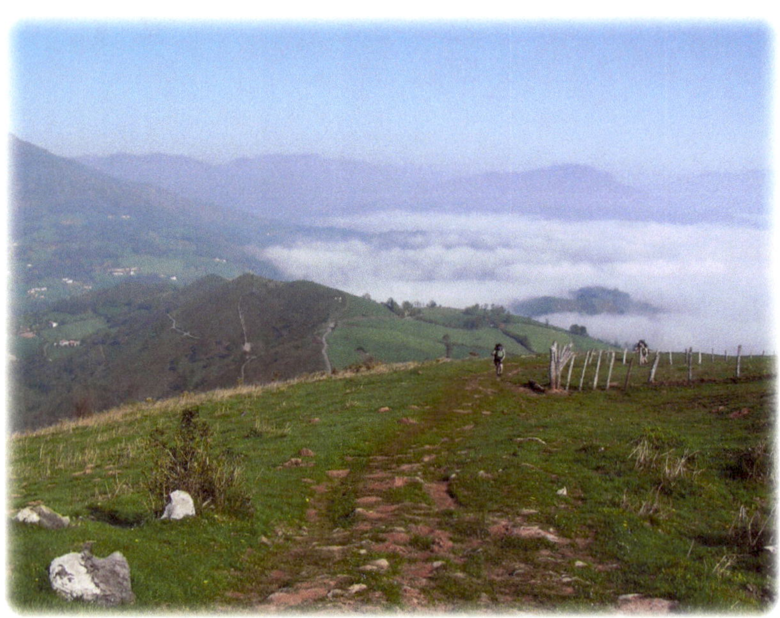

Long climb

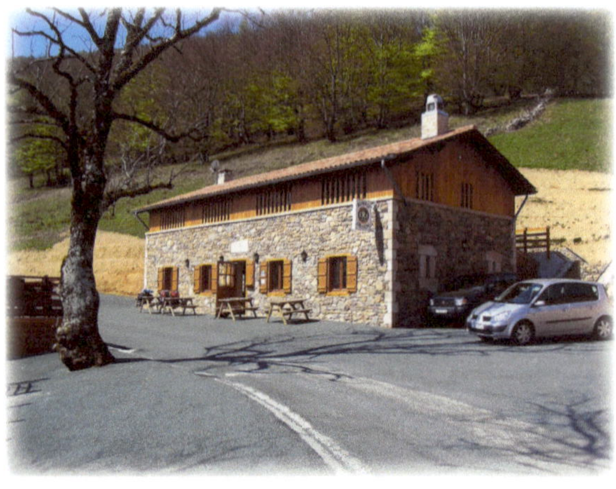

Orisson

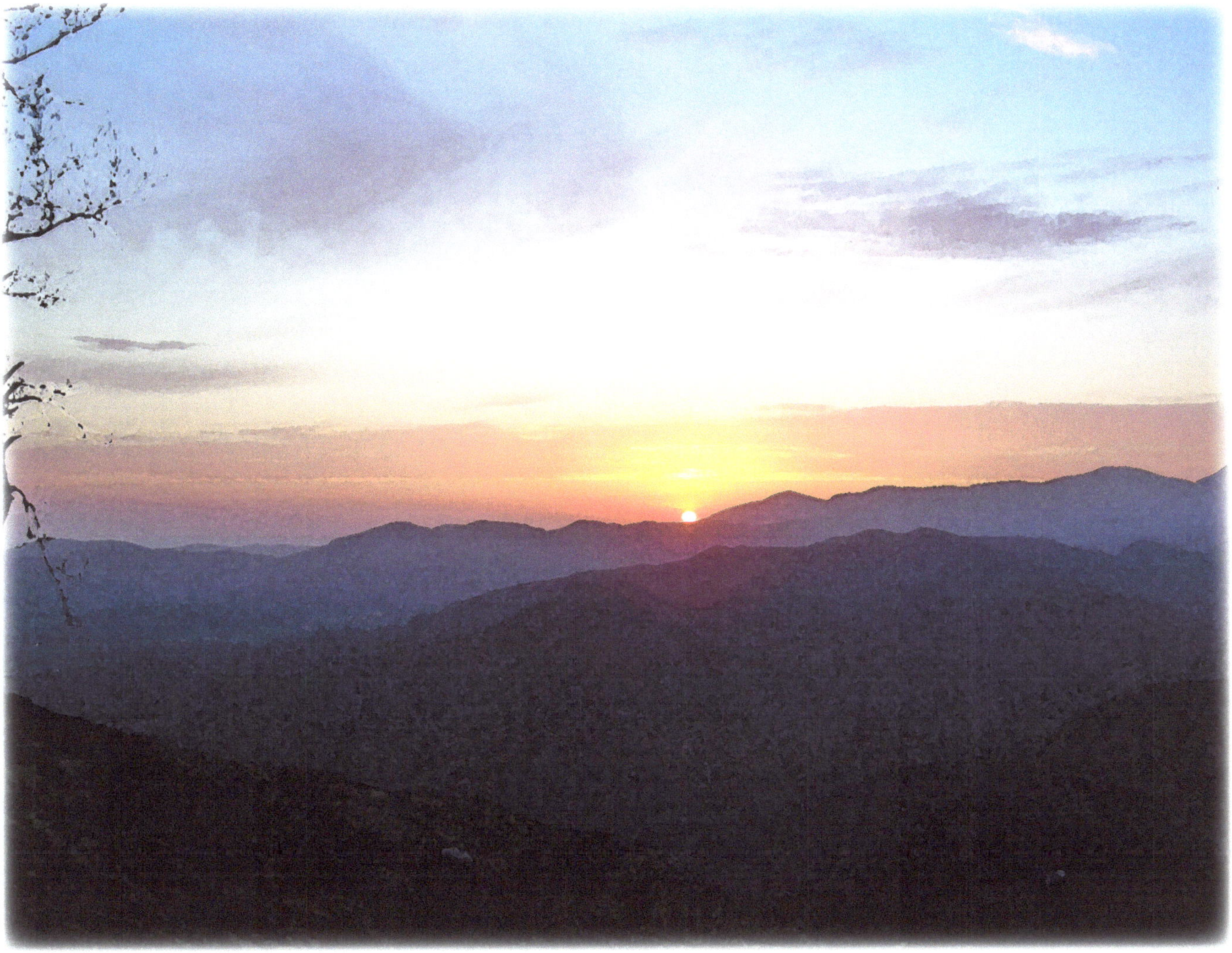

Sunrise at Orisson--high in the Pyrenees Mountains.

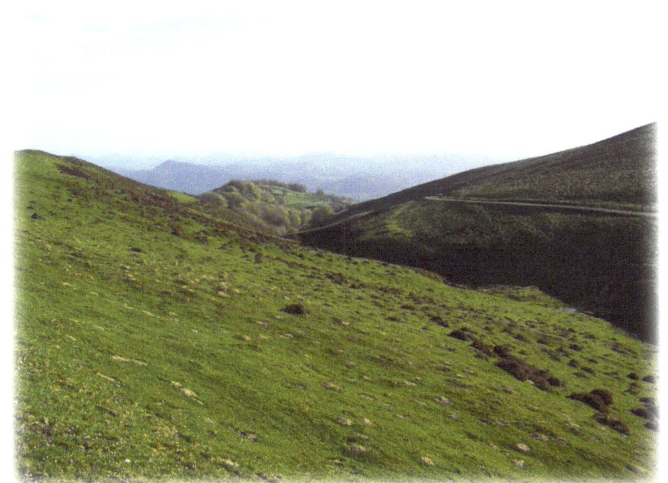

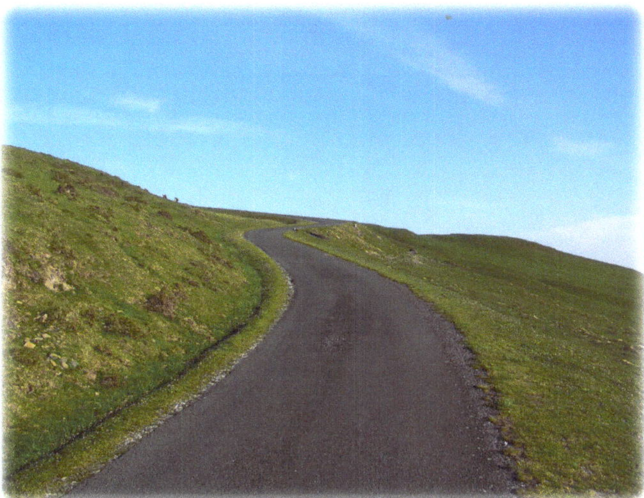

Route Napoleon leaving Orisson

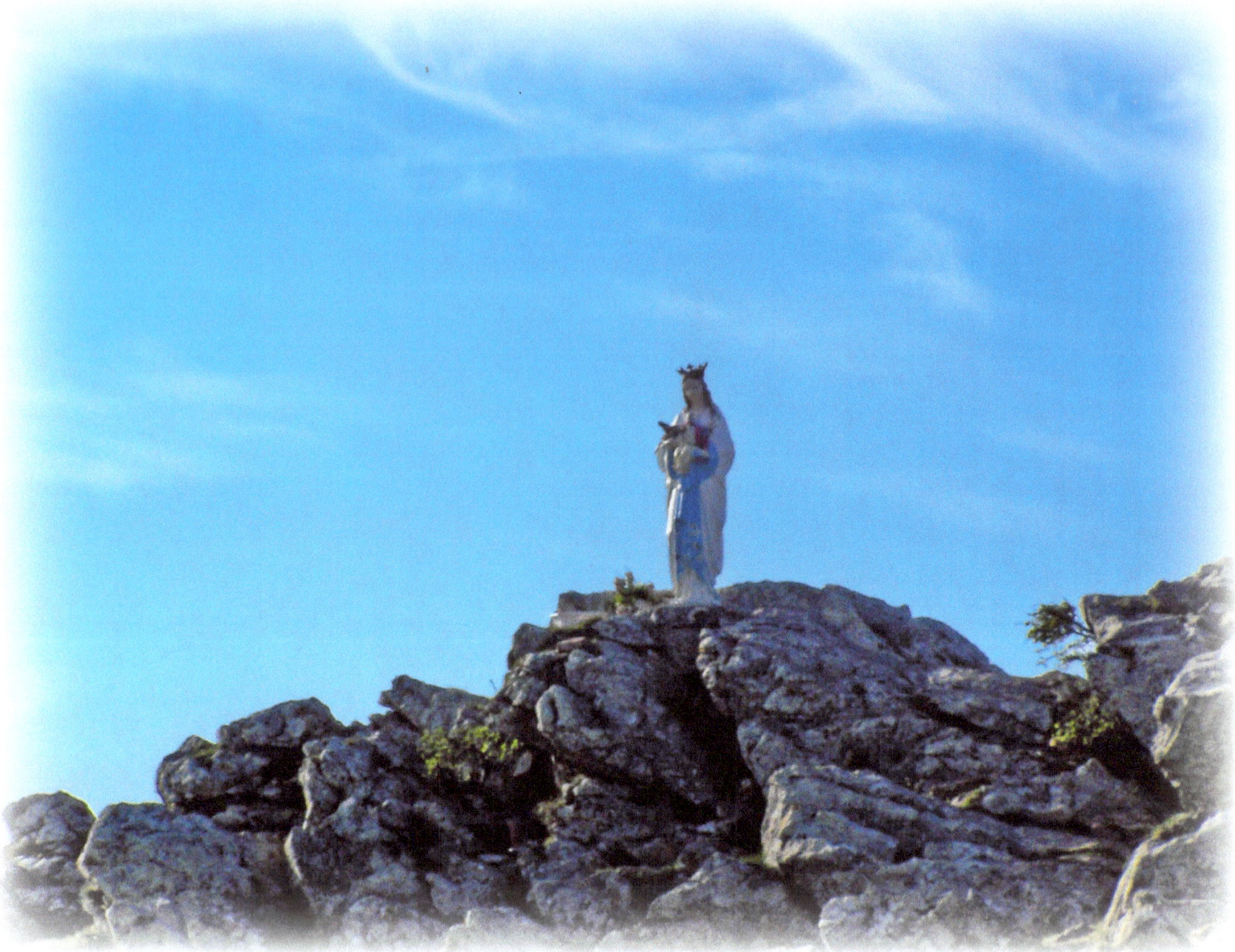

Vierge D'Orisson

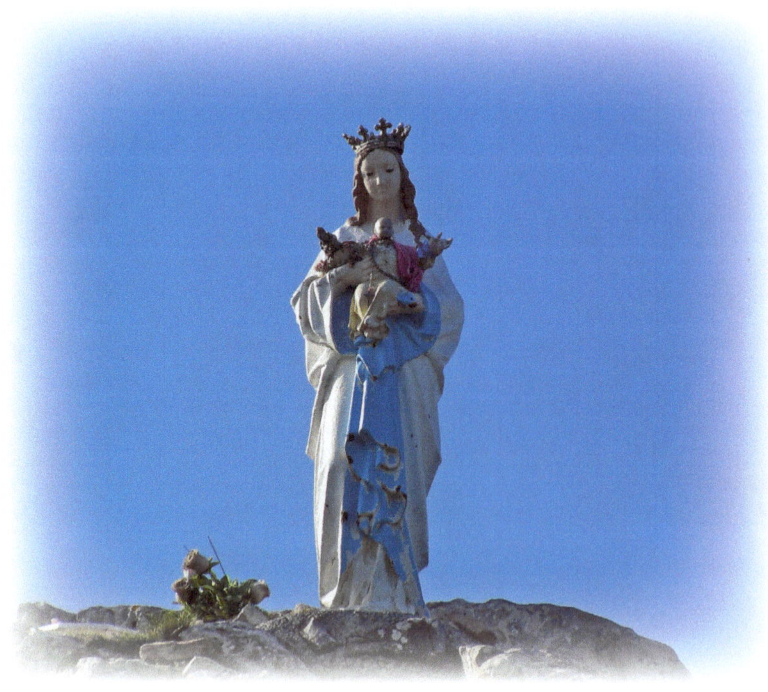

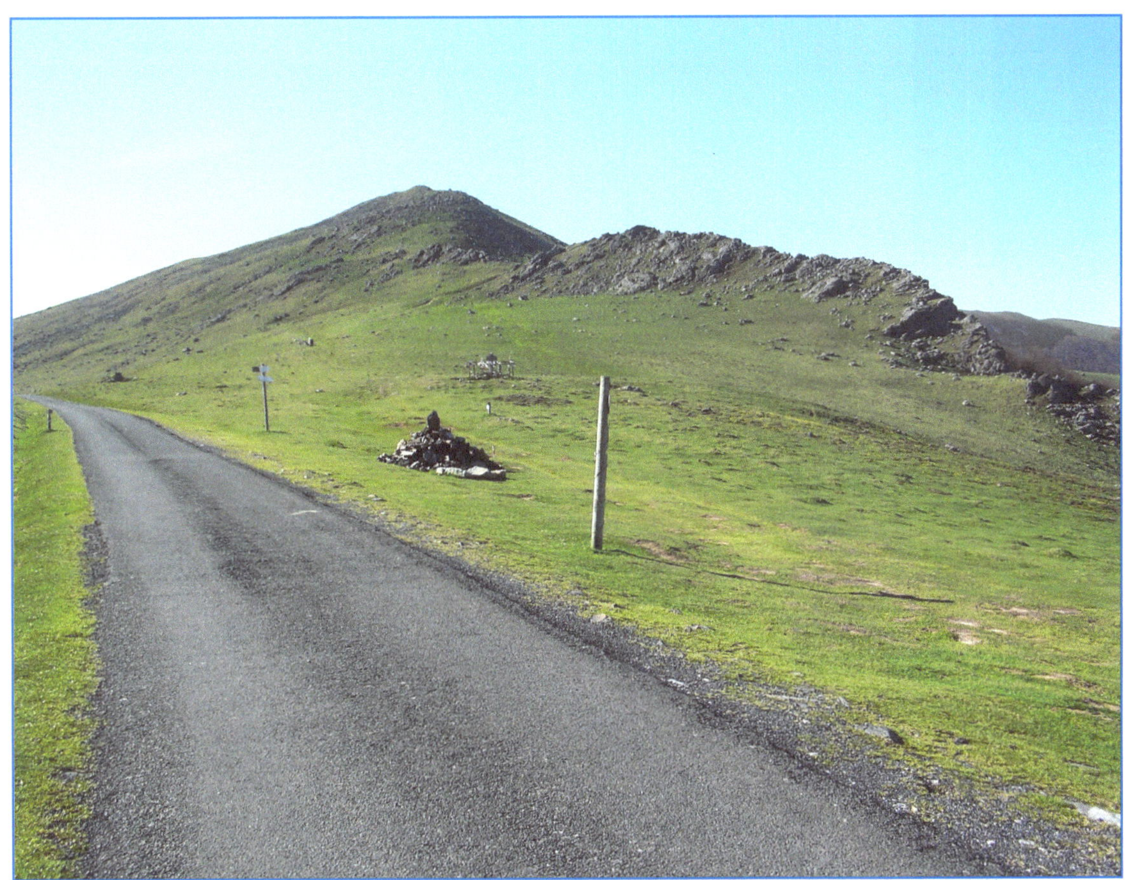

Where the Camino trail leaves the road

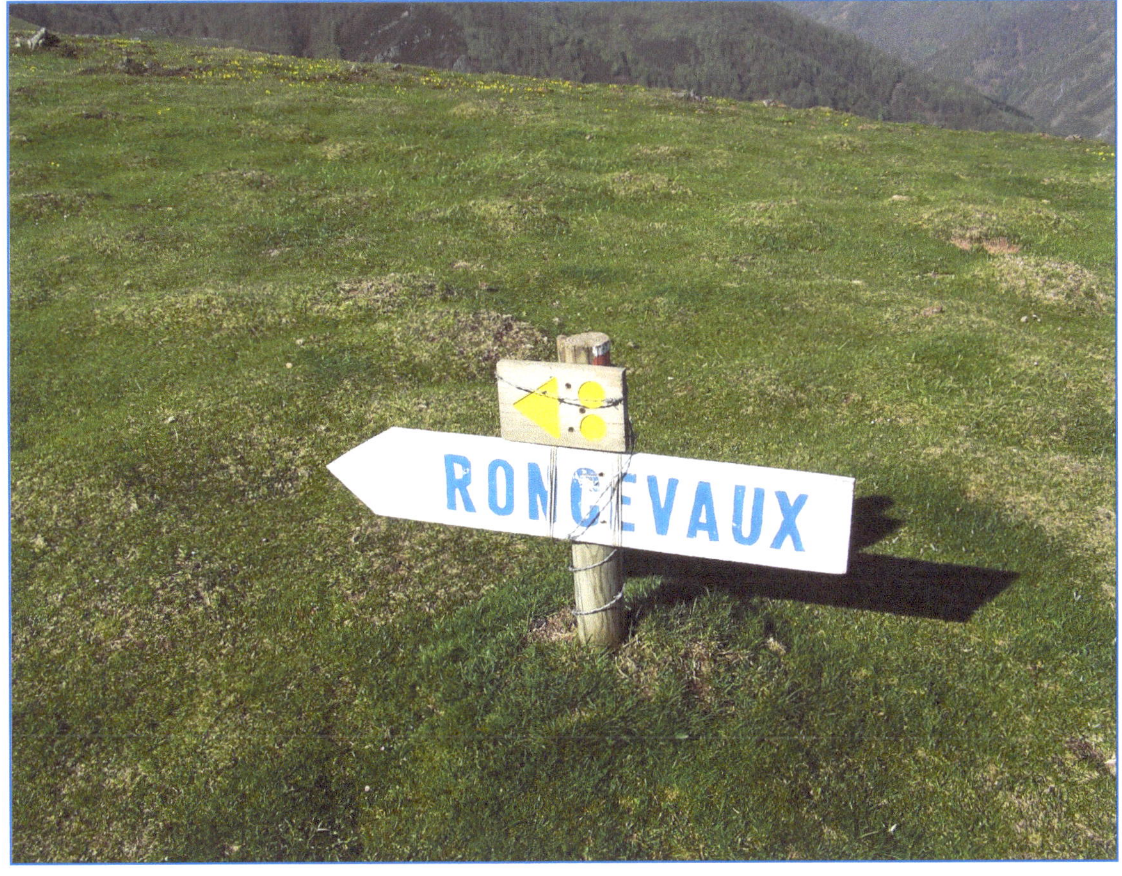

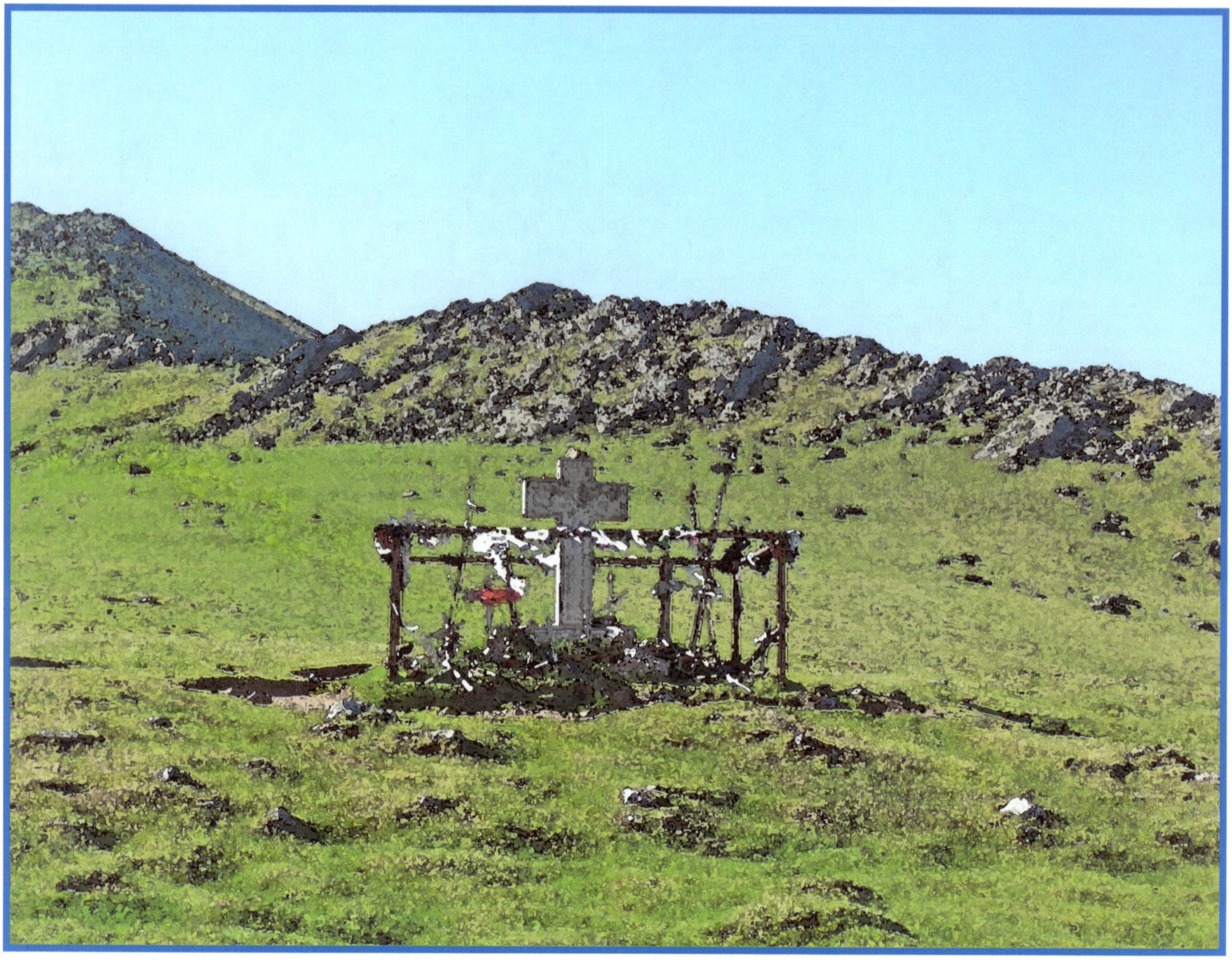

Camino marker

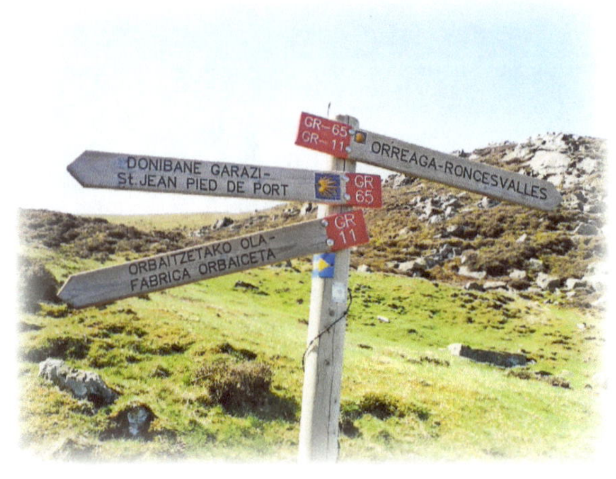

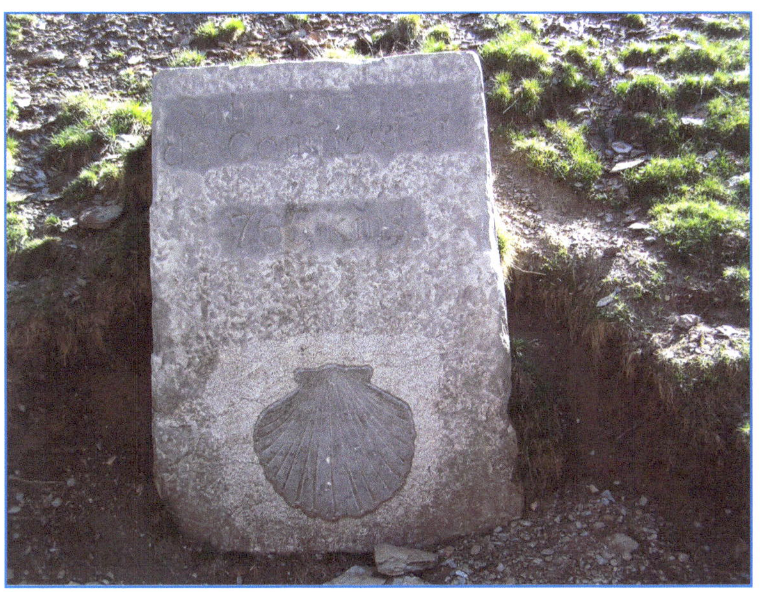

765 Kms to Santiago !

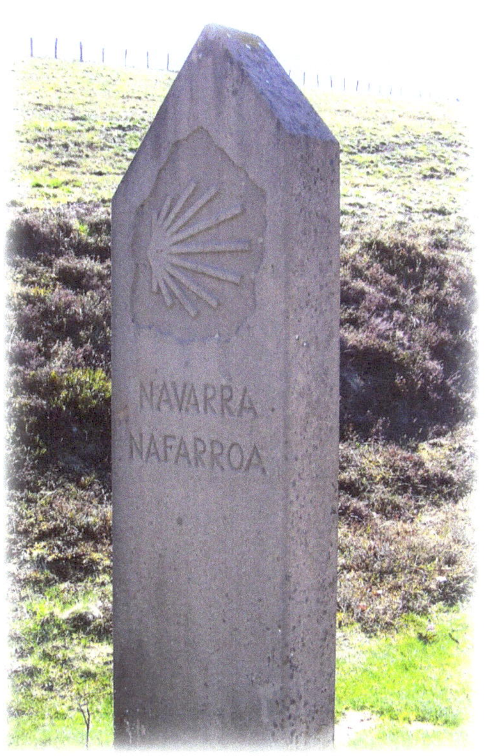

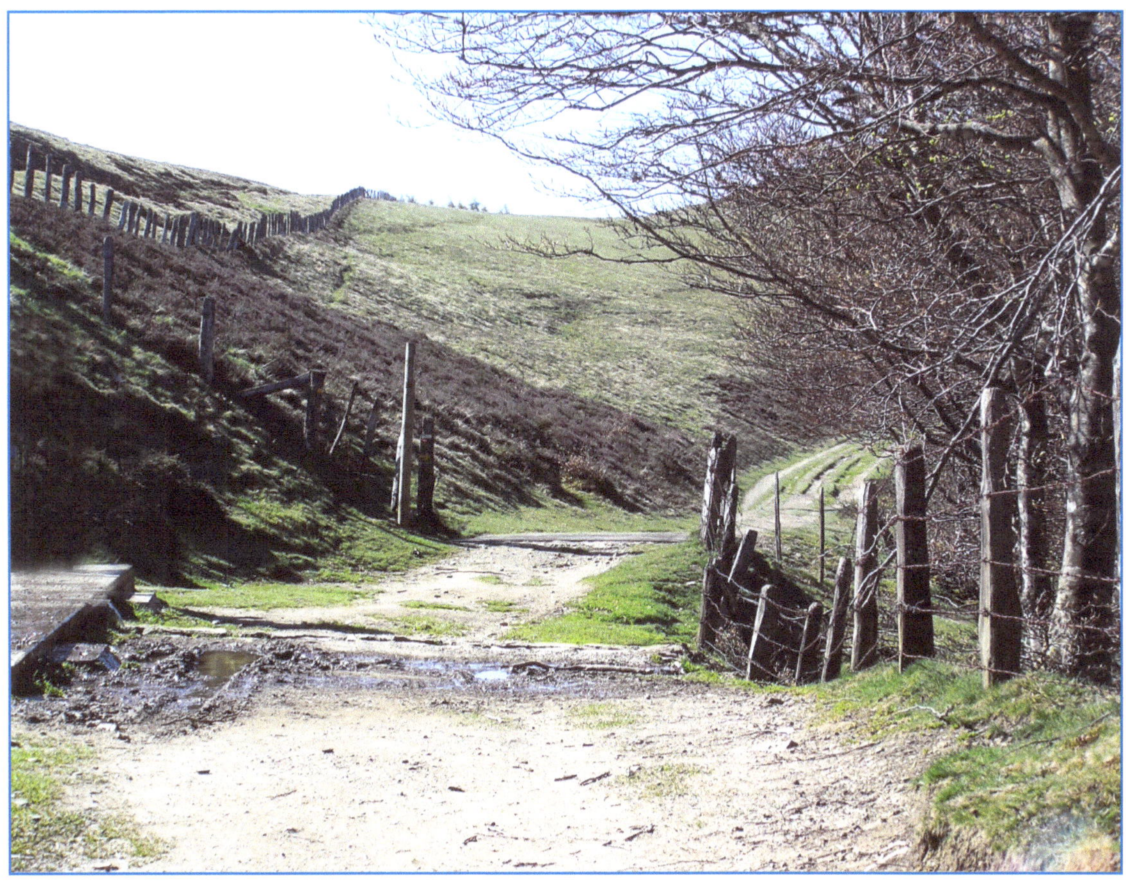

Border between France and Spain

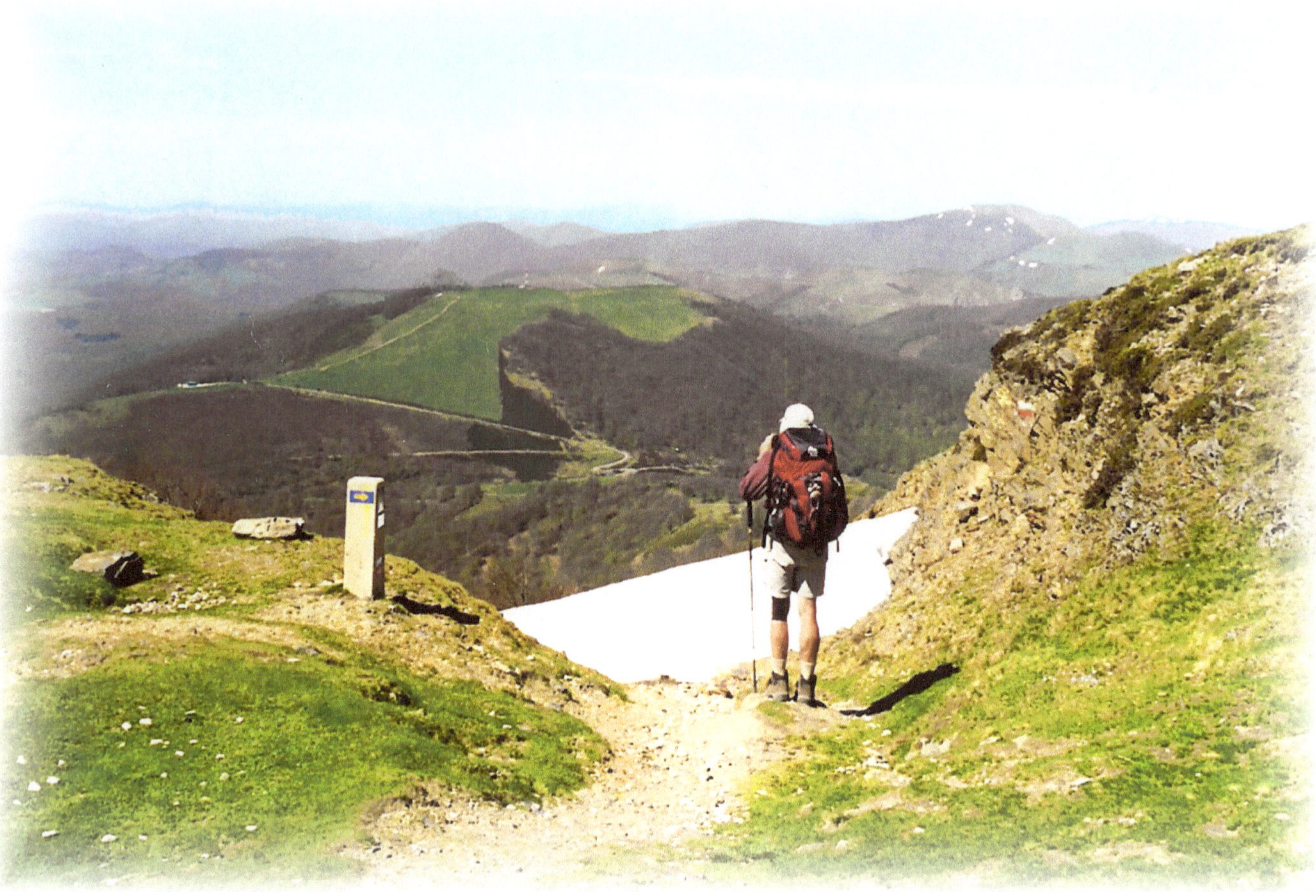

Pilgrim

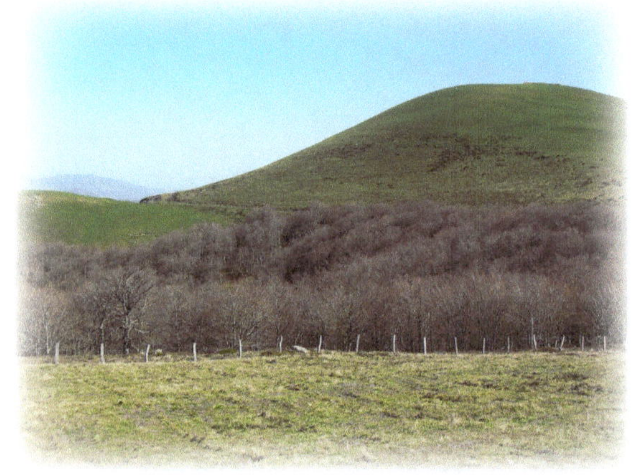

Along the Route Napoleon

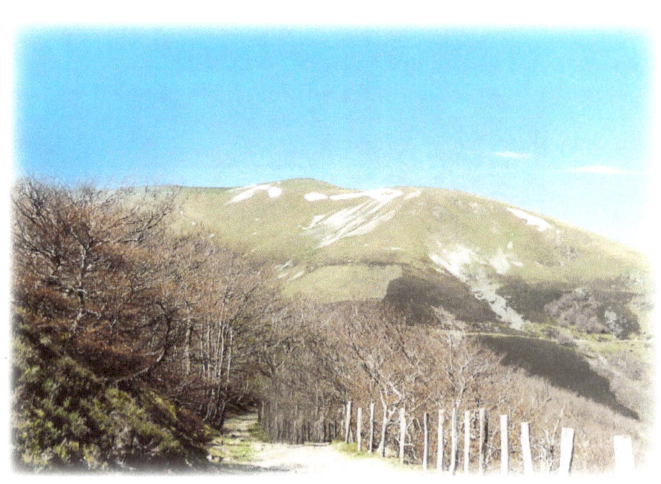

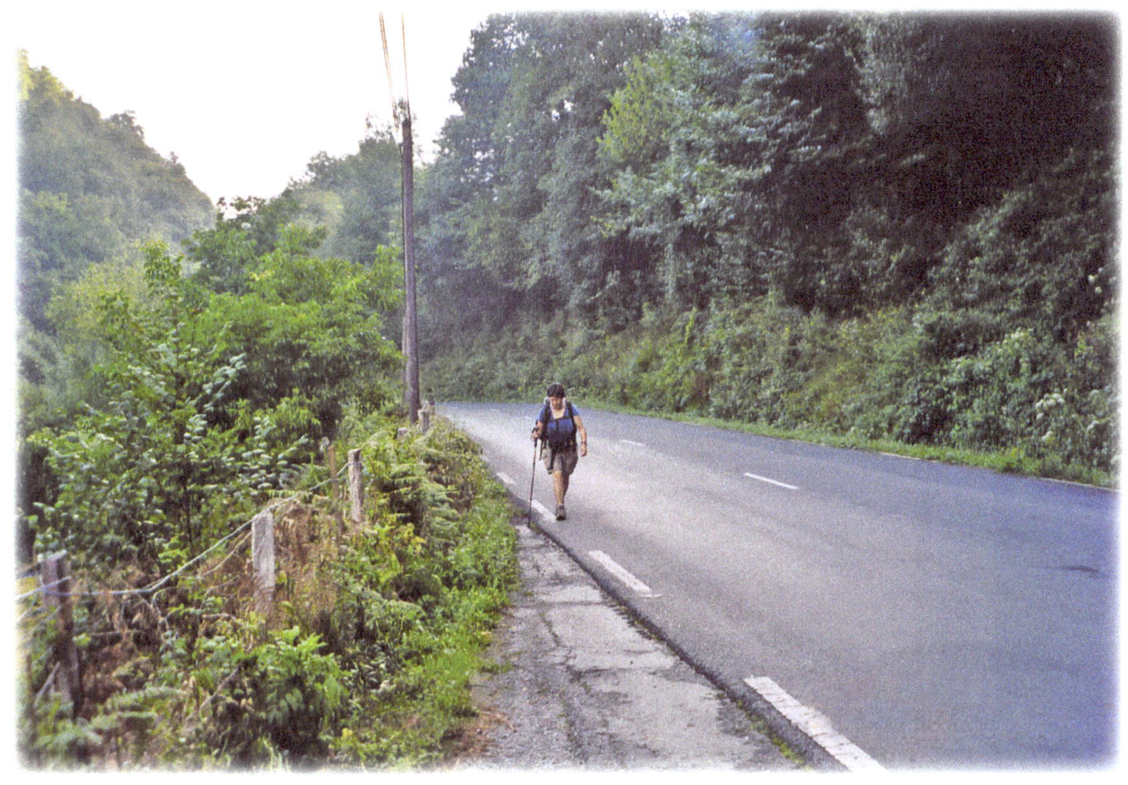

The Road Route follows the main highway through Arneguy, Valcarlos, and then over the Ibaneta Pass. It is the original pilgrim's path to Roncesvalles.

It was along this route that Charlemagne's forces were defeated while retreating from Spain

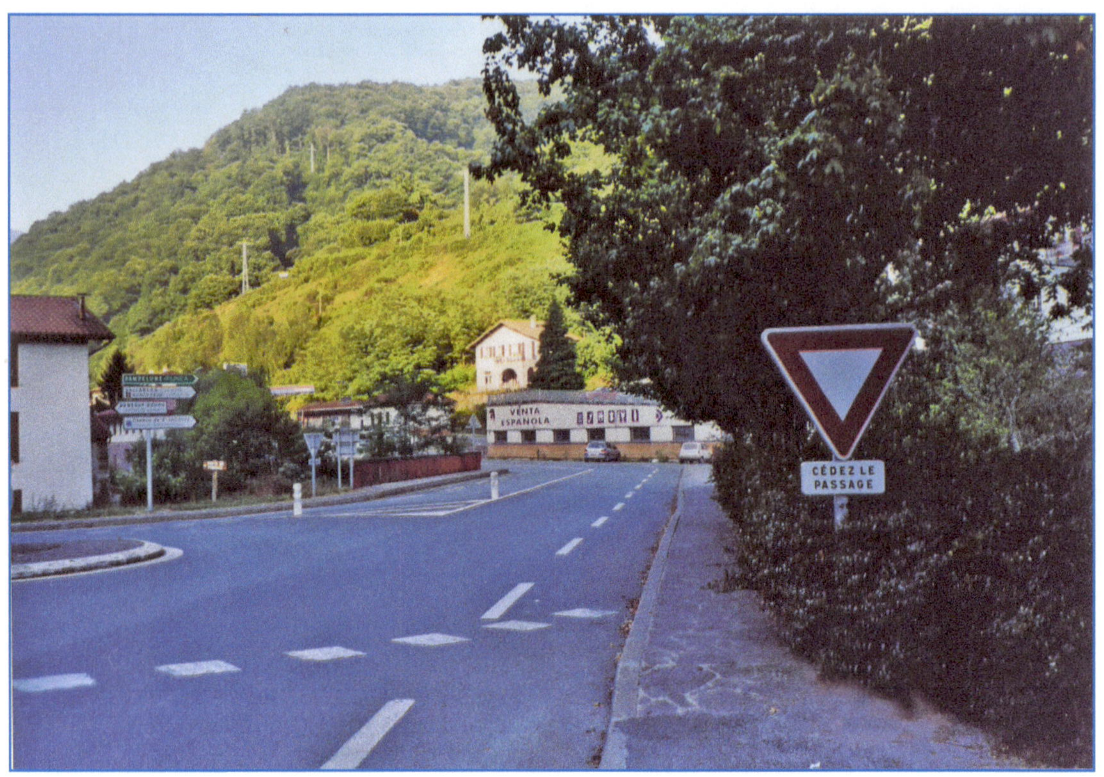

French-Spanish Border at Arneguy

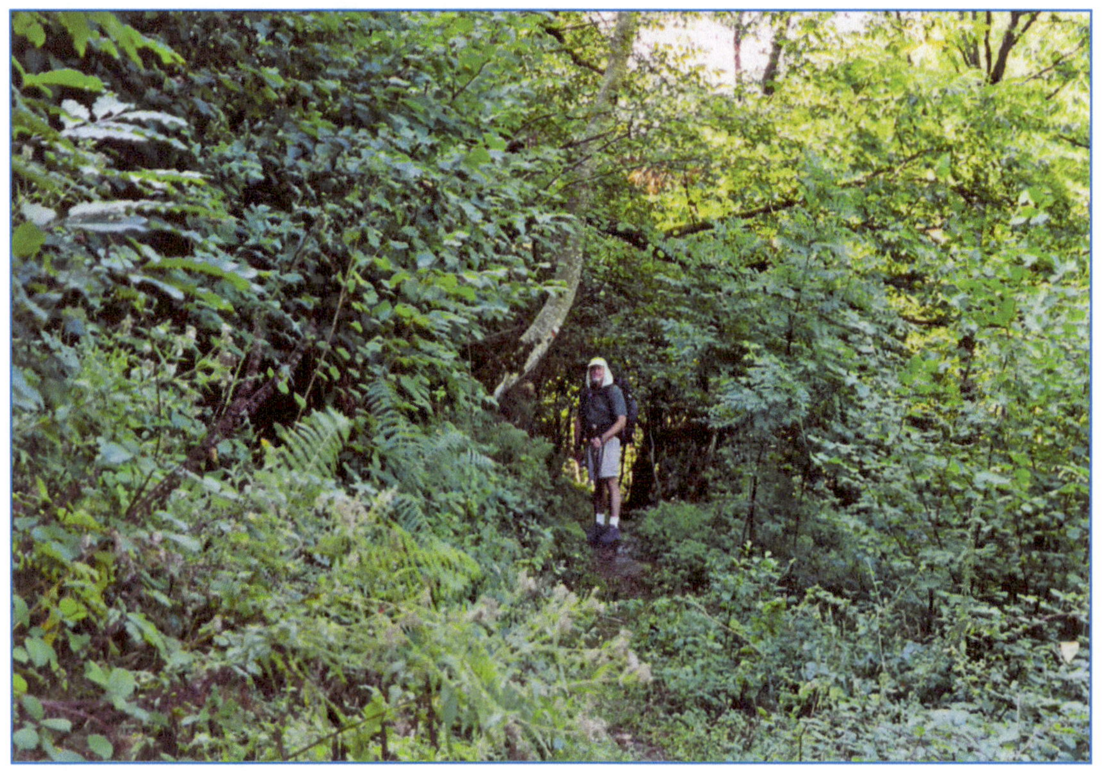

Off road section of the Road Route

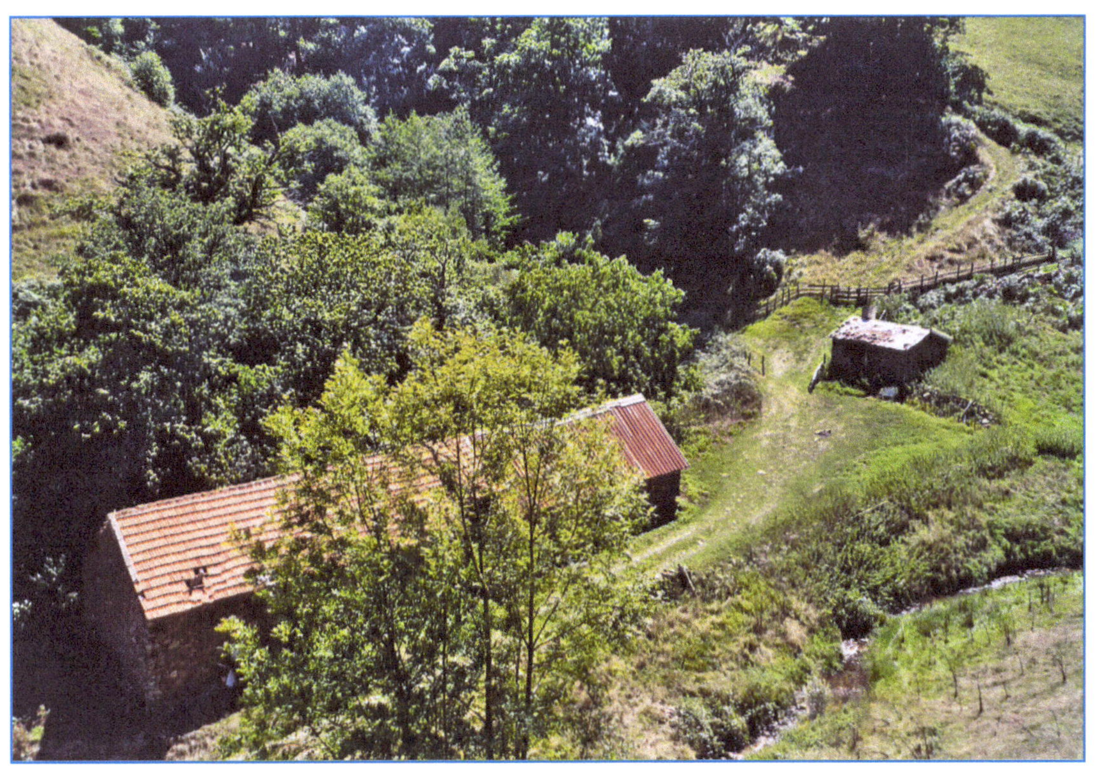

View from the Camino

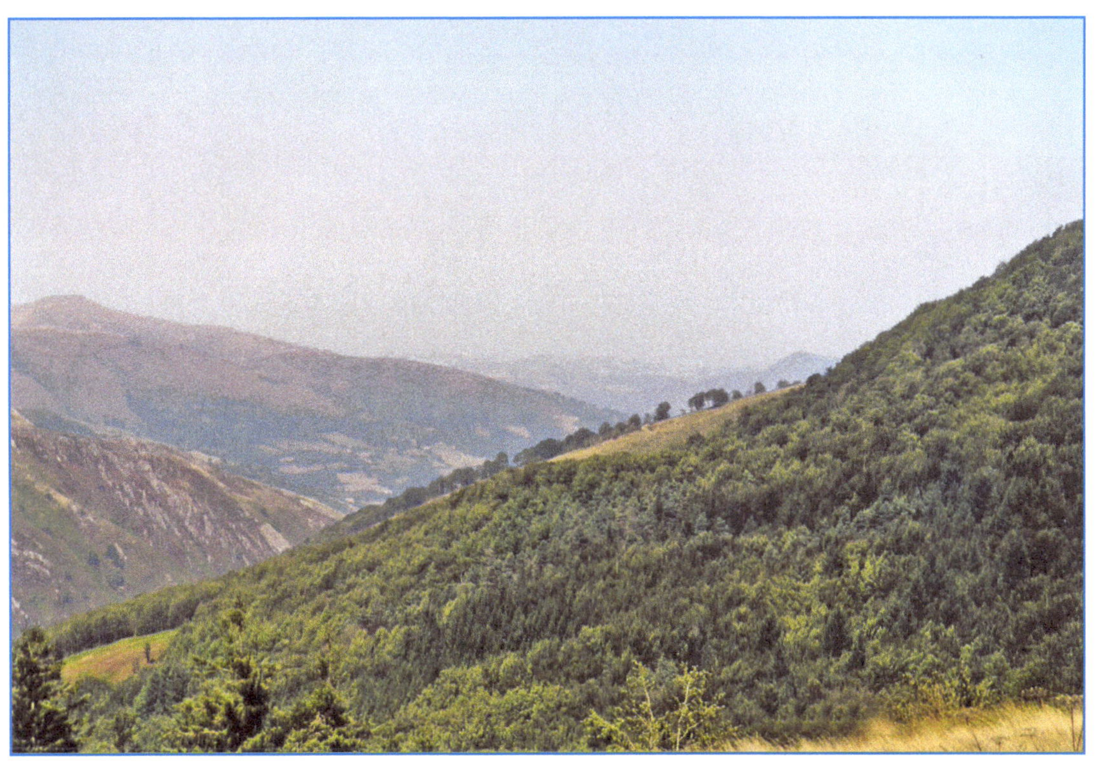

Looking back toward France

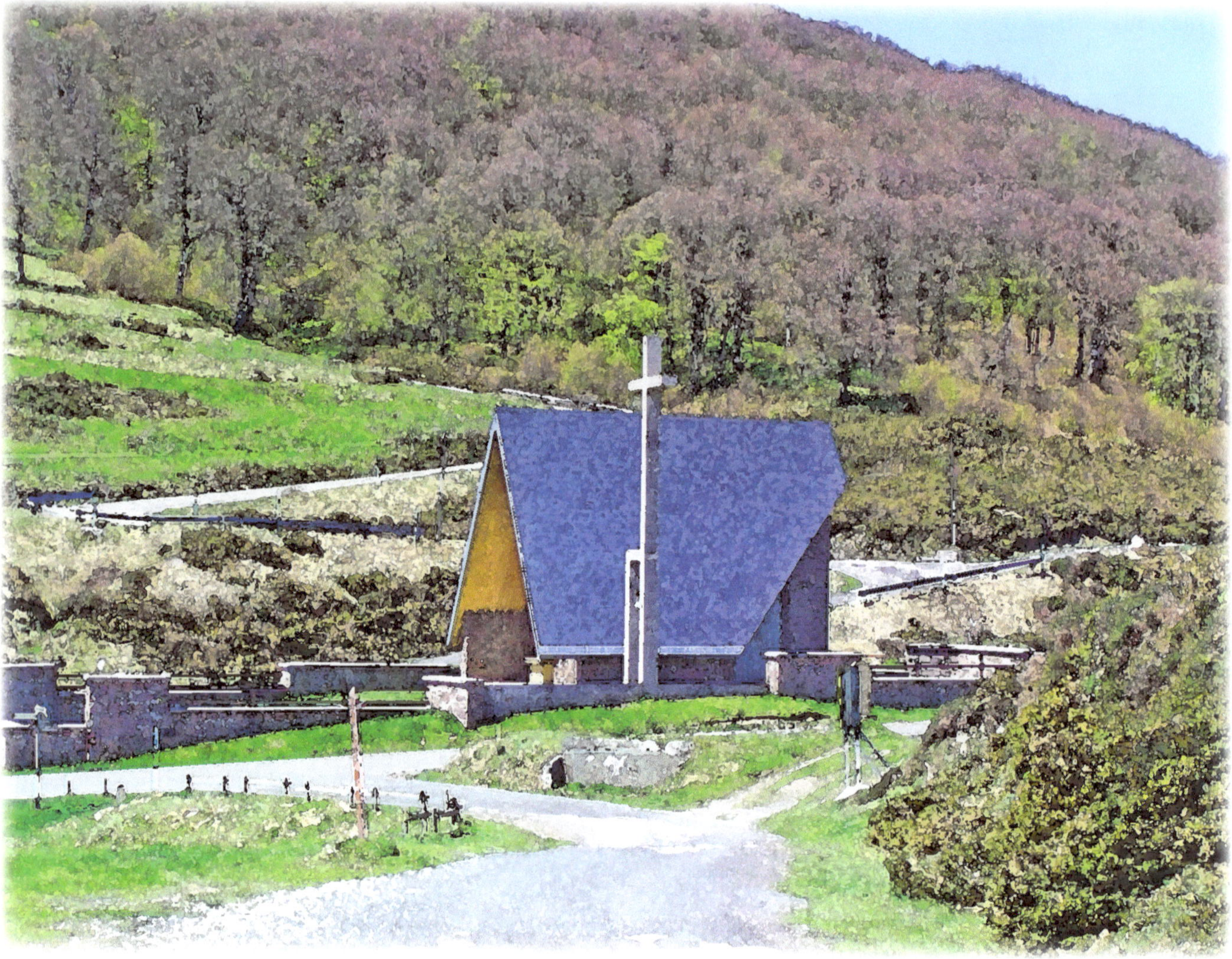

Where the trails meet-The chapel at Ibaneta Pass

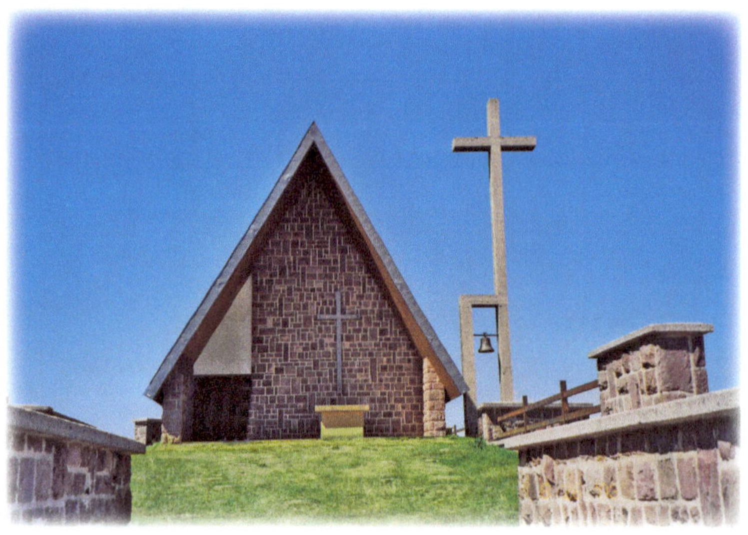

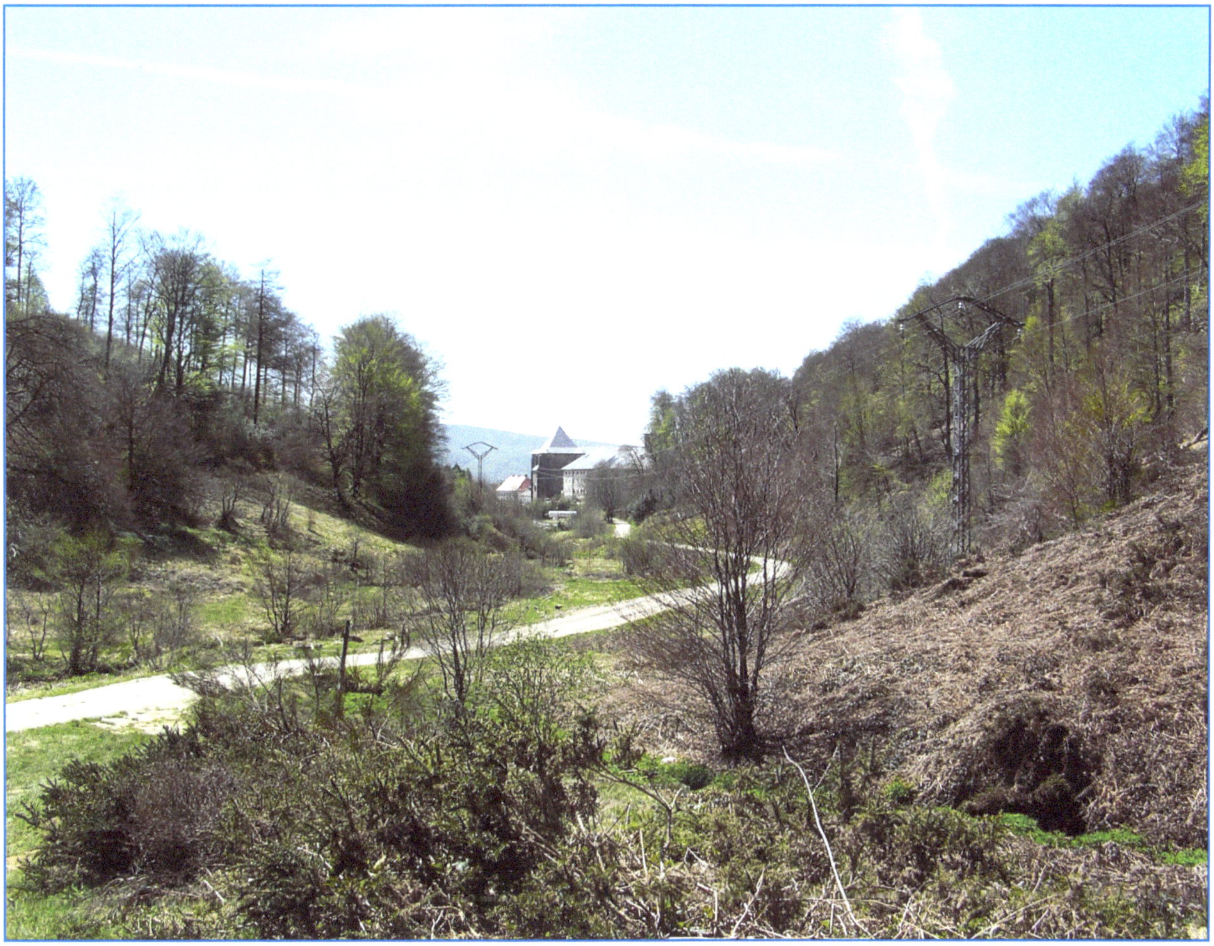

Trail into Roncesvalles

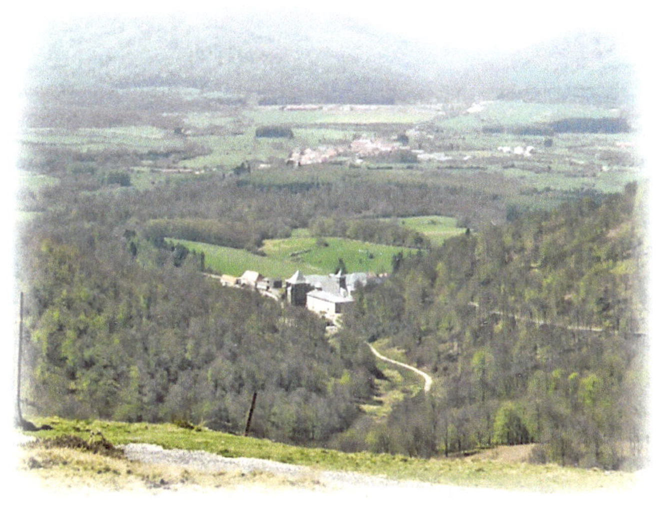

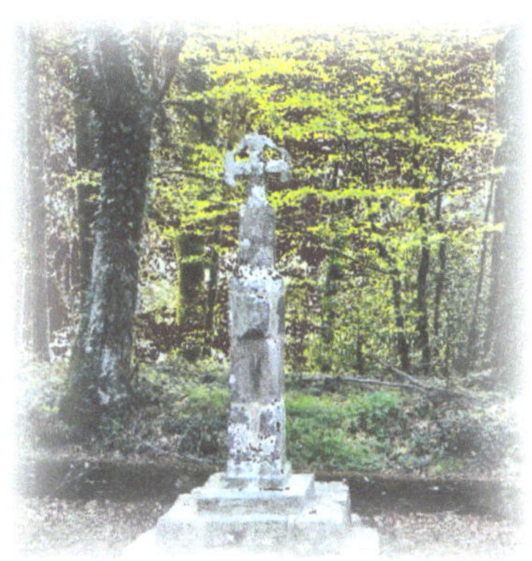

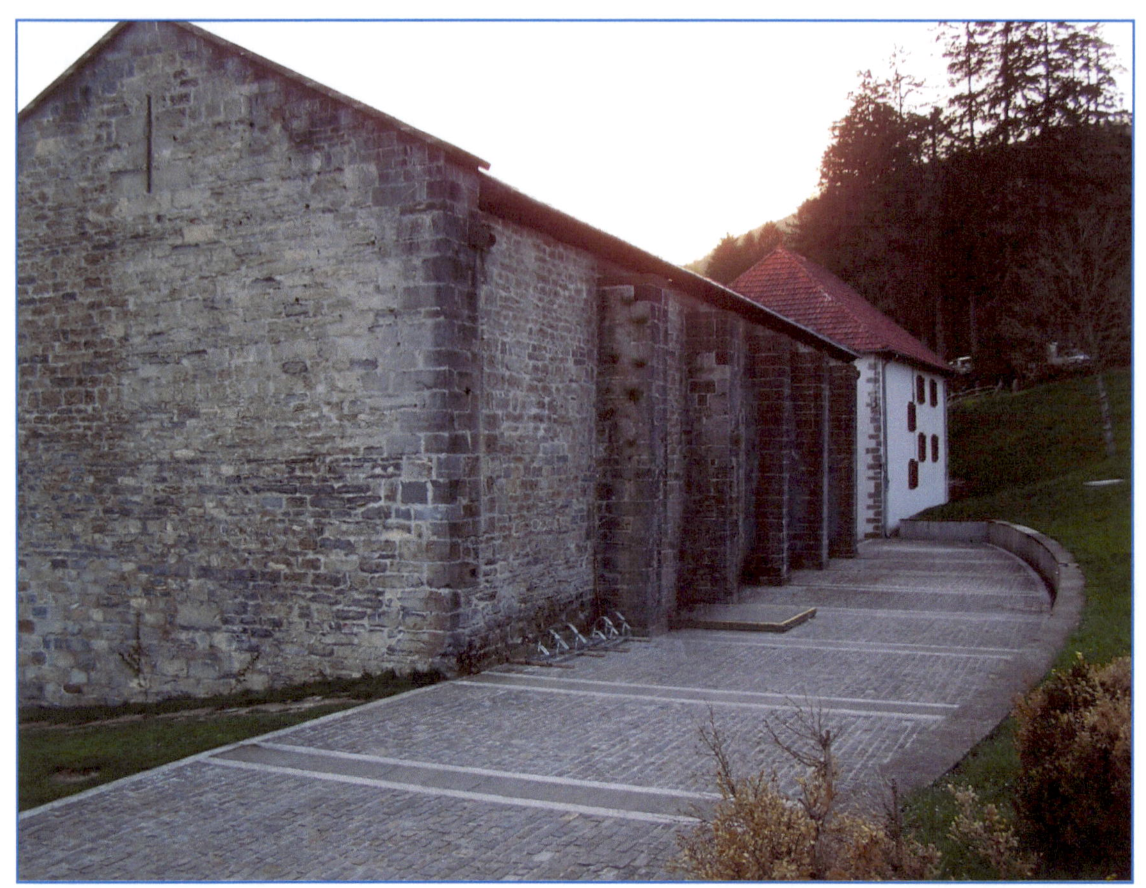

Roncesvalles Albergue

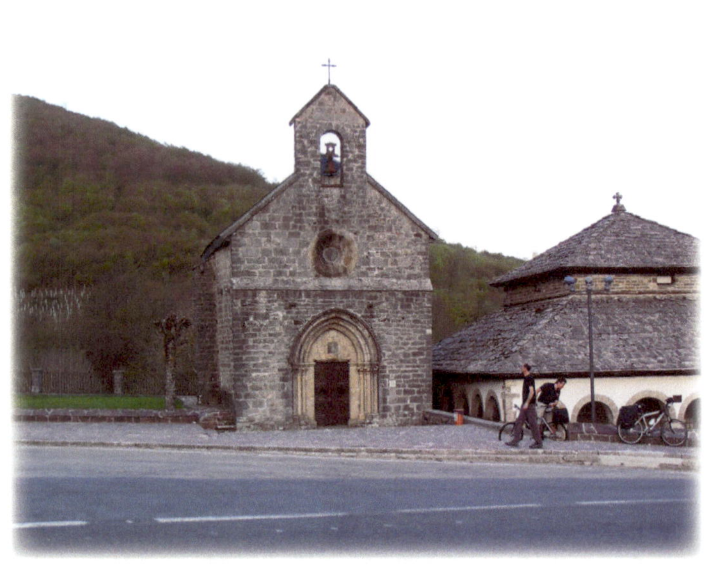

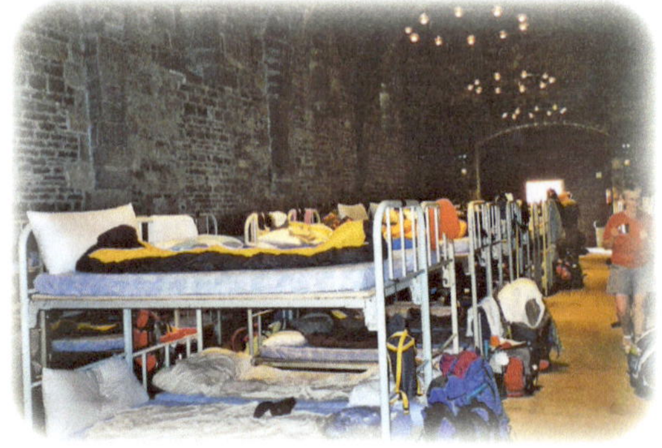

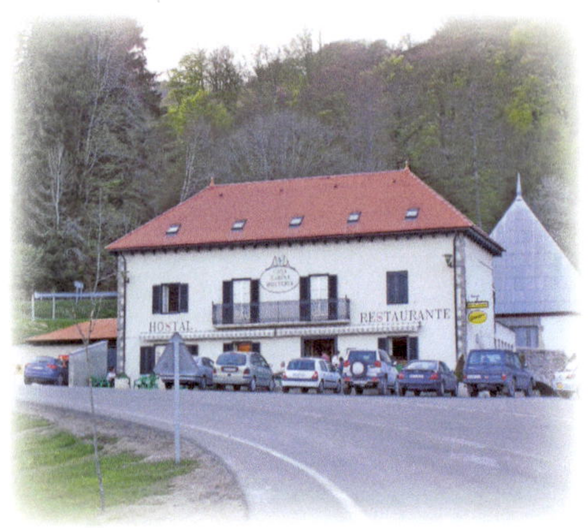

Roncesvalles

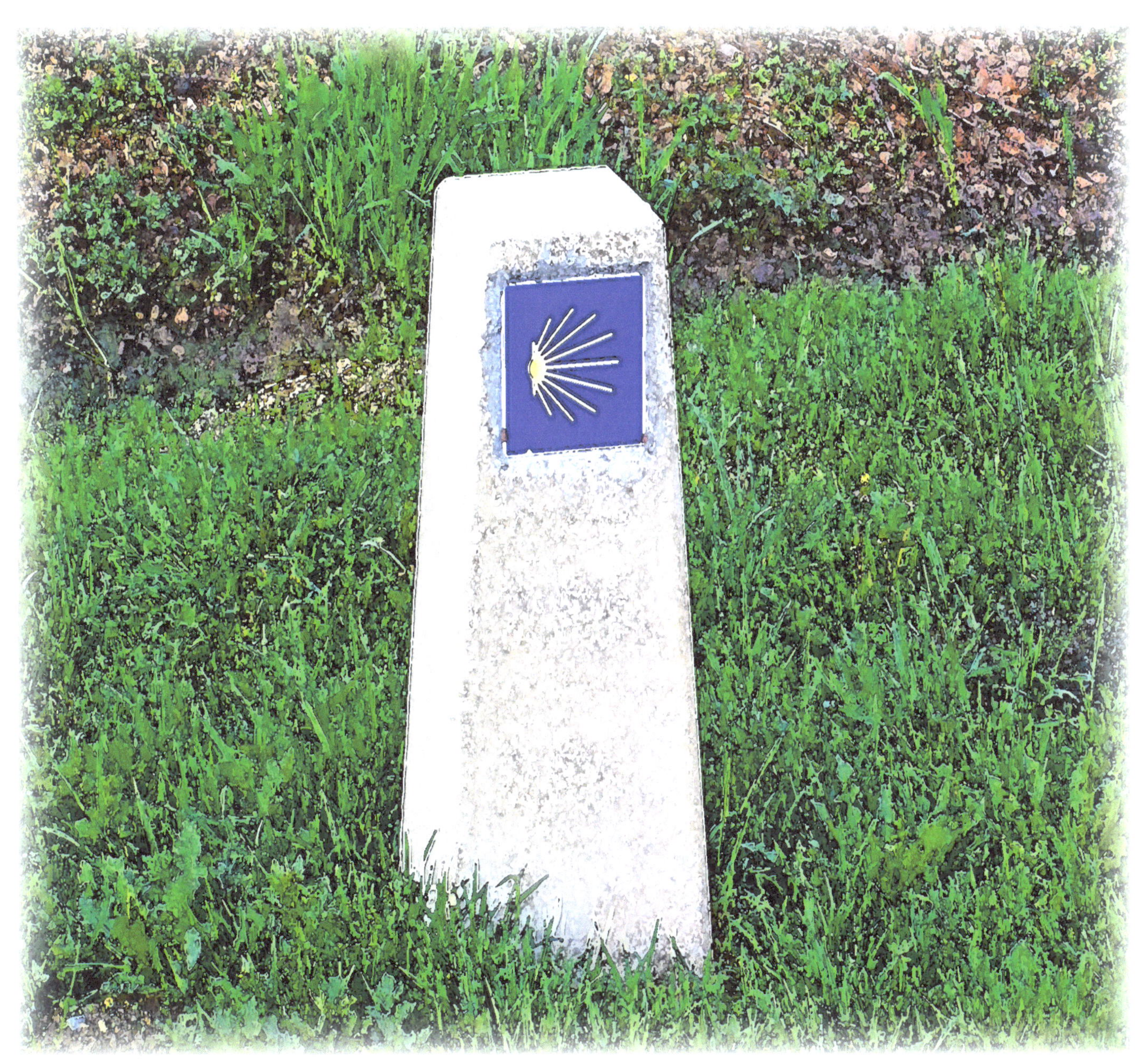

Camino Marker

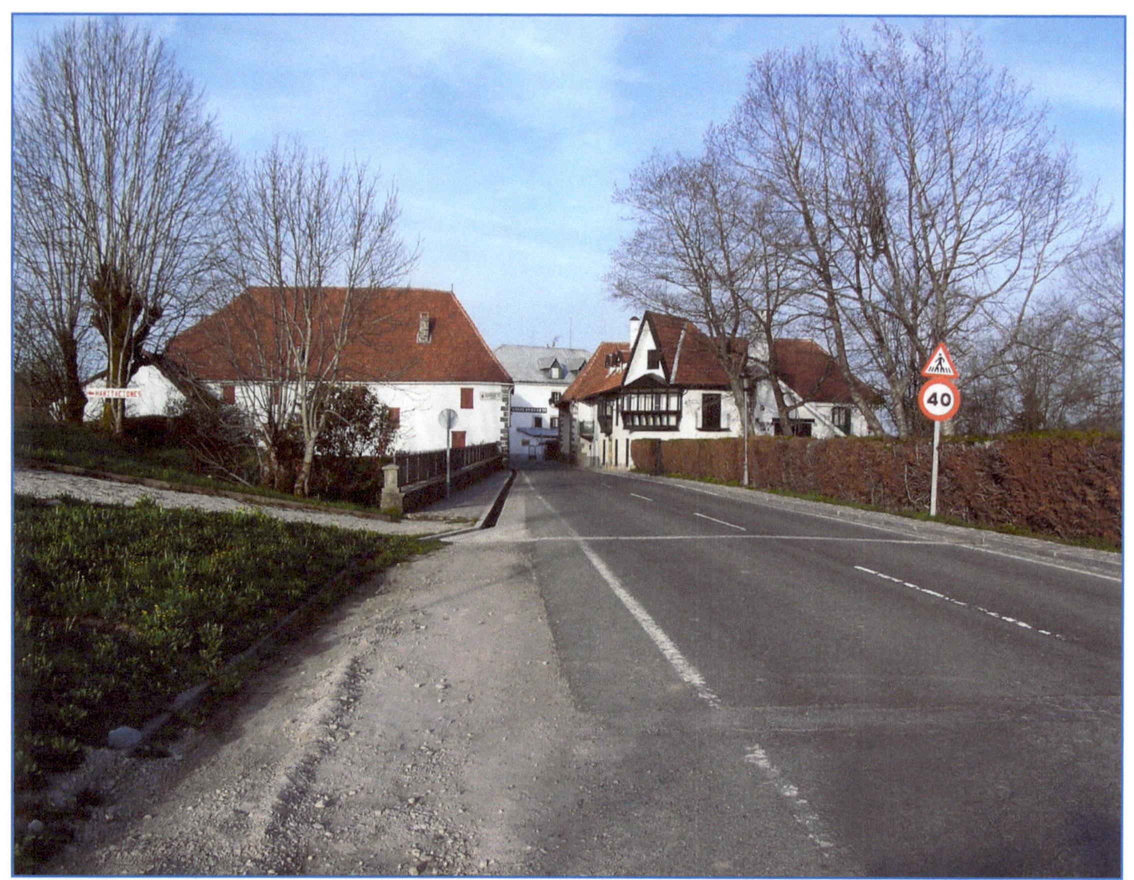

Entering Burguete

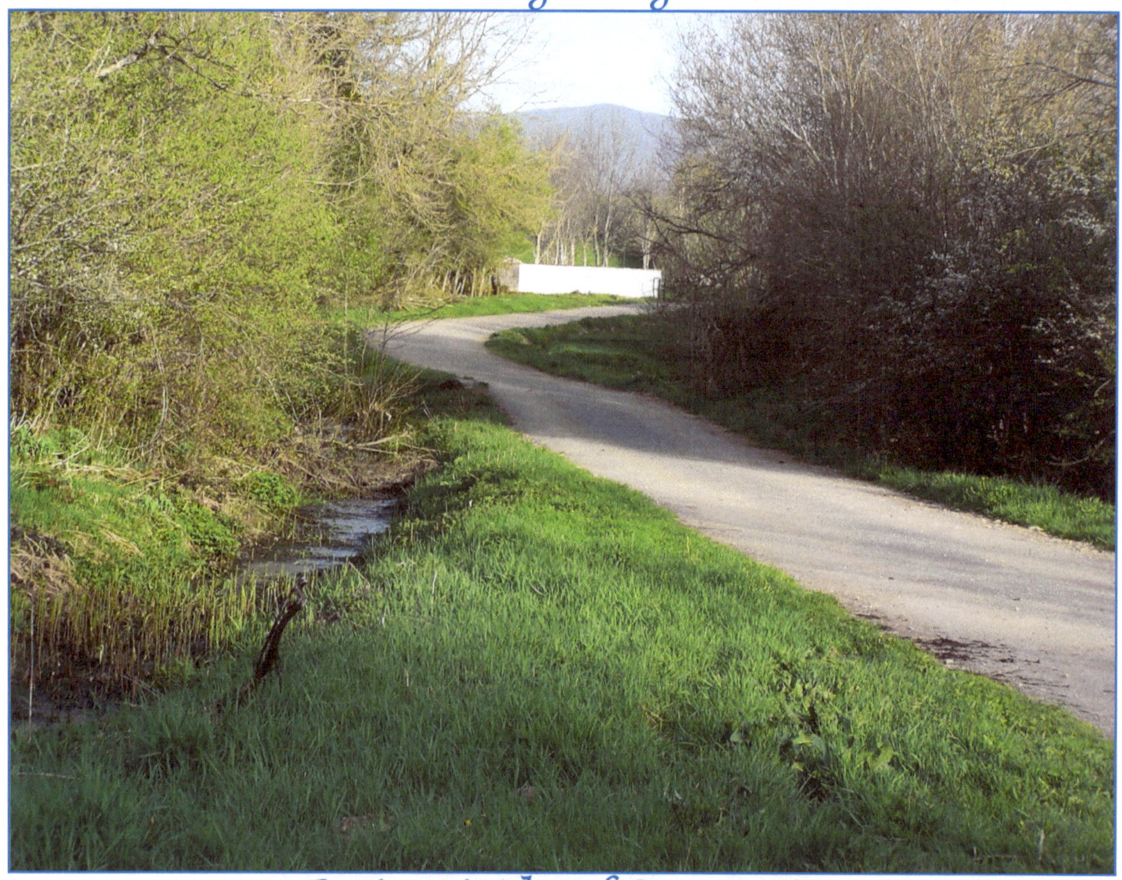

Just outside of Burguete

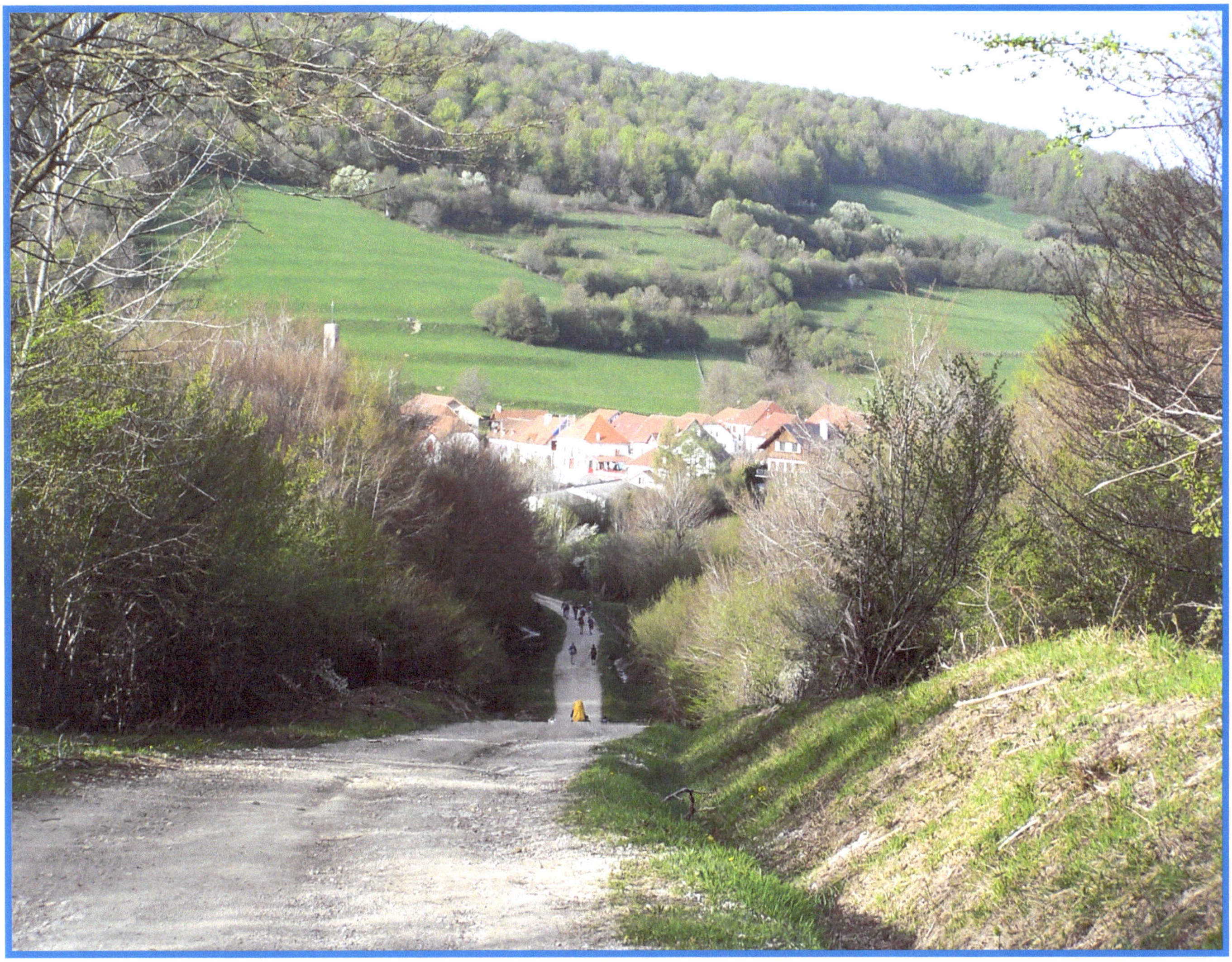

Approaching Espinal

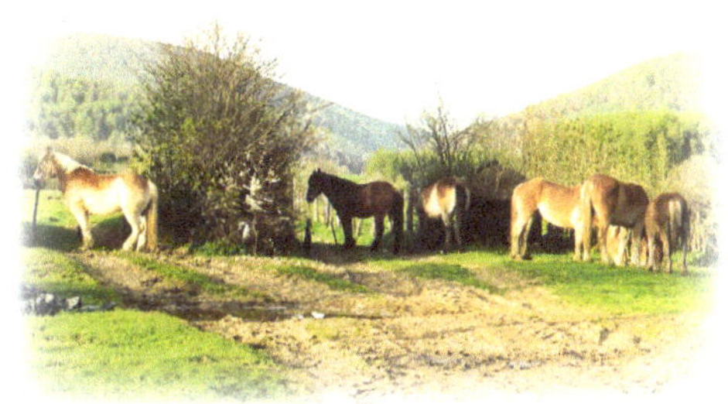

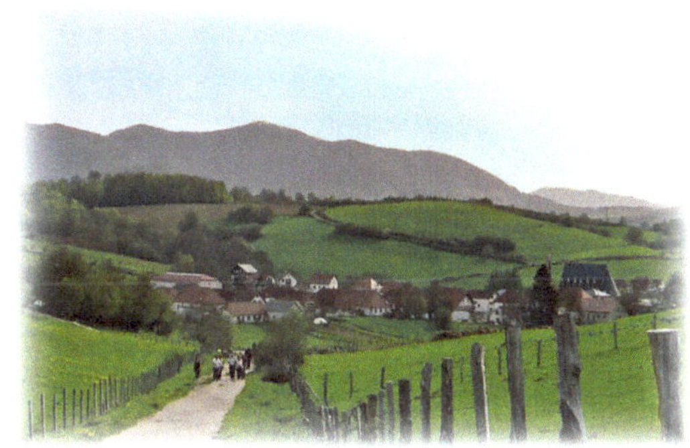

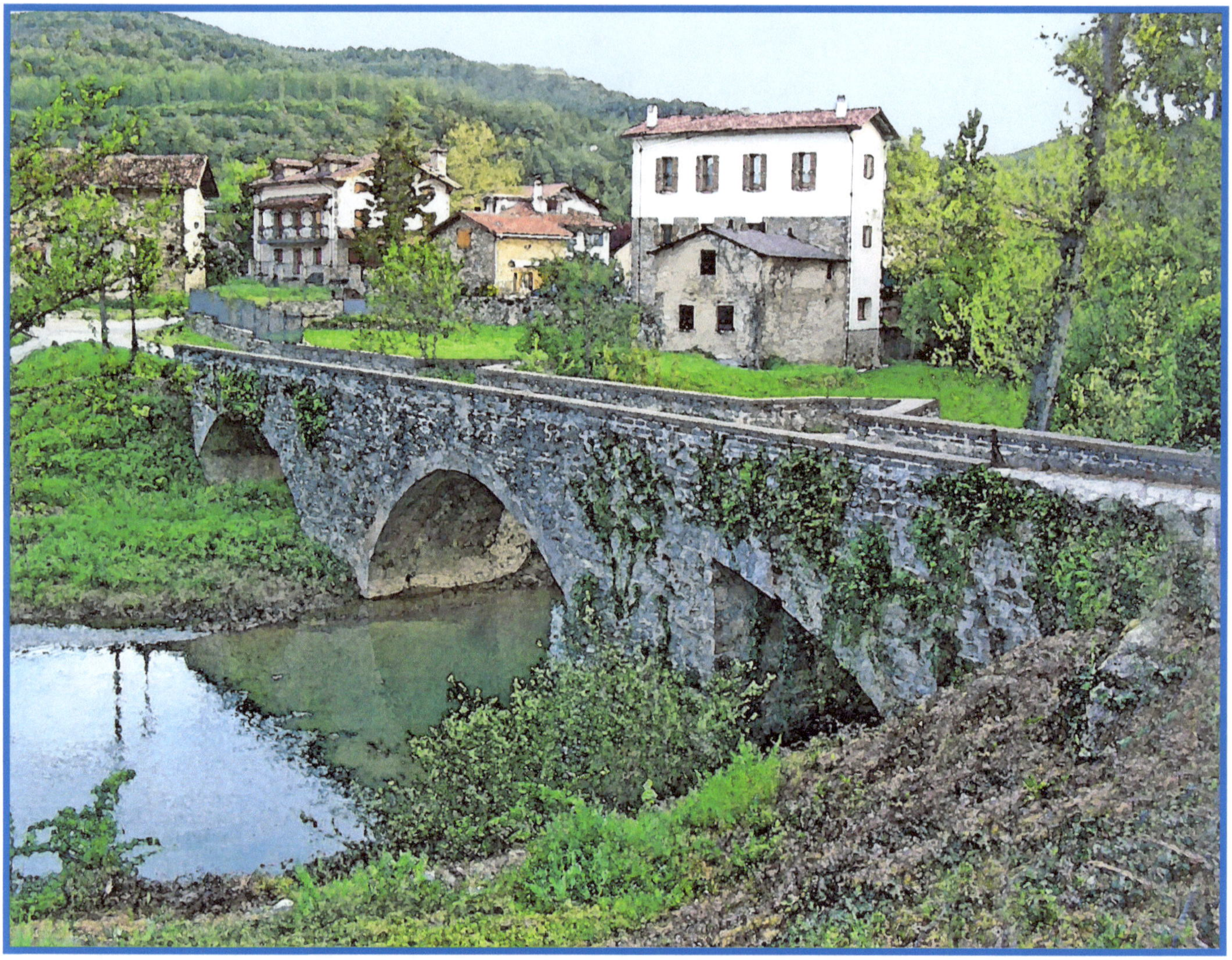

Puente de los Bandidos-Larrasoana

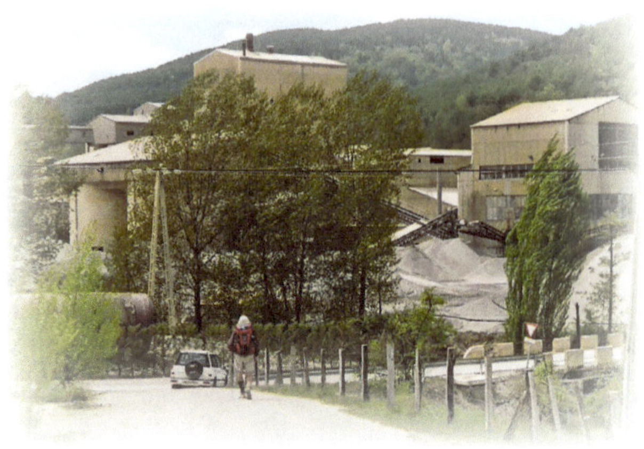

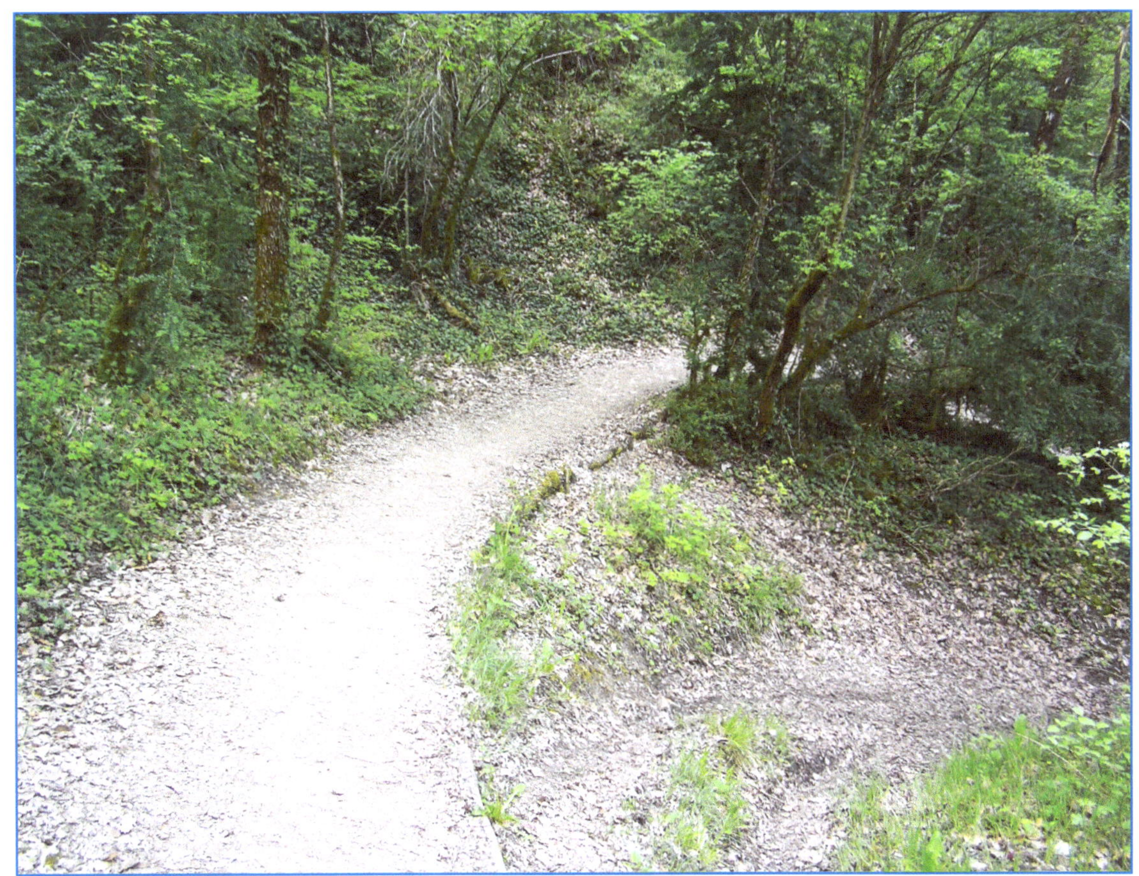

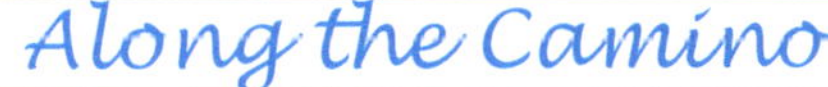
Along the Camino

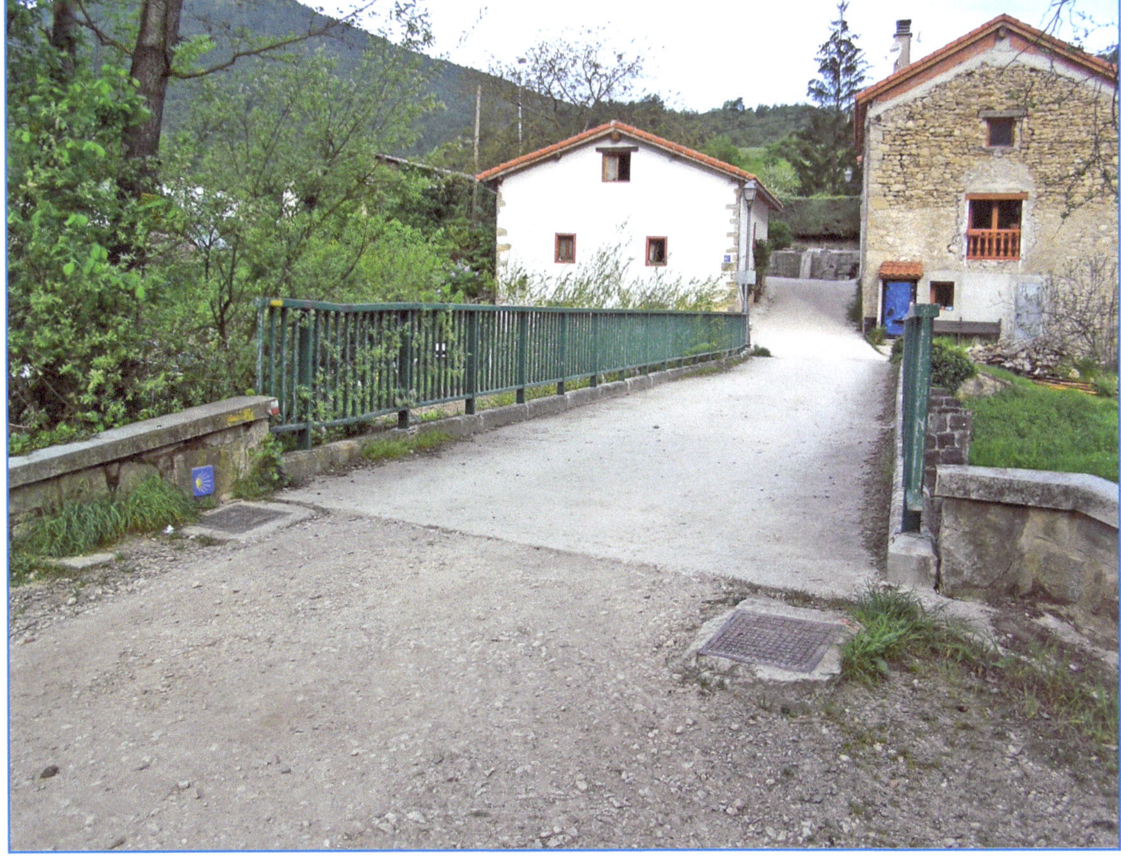

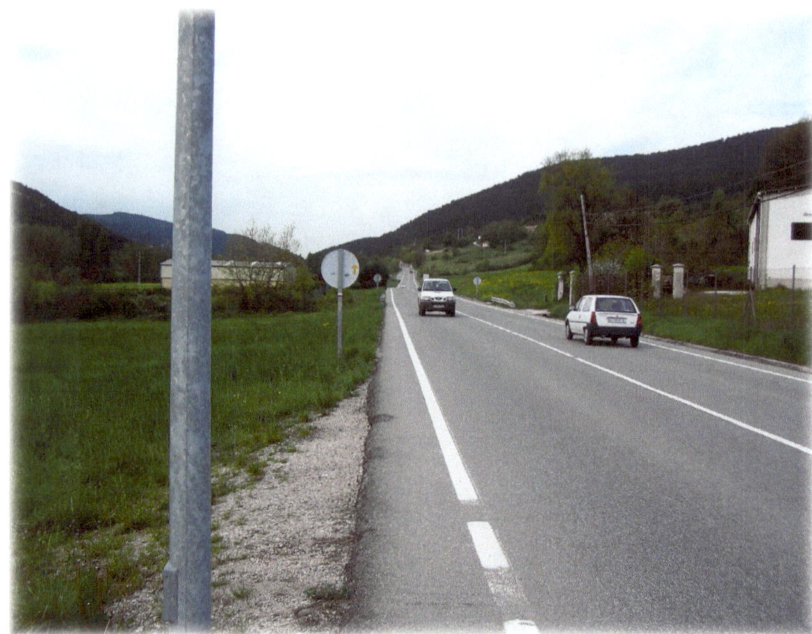

Camino along the main highway

View from the Camino

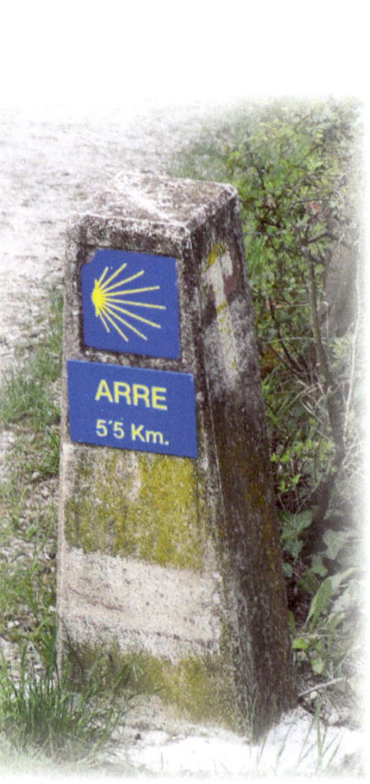

Camino trail marker

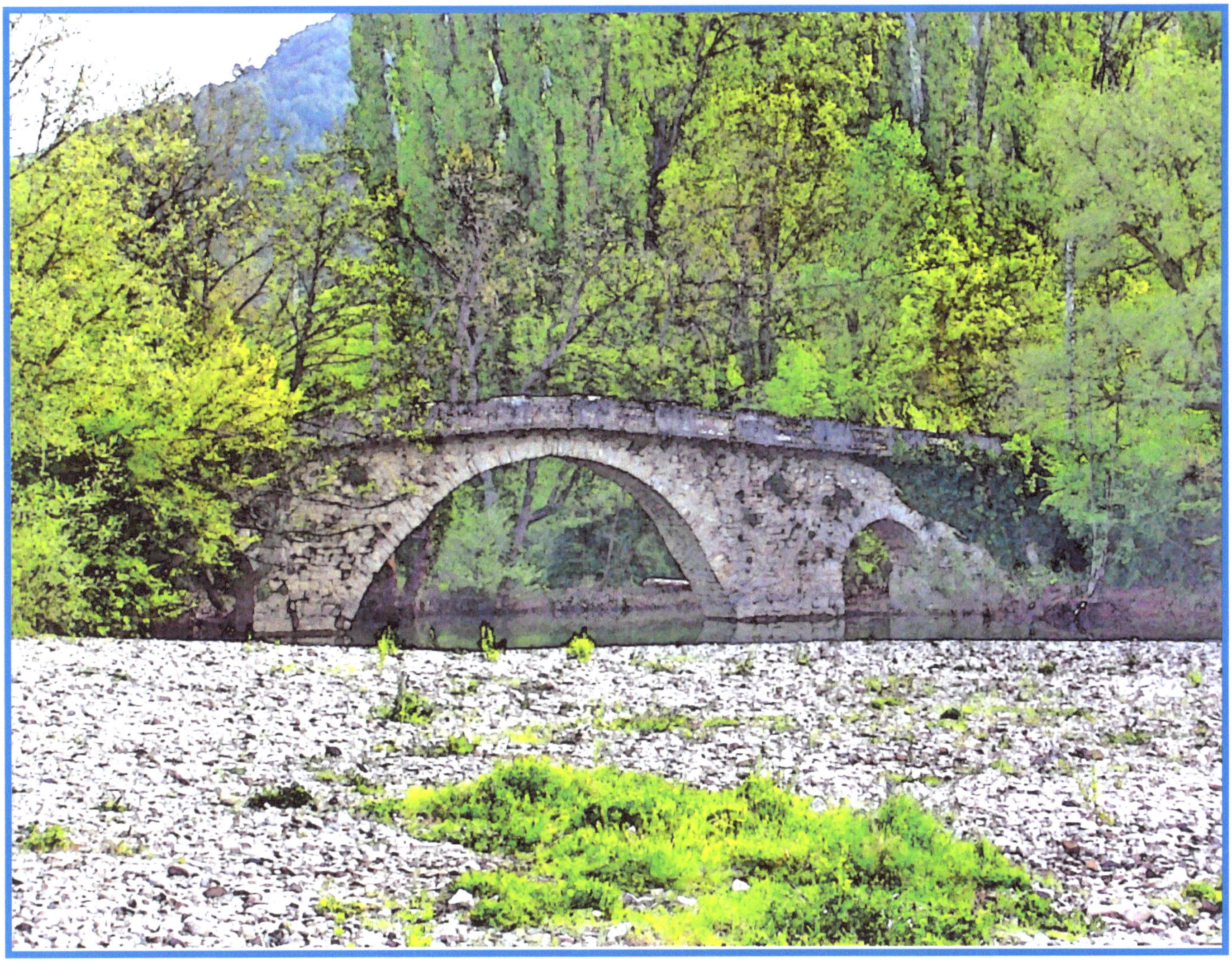

Bridge at Irotz

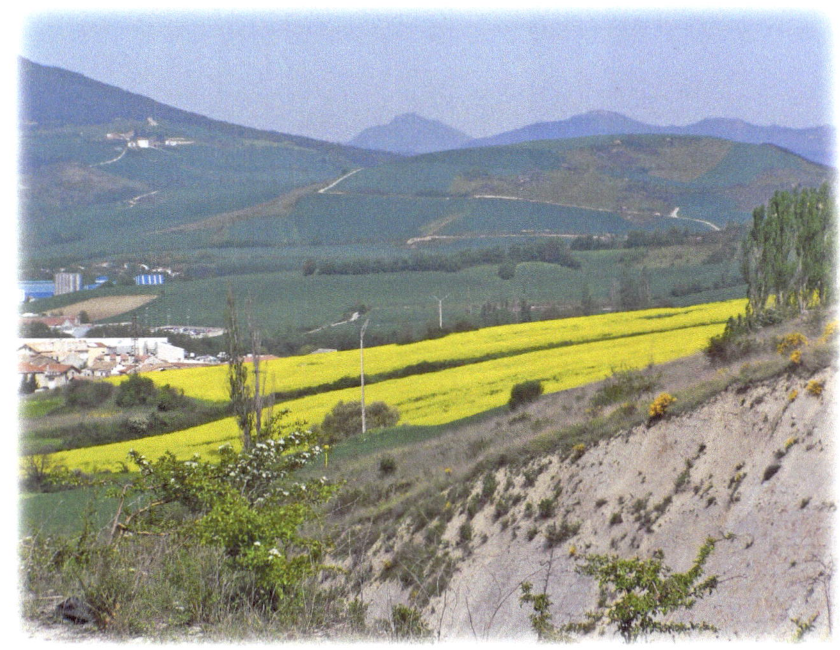

View from the Camino

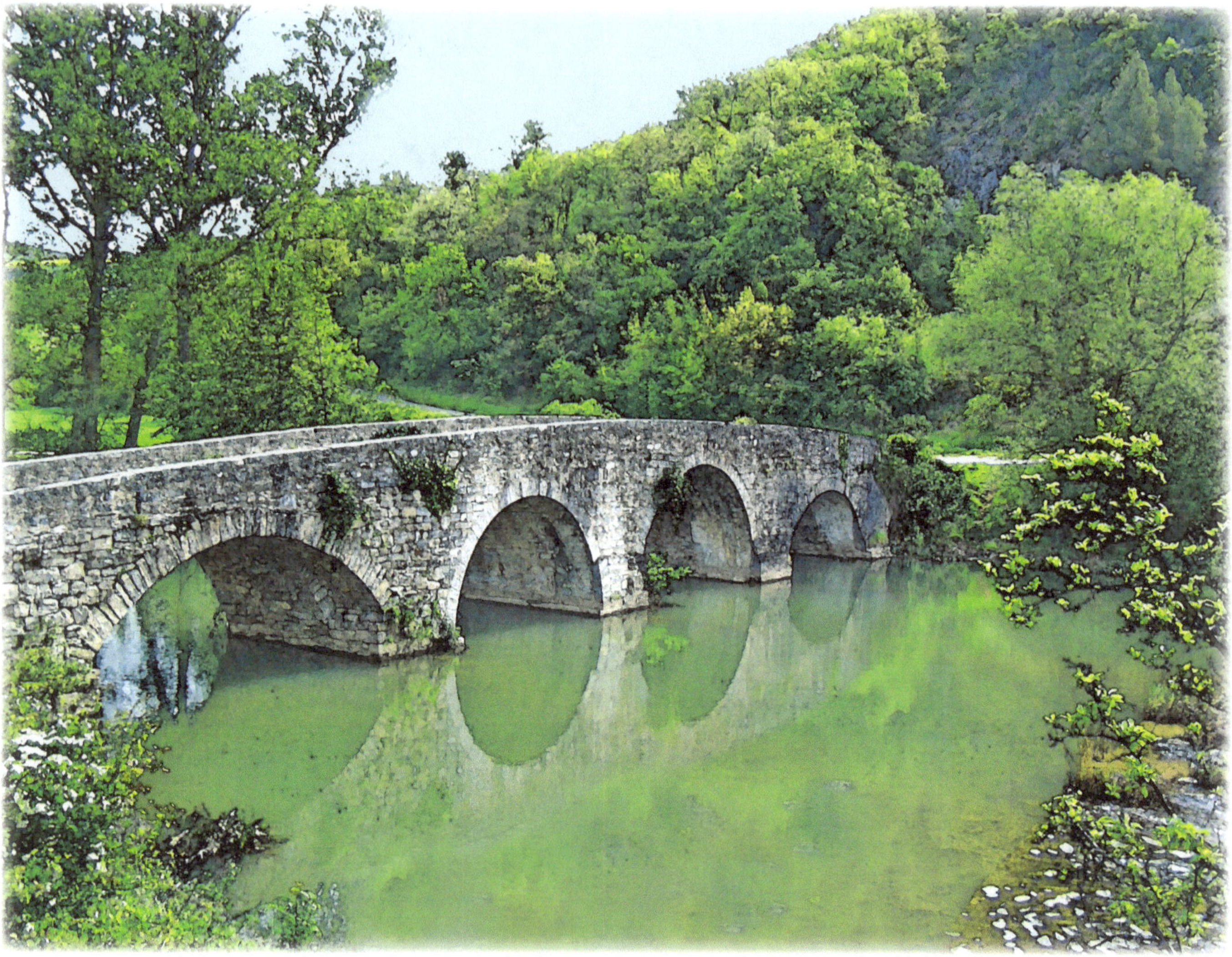

Bridge at Trinidad de Arre

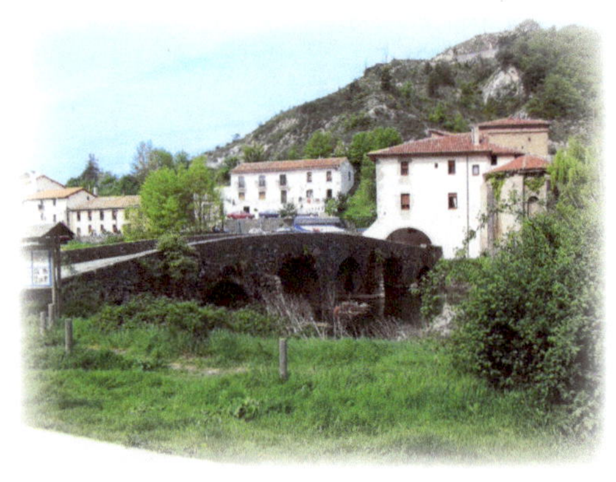

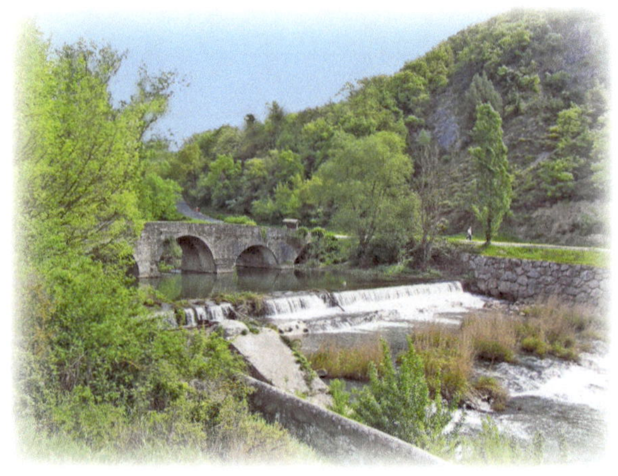

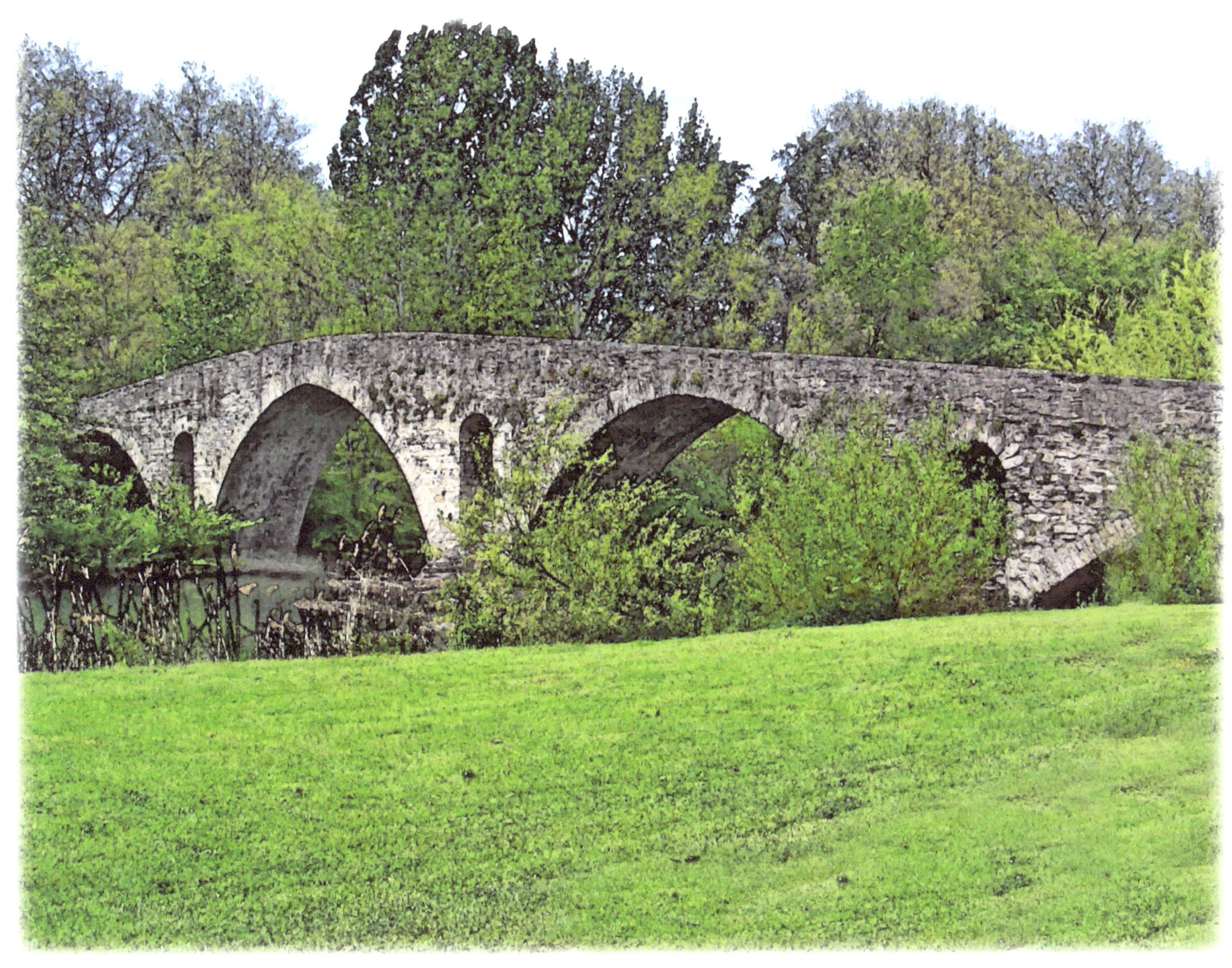

Puente de la Magdalena into Pamplona

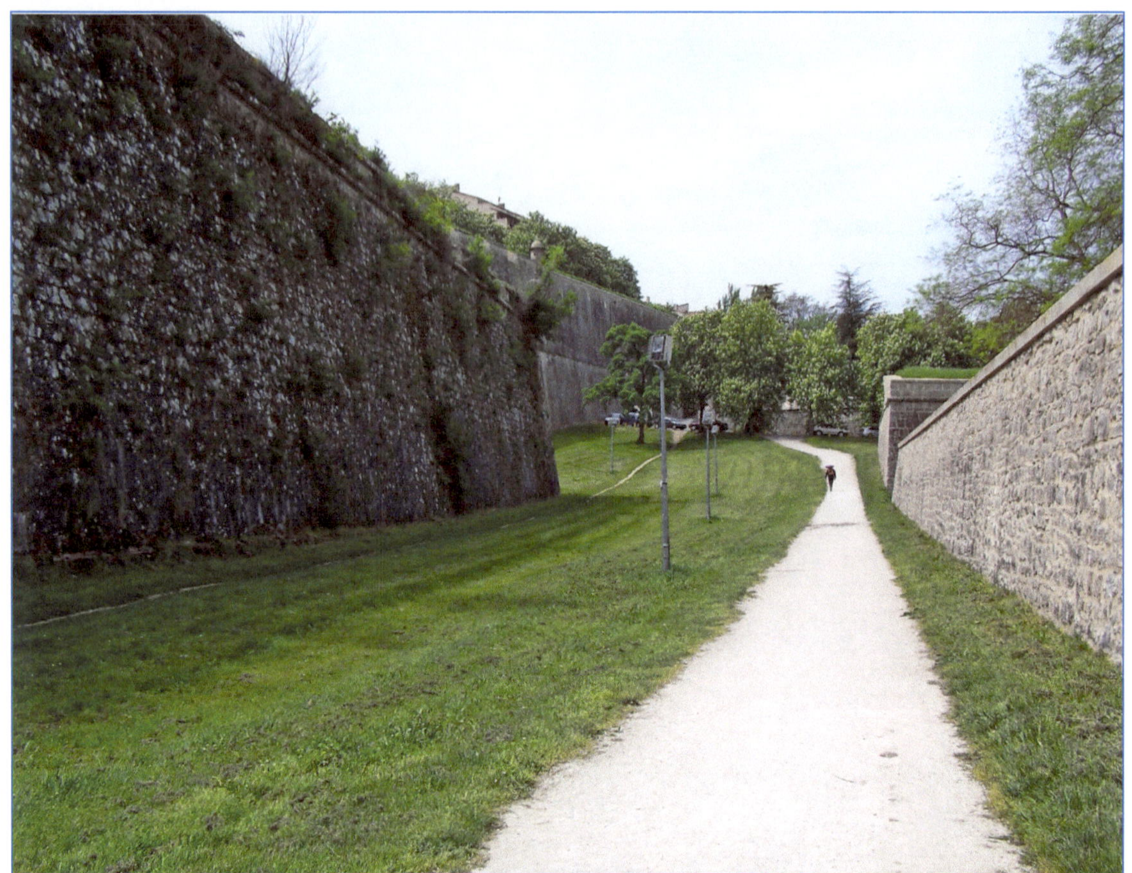

Pamplona City walls

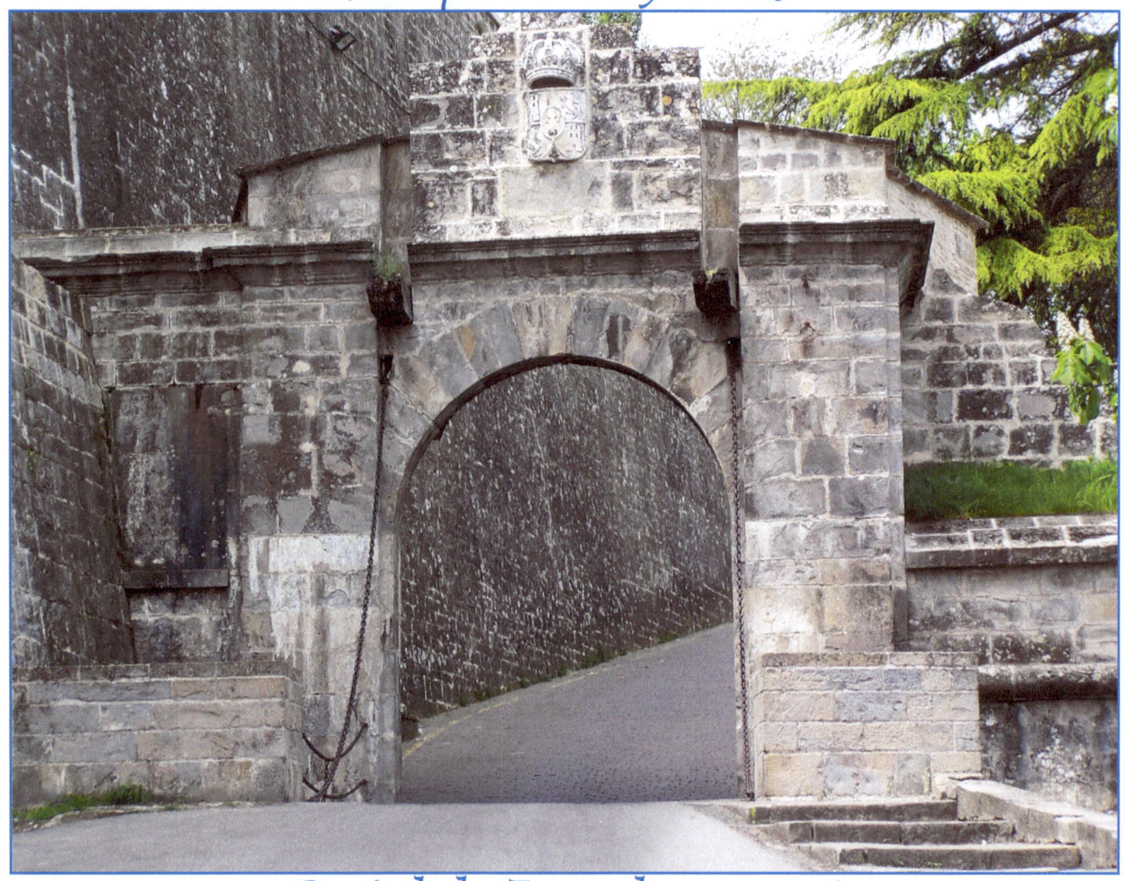

Portal de Zumalacarregi

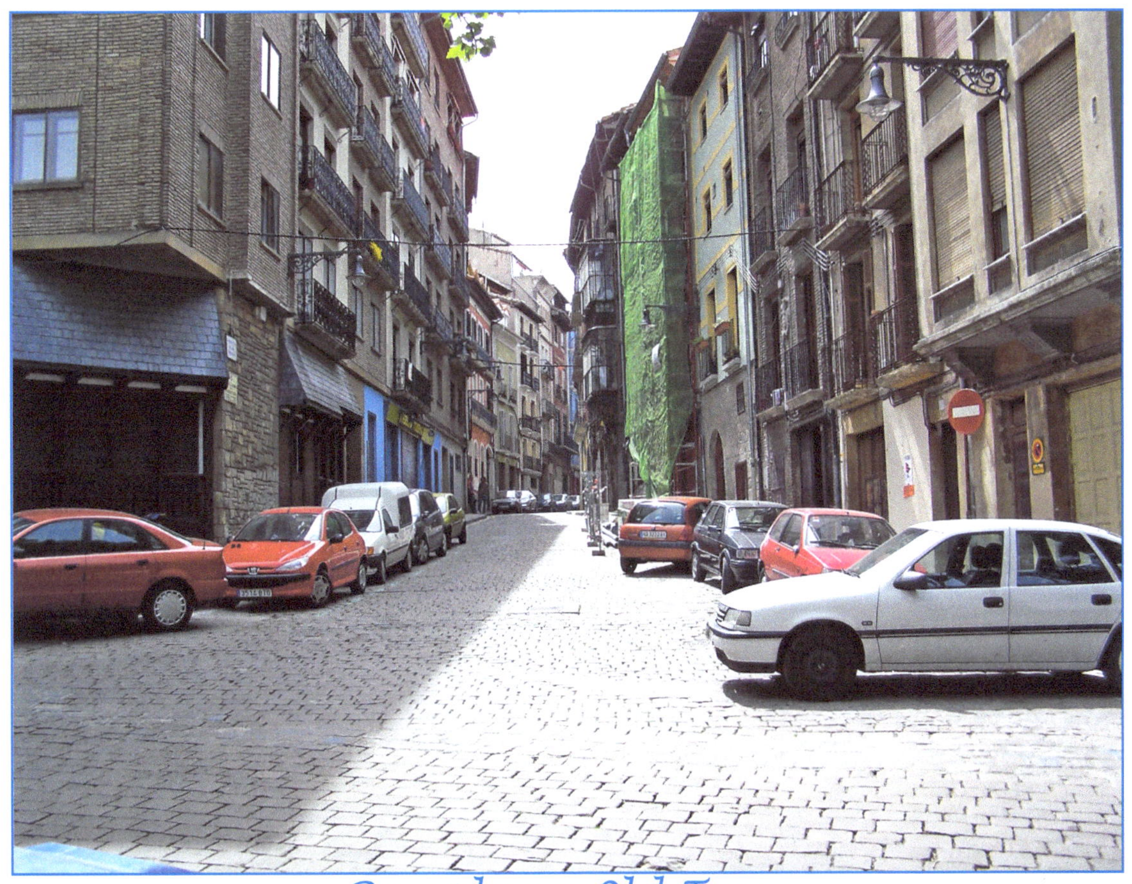

Pamplona Old Town

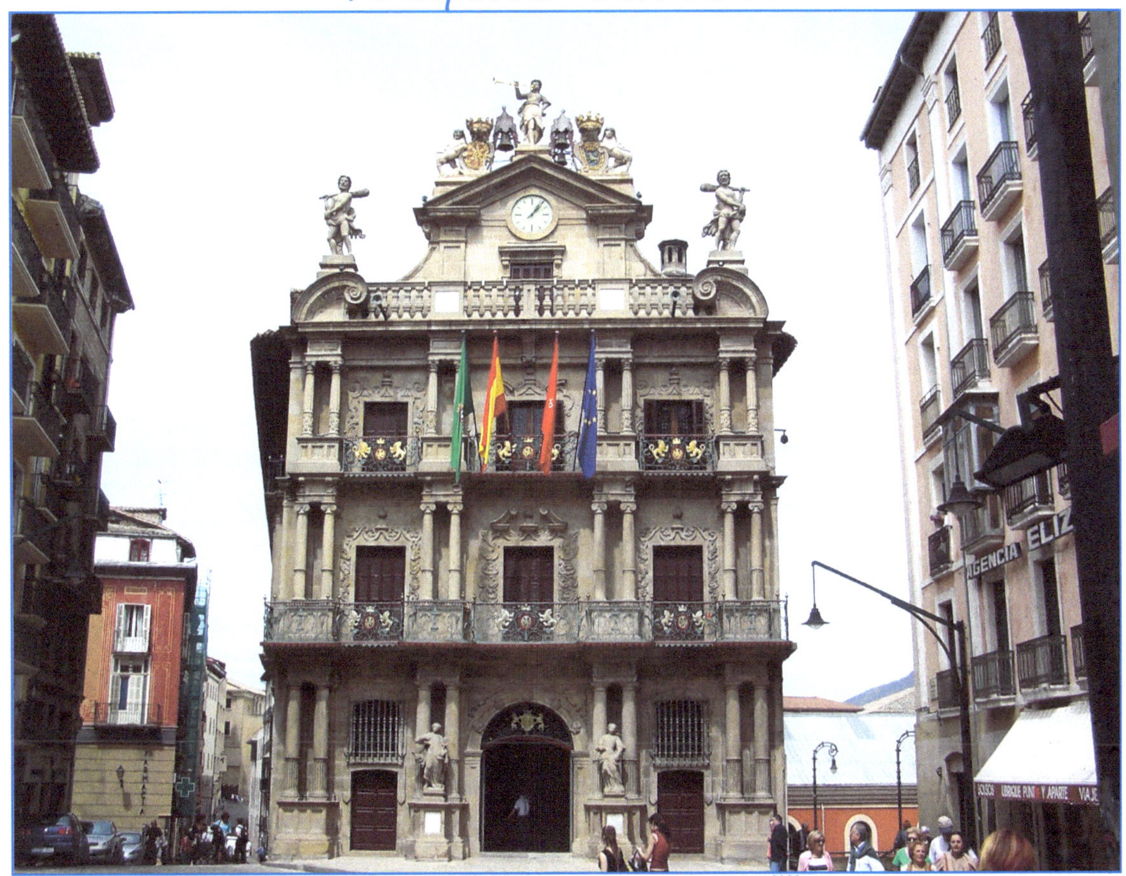

Pamplona Town Hall

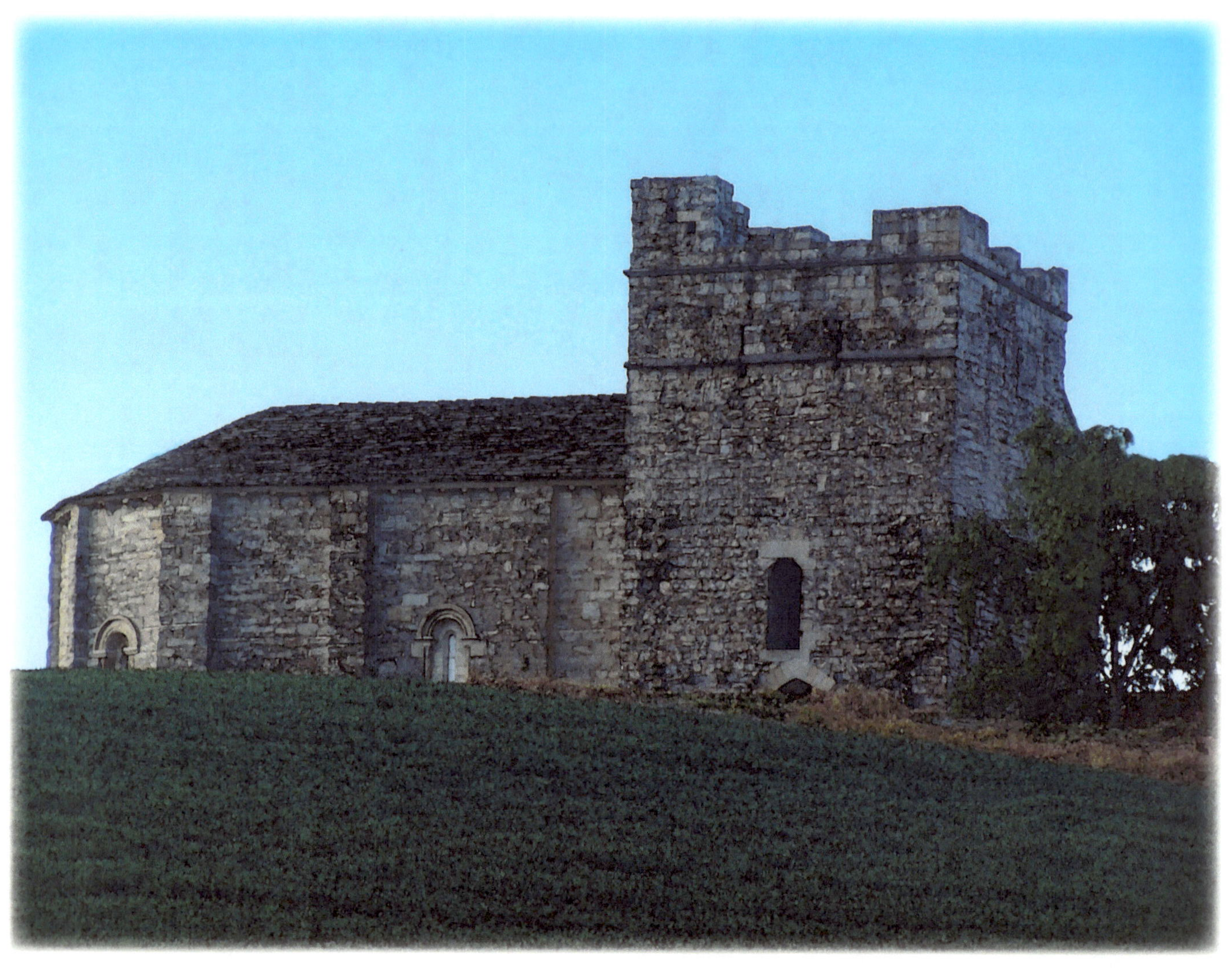

Cizur Menor

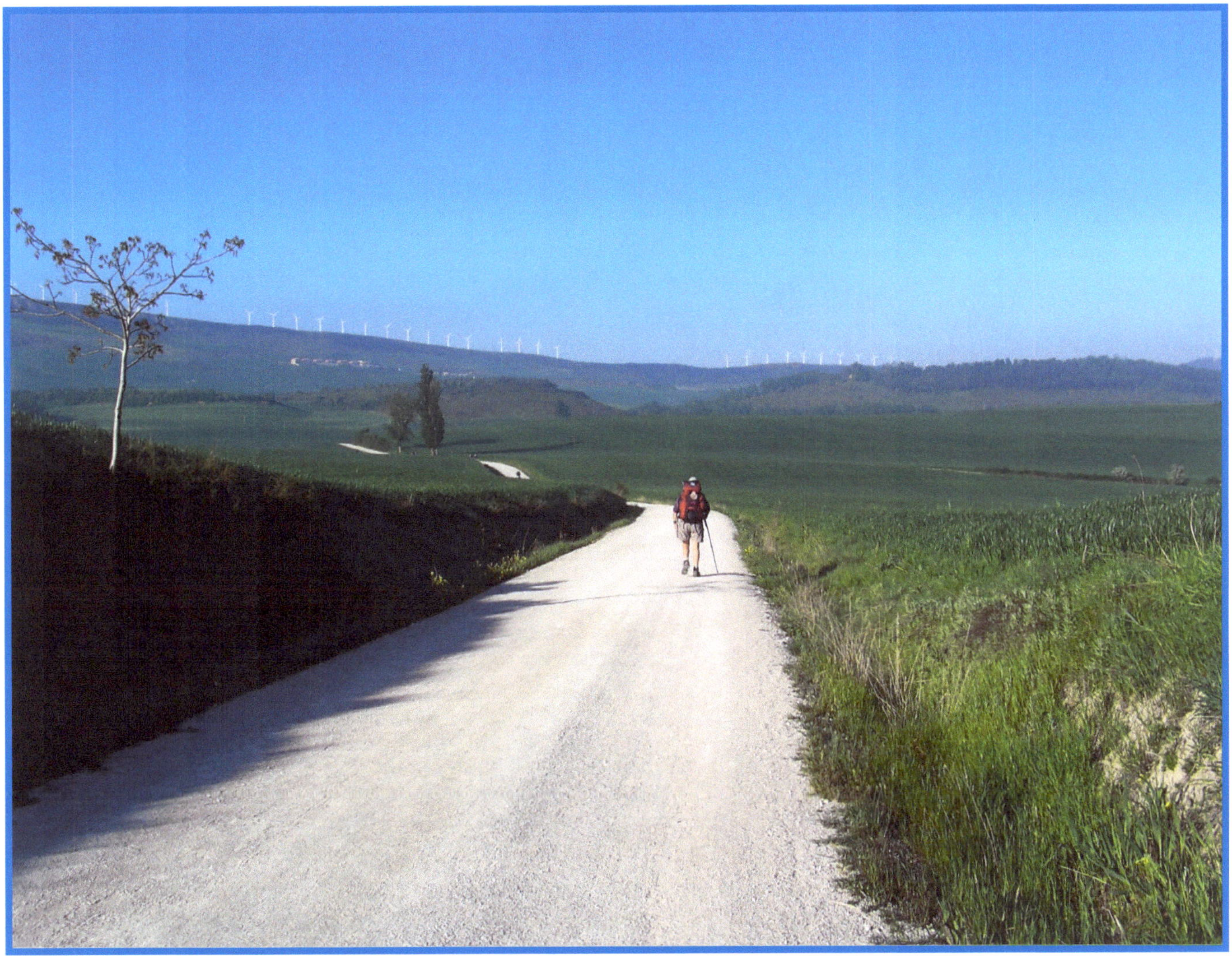

Perfect day on the Camino

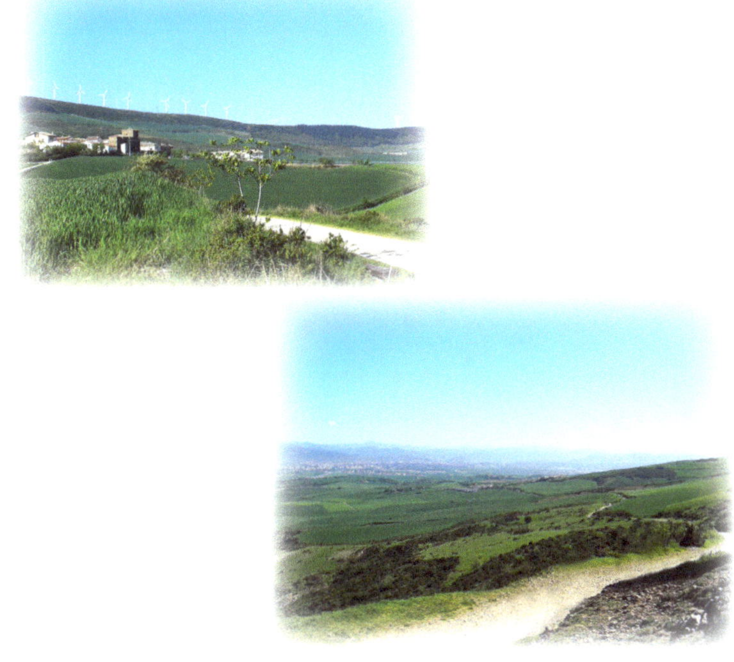

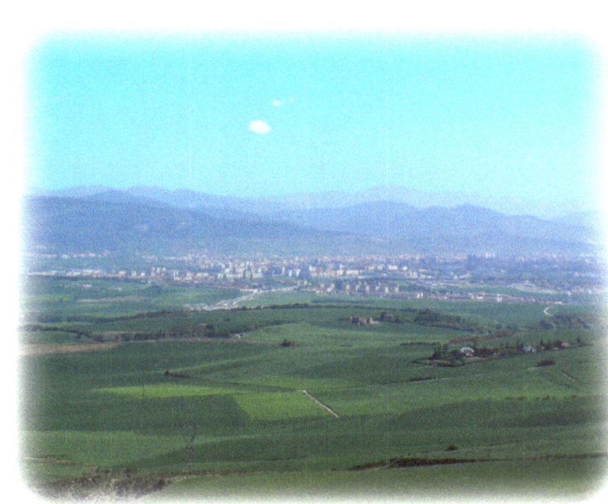

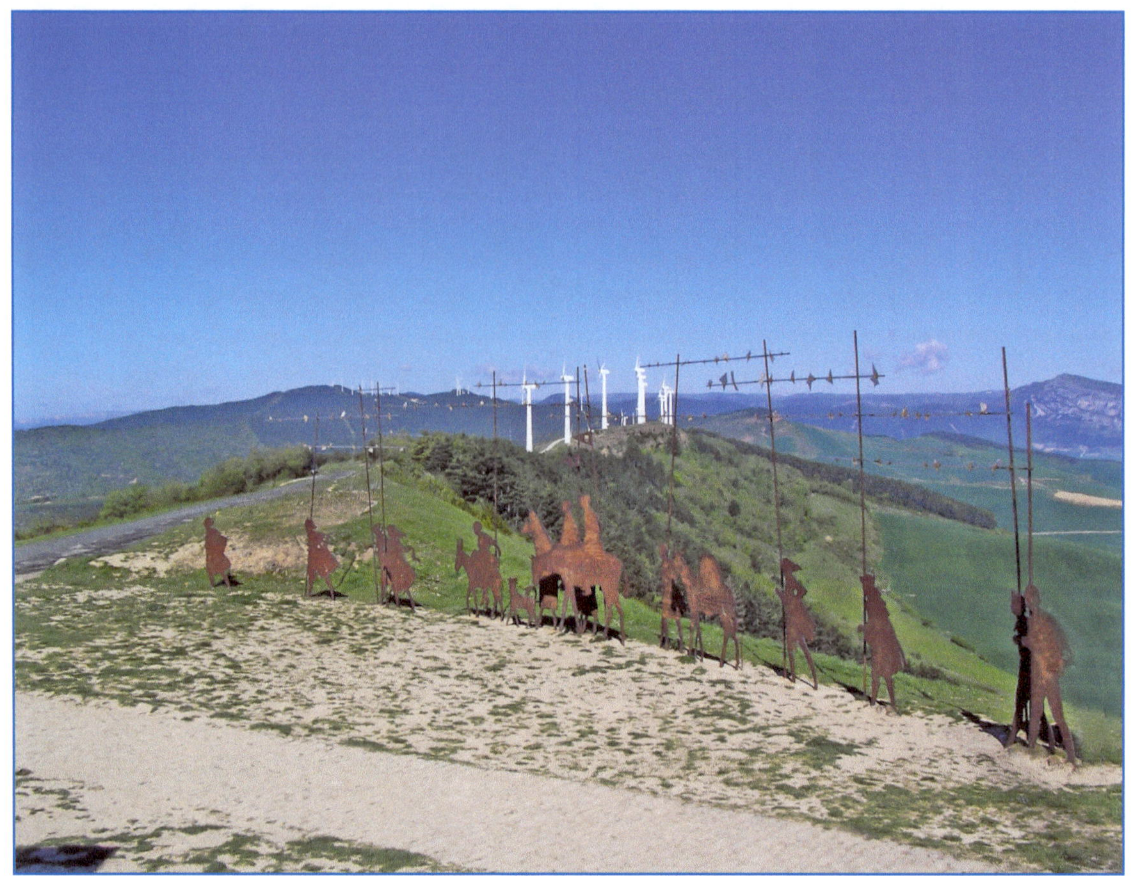

Alto del Perdon

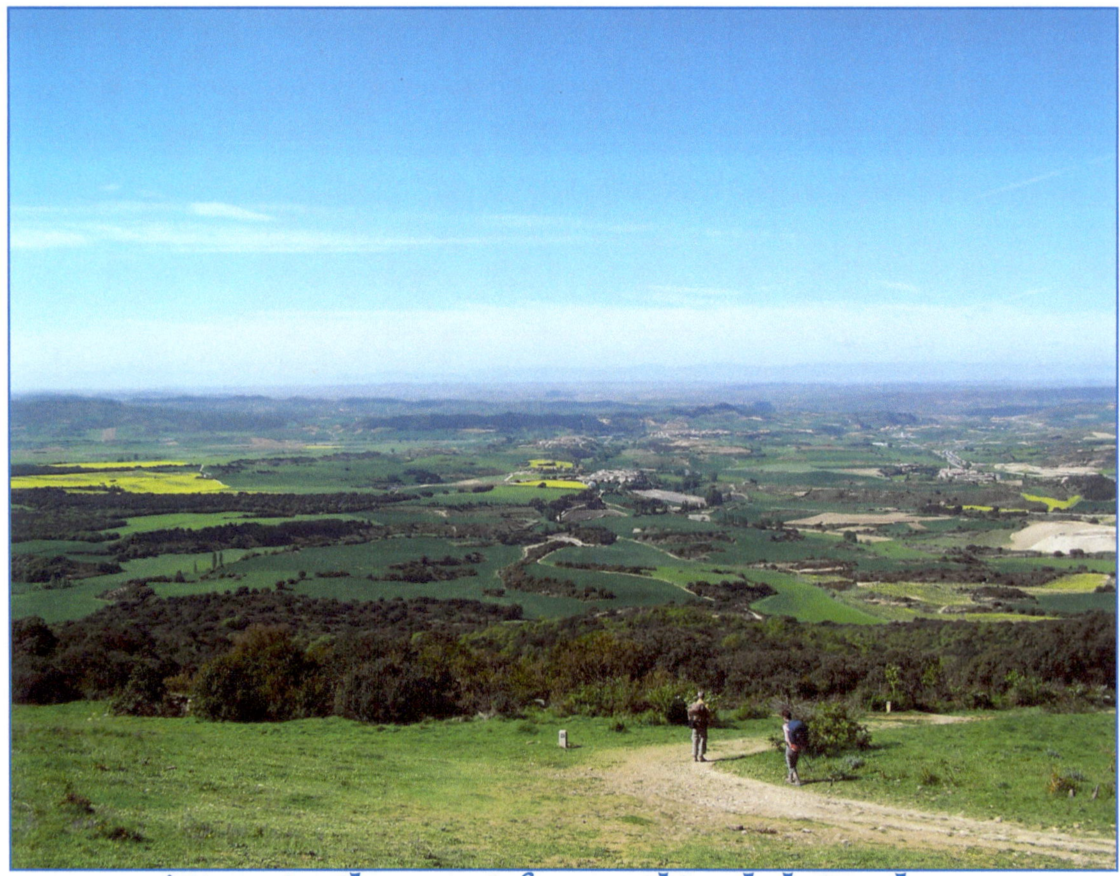

View to the west from Alto del Perdon

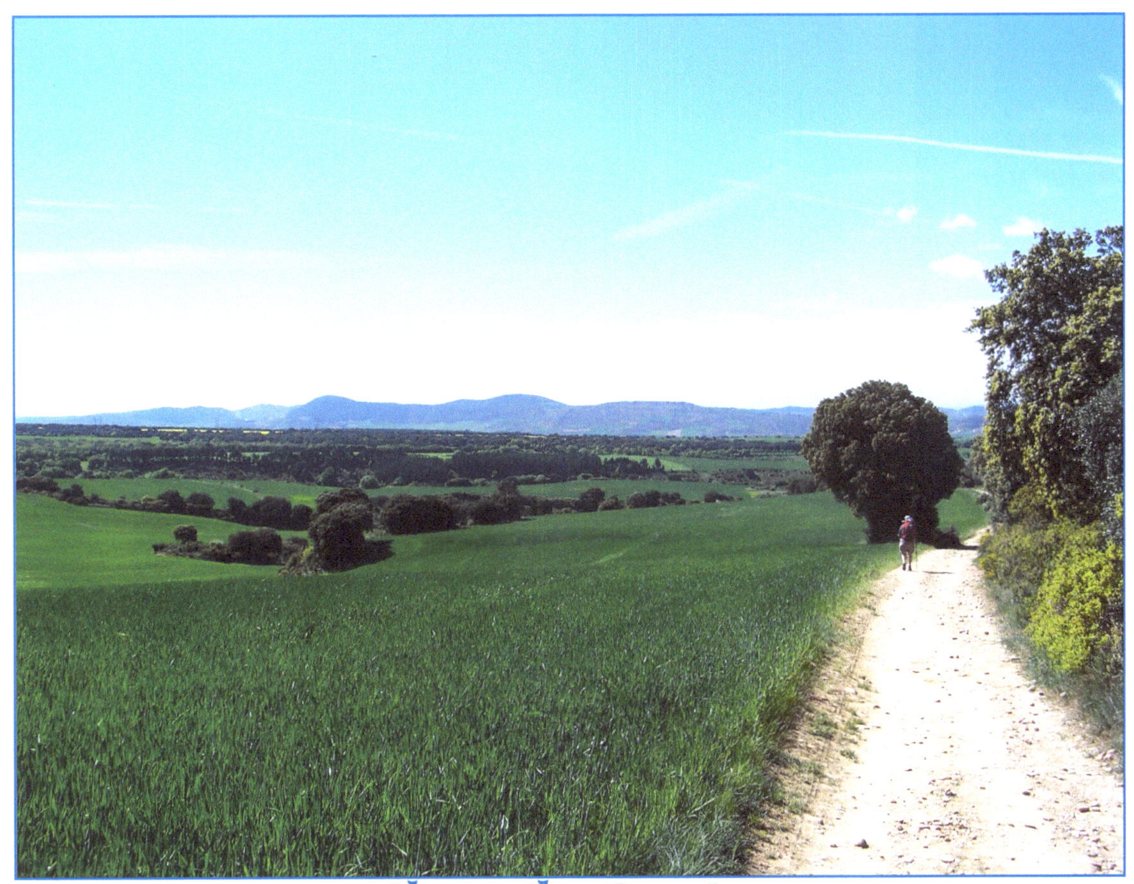

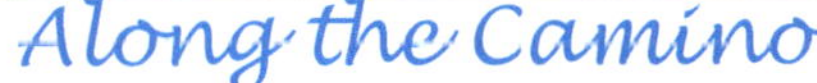
Along the Camino

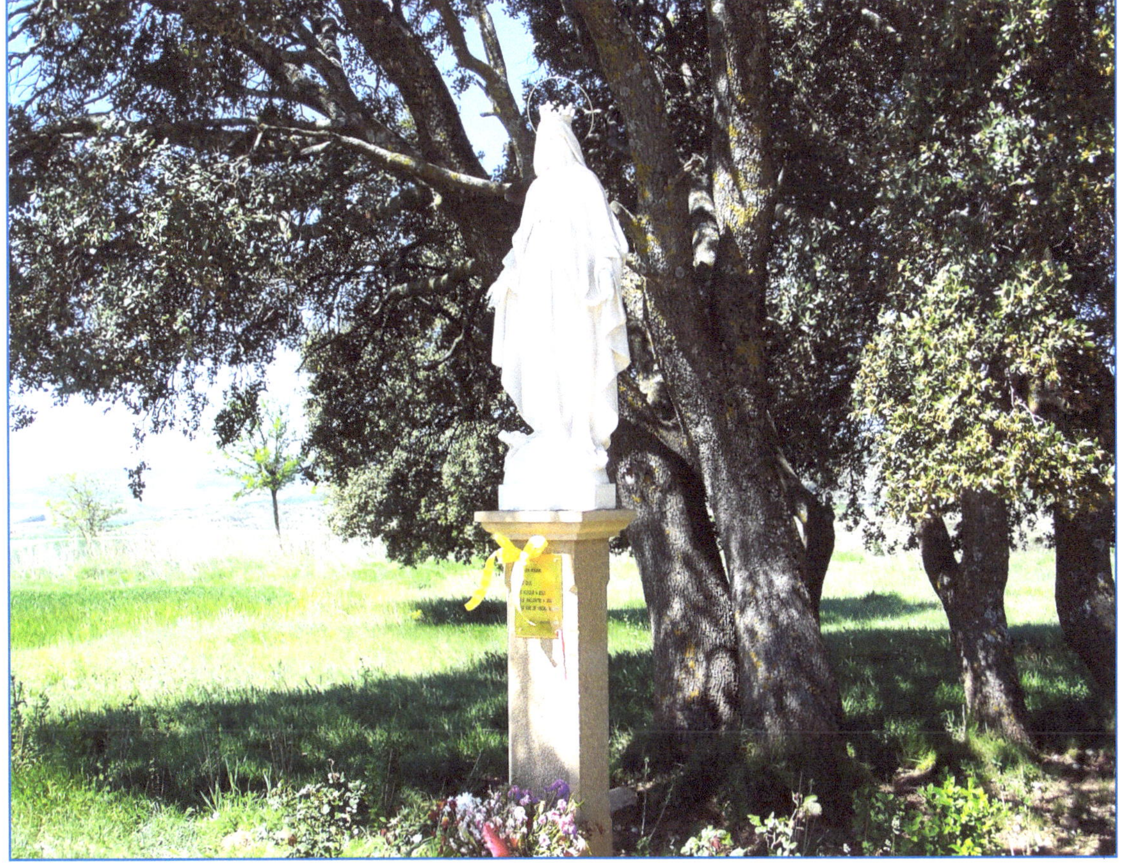

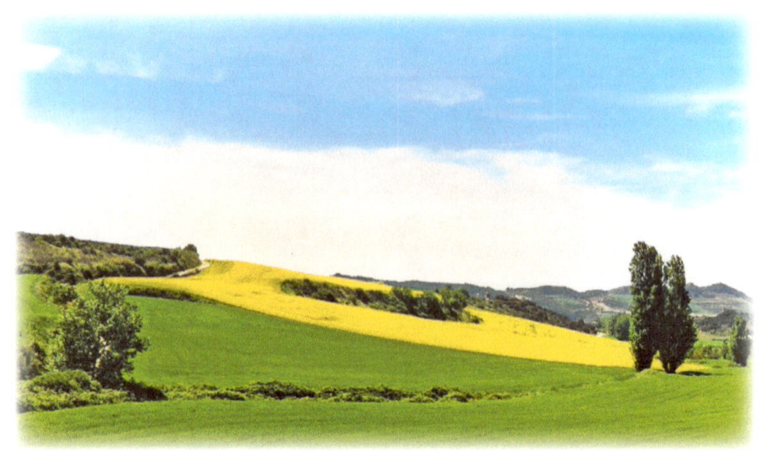

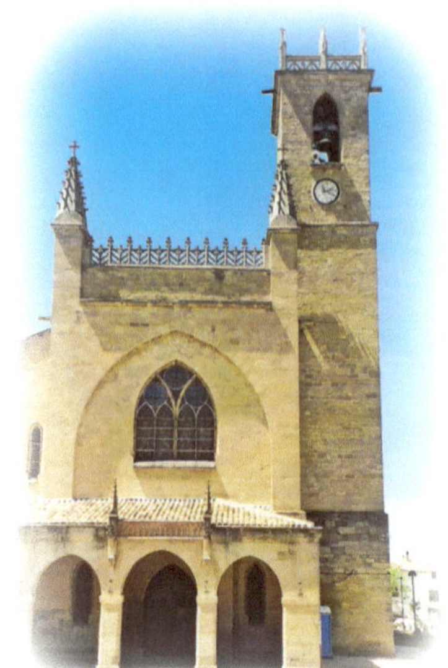

Obanos

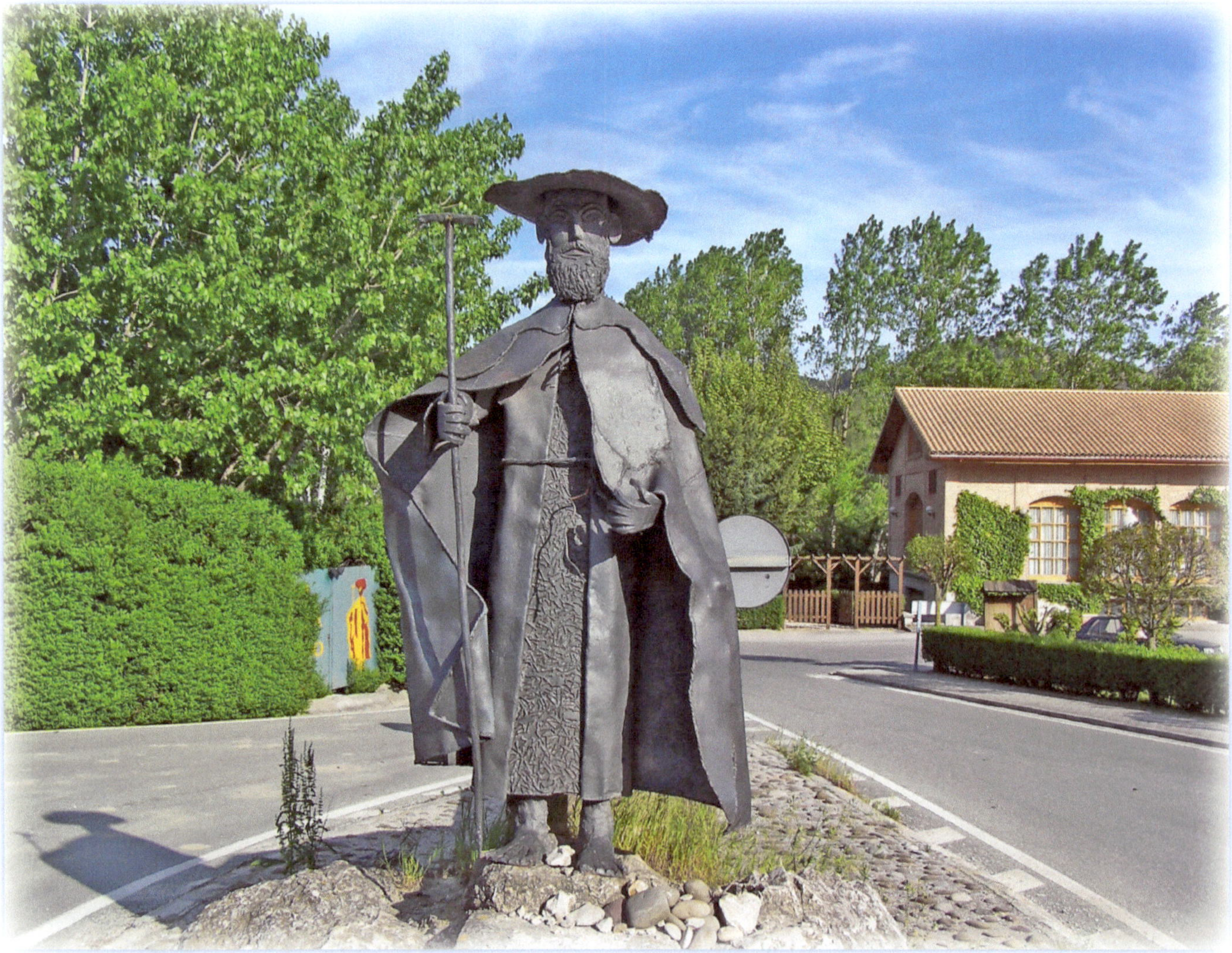

St. James-Puente la Reina

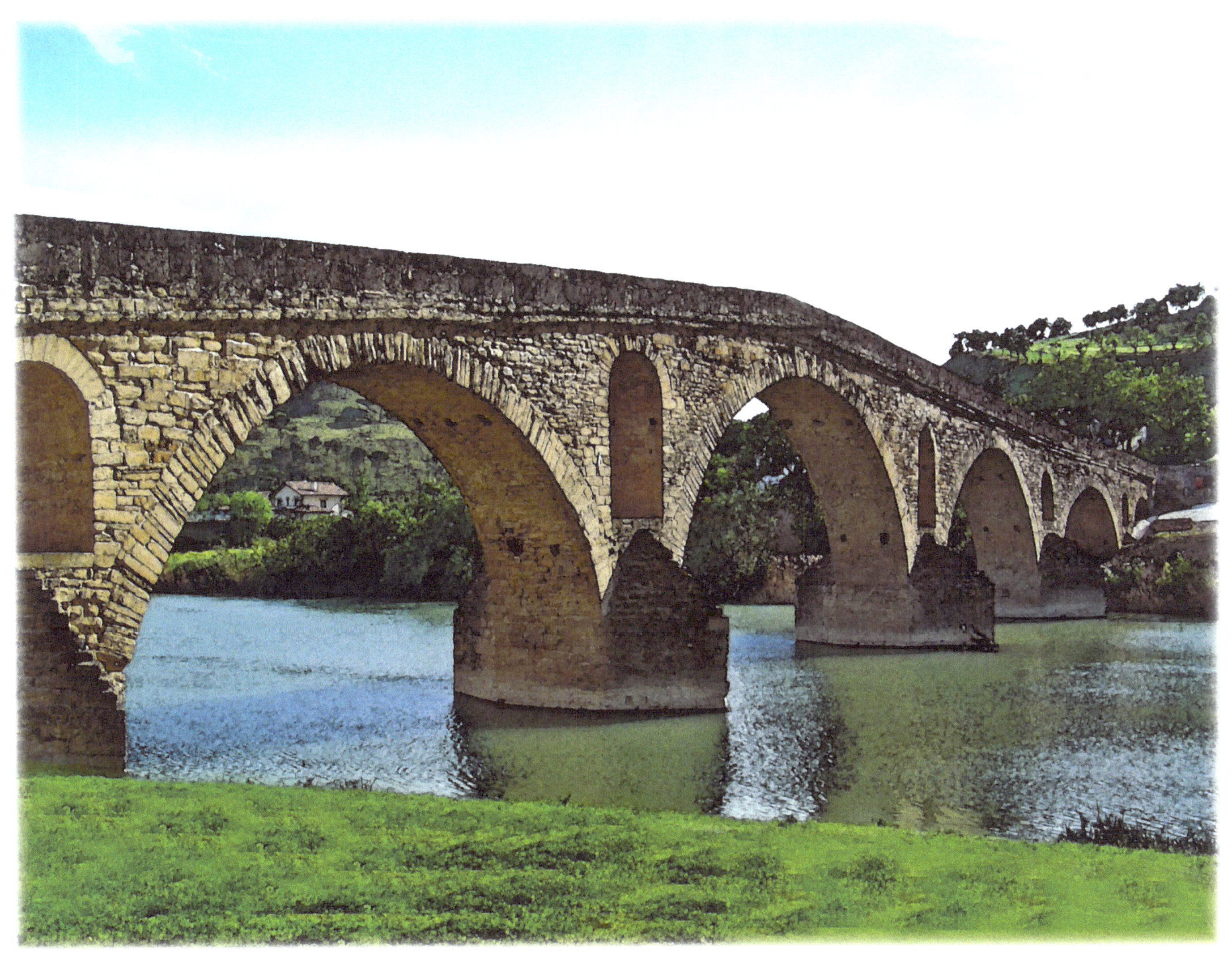

Puente la Reina

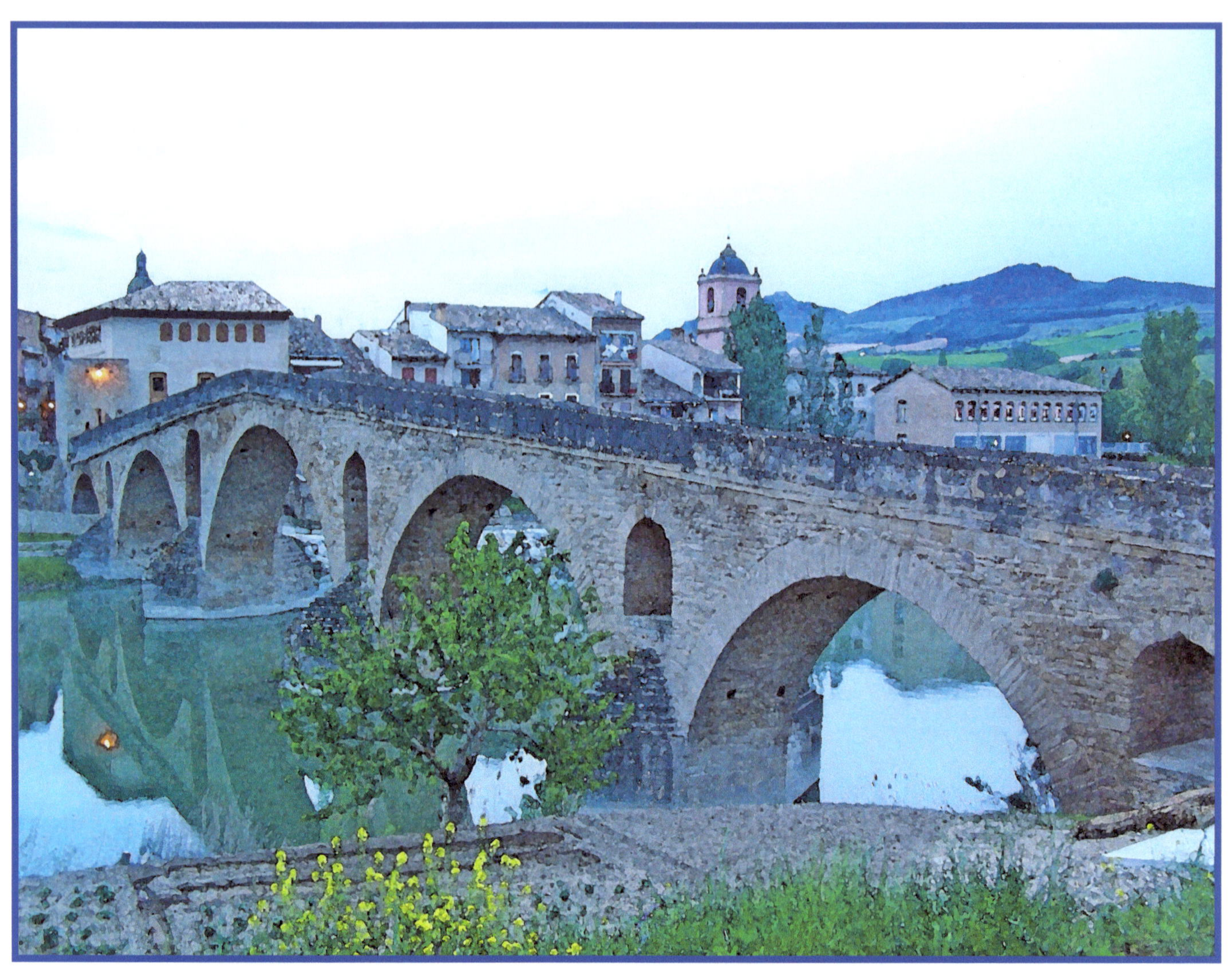

Early morning-Leaving Puente la Reina

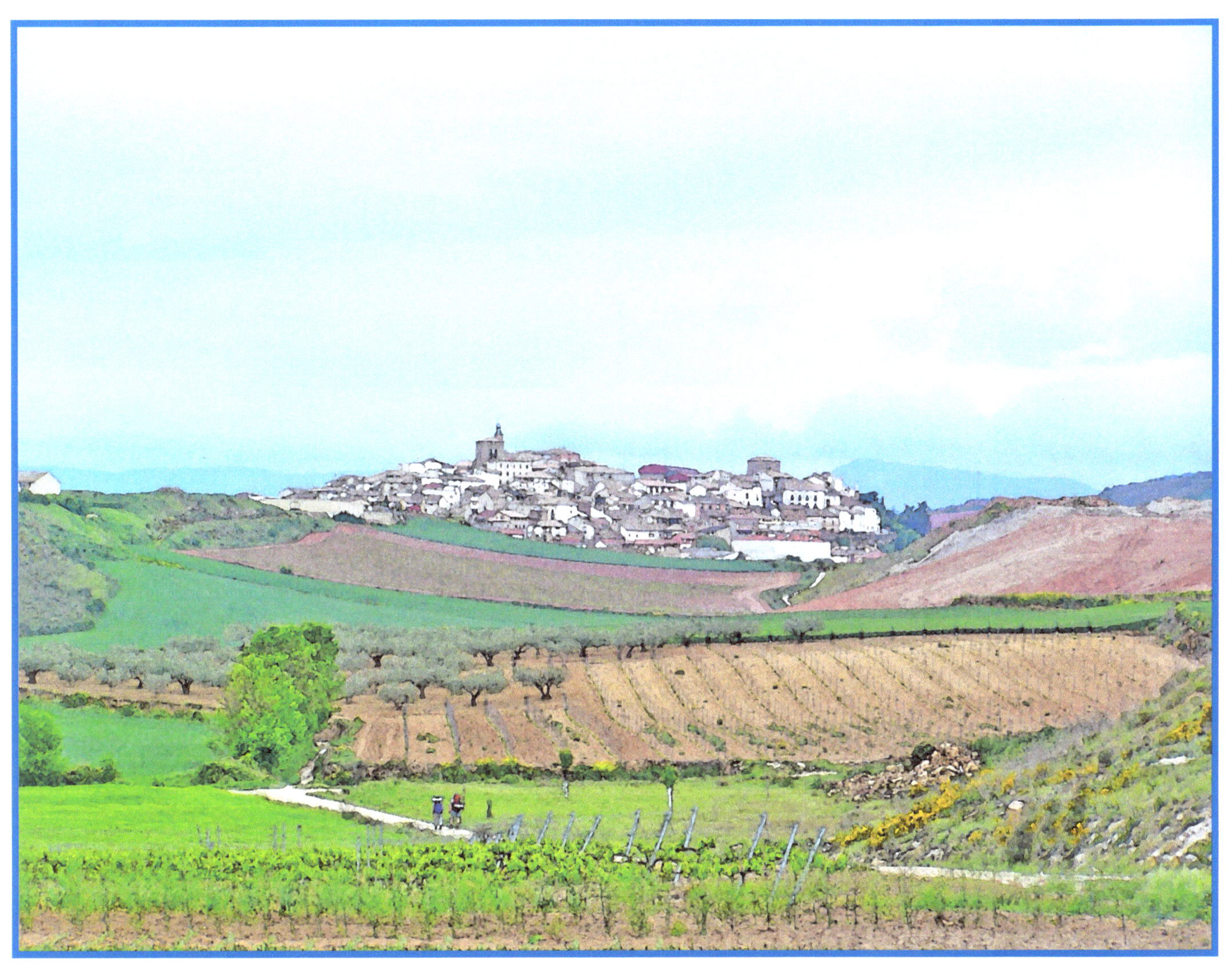

Pilgrims approaching Cirauqui

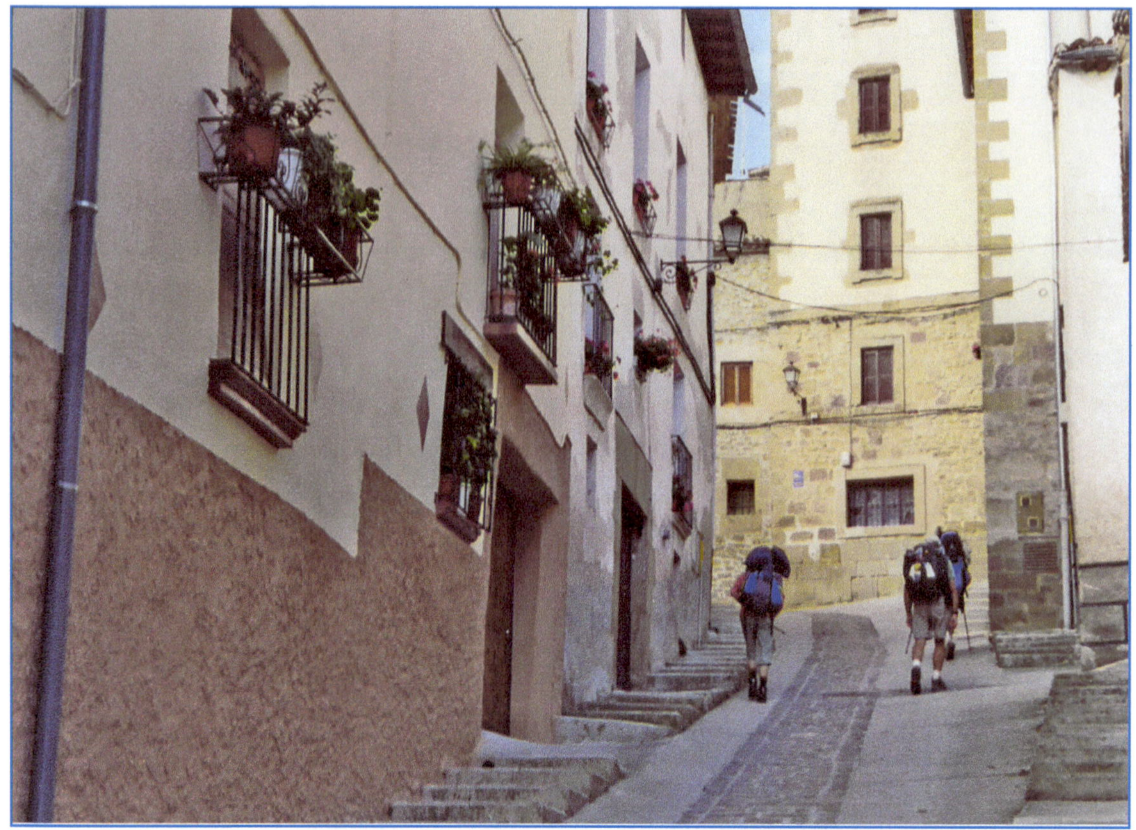

Camino through Cirauqui

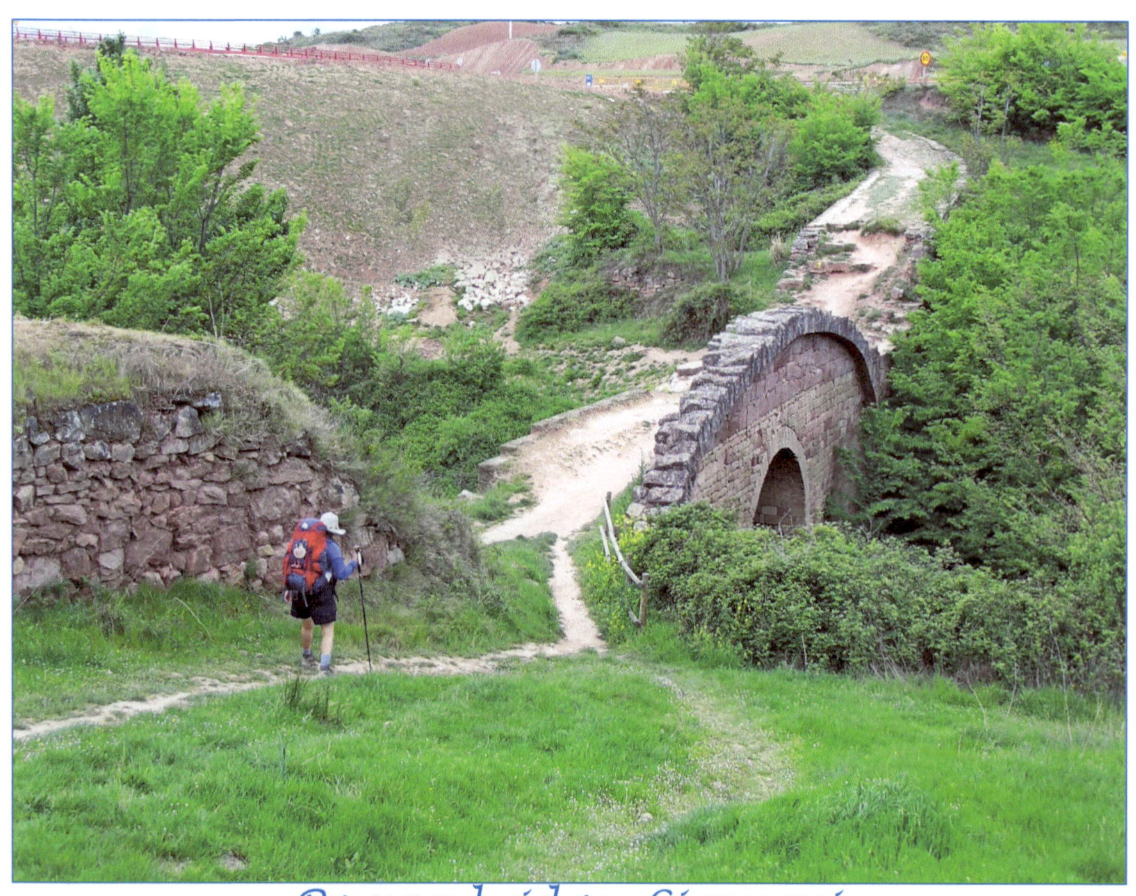

Roman bridge -Cirauqui

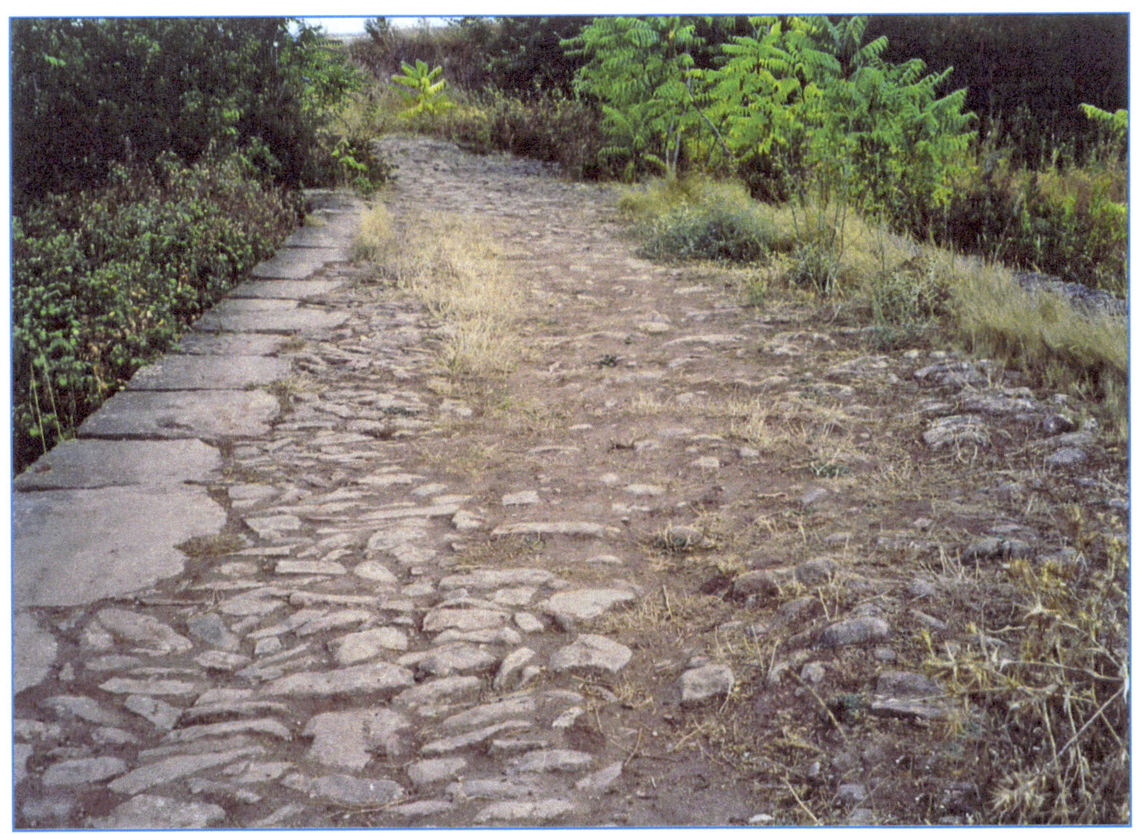

Roman roadbed outside of Cirauqui

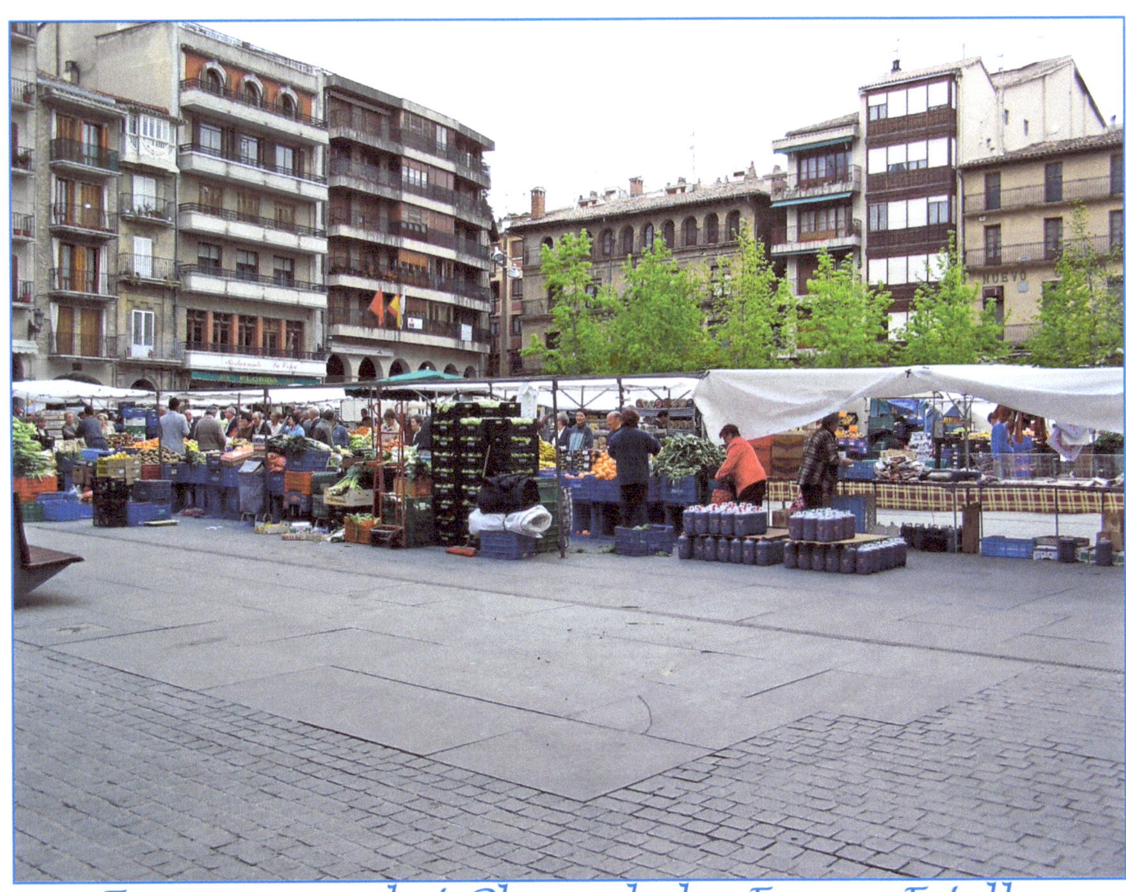

Farmers market-Plaza de los Fueros-Estella

Early morning sunrise-Estella

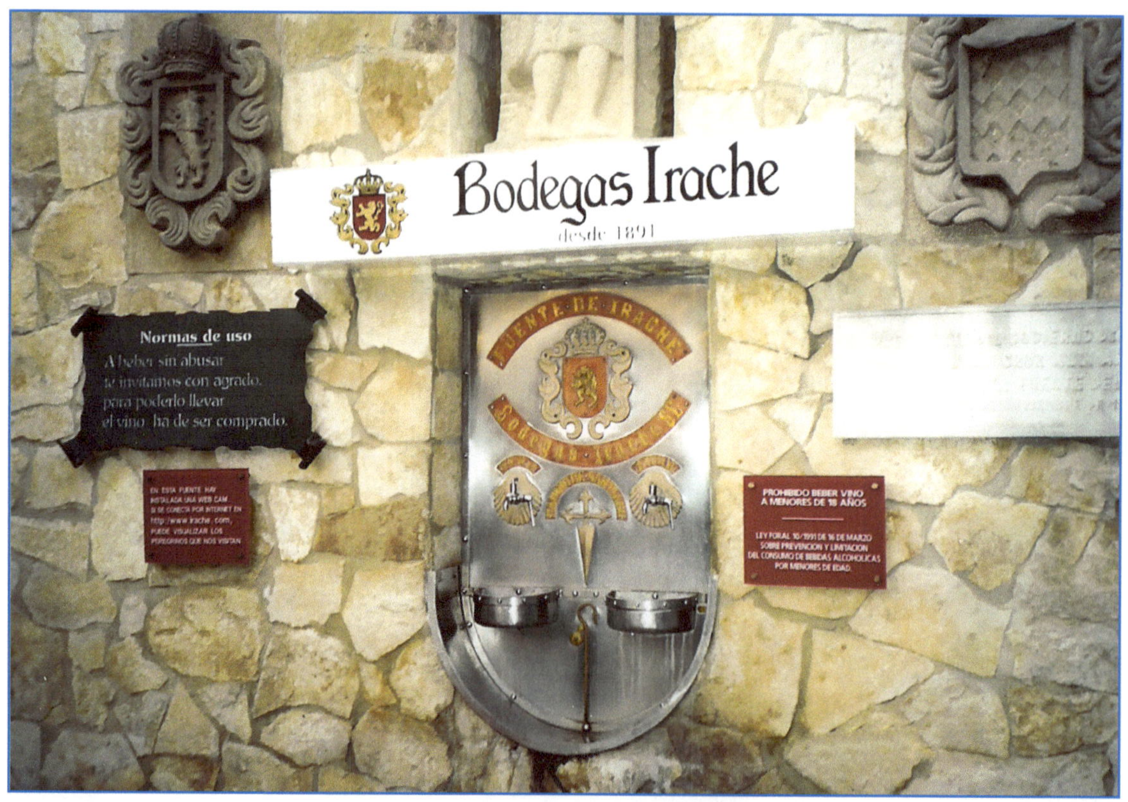

Fuente del Vino

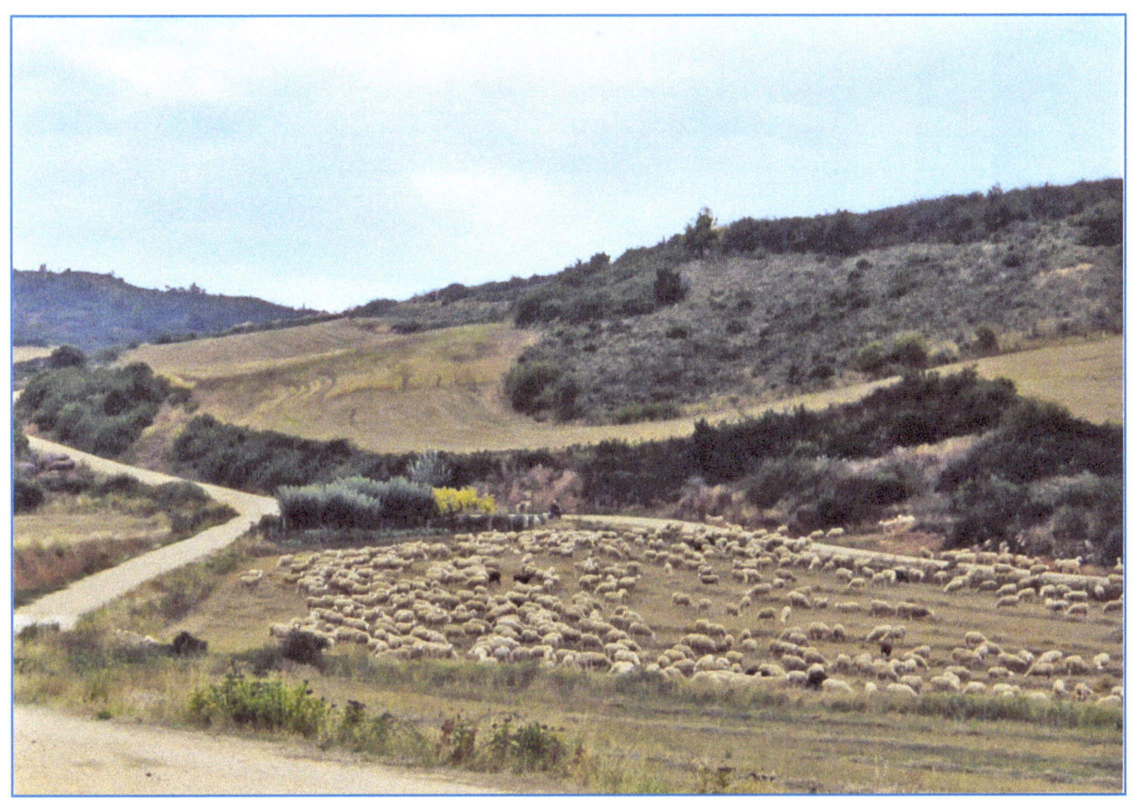

Camino just prior to Luquin

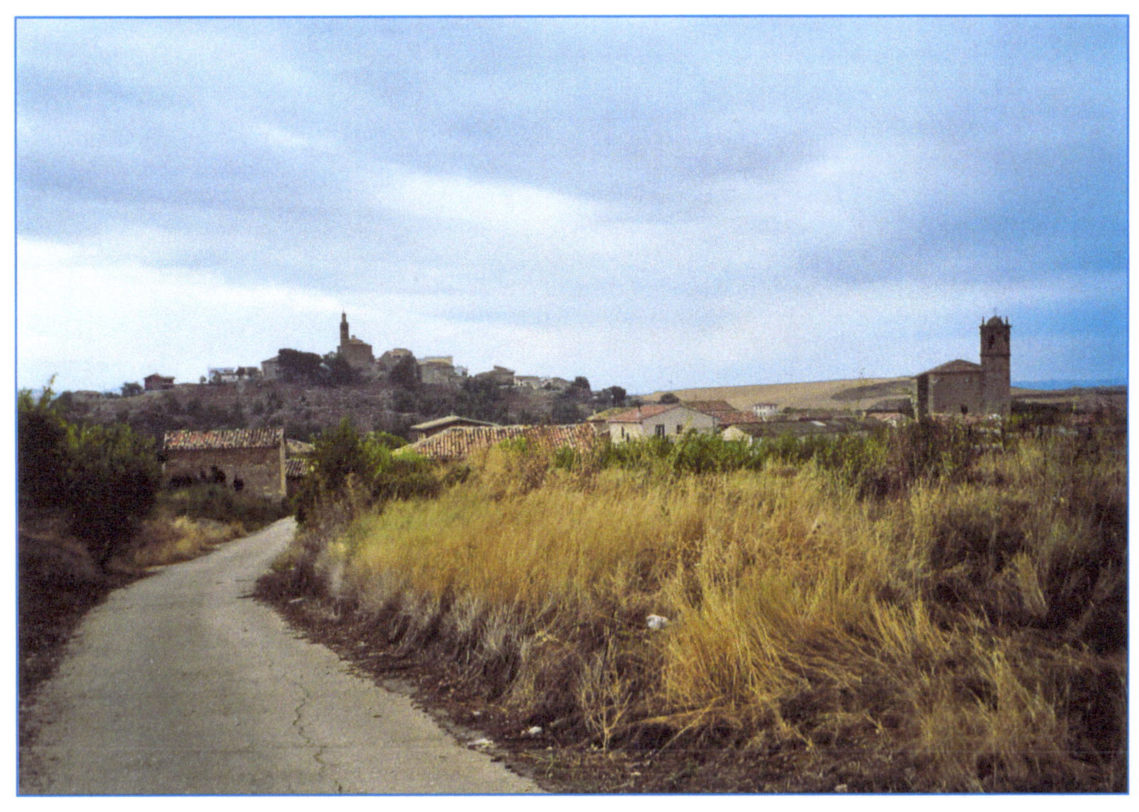

Camino into Sansol

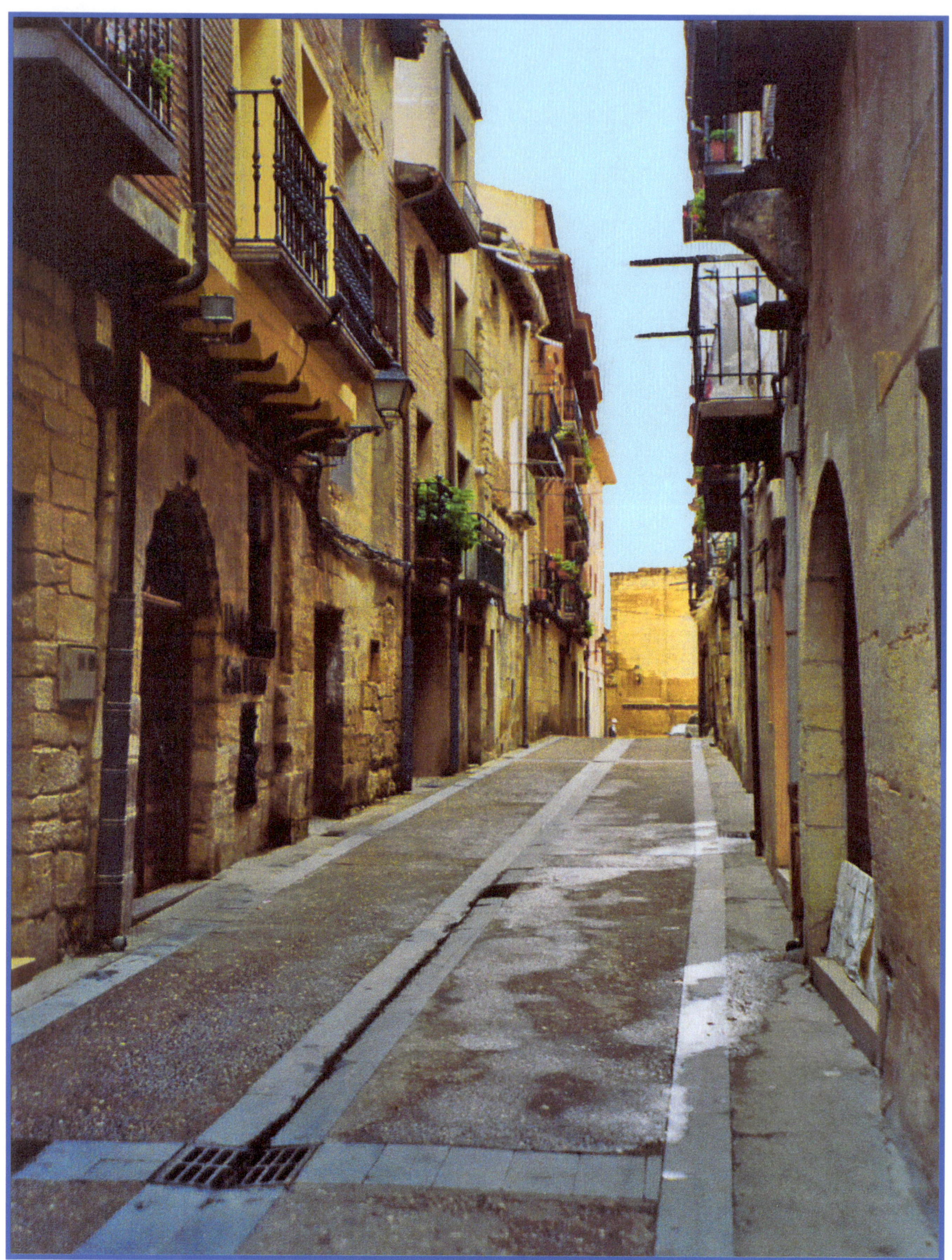

Viana

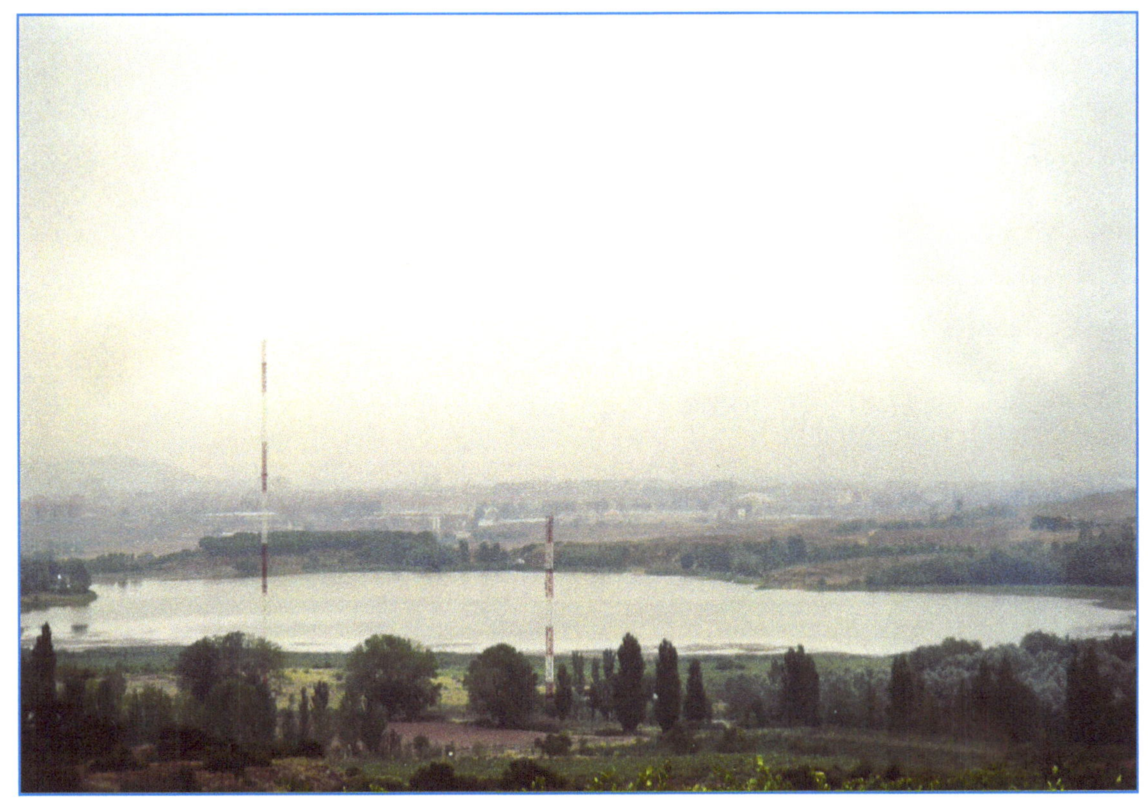

Looking back toward Logrono

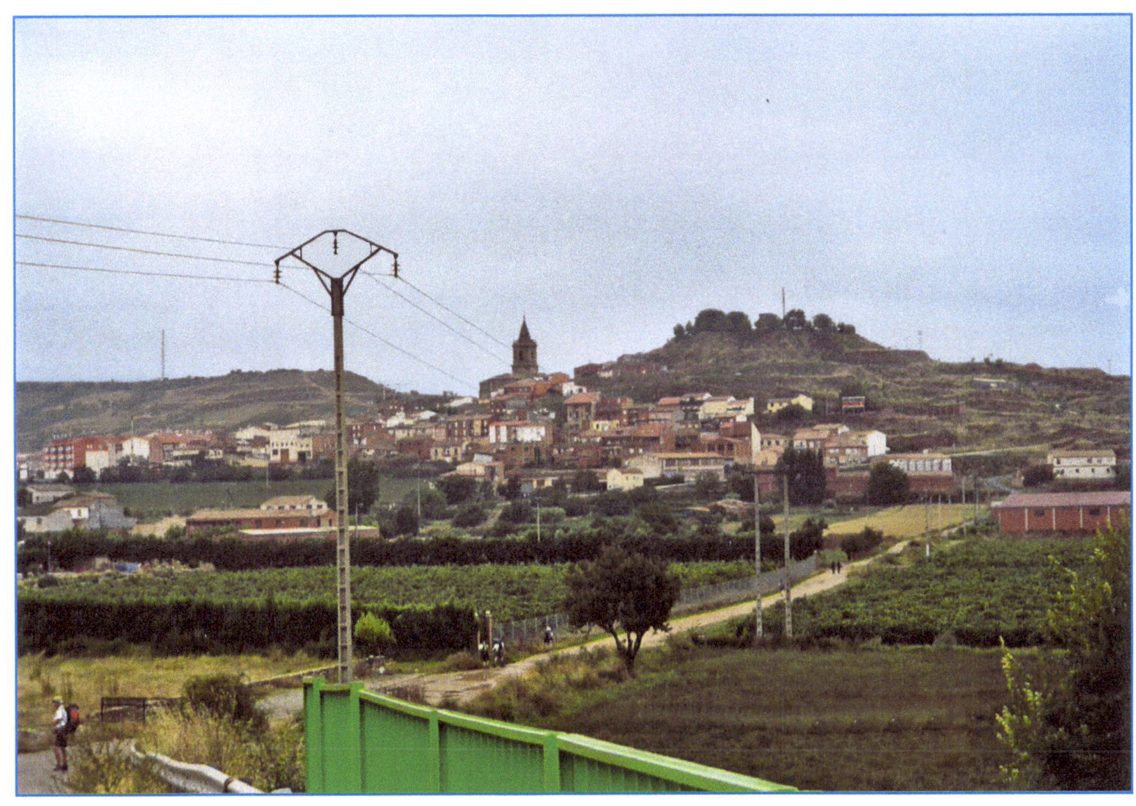

Approaching Navarrete

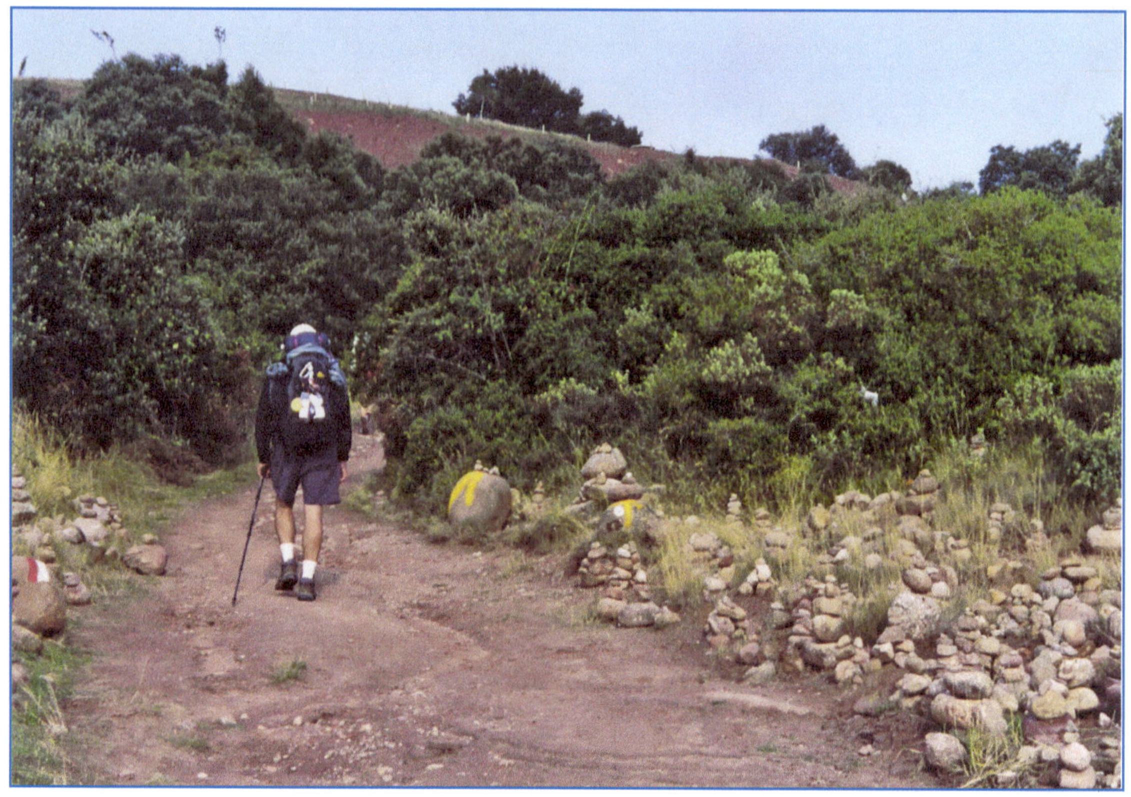

Poyo de Roldan-Roland's bench

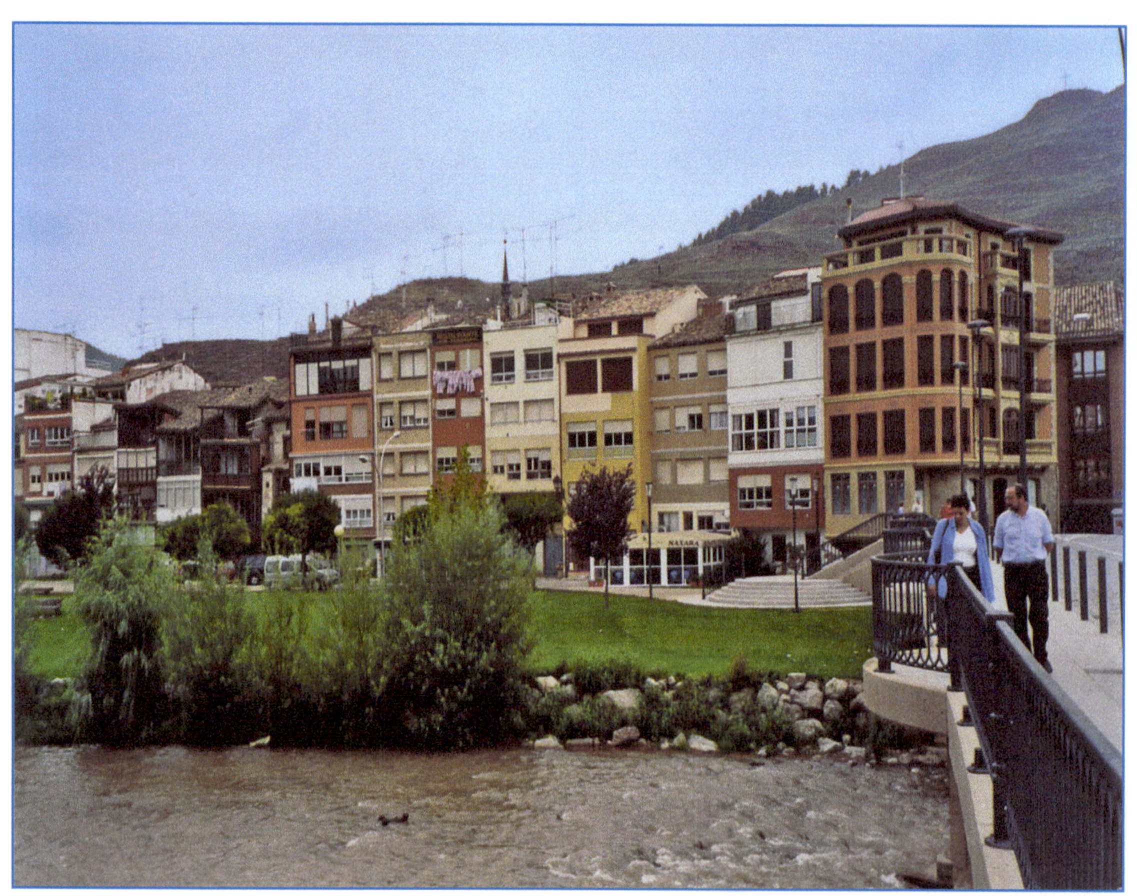

Najera

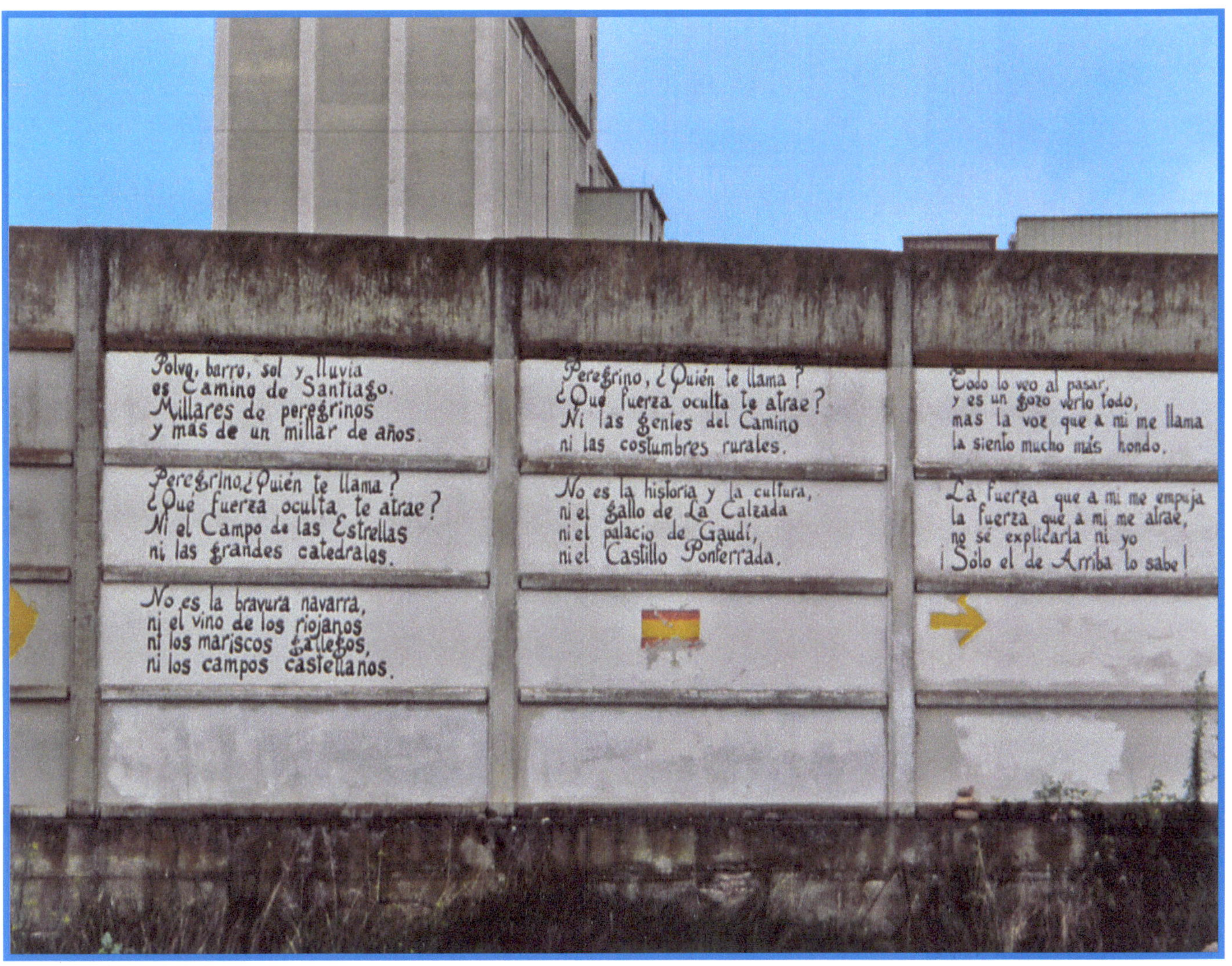

Pilgrim's poem on a factory wall just outside Najera

Dust, mud, sun and rain
Camino de Santiago
Thousands of pilgrims
And more than a thousand years

Pilgrim, who calls you?
What hidden force attracts you?
Not the fields of stars
Not the grand cathedrals.

It isn't the brave Navarra,
Nor the wine of the Riojanos,
Nor the Galician seafood
Nor the Castillian fields

Pilgrim, who calls you?
What hidden force attracts you?
Not the people of the Camino
Nor the rural customs.

It isn't the history or culture
Nor the hen of La Calzada
Nor the Palace of Gaudi
Nor the Castle of Ponferrada

I see it all in passing
It is a pleasure to see it all
Plus the voice that calls me
I feel much deeper.

The force that pushes me
The force that attracts me
I can't even explain
Only the One above knows!

EGB

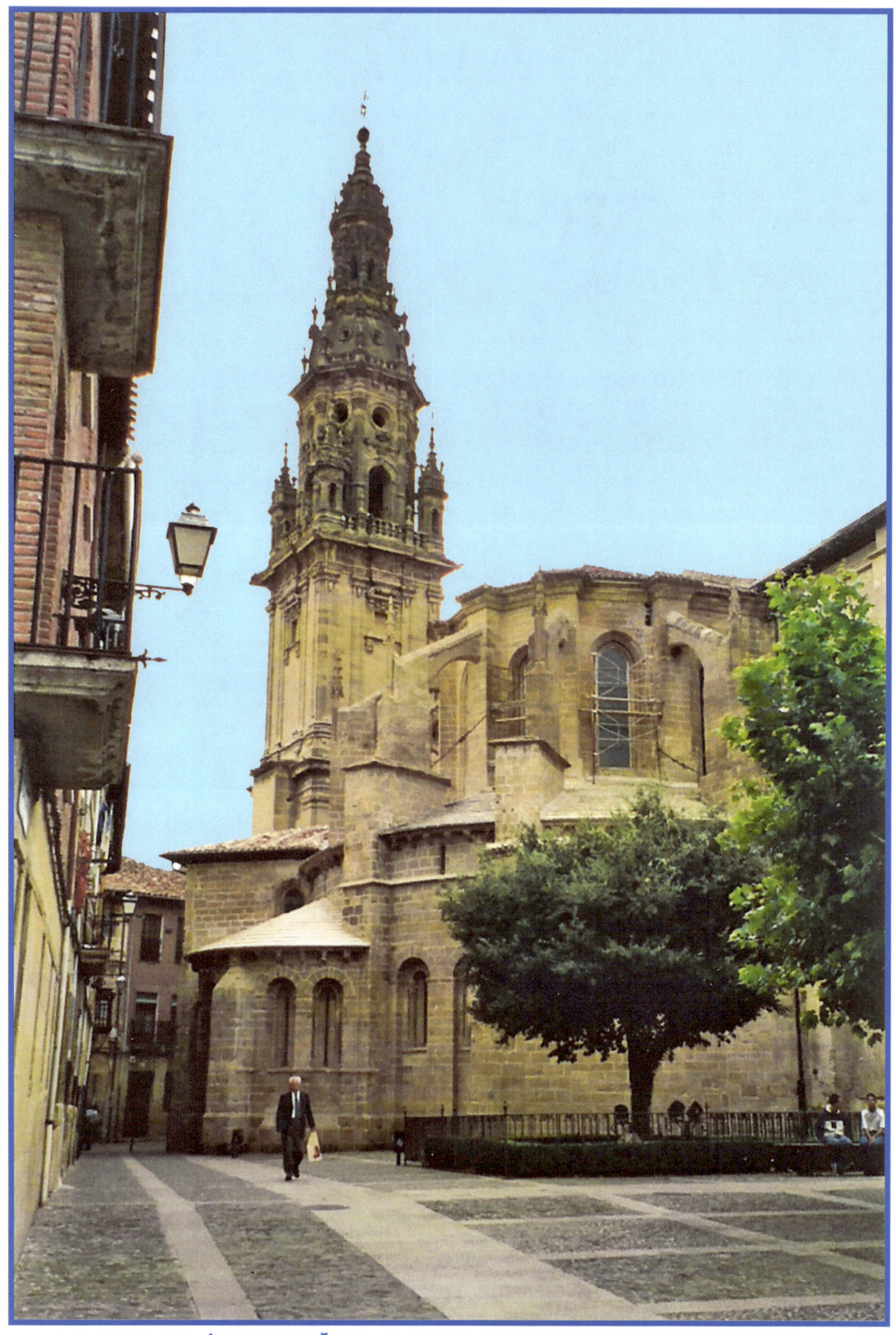

Main Plaza - Santo Domingo

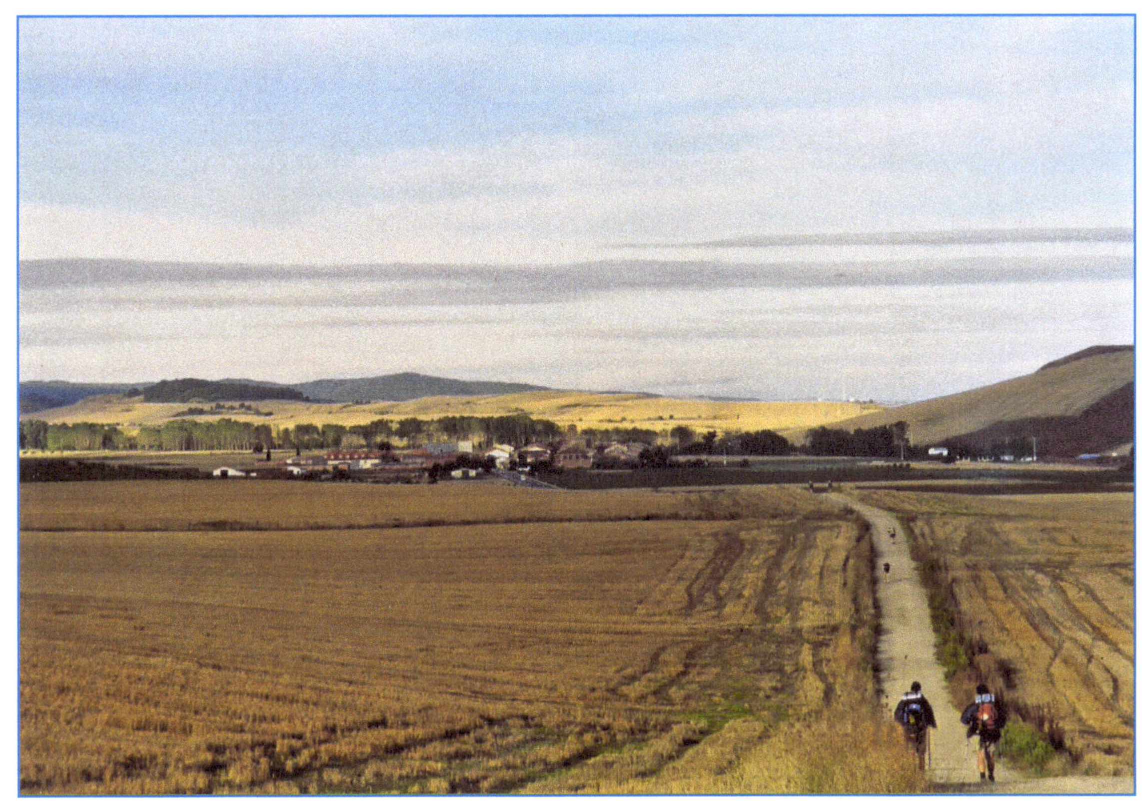

Long downhill toward Belorado

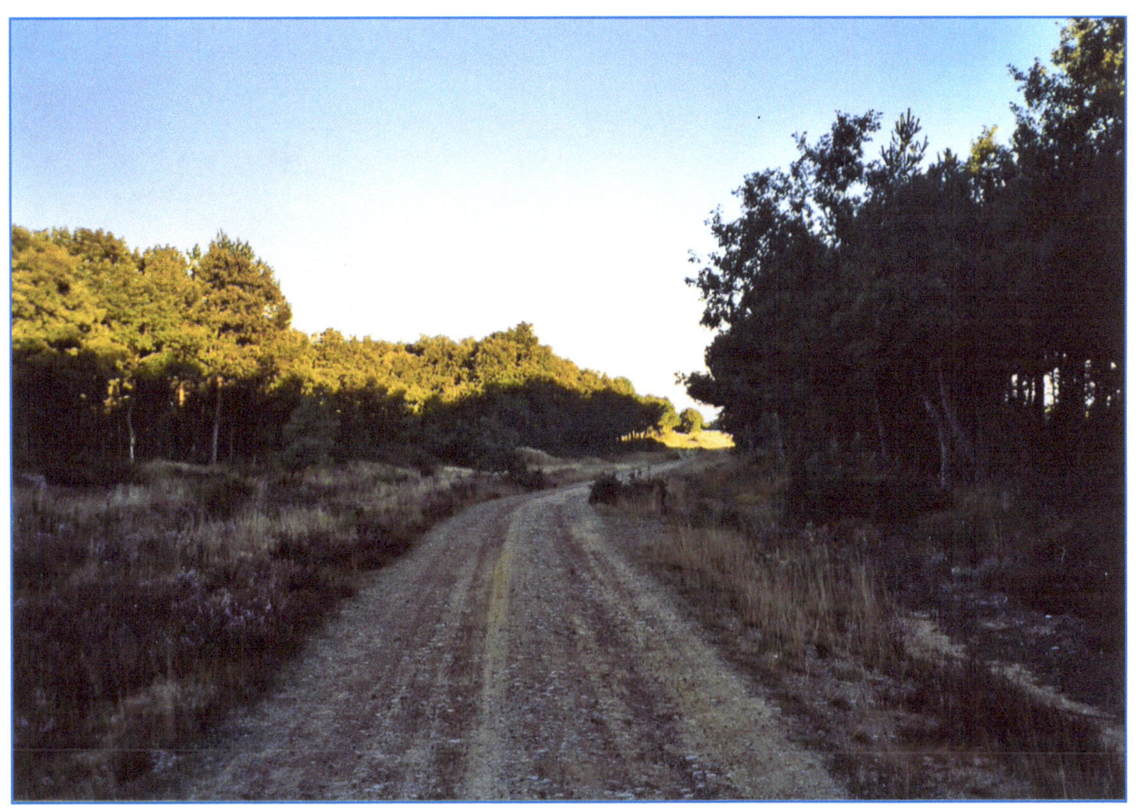

Early morning outside of Villafranca de Montes de Oca

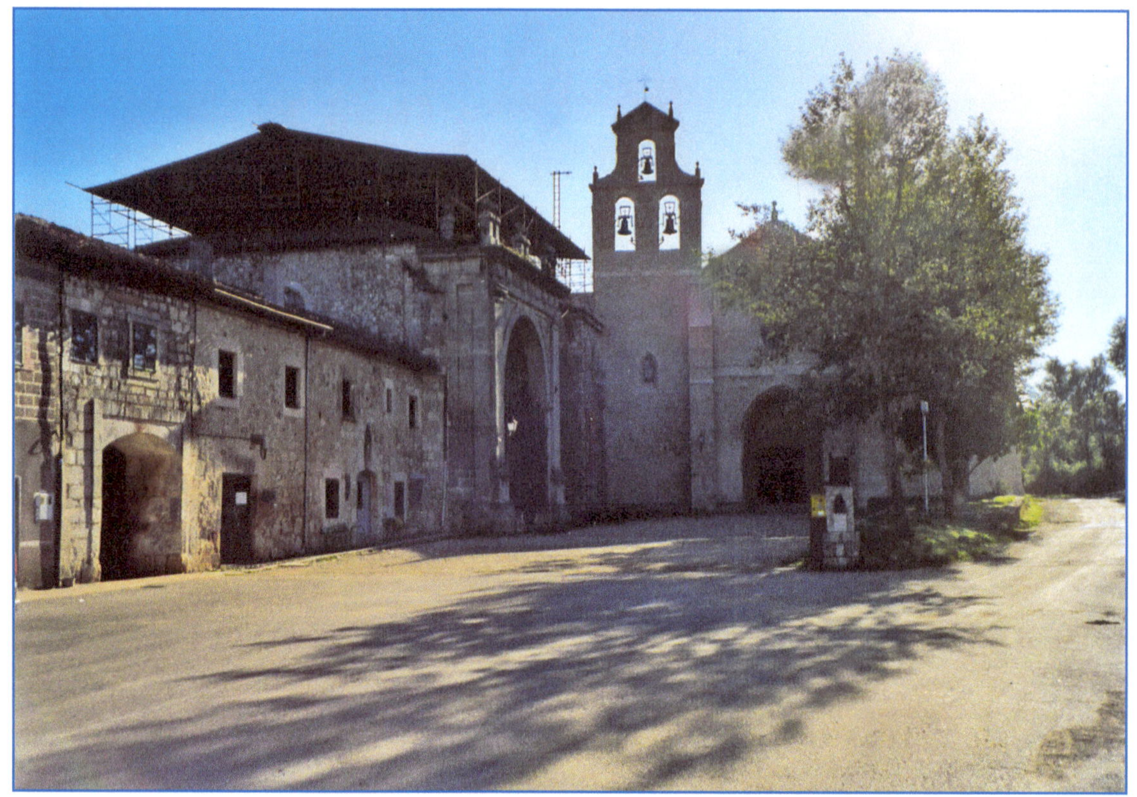

San Juan de Ortega

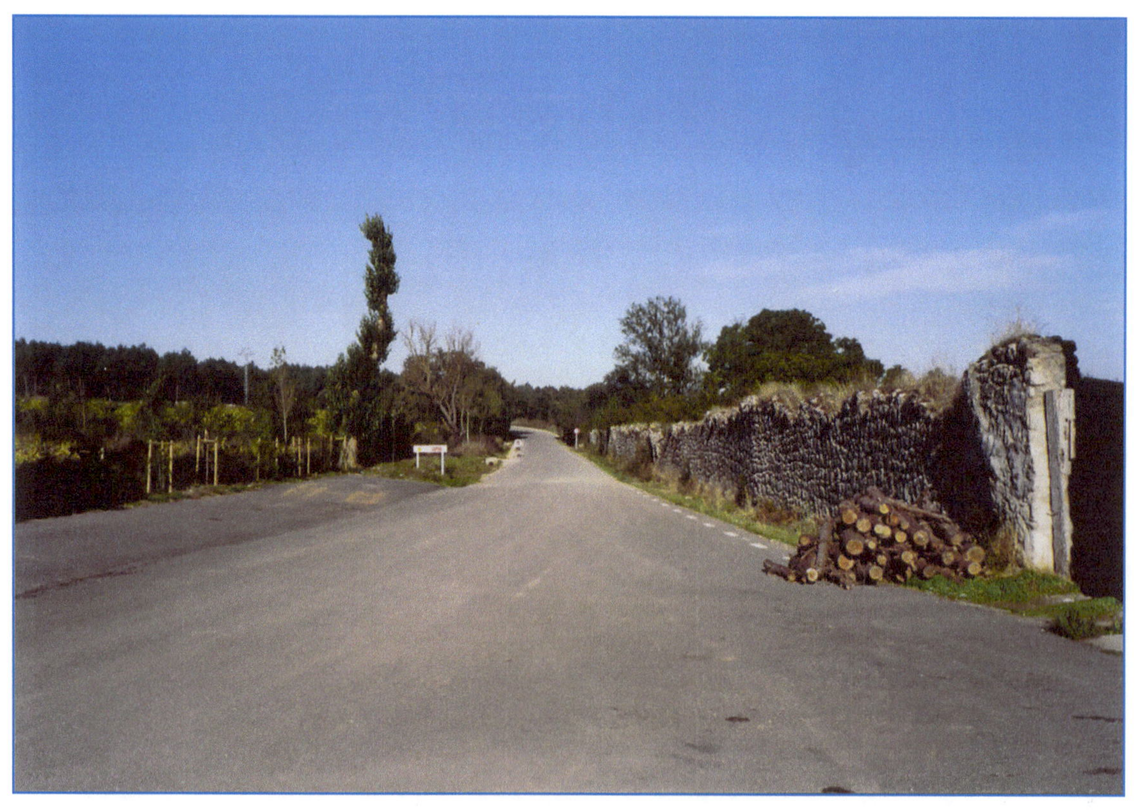

Camino leaving San Juan de Ortega

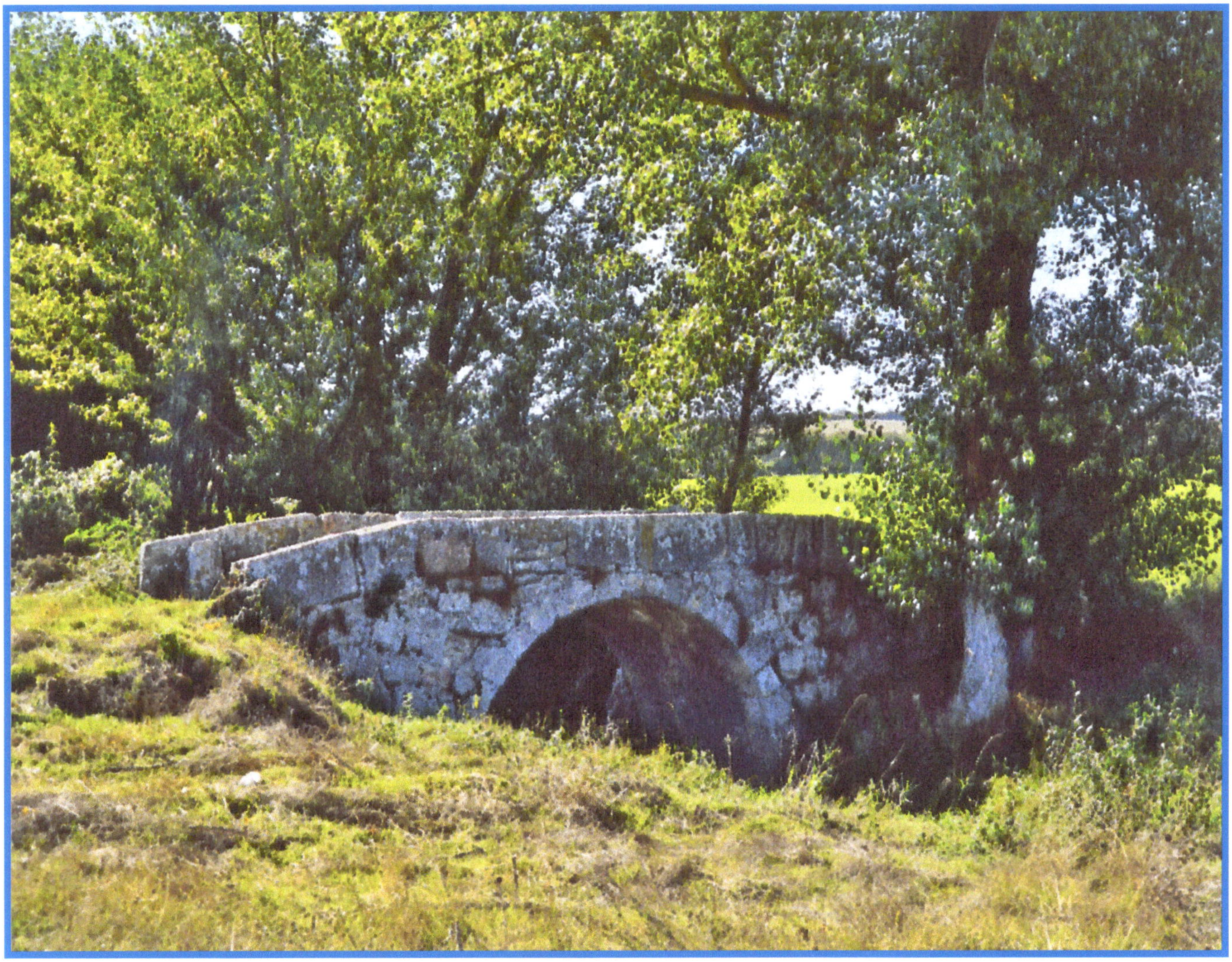

Puente de San Juan de Ortega

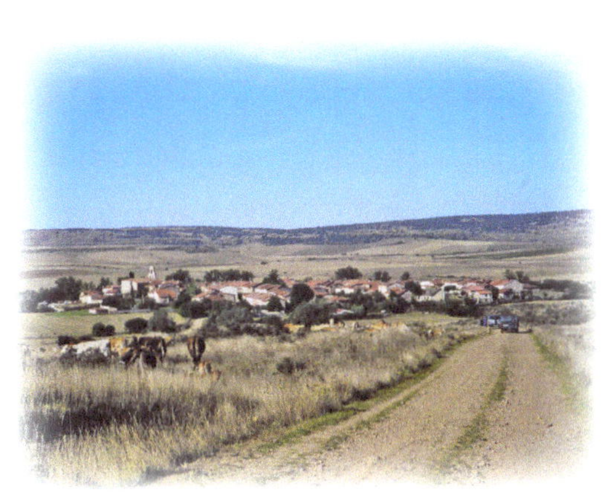

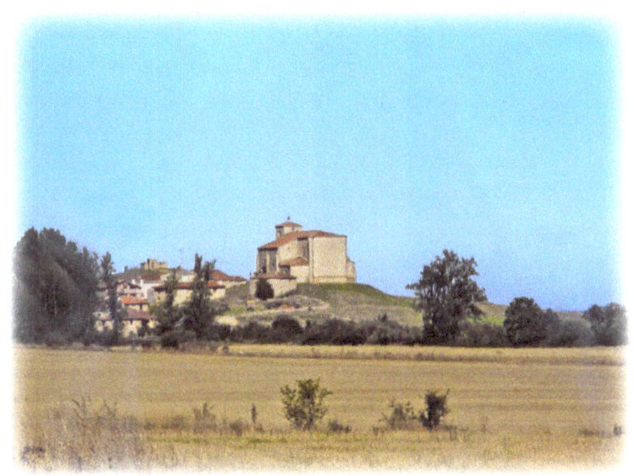

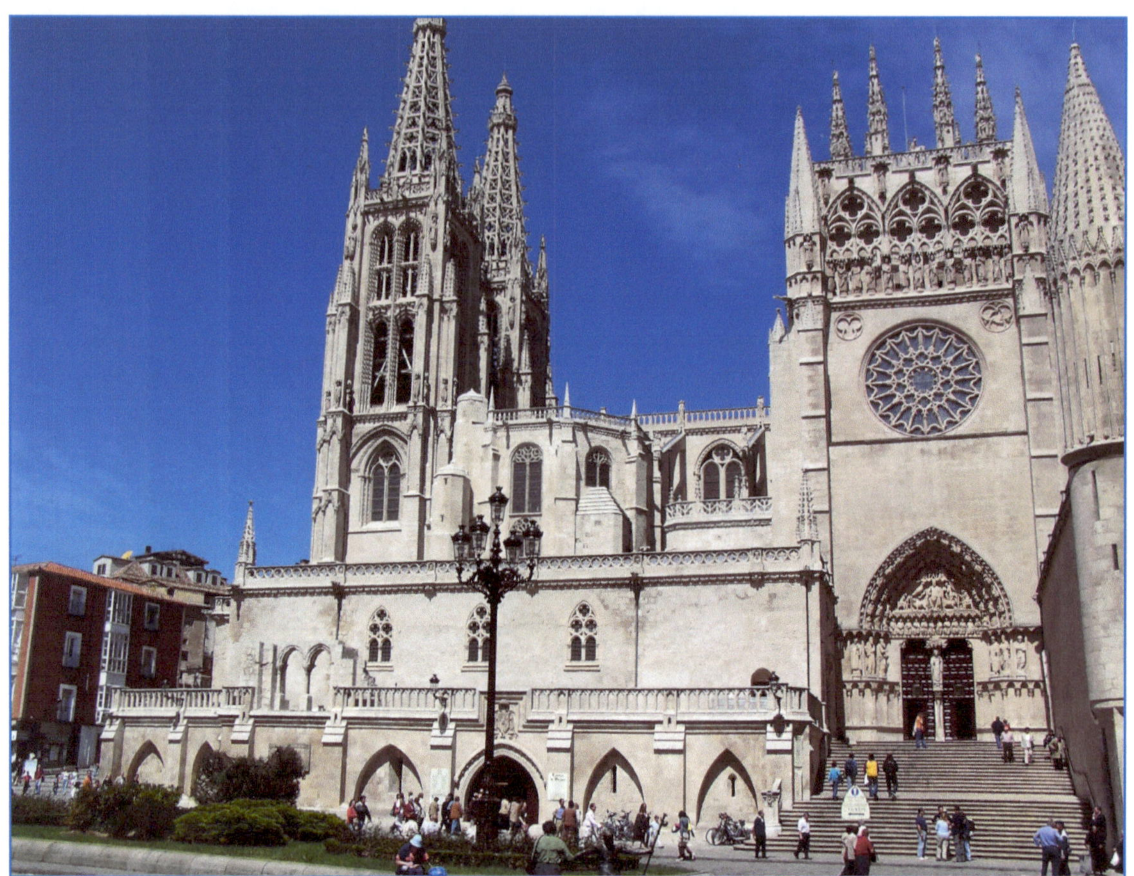

Burgos Cathedral de Santa María

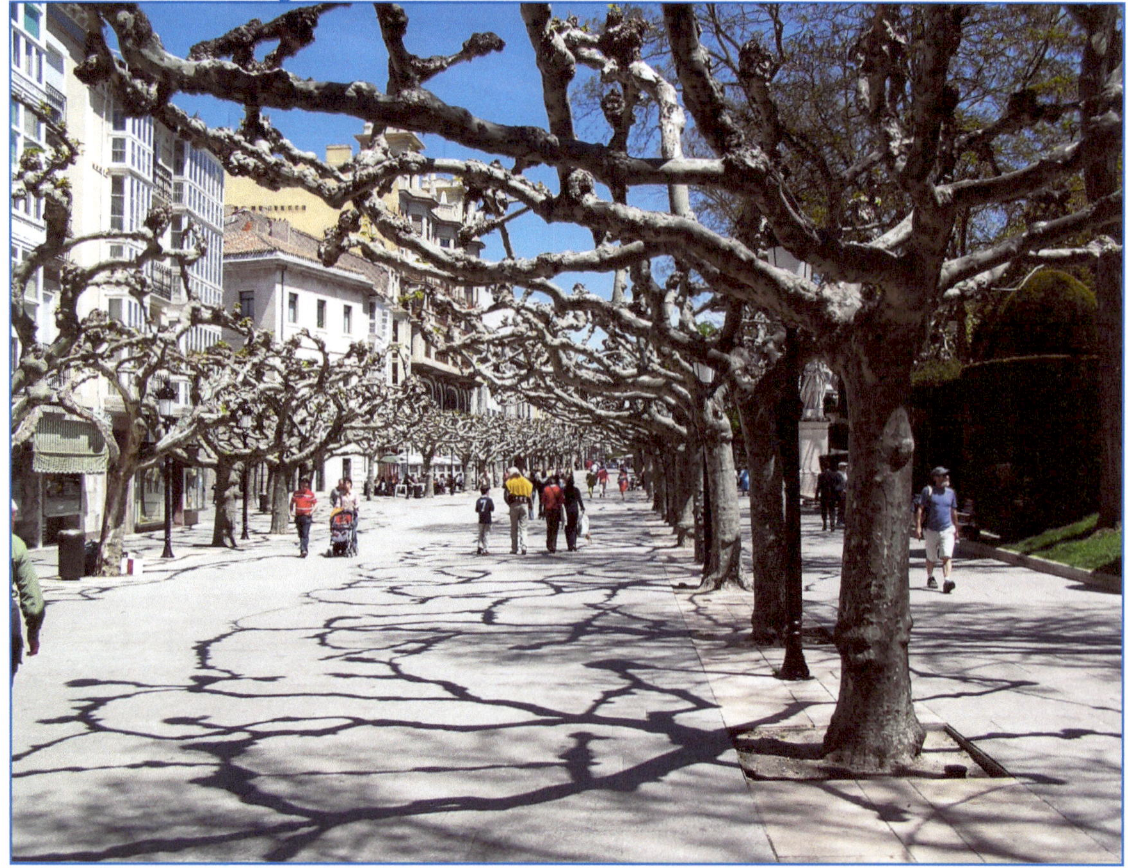

Tree-lined walk through Burgos

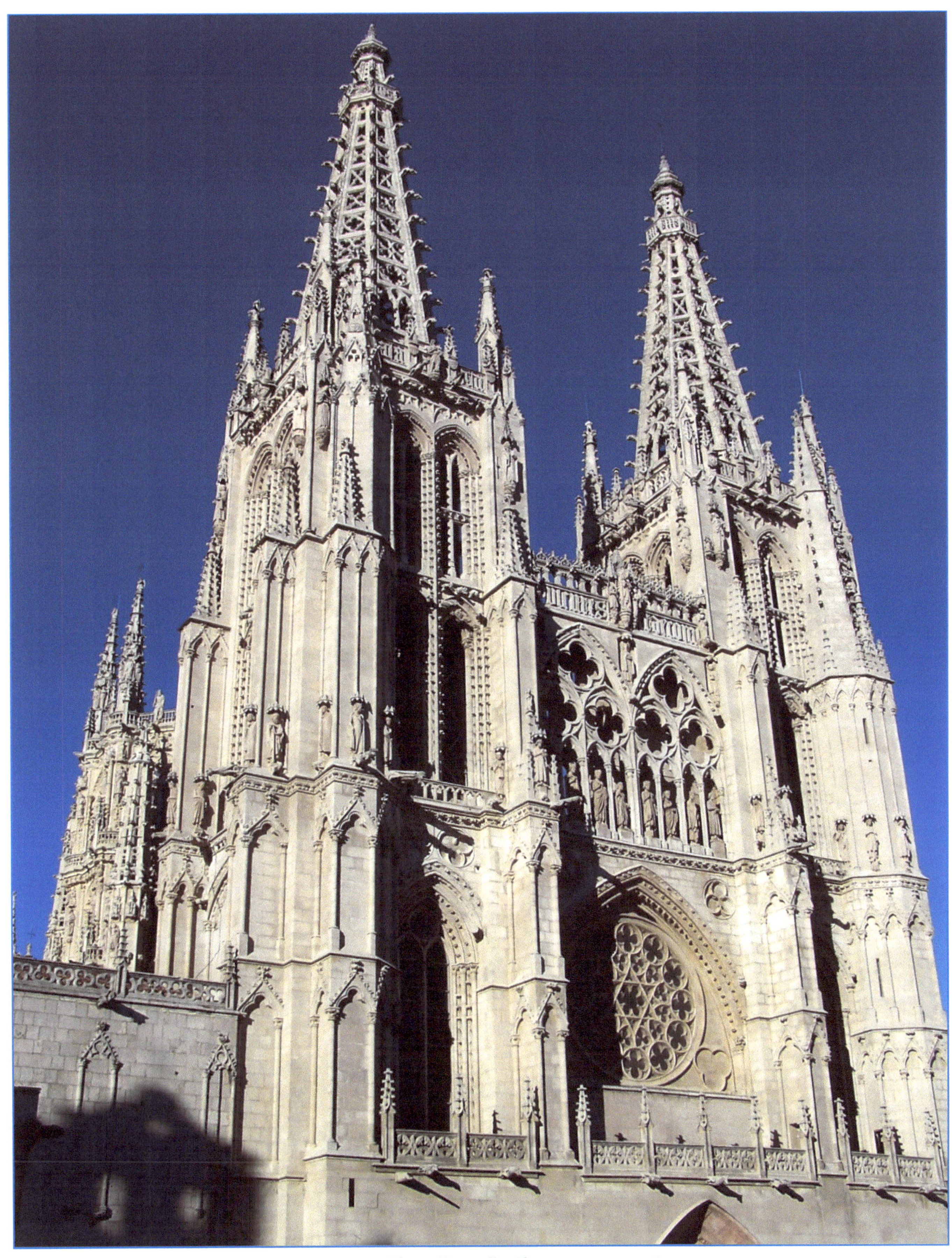

Burgos Cathedral de Santa Maria

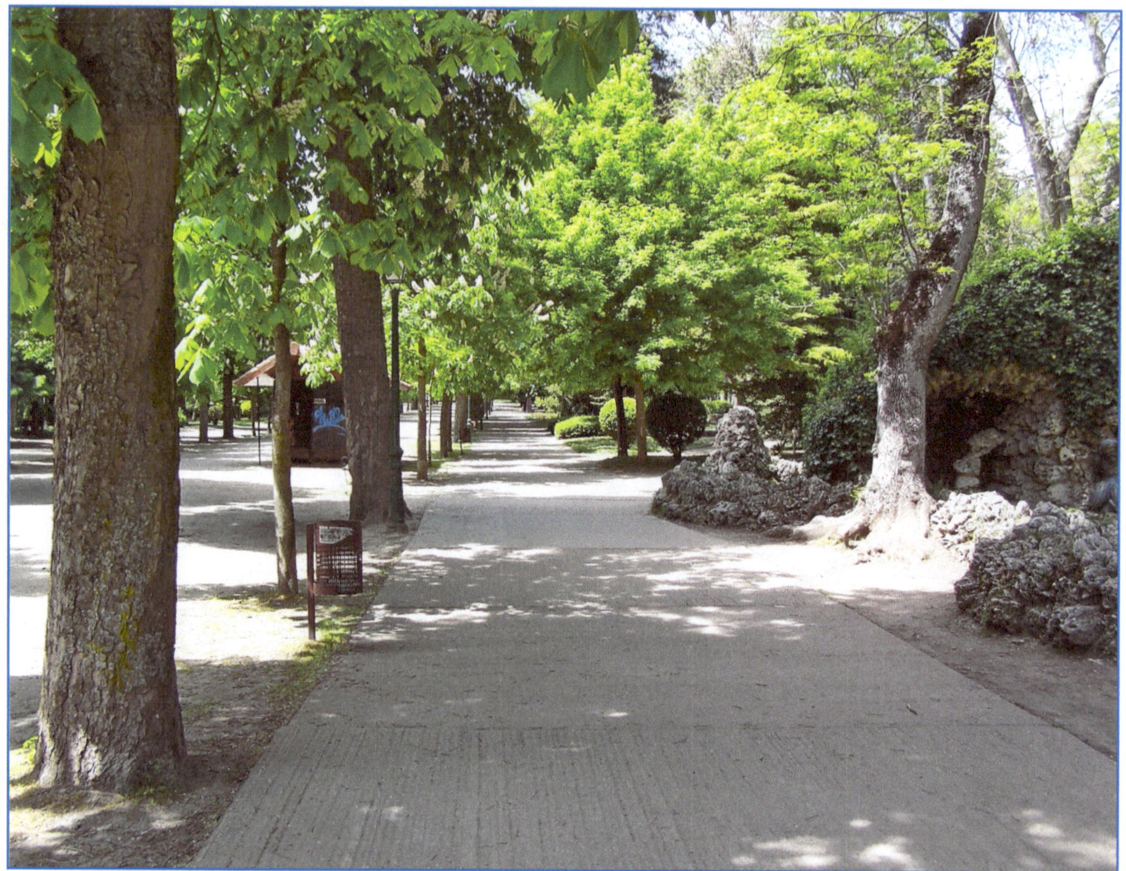

Approaching the Burgos Albergue

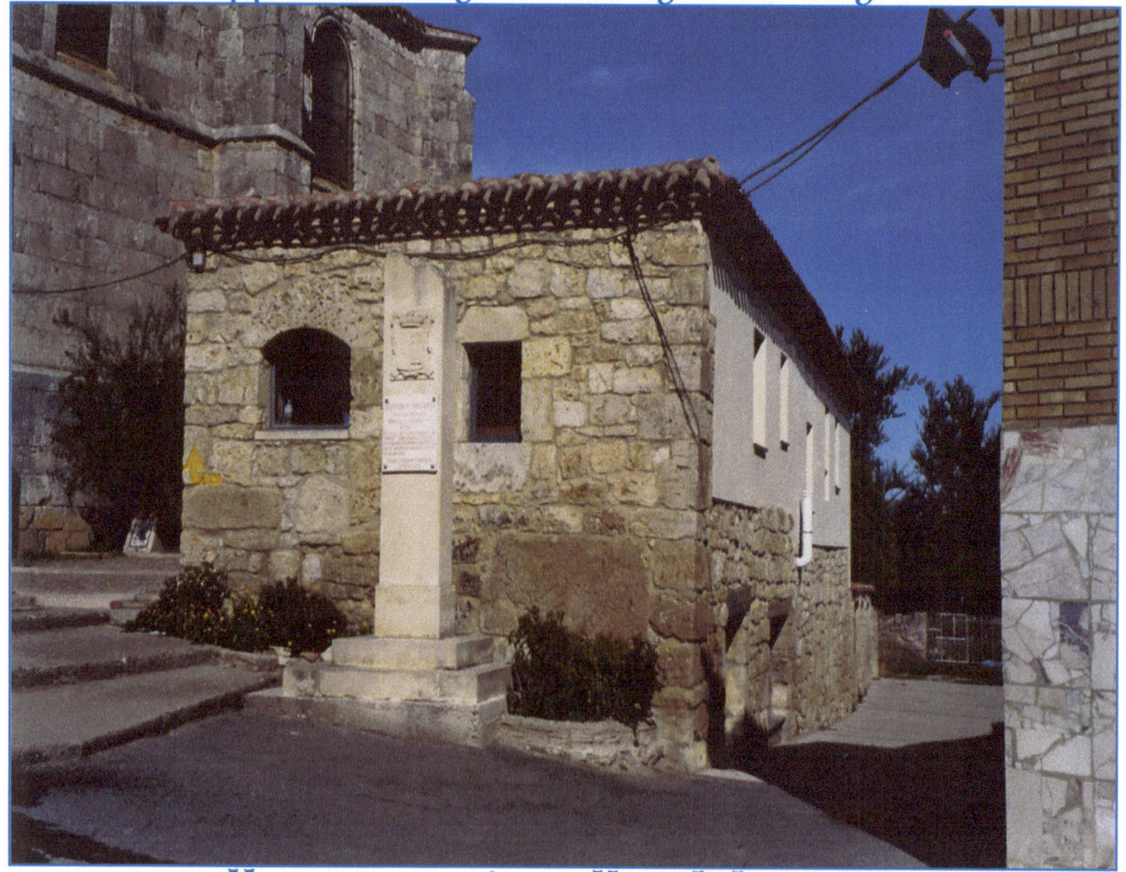

Albergue in Hornillos del Camino

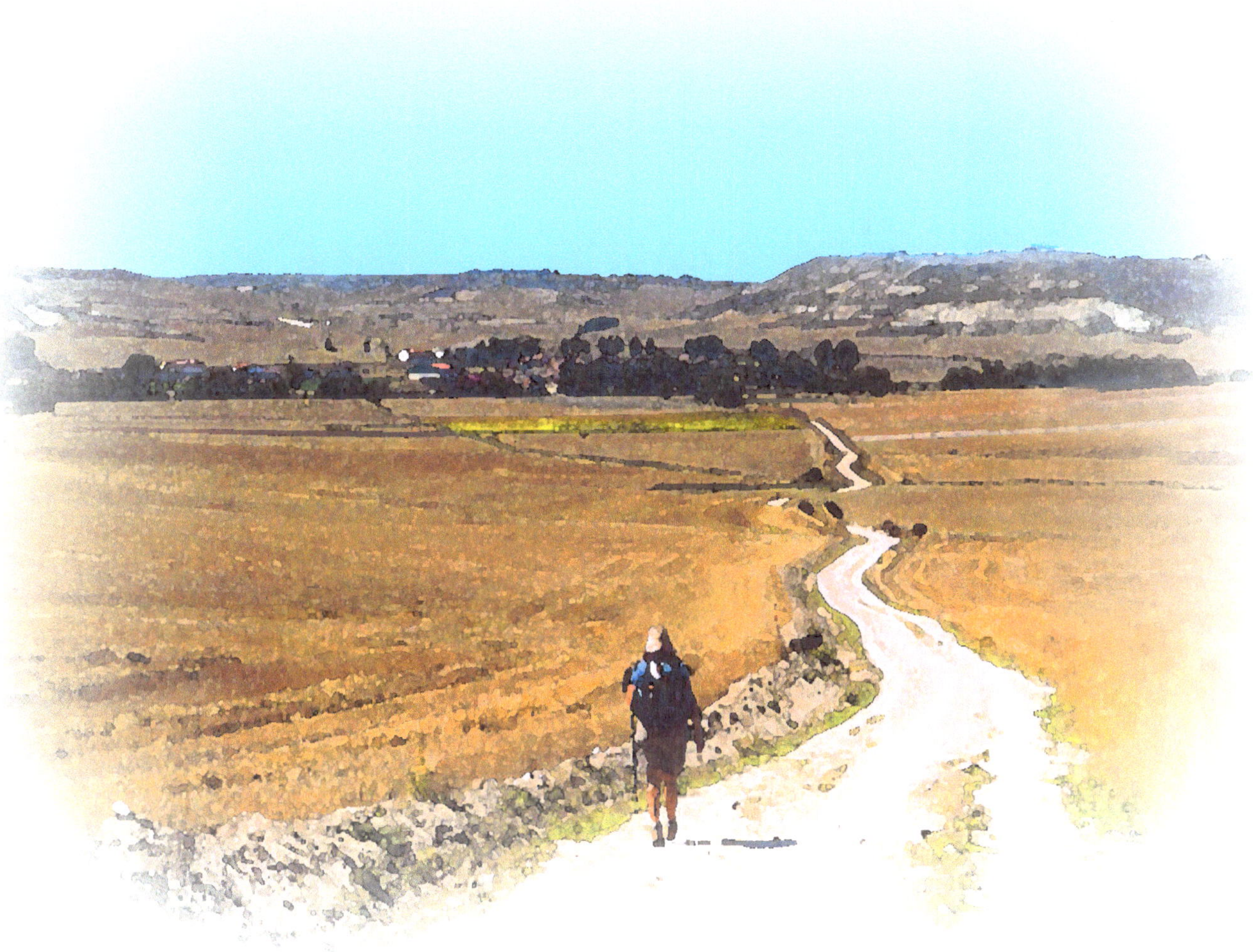

Camino into Hornillos del Camino

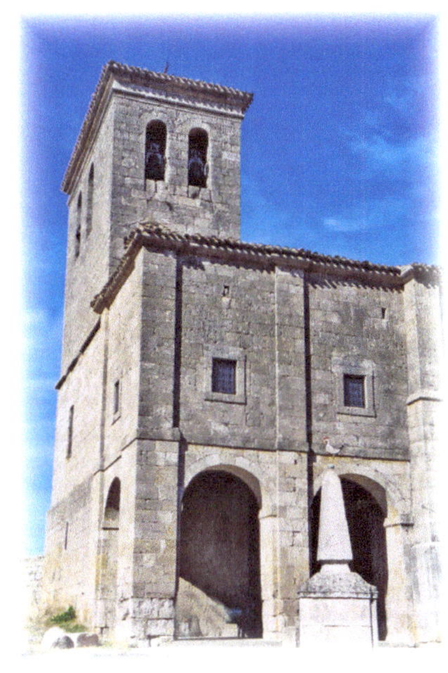

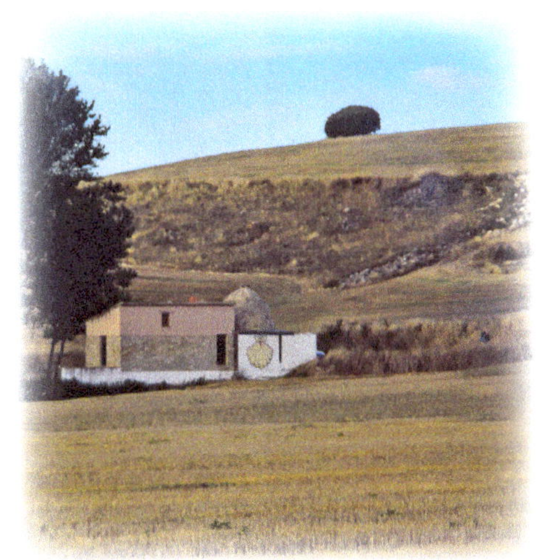

San Bol Albergue

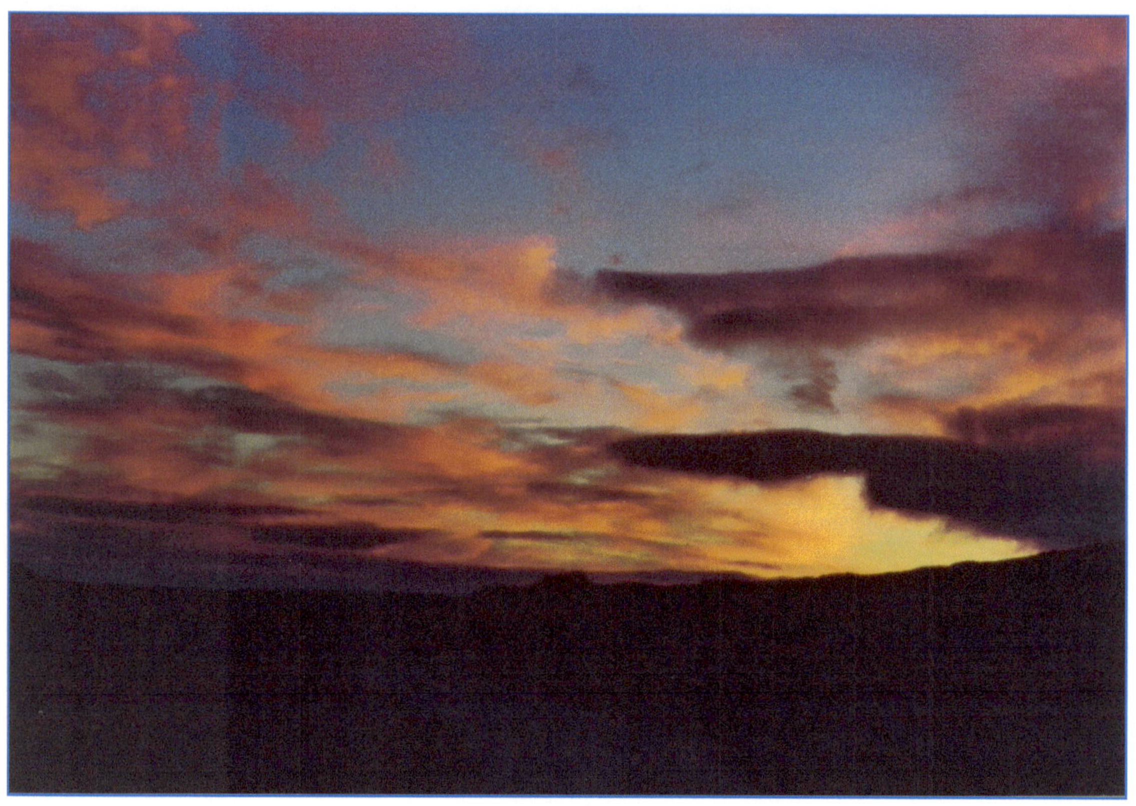

Early morning Hornillos del Camino

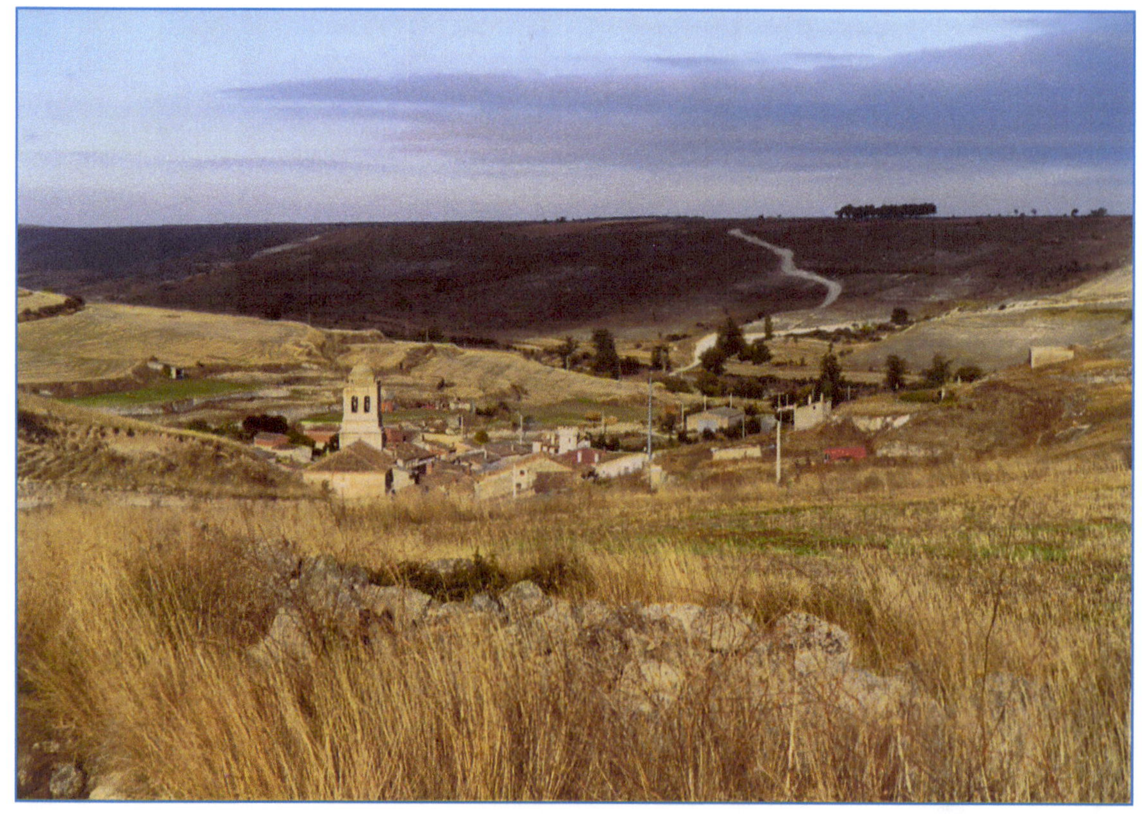

Hontanas

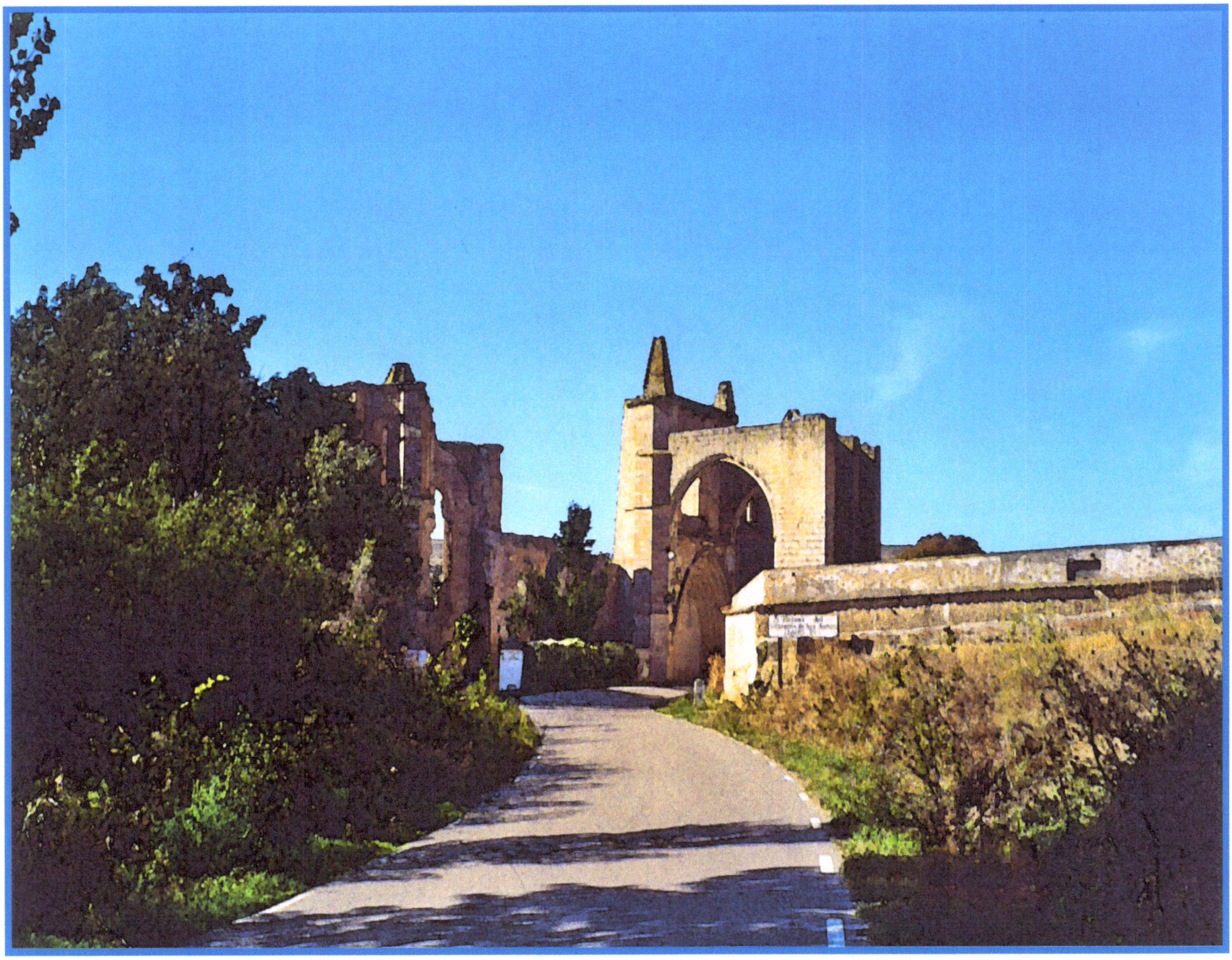

Monastery San Anton

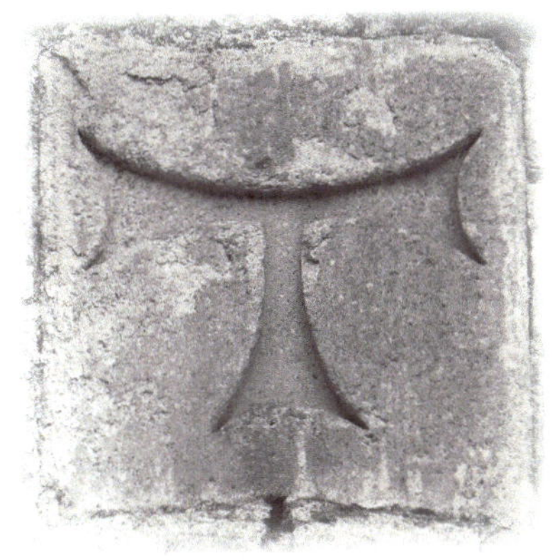

The "Tau" was the symbol for the Order of San Anton - an Order known for their ability to heal.

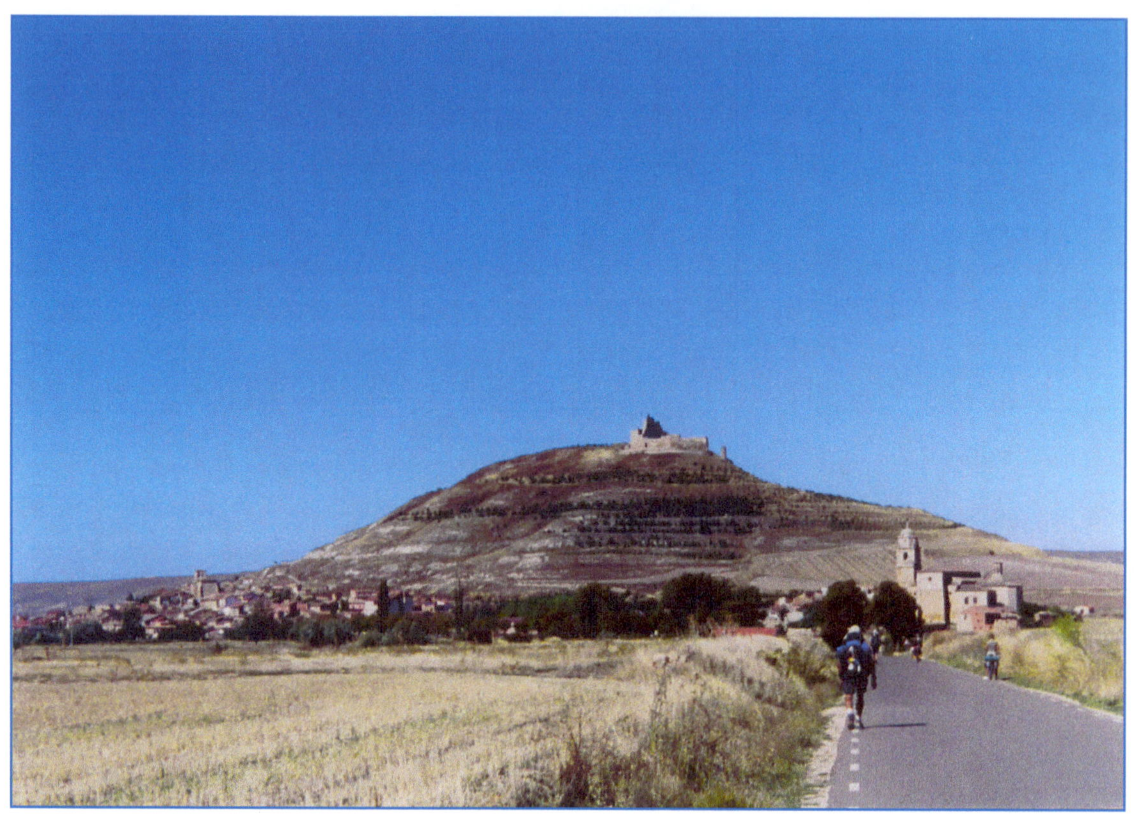

Approaching Castrojeriz

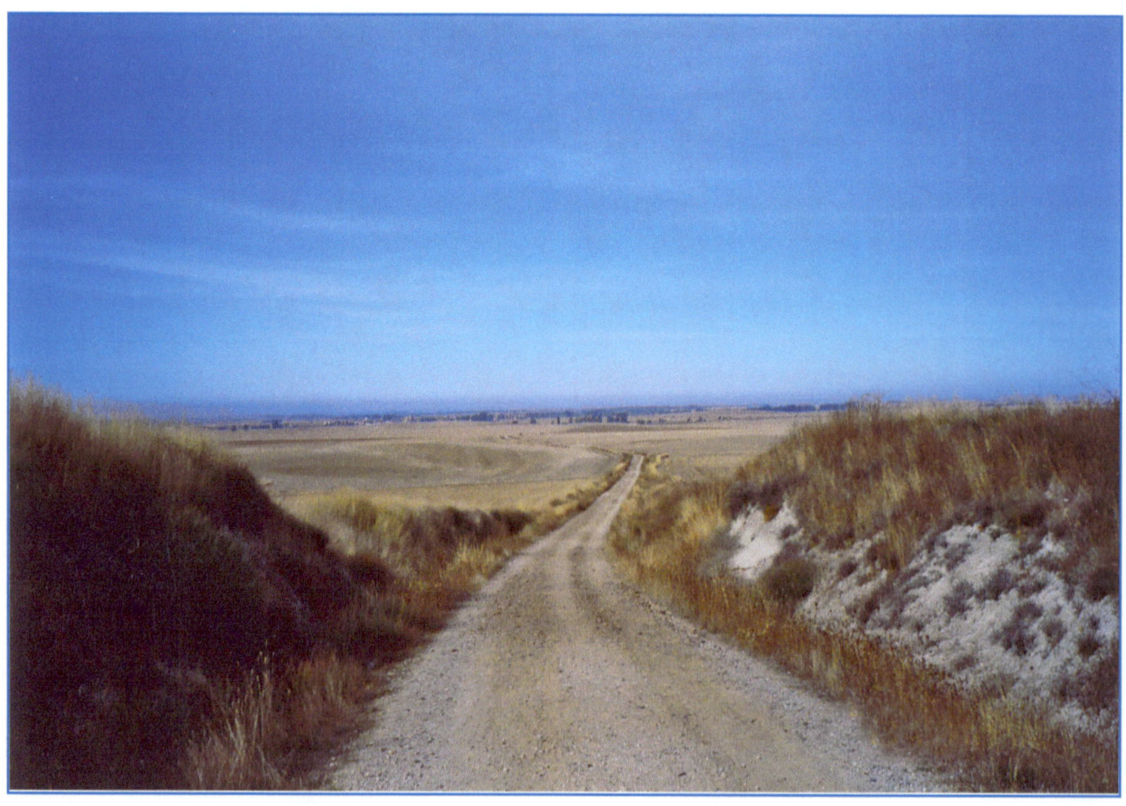

Early morning approaching Ermita de San Nicolas

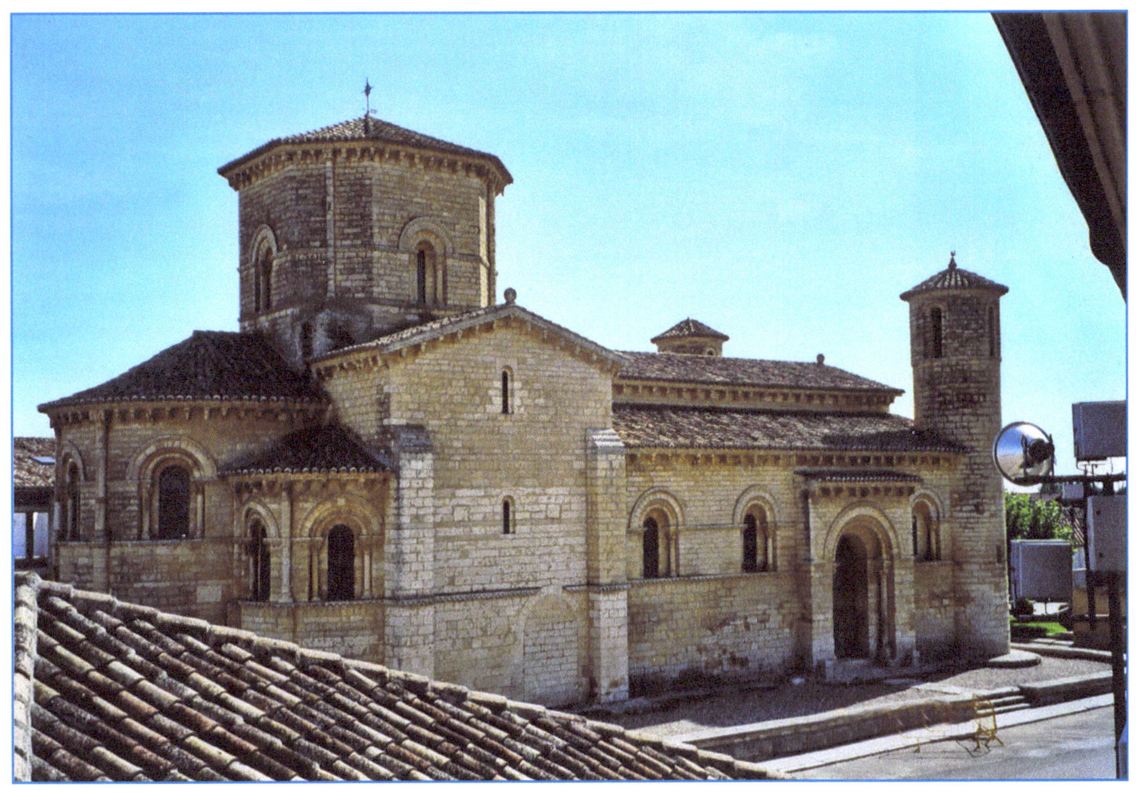

Fromista-Iglesia de San Martin

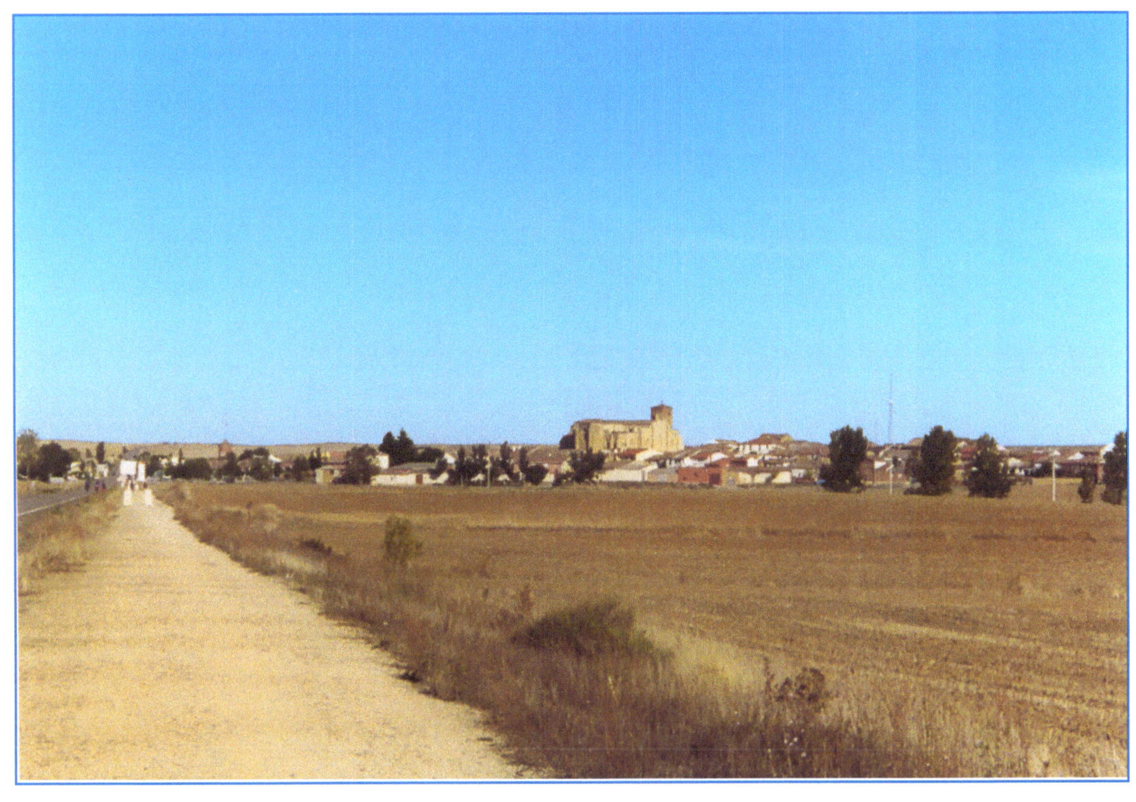

Camino approaching Villalcazar de Sirga

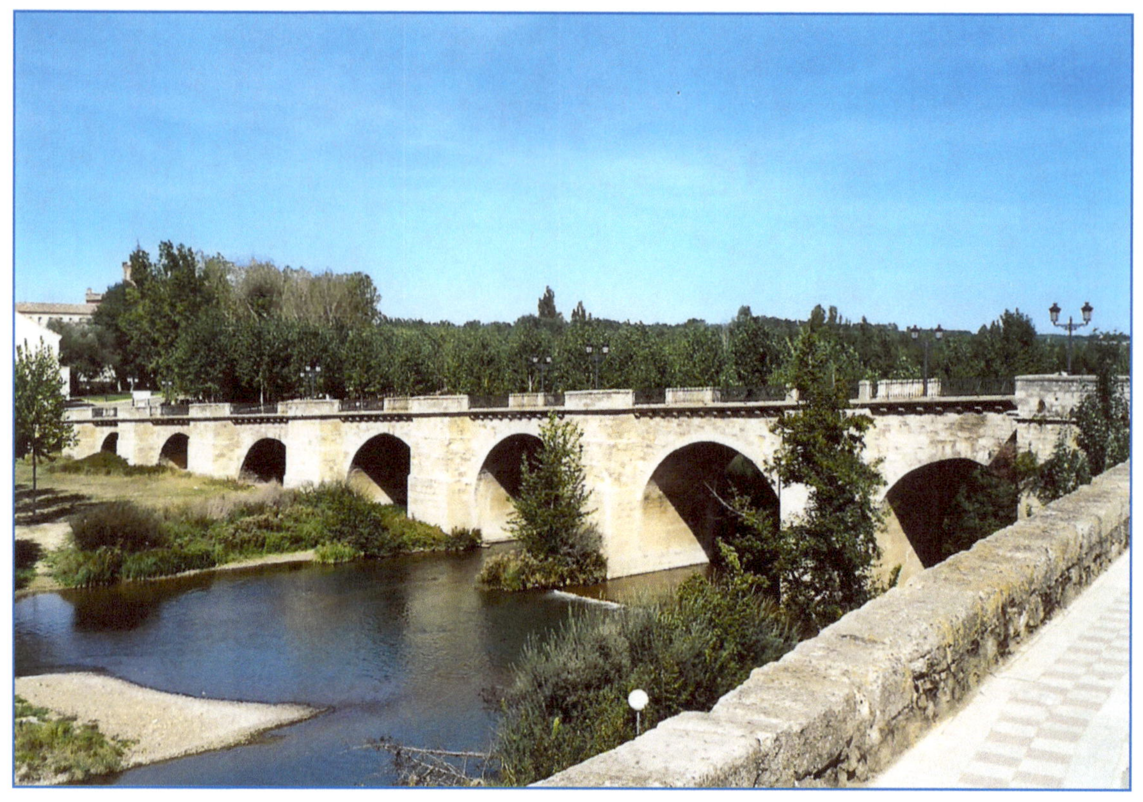

Carrion de los Condes Rio Carrion

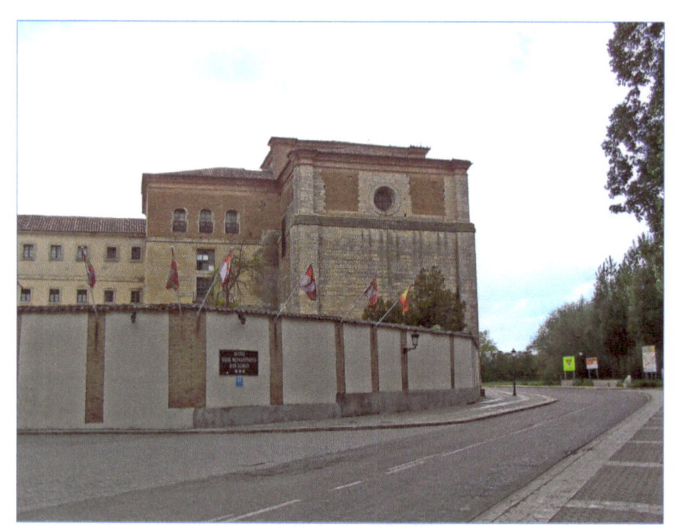

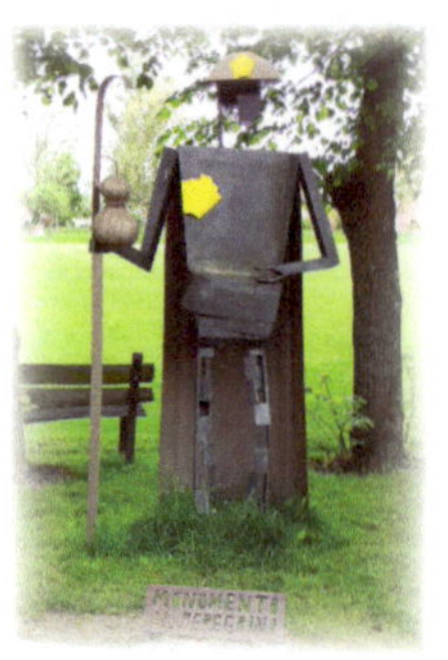

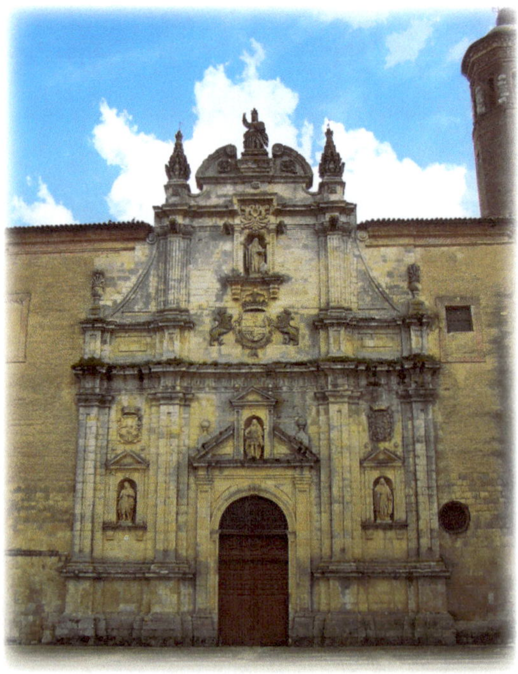

Carrion de los Condes-Monasterio de San Zoilo

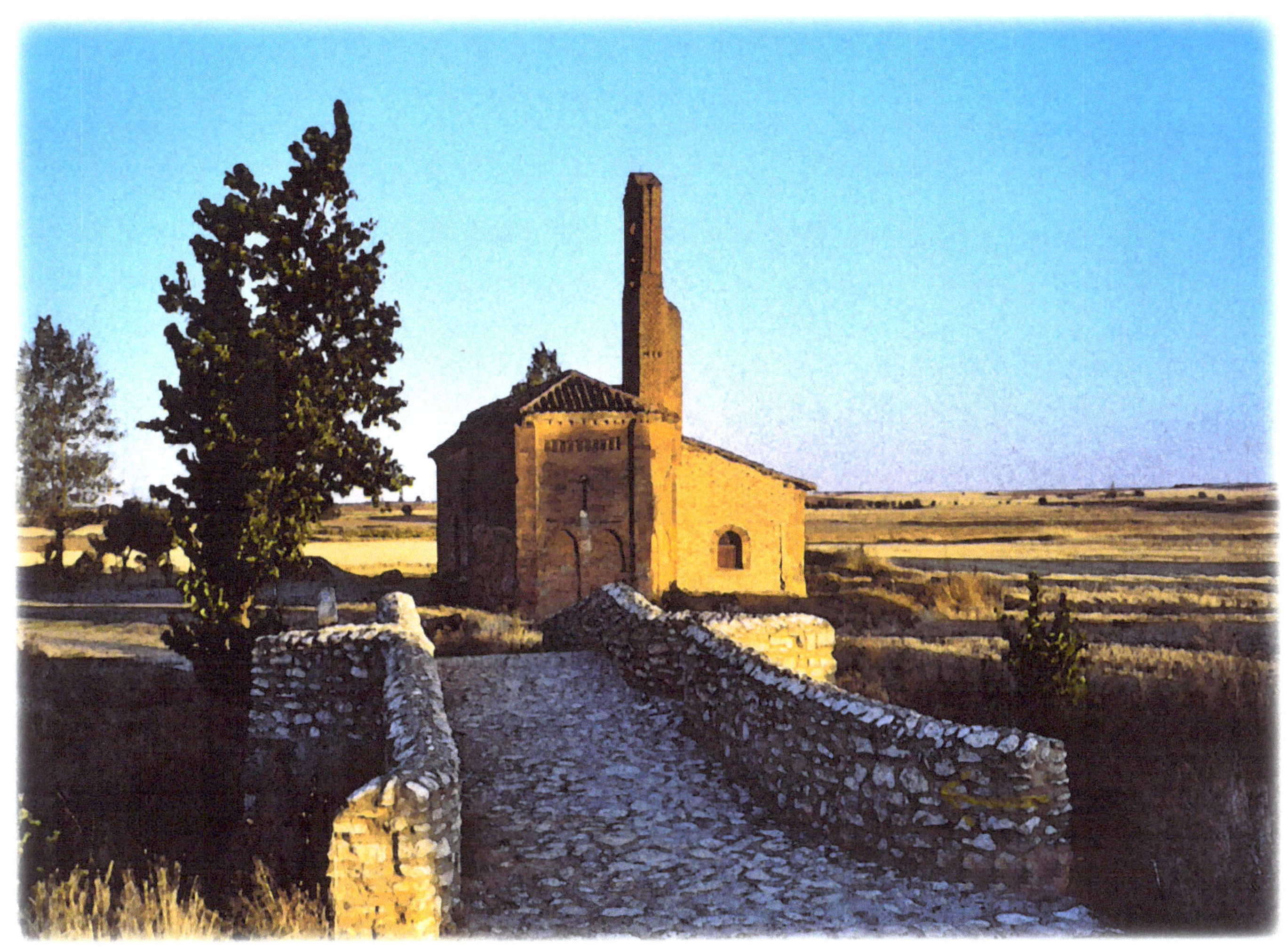

Ermita de la Virgen del Puente

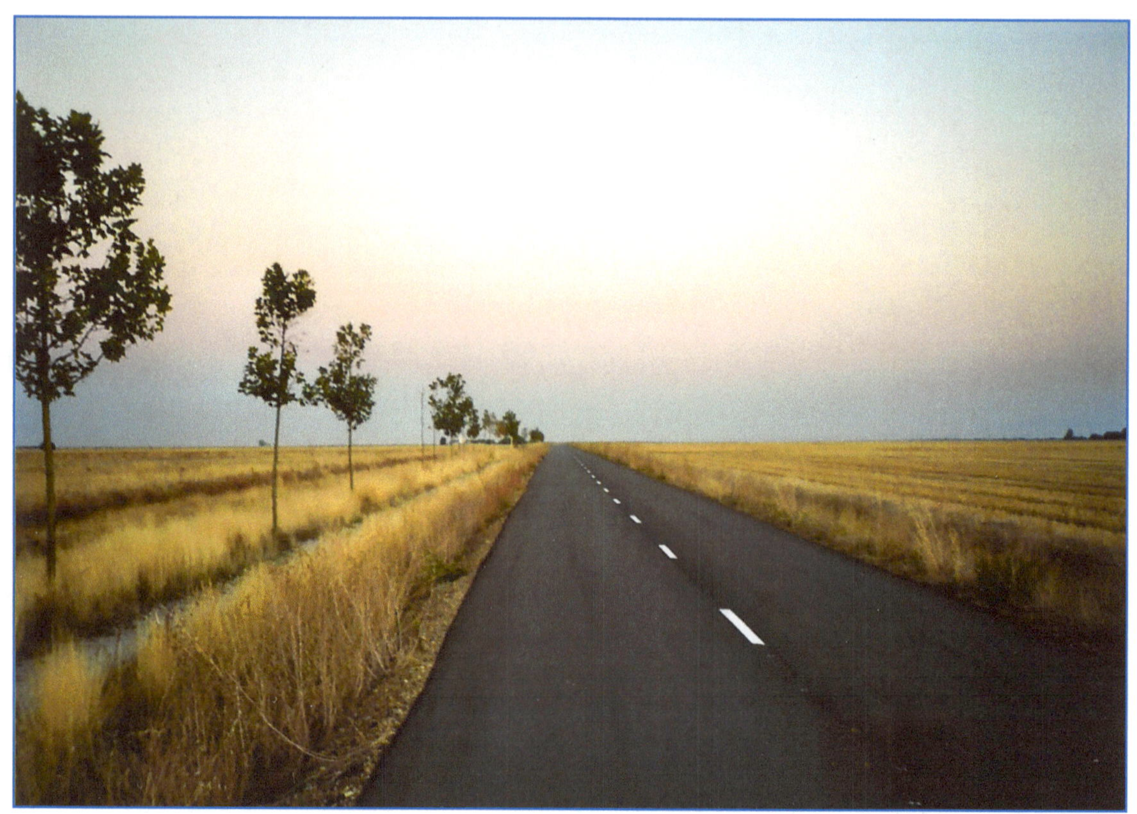

Early morning out of El Burgo Ranero

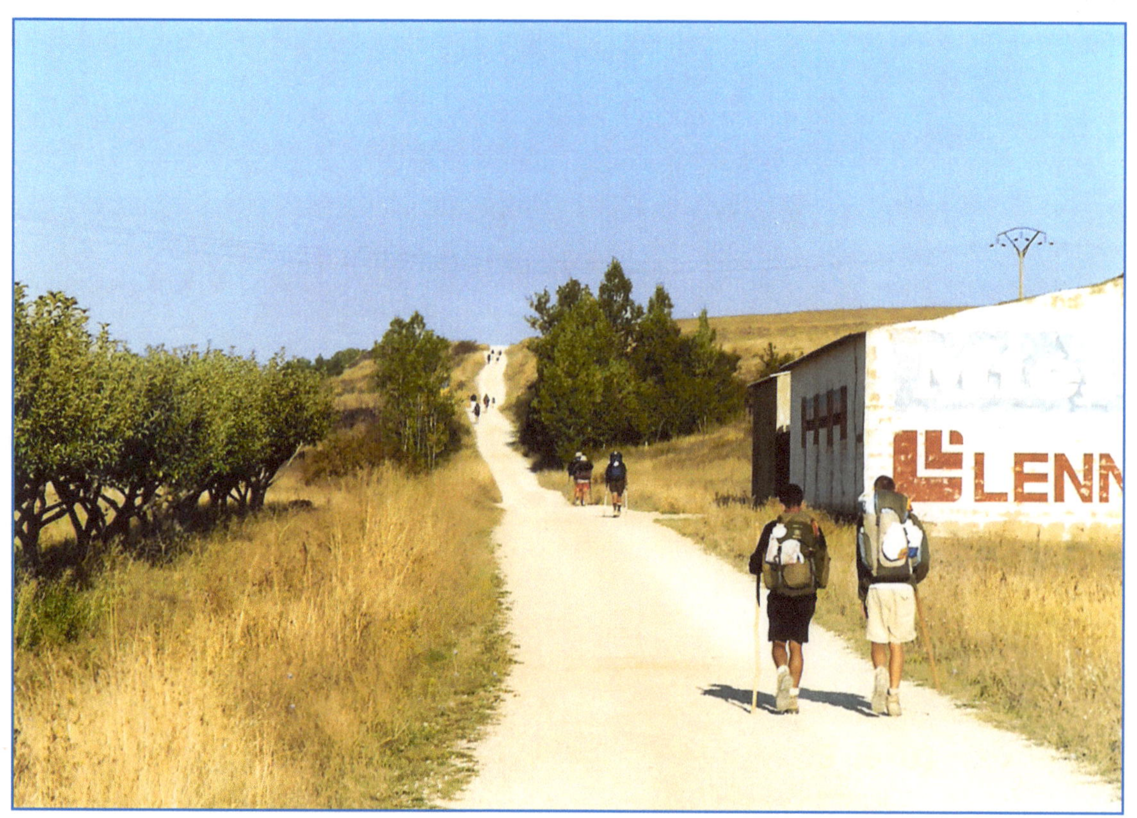

Nearing Leon

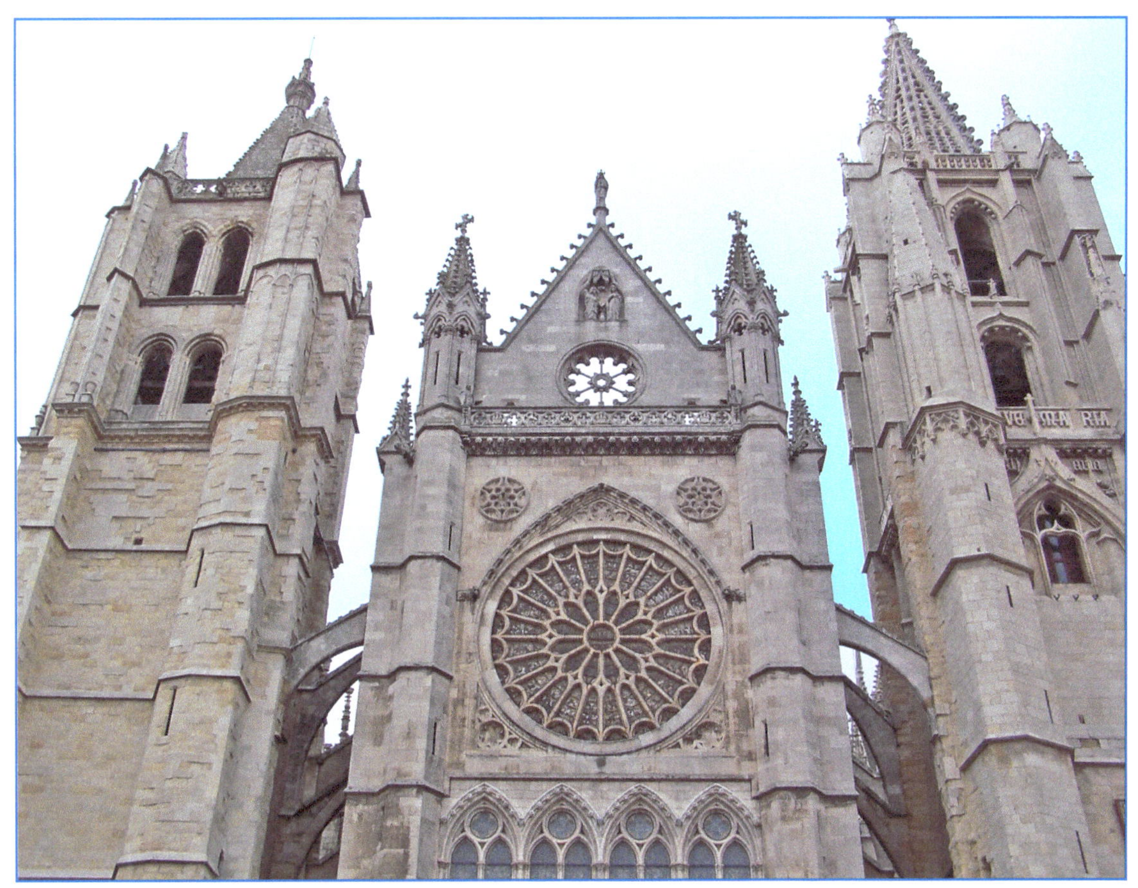

Leon Cathedral

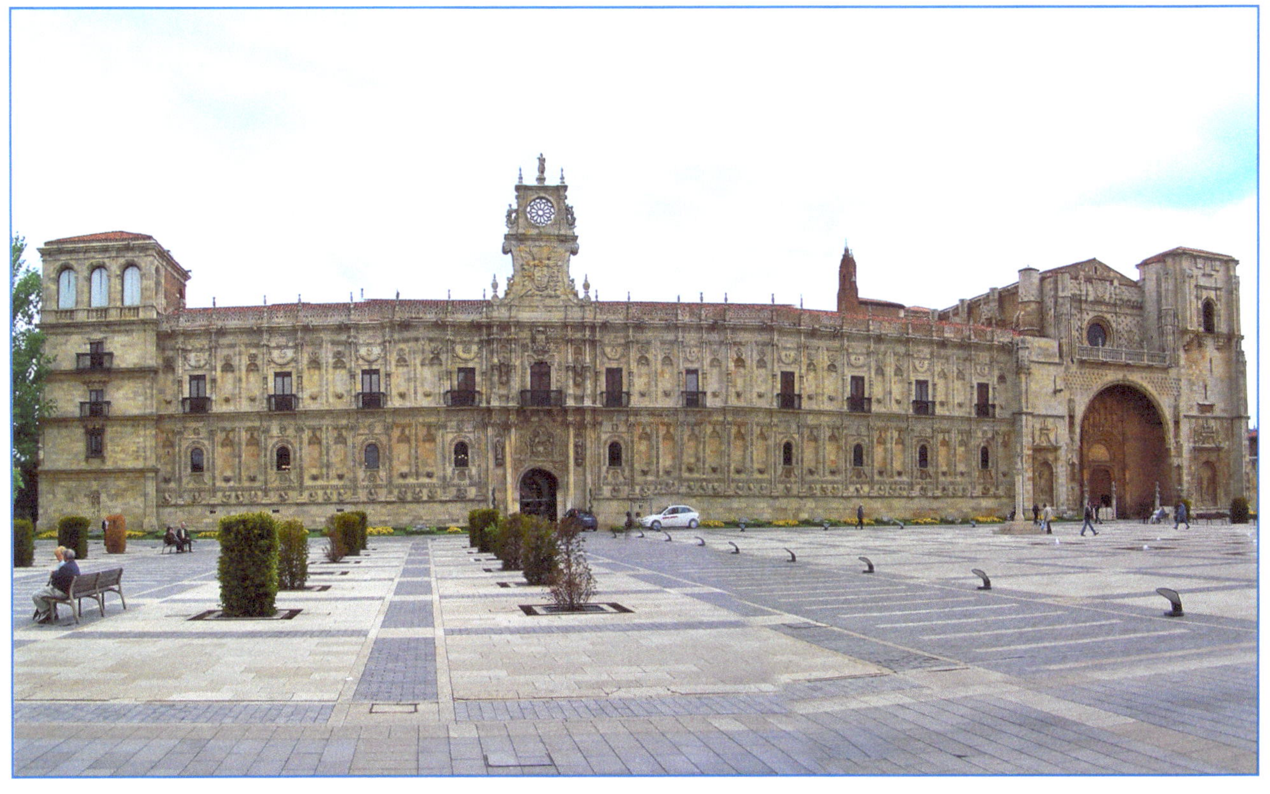

Parador San Marcos-Leon

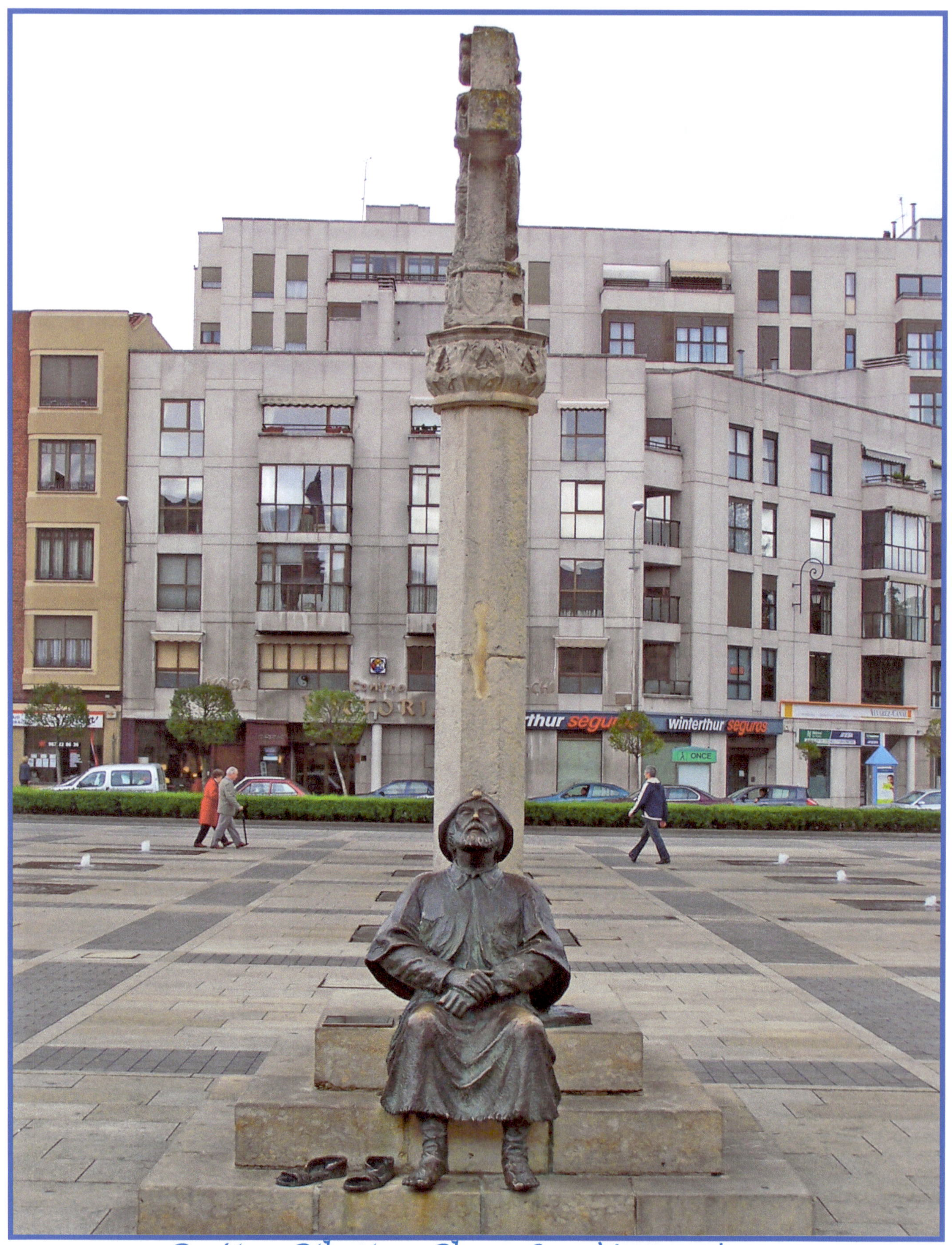

Resting Pilgrim--Plaza San Marcos-Leon

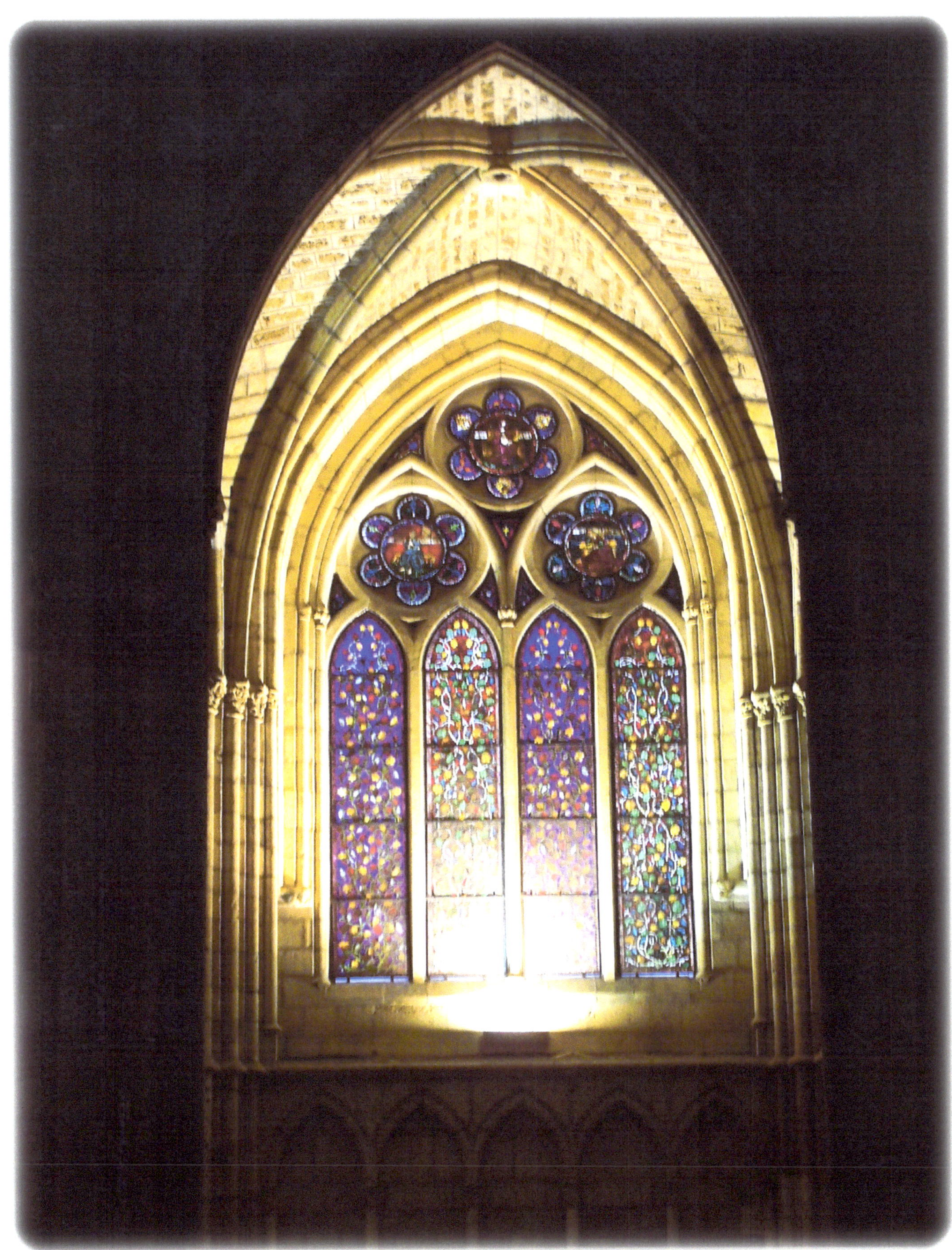

Leon Cathedral

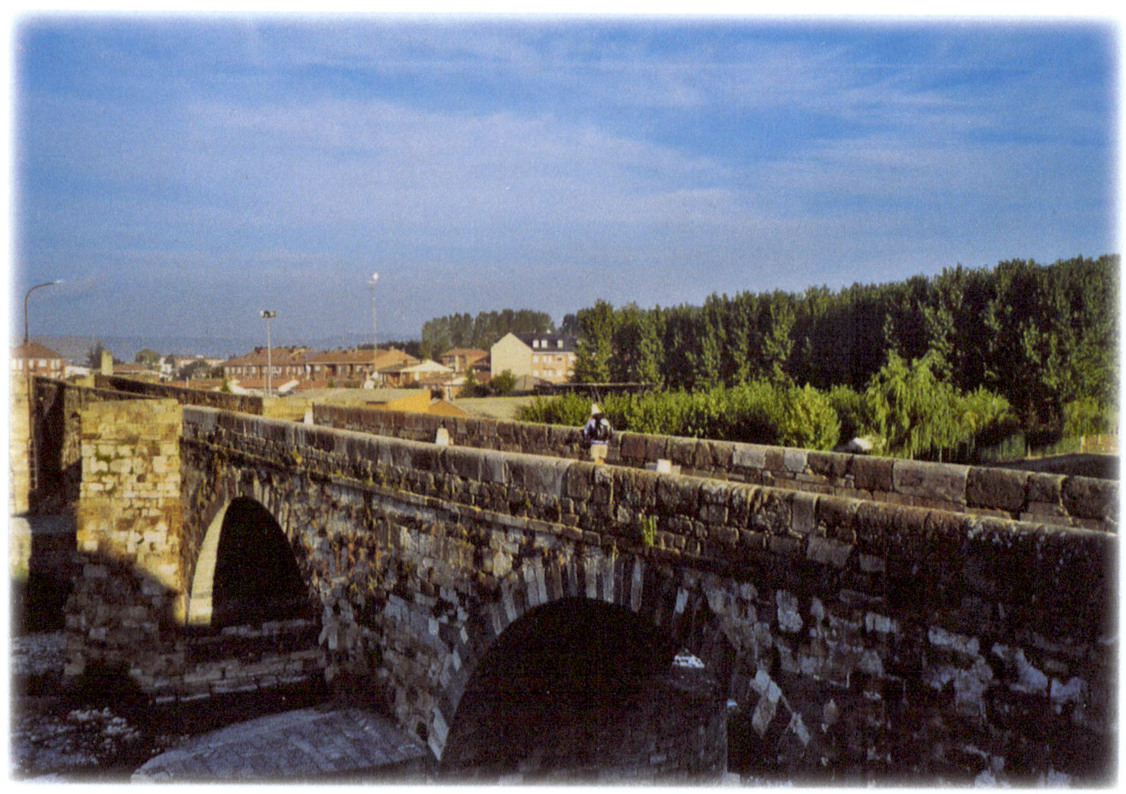

Puente de Orbigo-Hospital de Orbigo

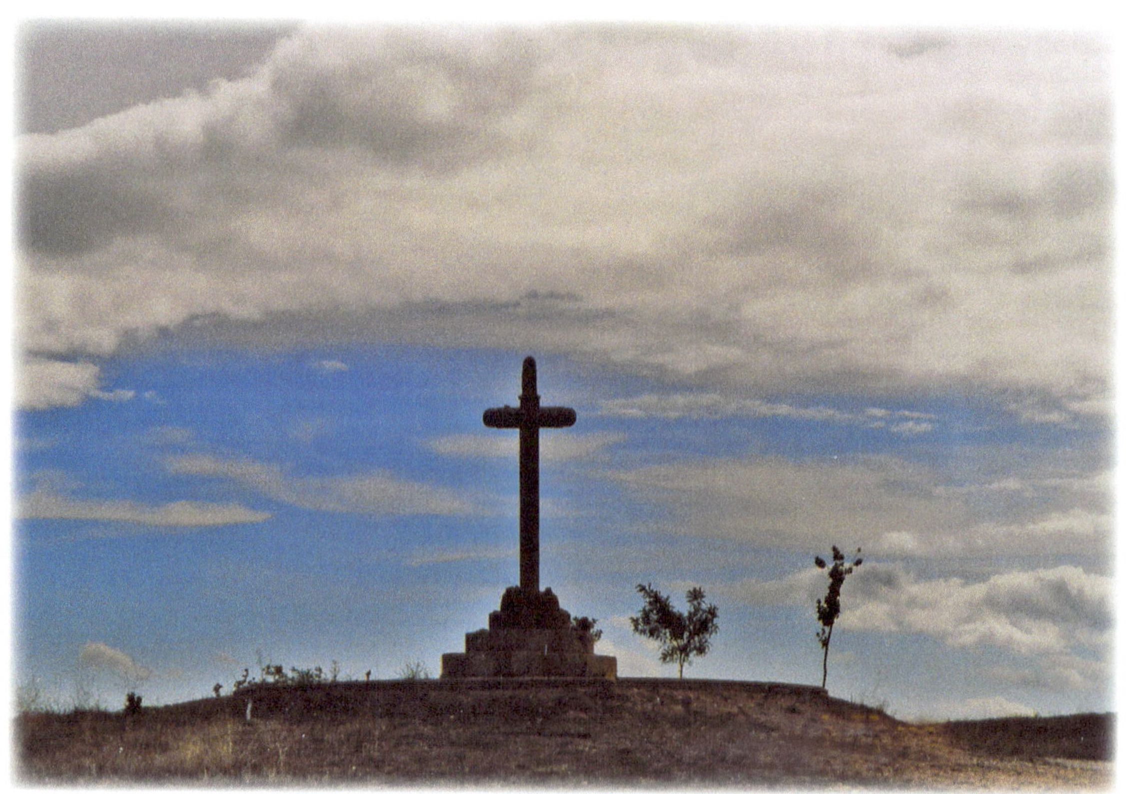

Crucero Santo Toribio

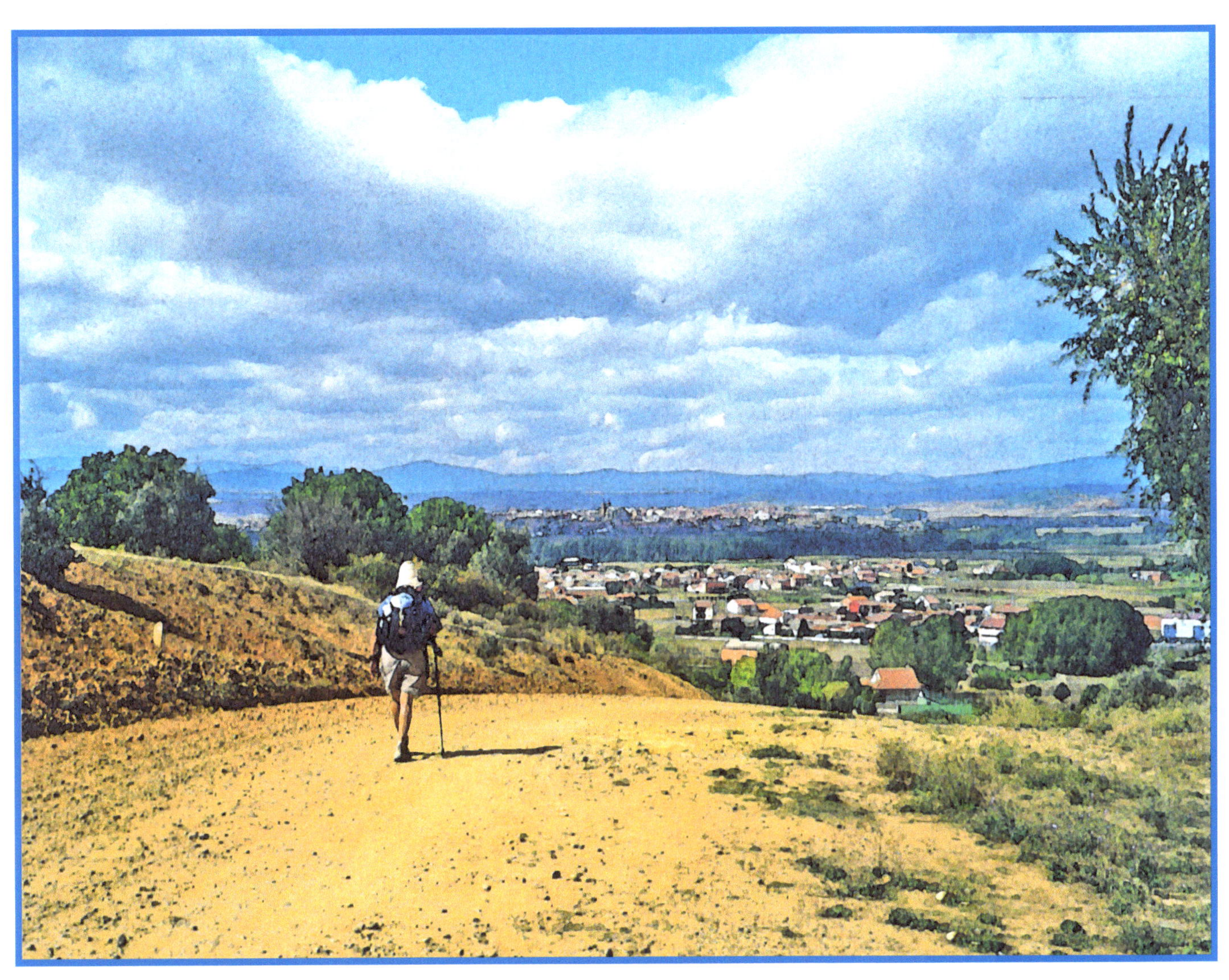

Camino into San Justo-Astorga in the distance

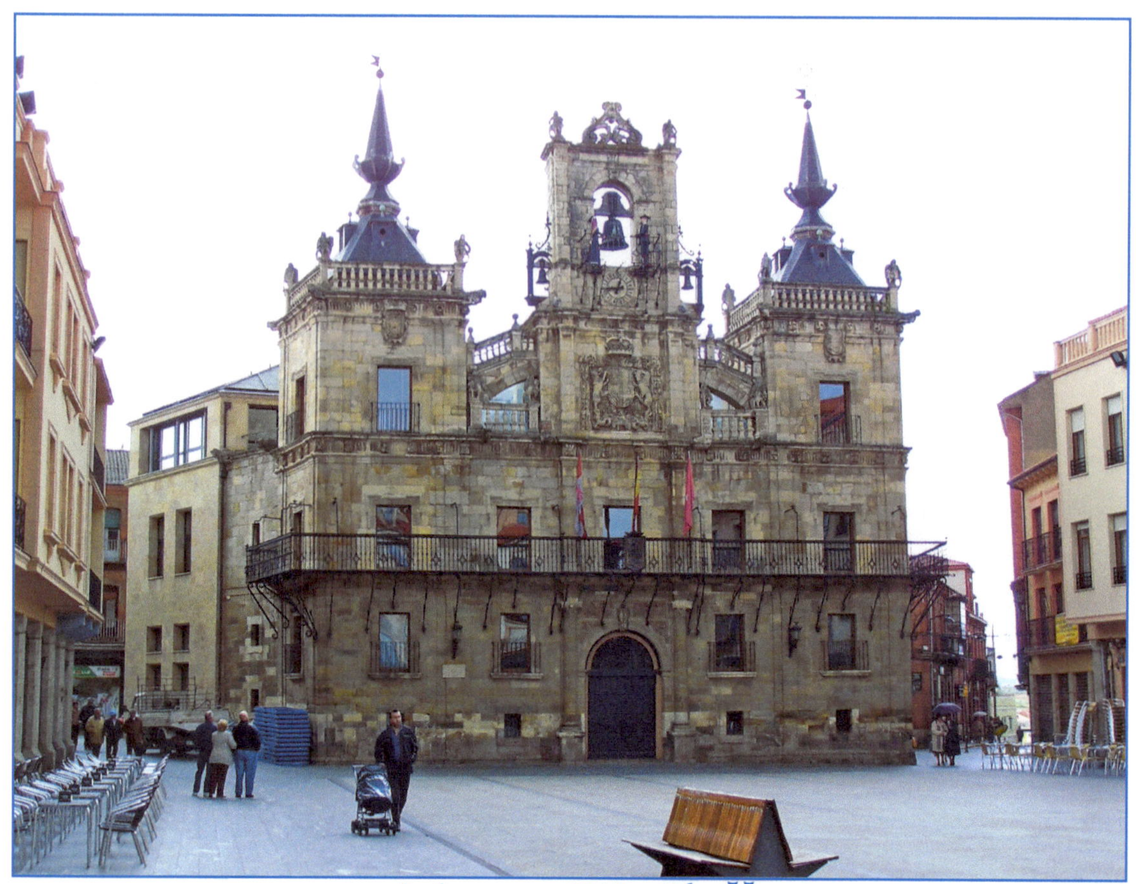

Astorga City Hall

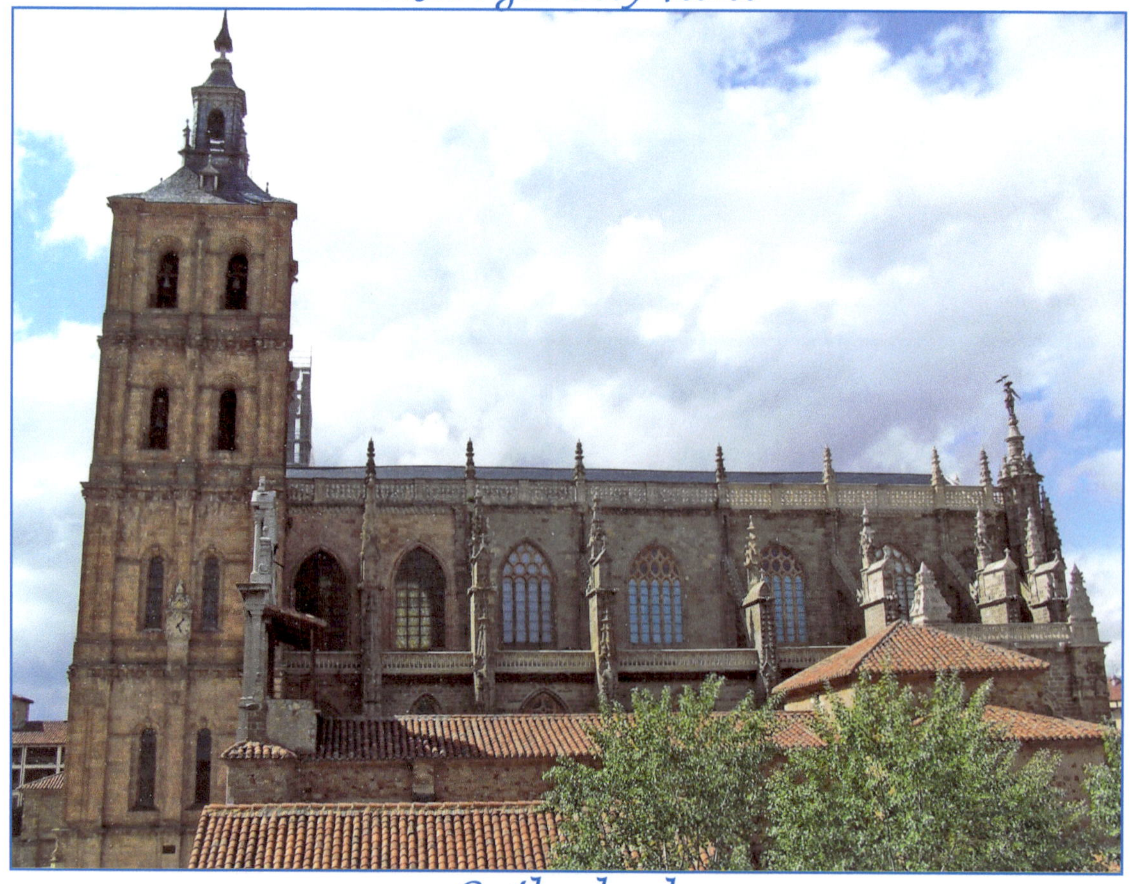

Cathedral

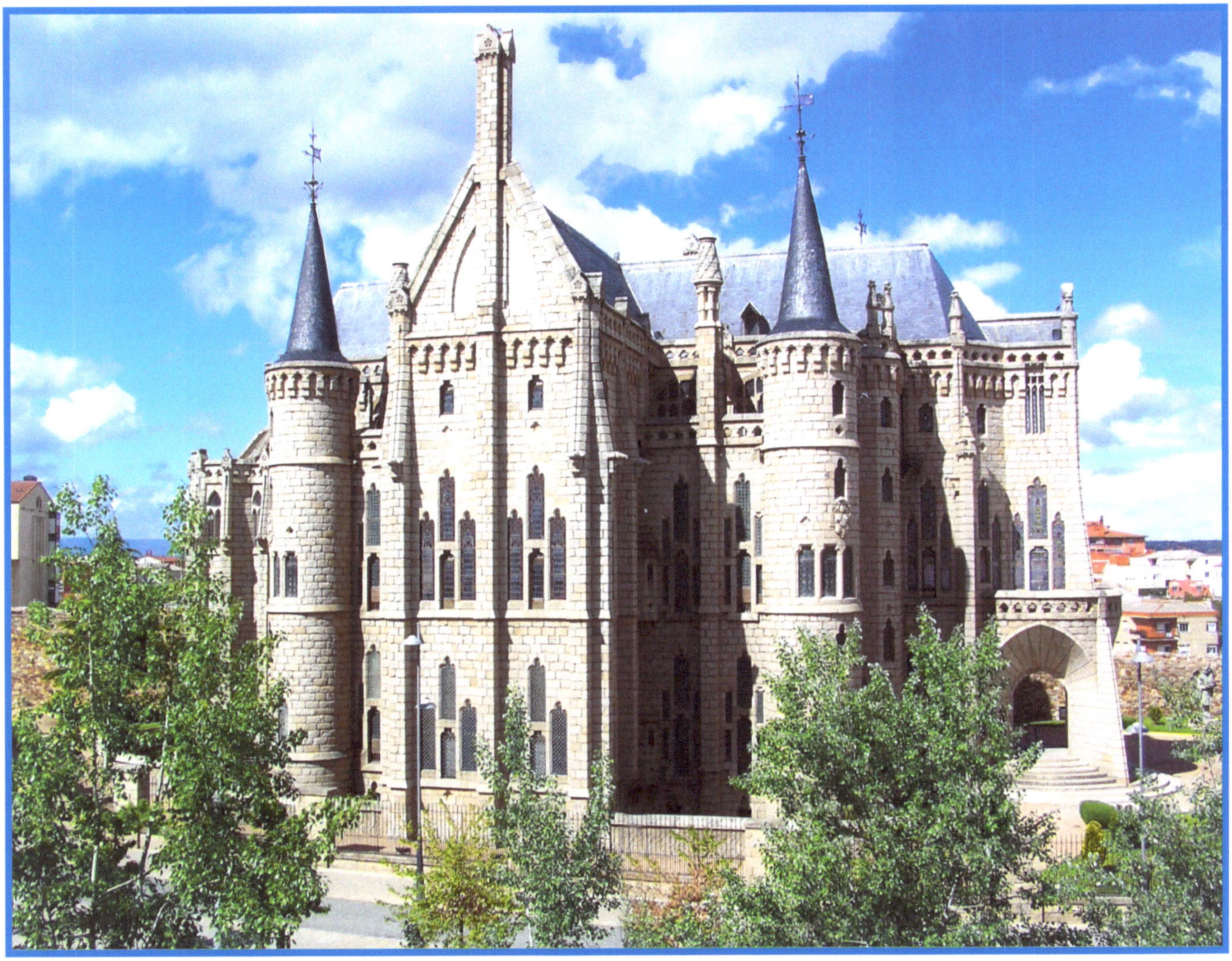

Palacio Episcopal-Designed by Antonio Gaudi

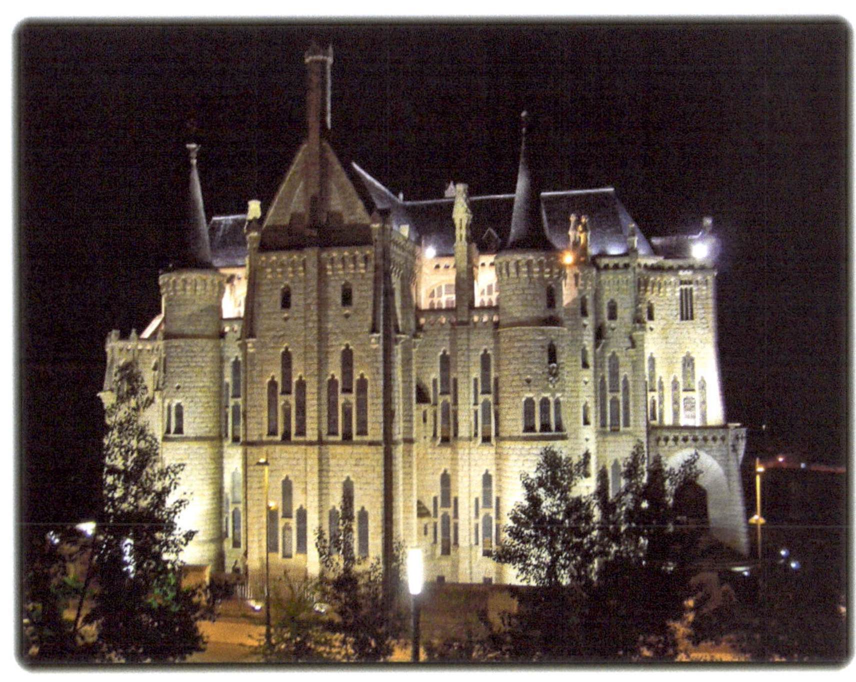

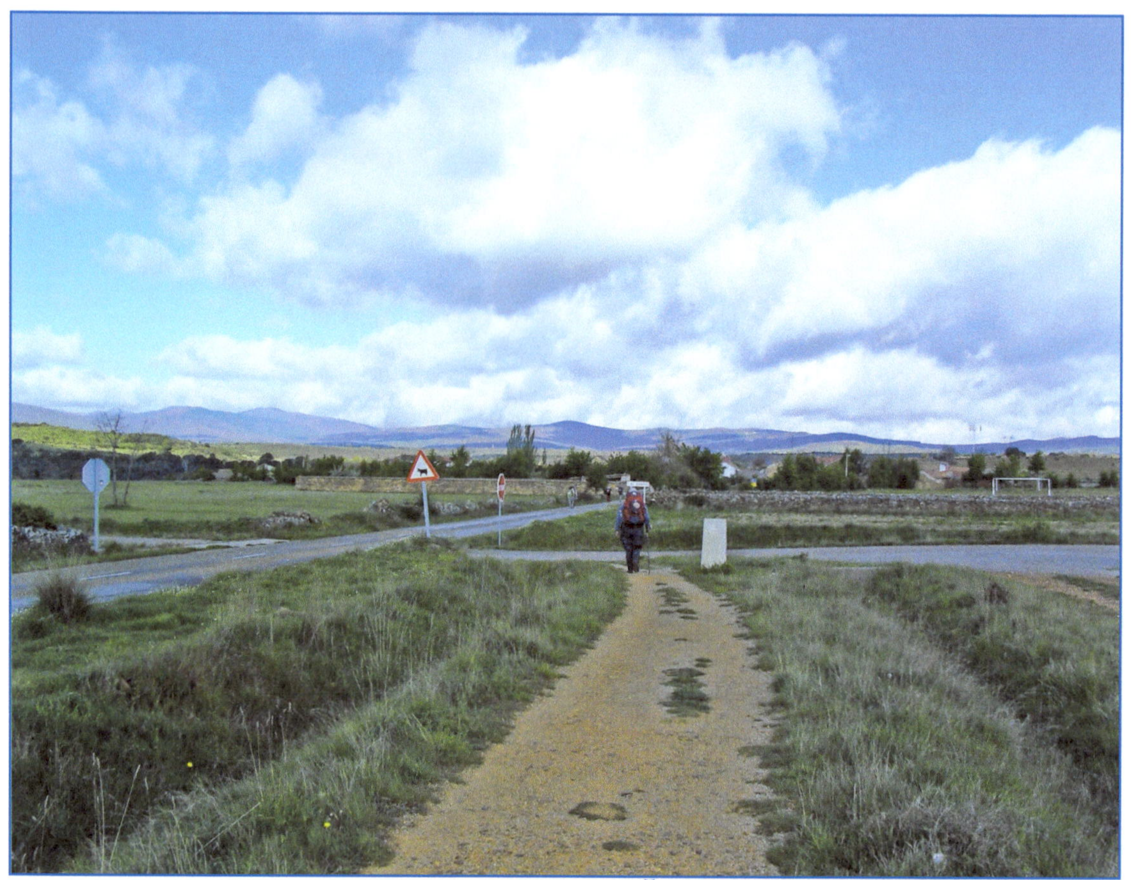

Camino into El Ganso

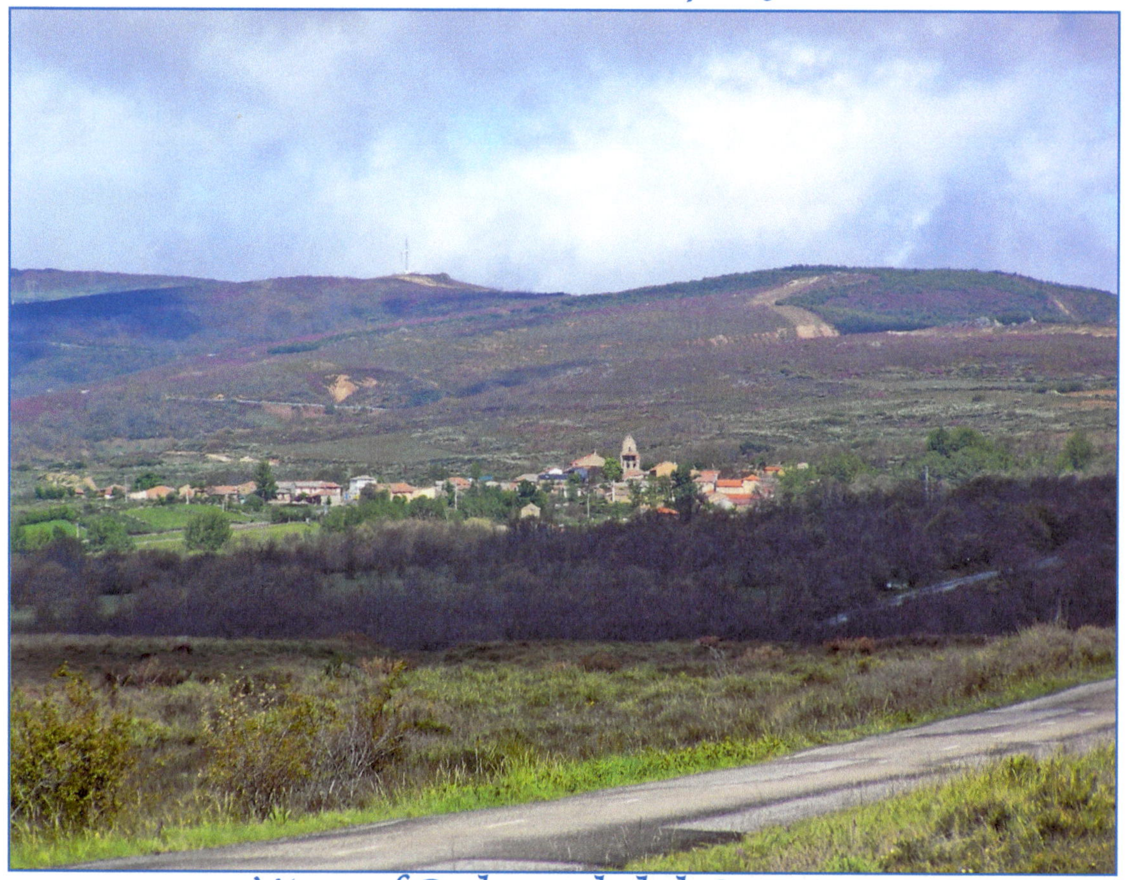

View of Rabanal del Camino

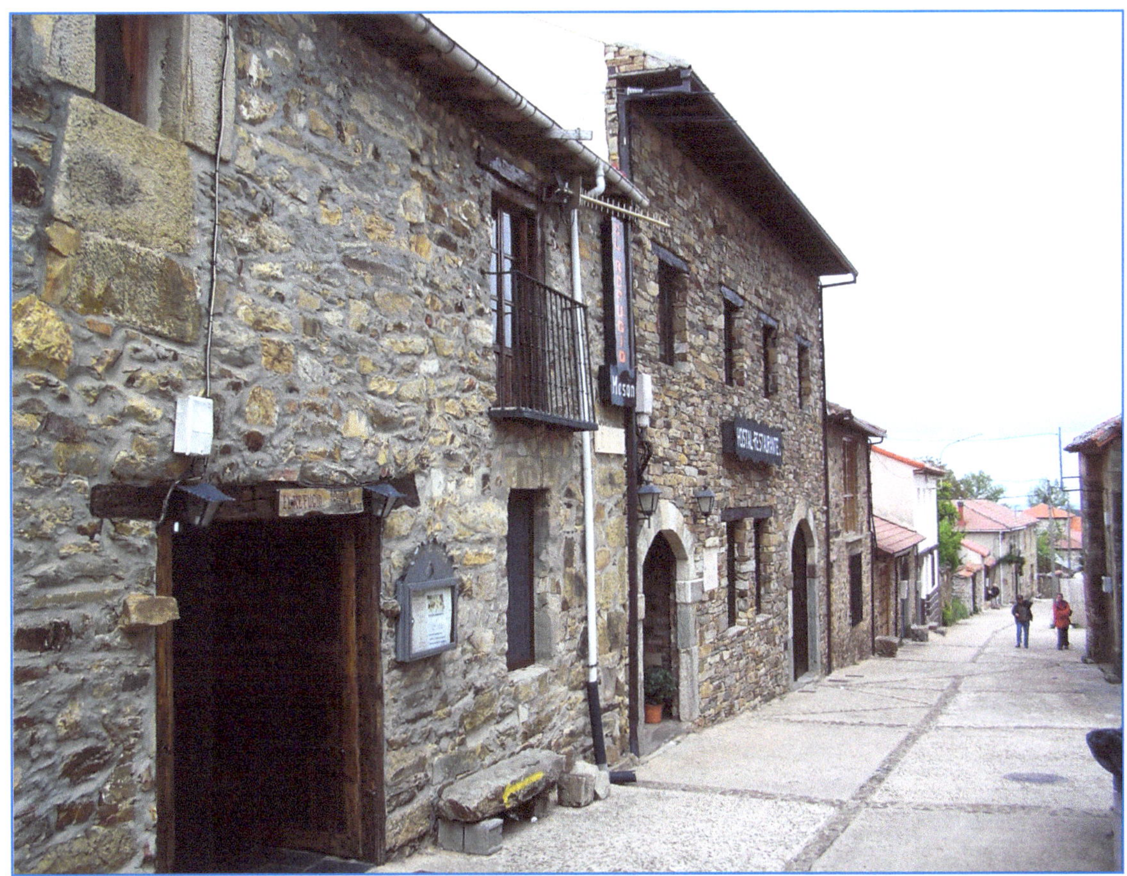

Rabanal del Camino-Main Street

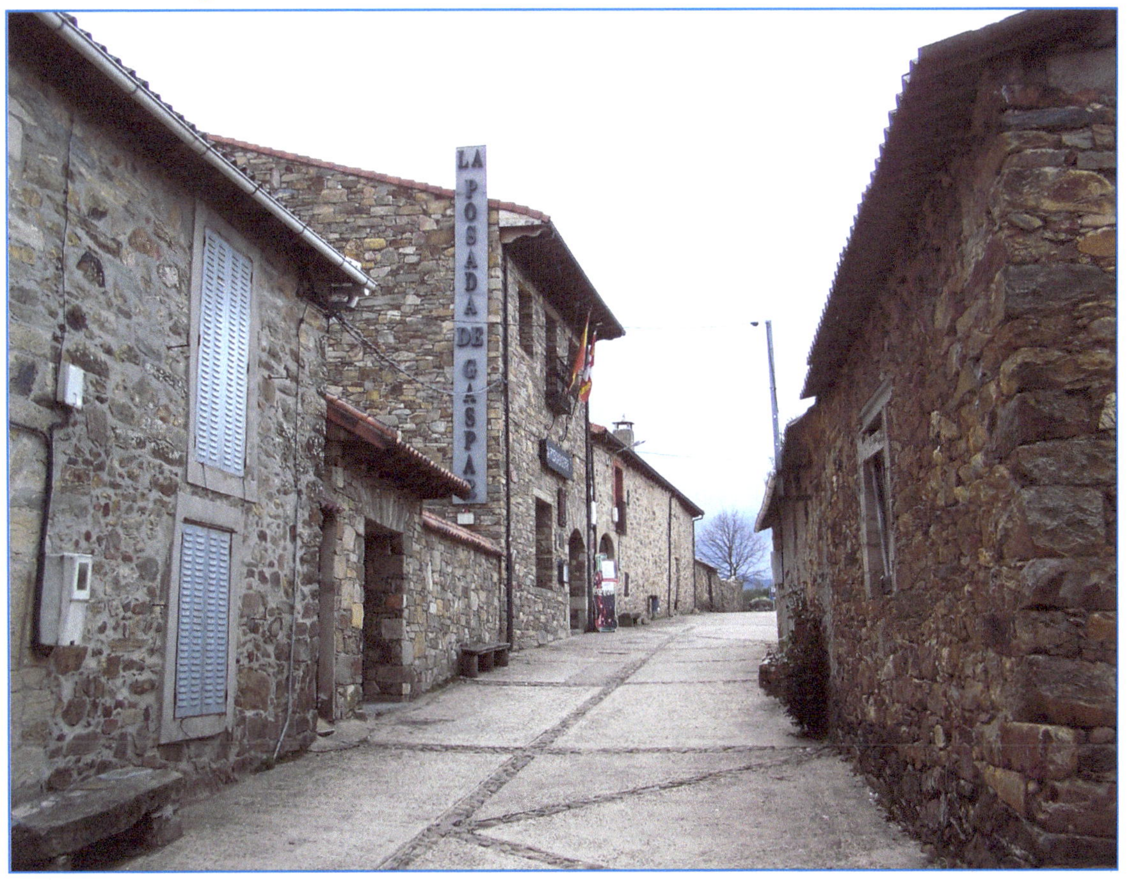

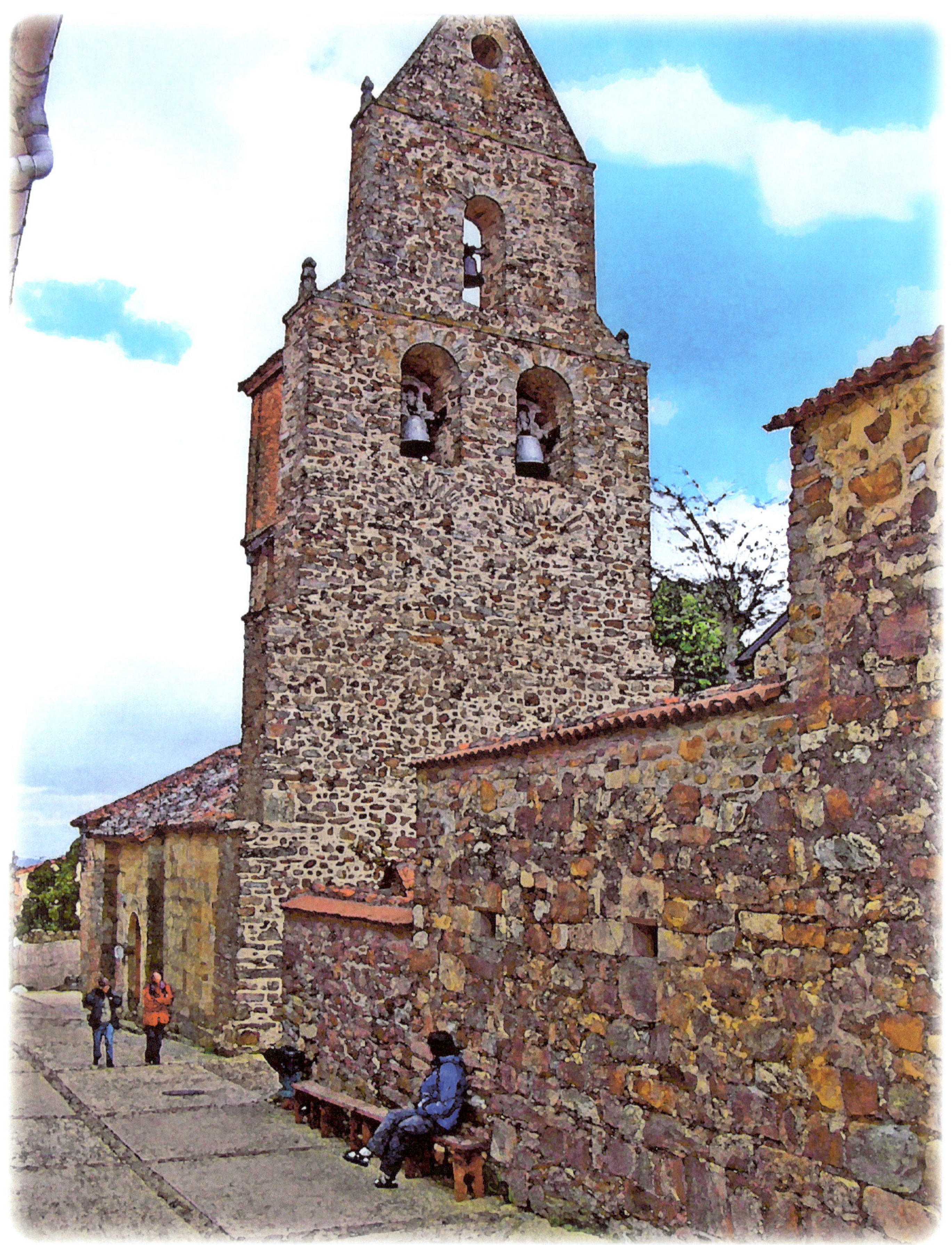

Rabanal del Camino Church

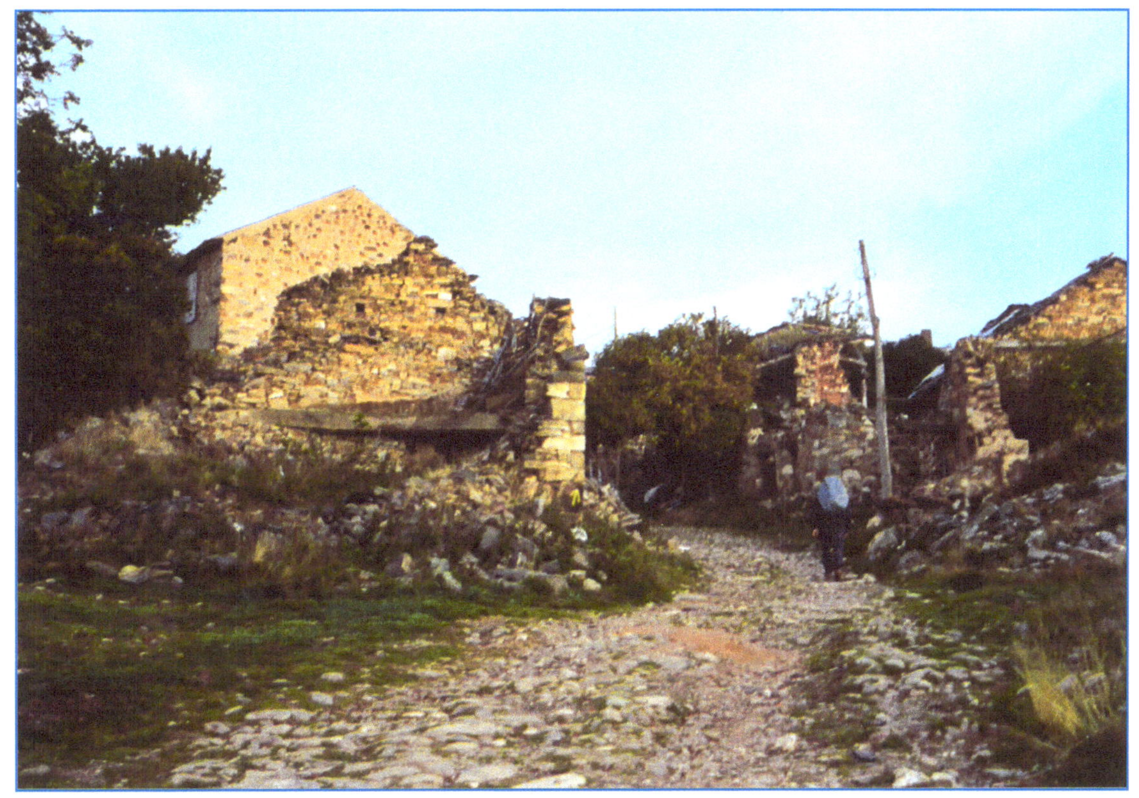

Foncebadon

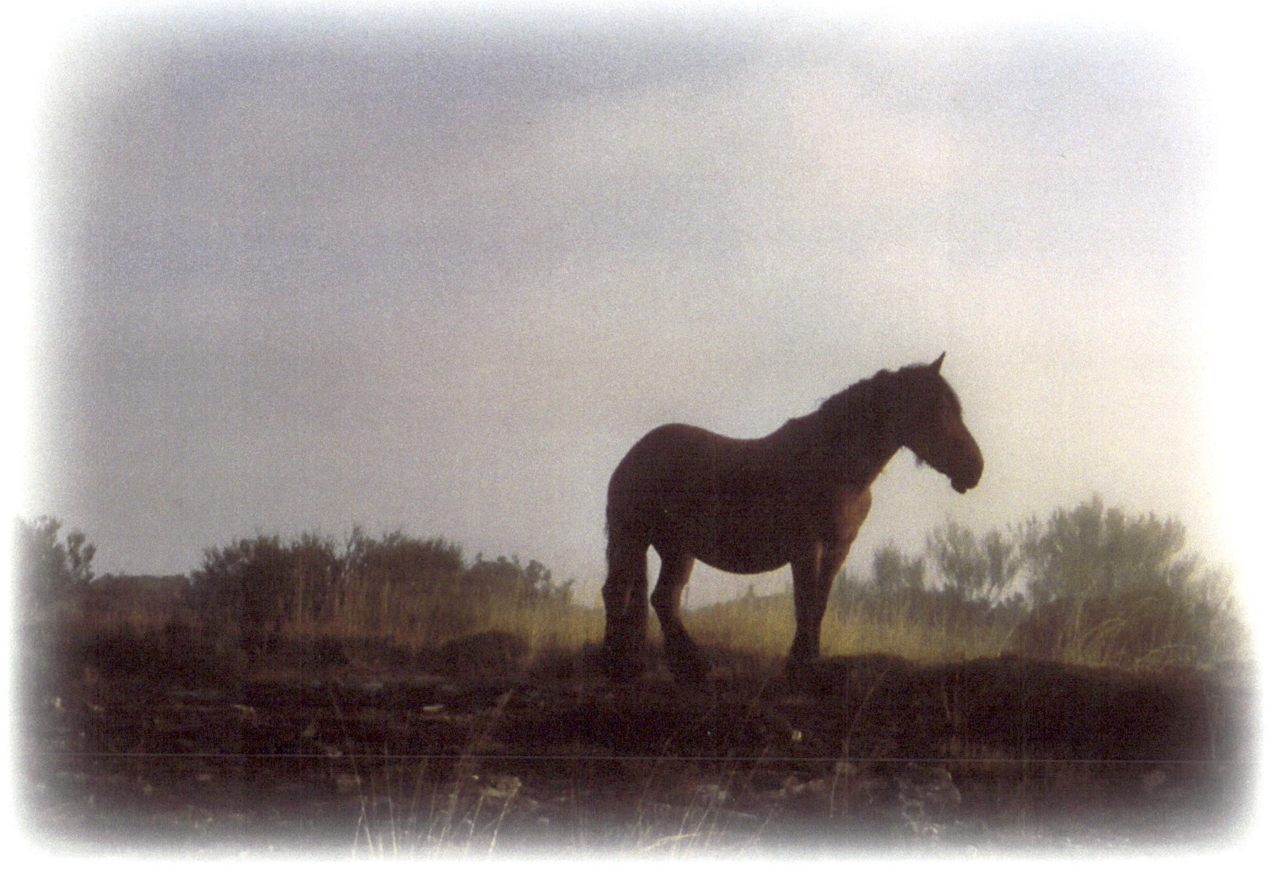

Horse in the clouds

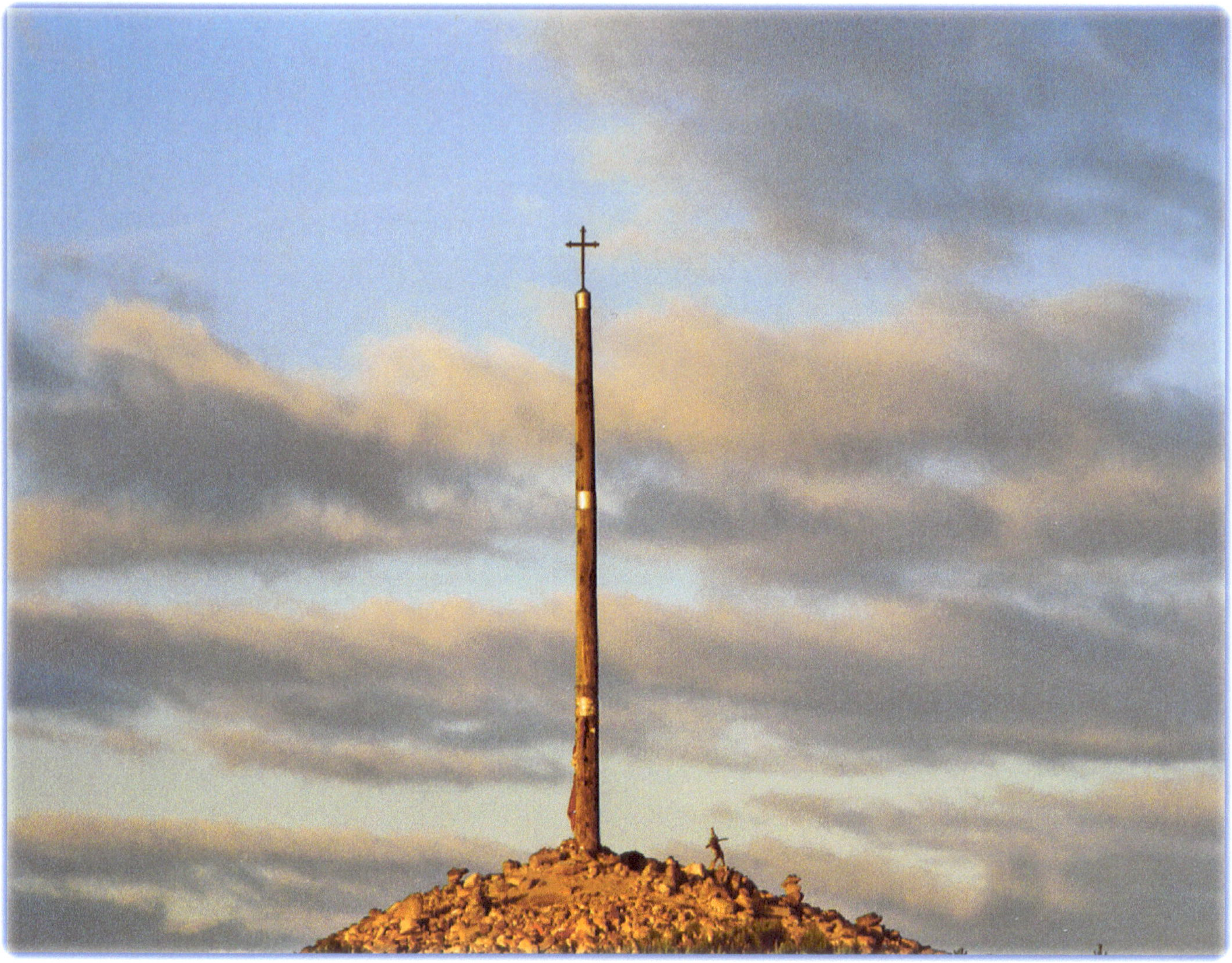

Cruz de Fierro-Highest point on the Camino

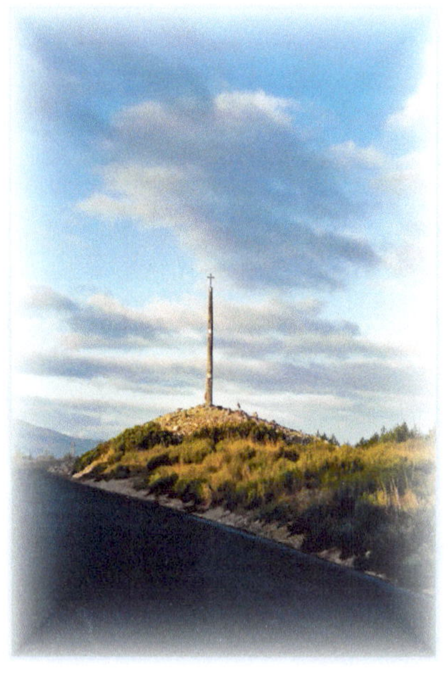

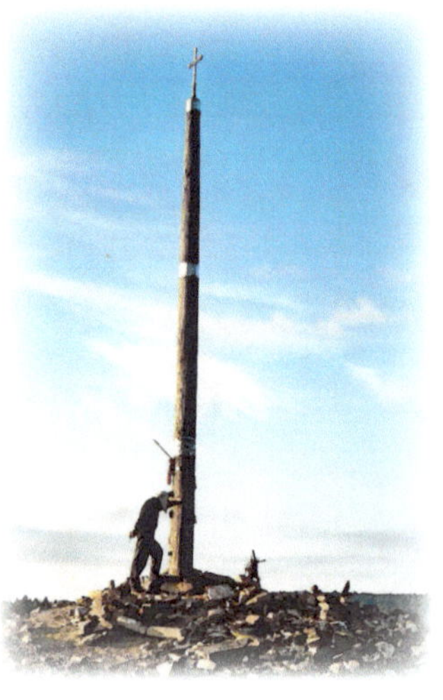

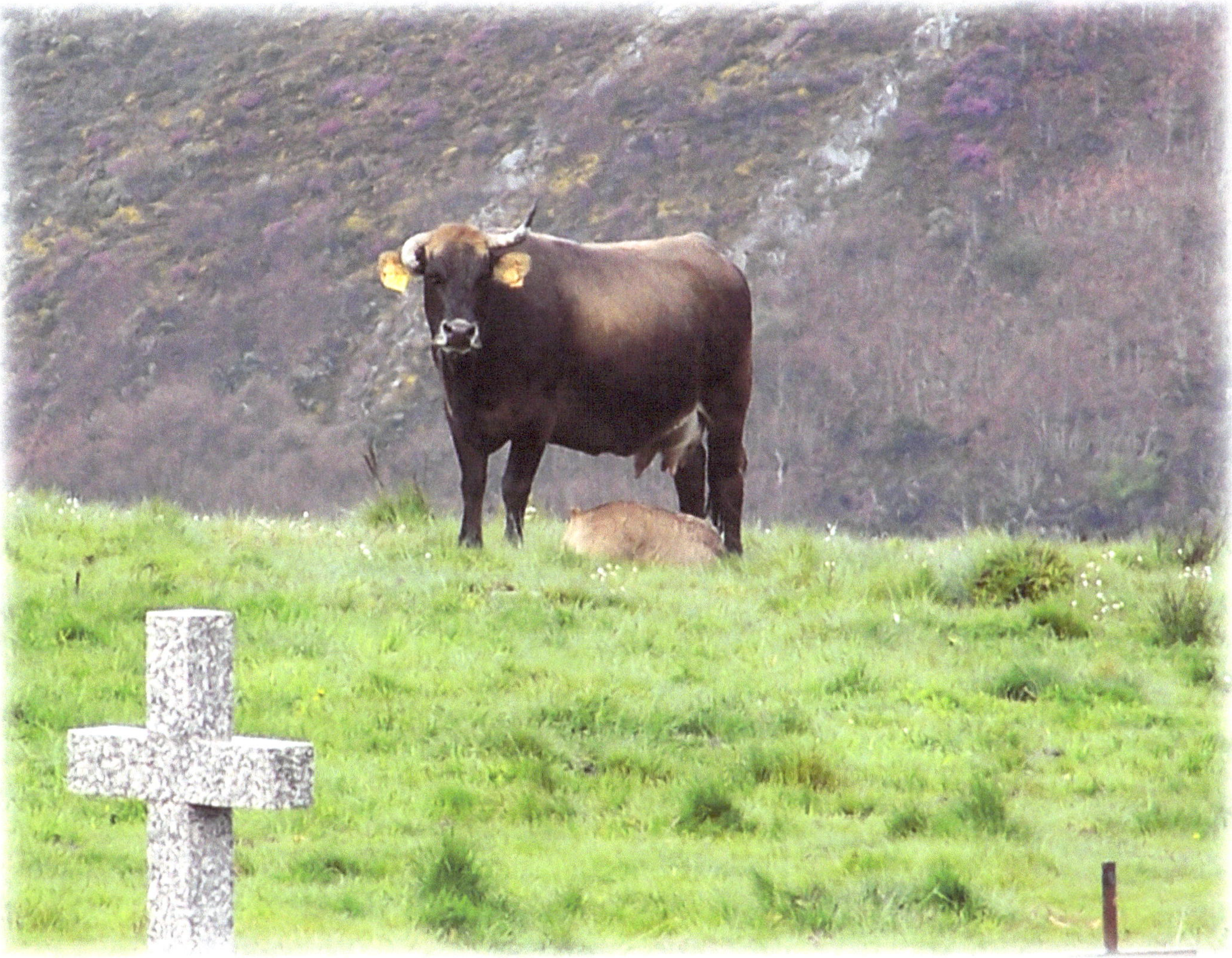

Mama-Baby-Cross

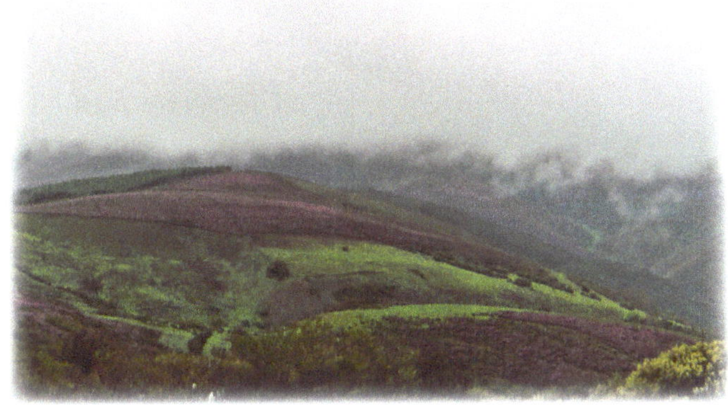

Cloud covered mountains approaching Manjarin

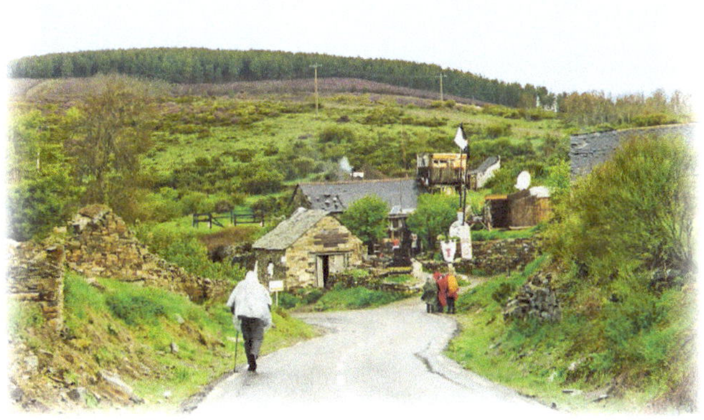

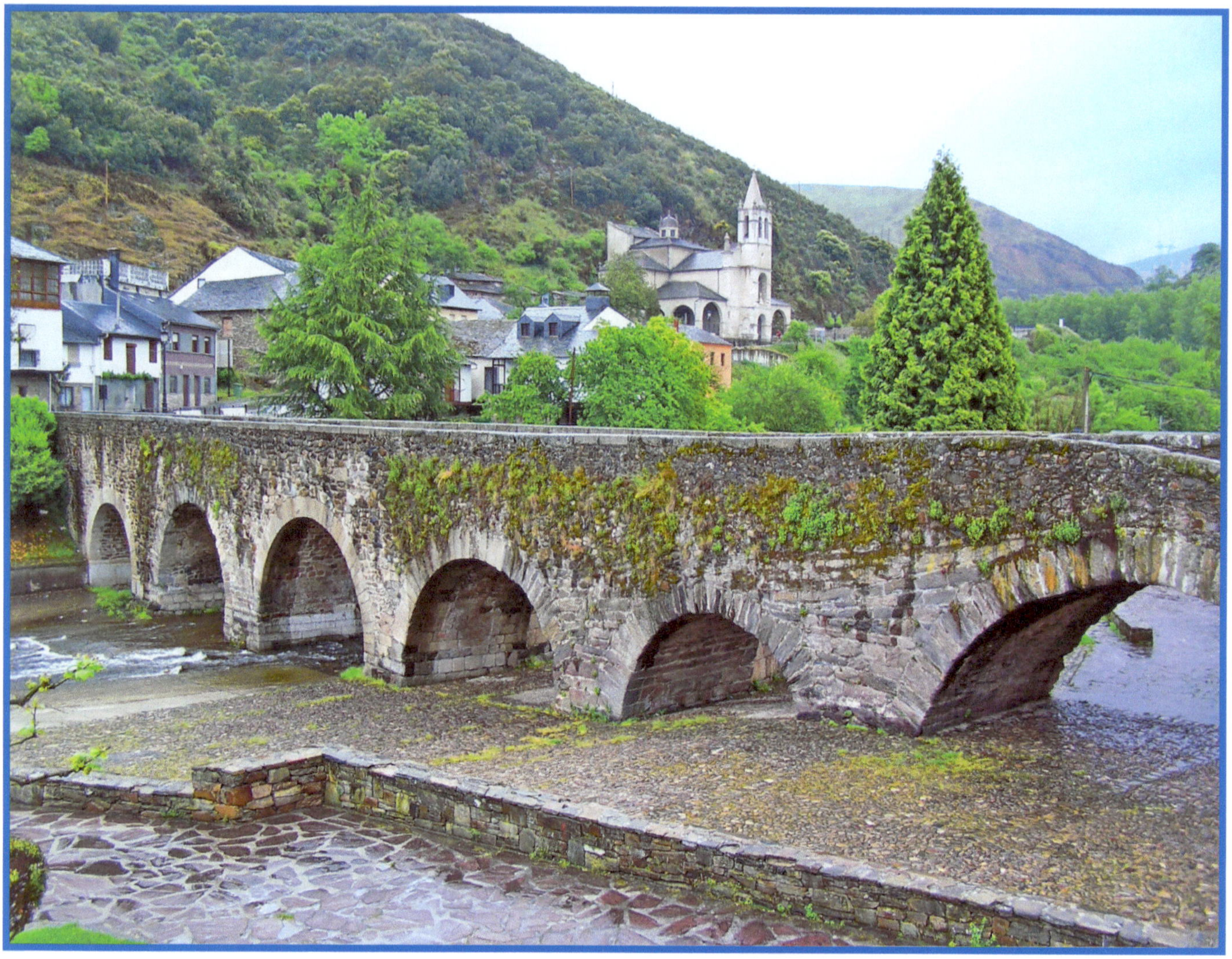

Medieval bridge-Molinaseca

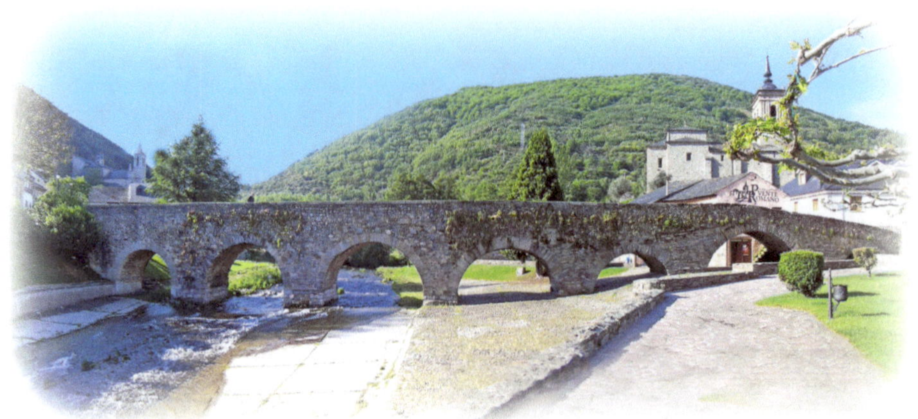

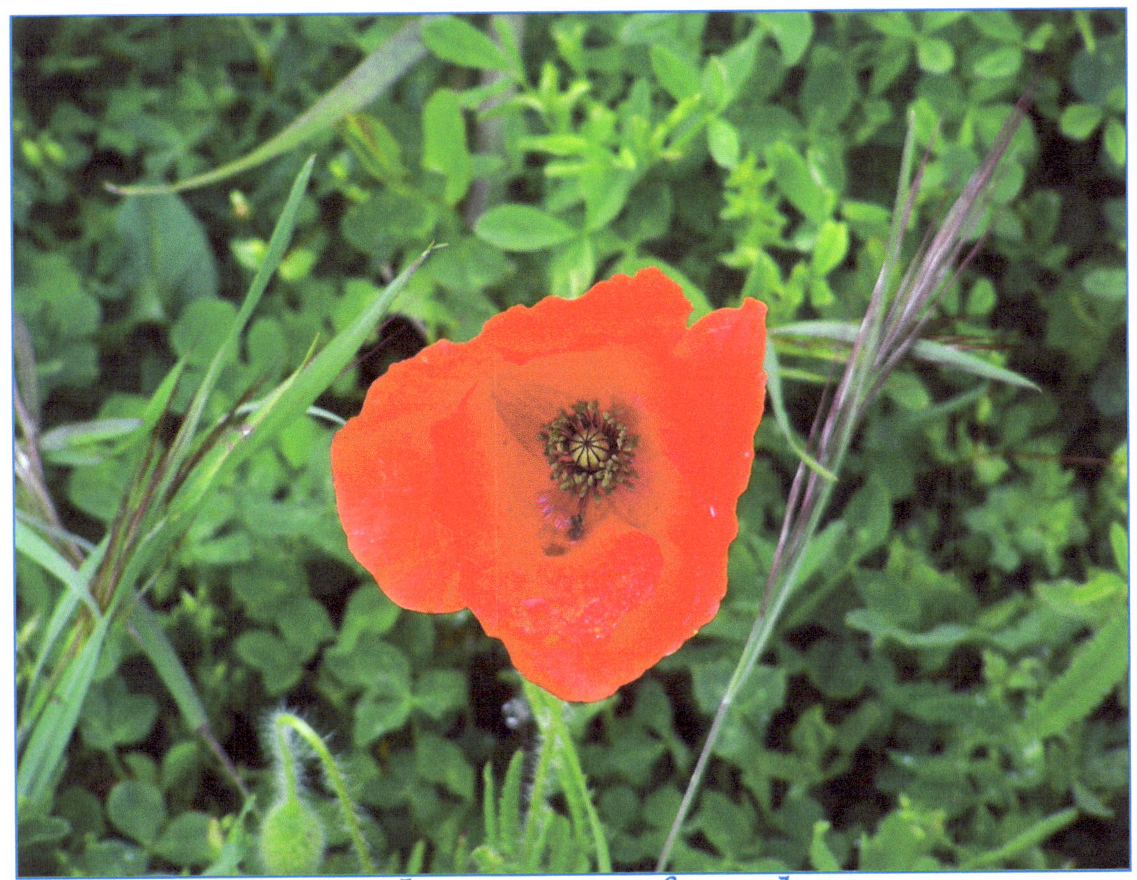

Red Poppy Ponferrada

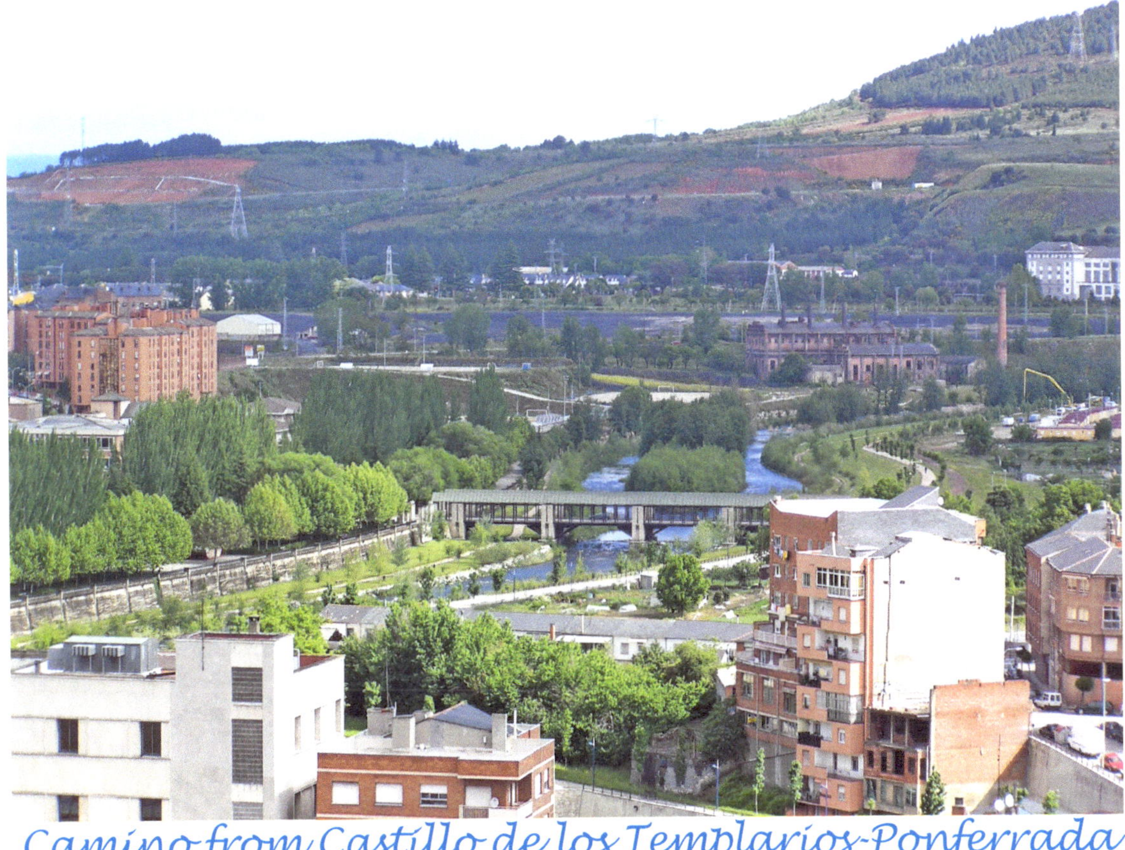

Camino from Castillo de los Templarios-Ponferrada

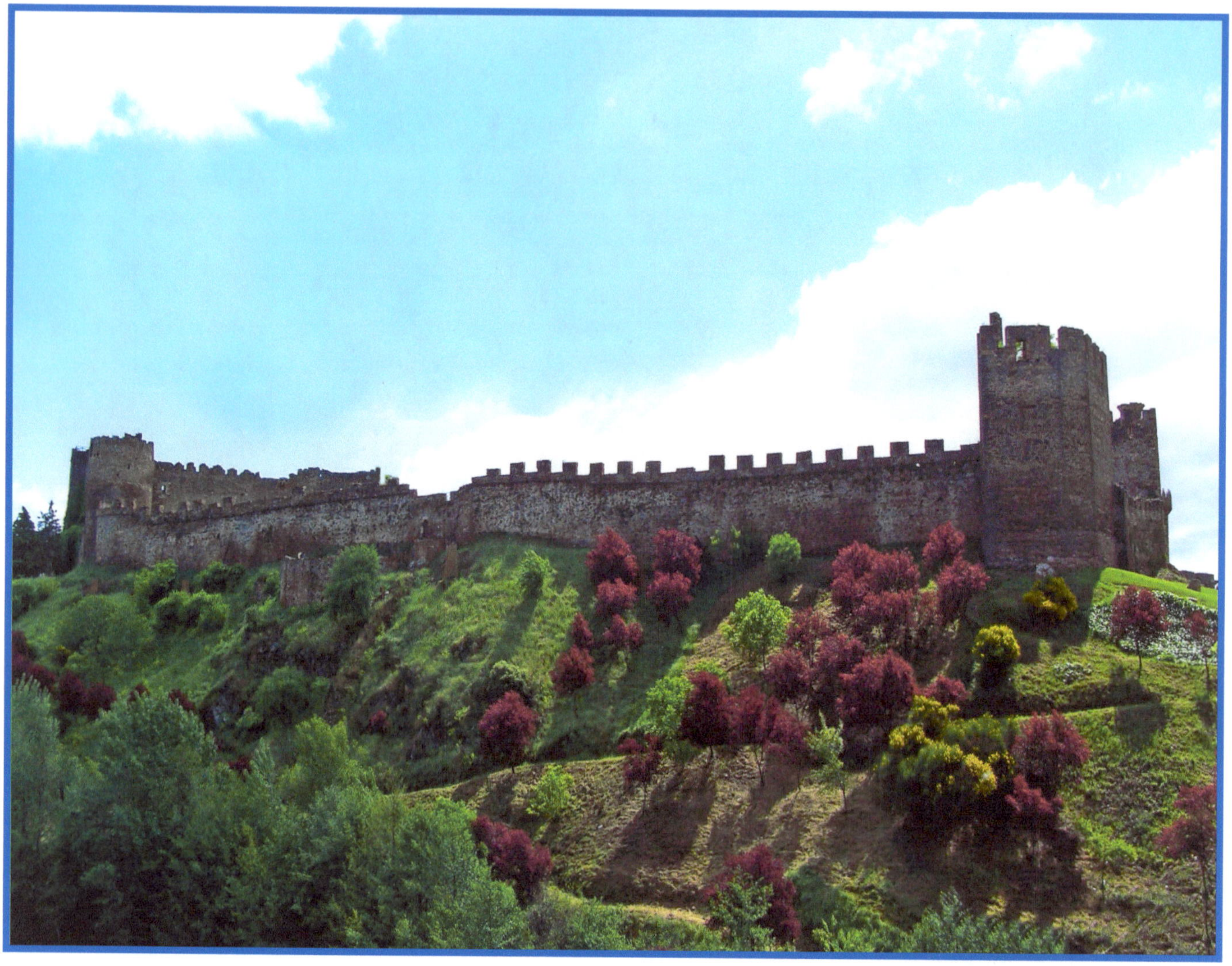

Castillo de los Templarios-Ponferrada

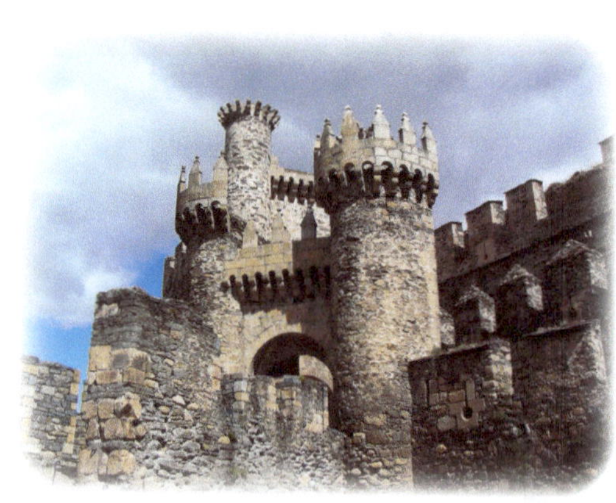

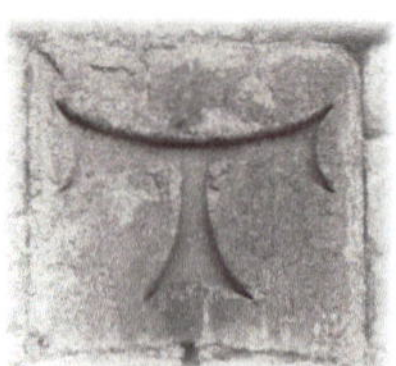

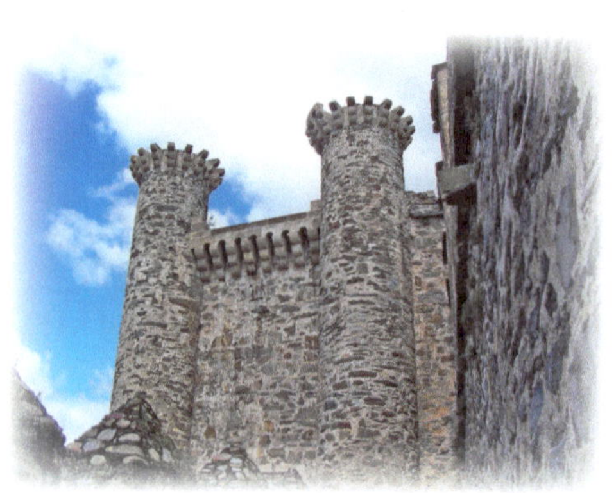

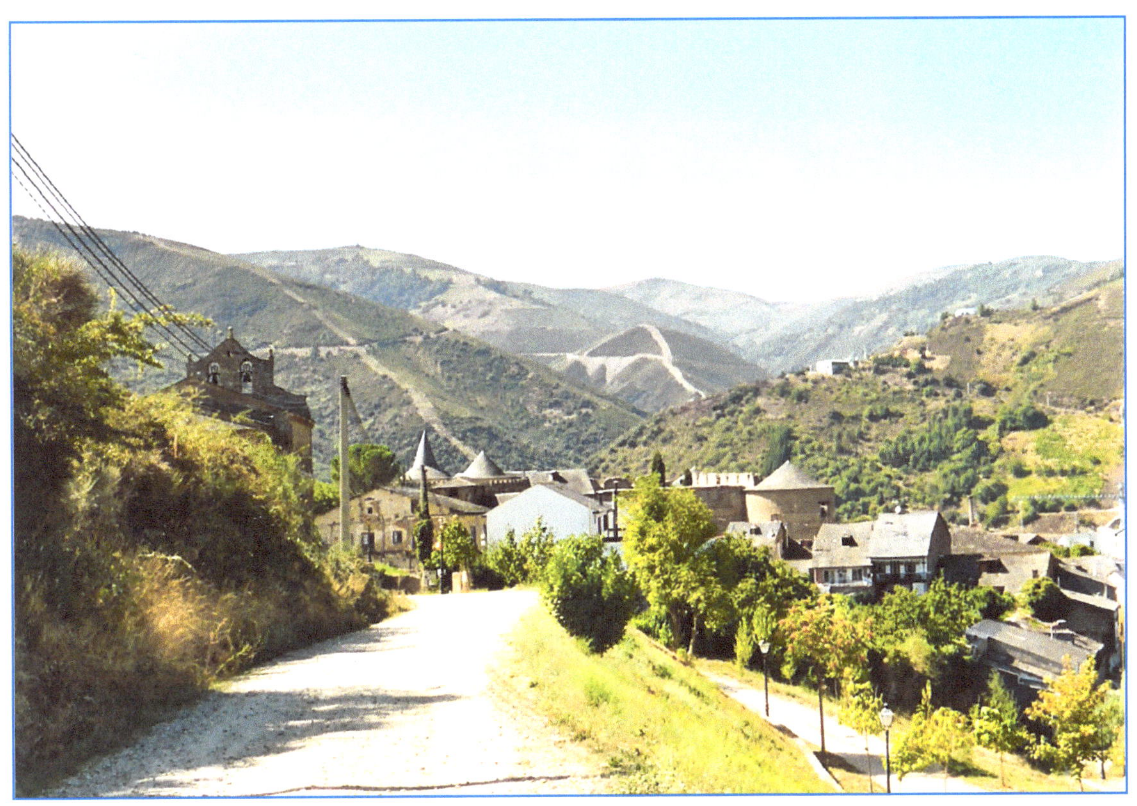

Camino into Villafranca del Bierzo

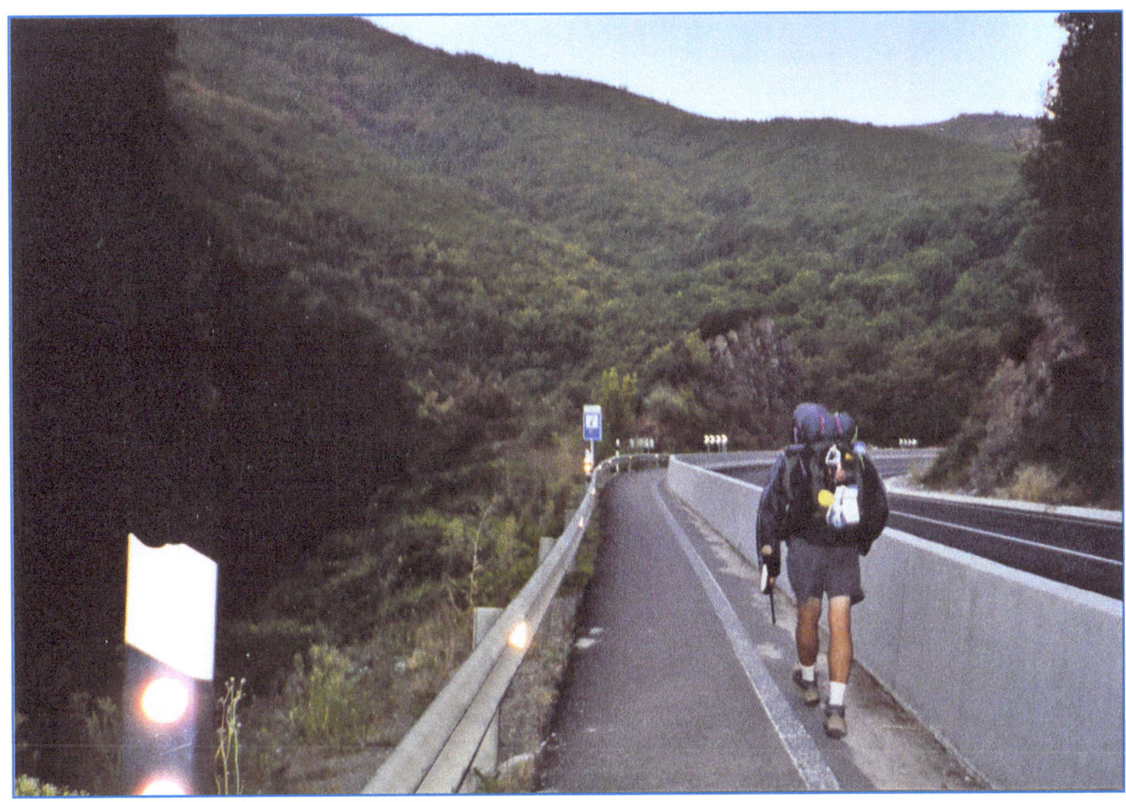

Early morning road route out of Villafranca del Bierzo

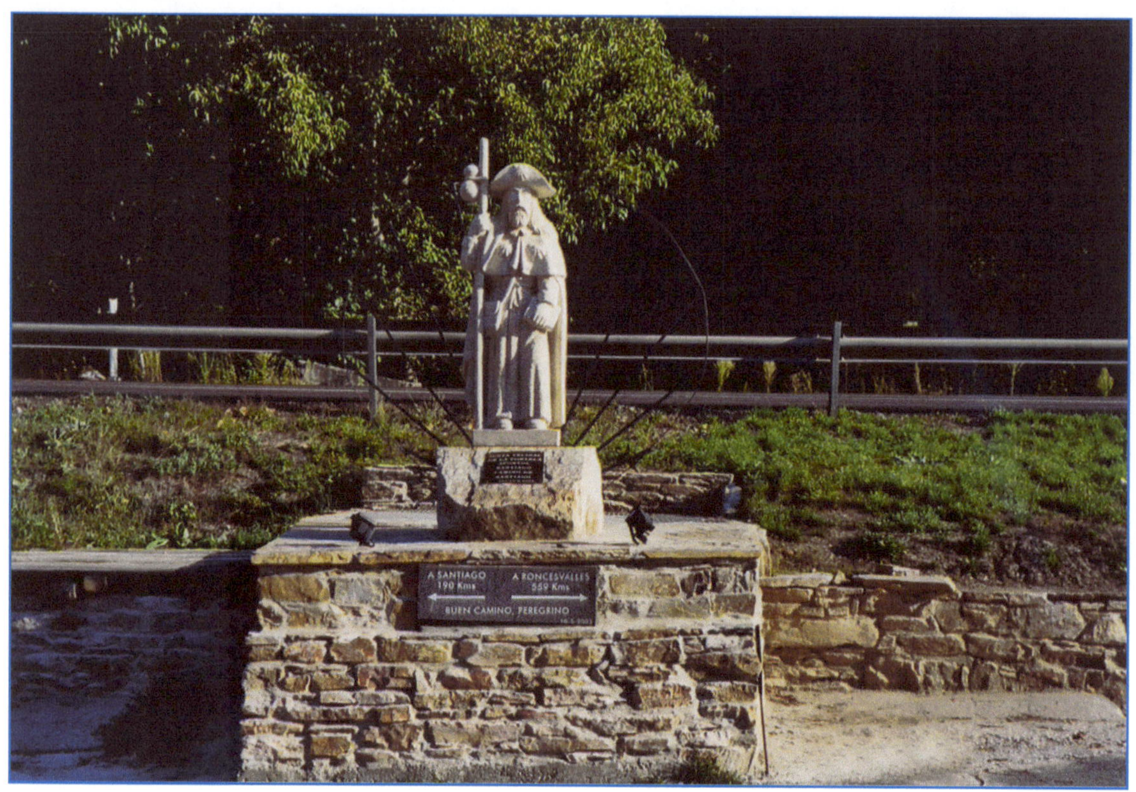

Pilgrim's monument-La Portela de Valcarce

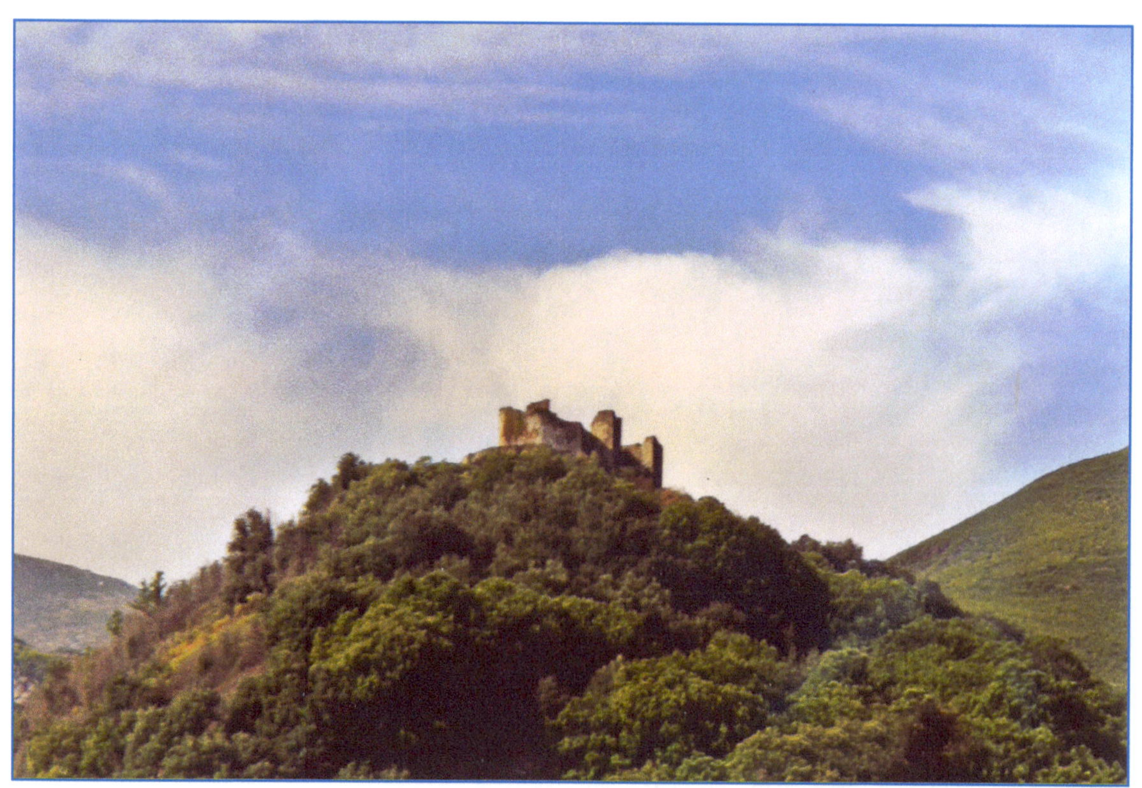

Castillo Saracin near Ruitelan

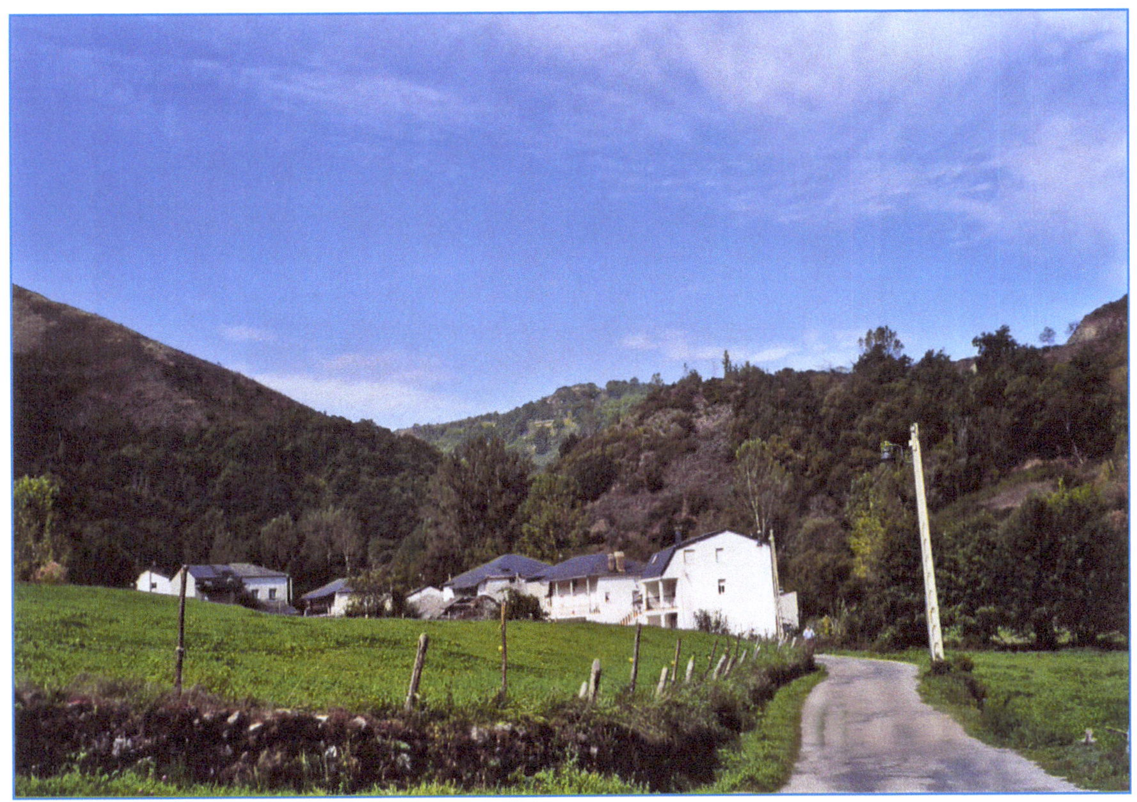

Herrerias

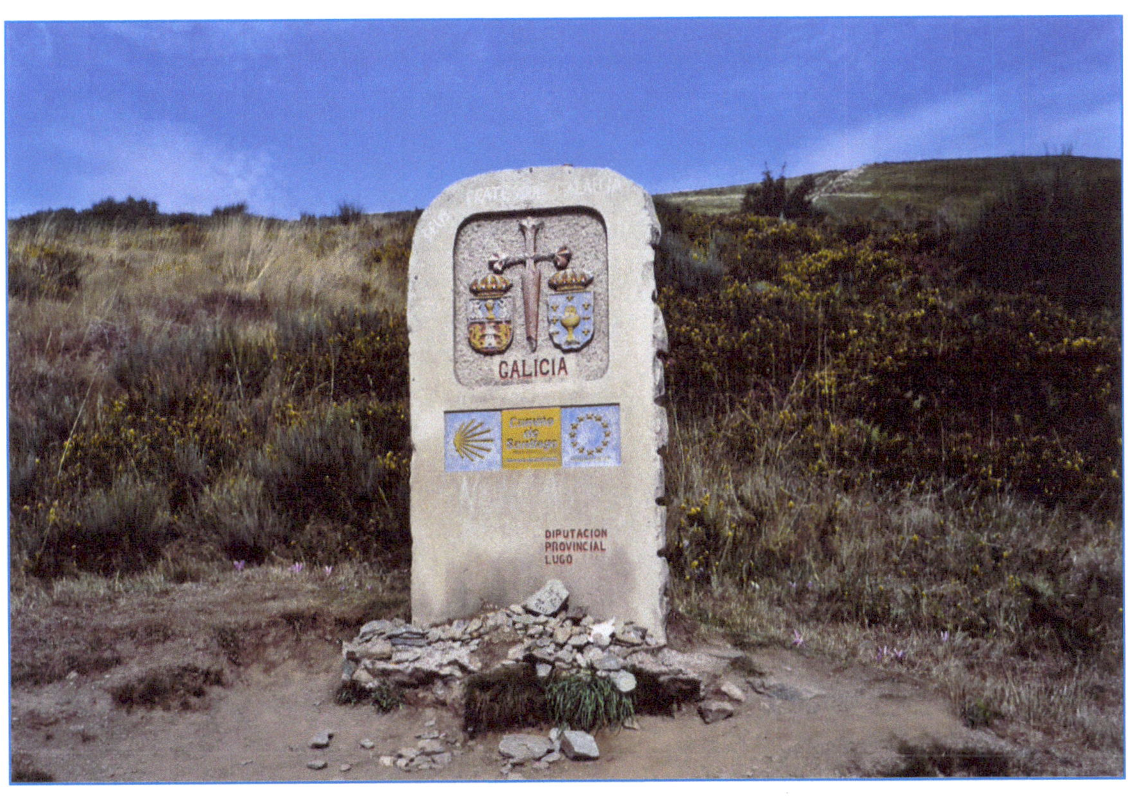

Entering Galicia just before O'Cebreiro

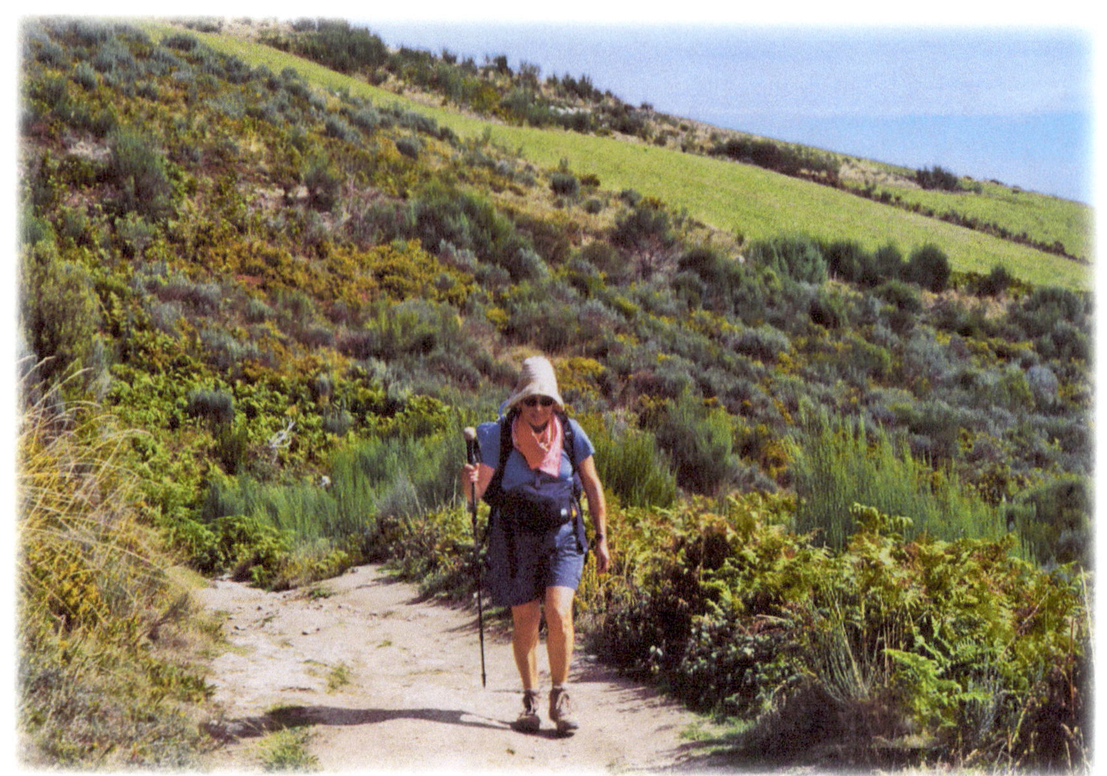

Last few steps into O'Cebreiro

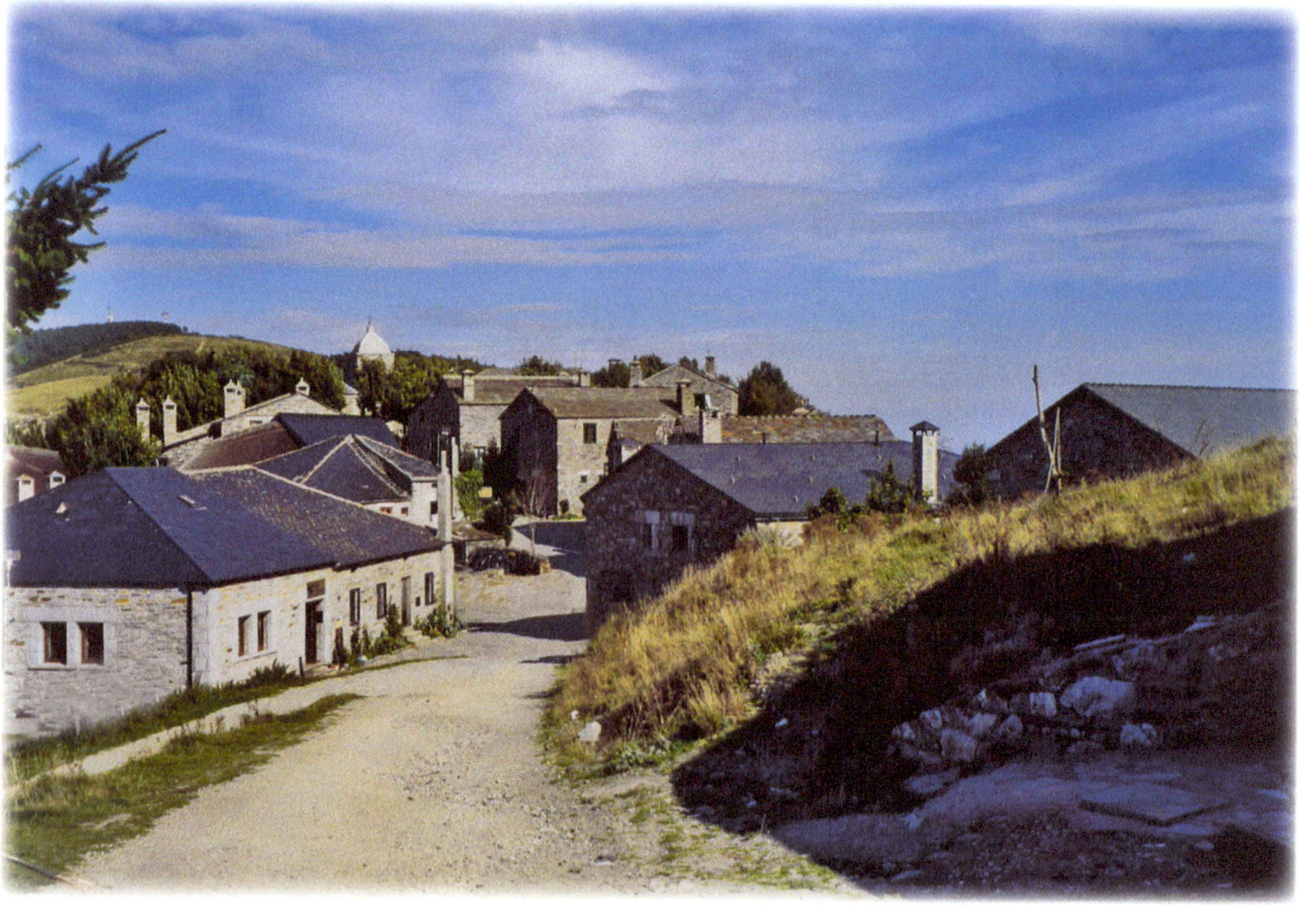

Mountain top village of O'Cebreiro

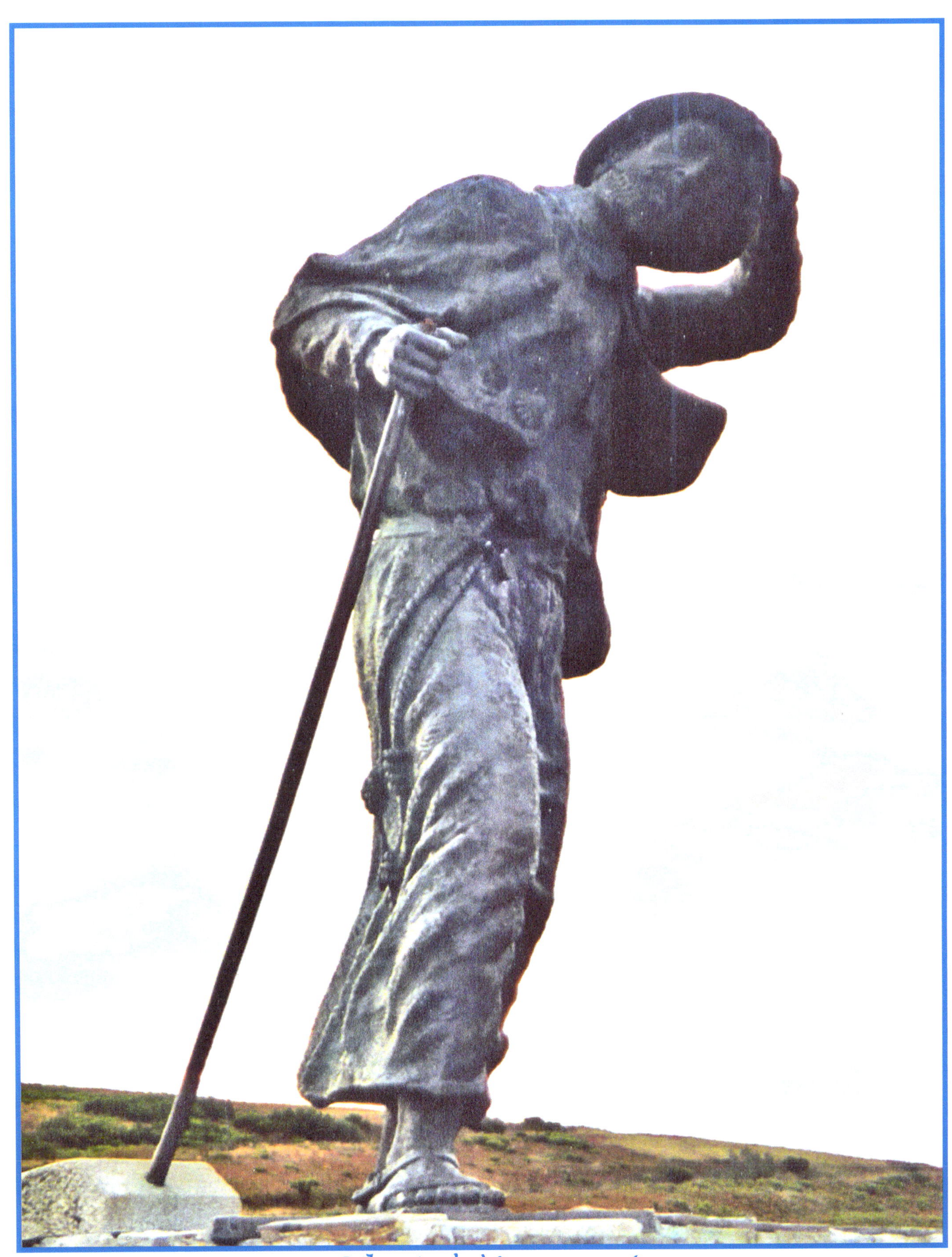

Pilgrim's Monument

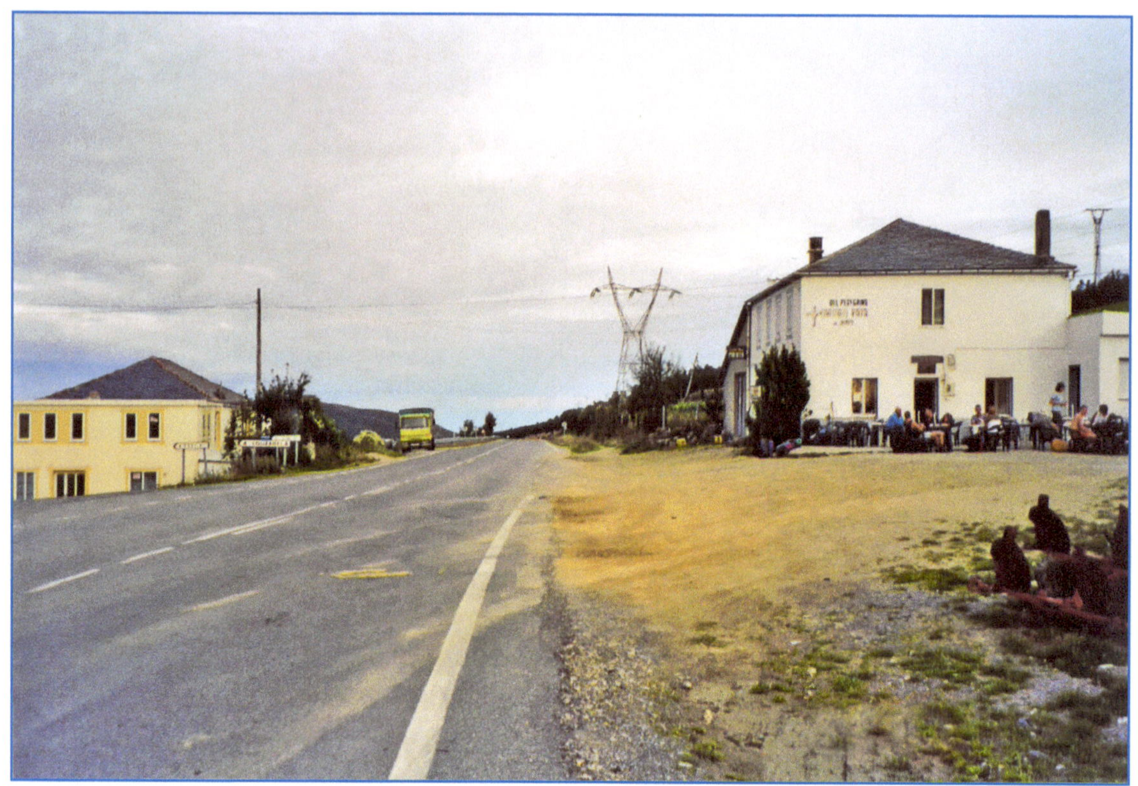

Alto do Poio-High point of the Camino in Galicia

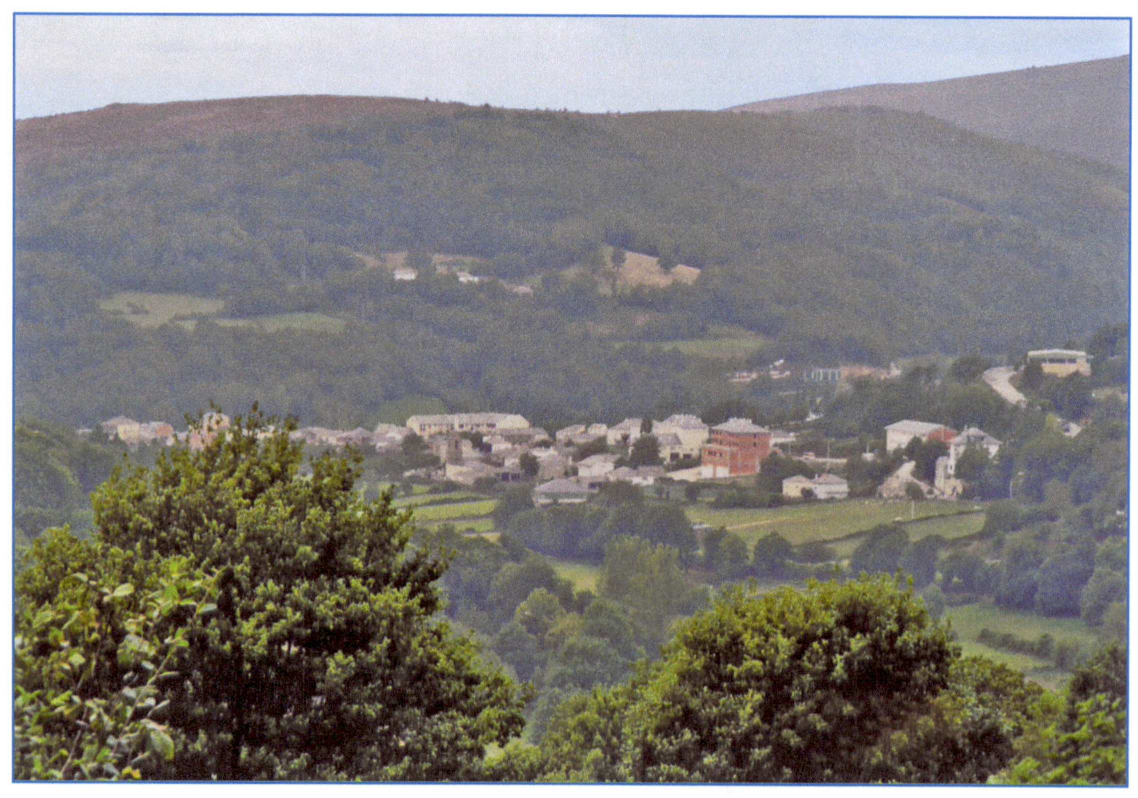

View of Triacastela

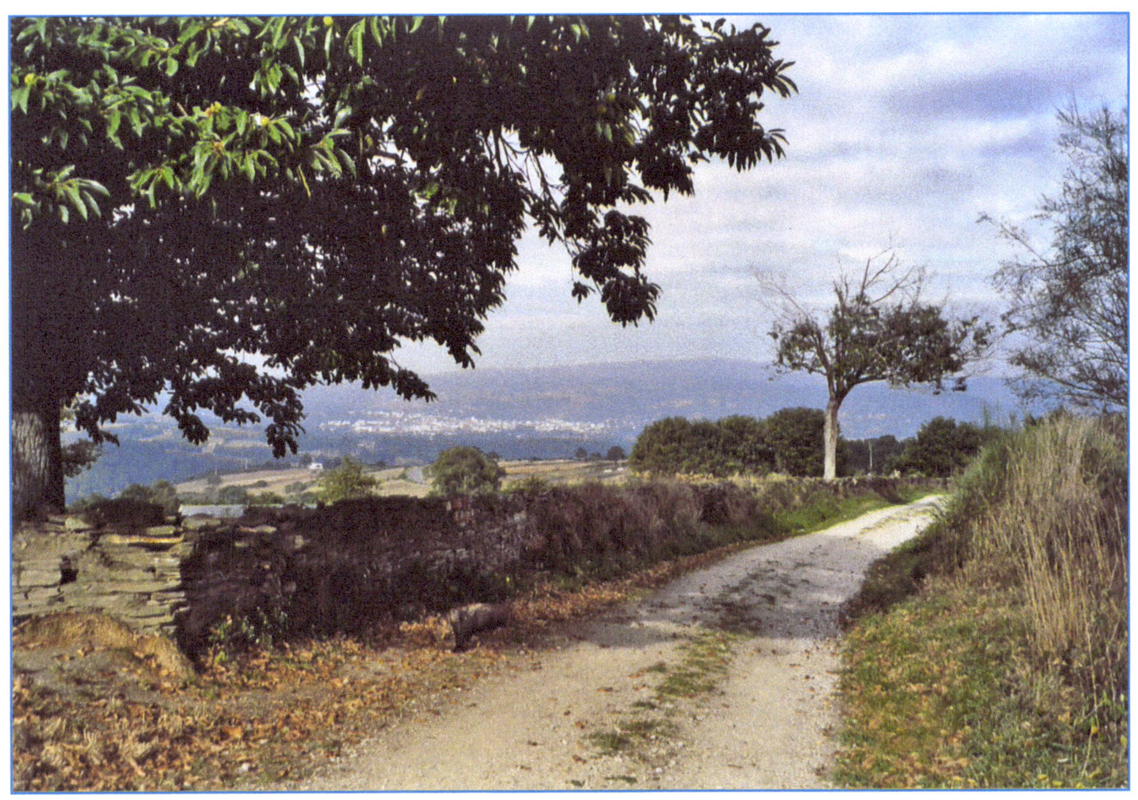

View of Sarria in the distance

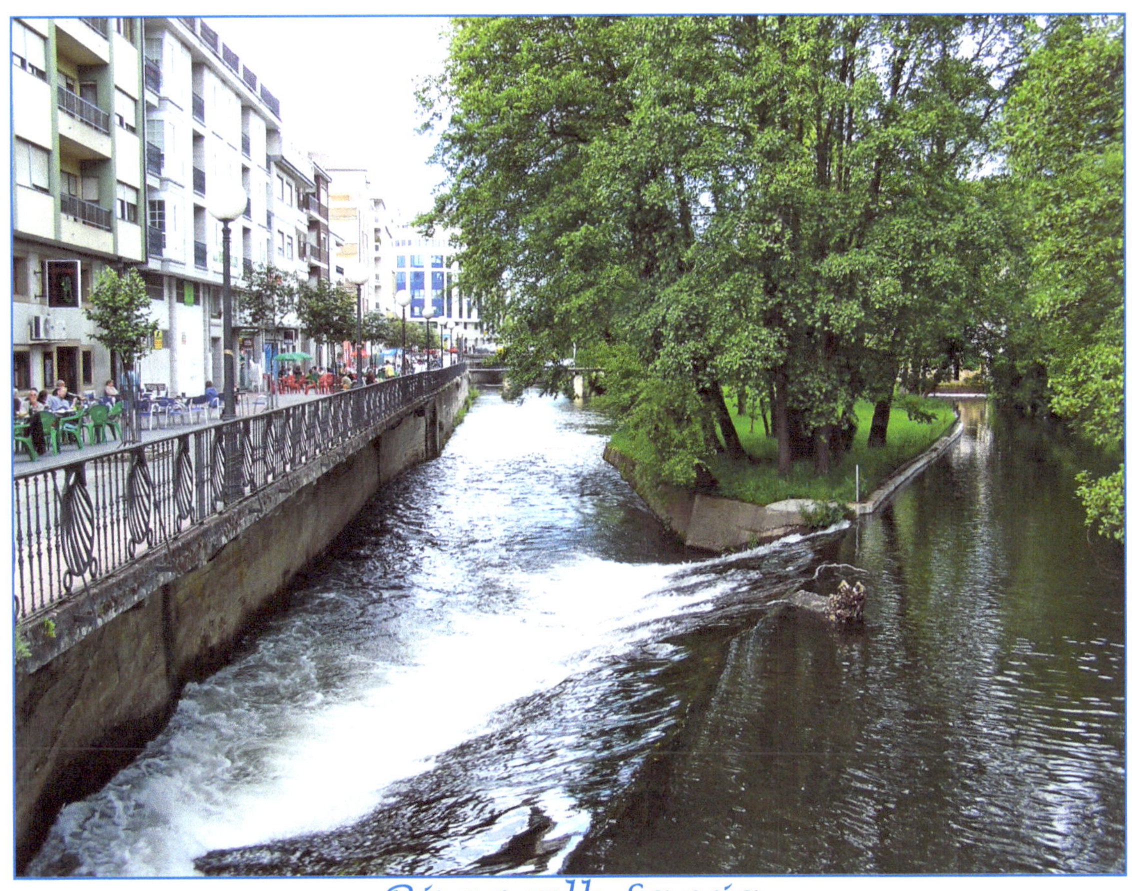

Riverwalk-Sarria

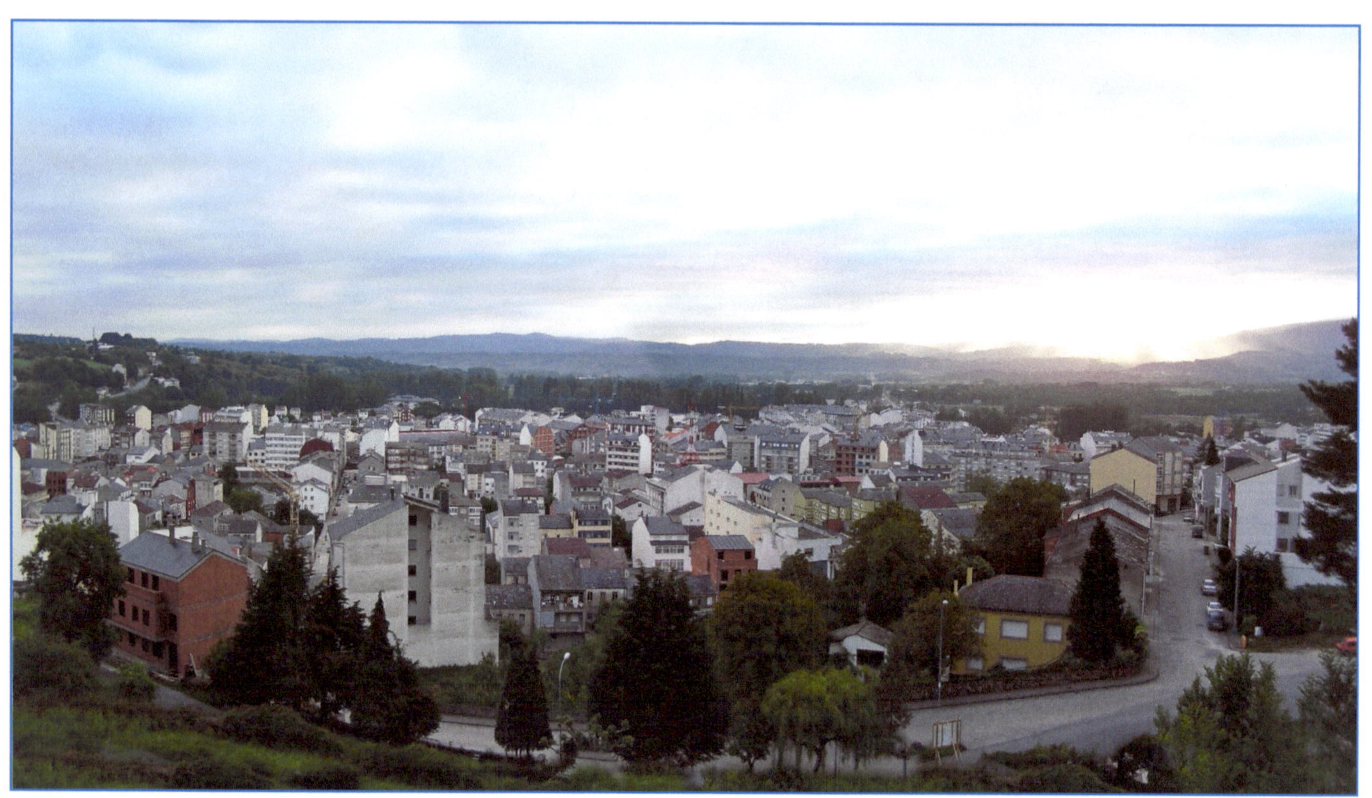

Early morning view leaving Sarria

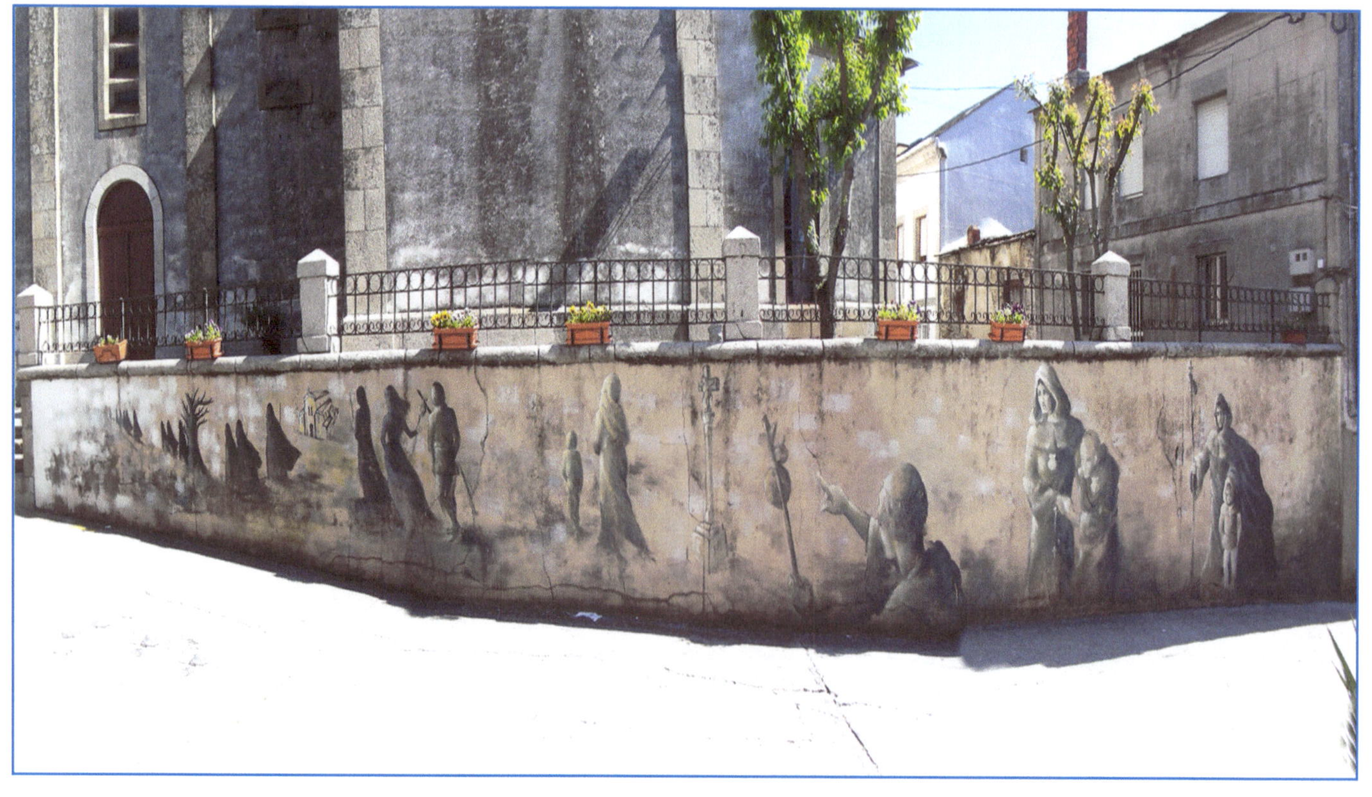

Pilgrim mural at the Church of Santa Marina-Sarria

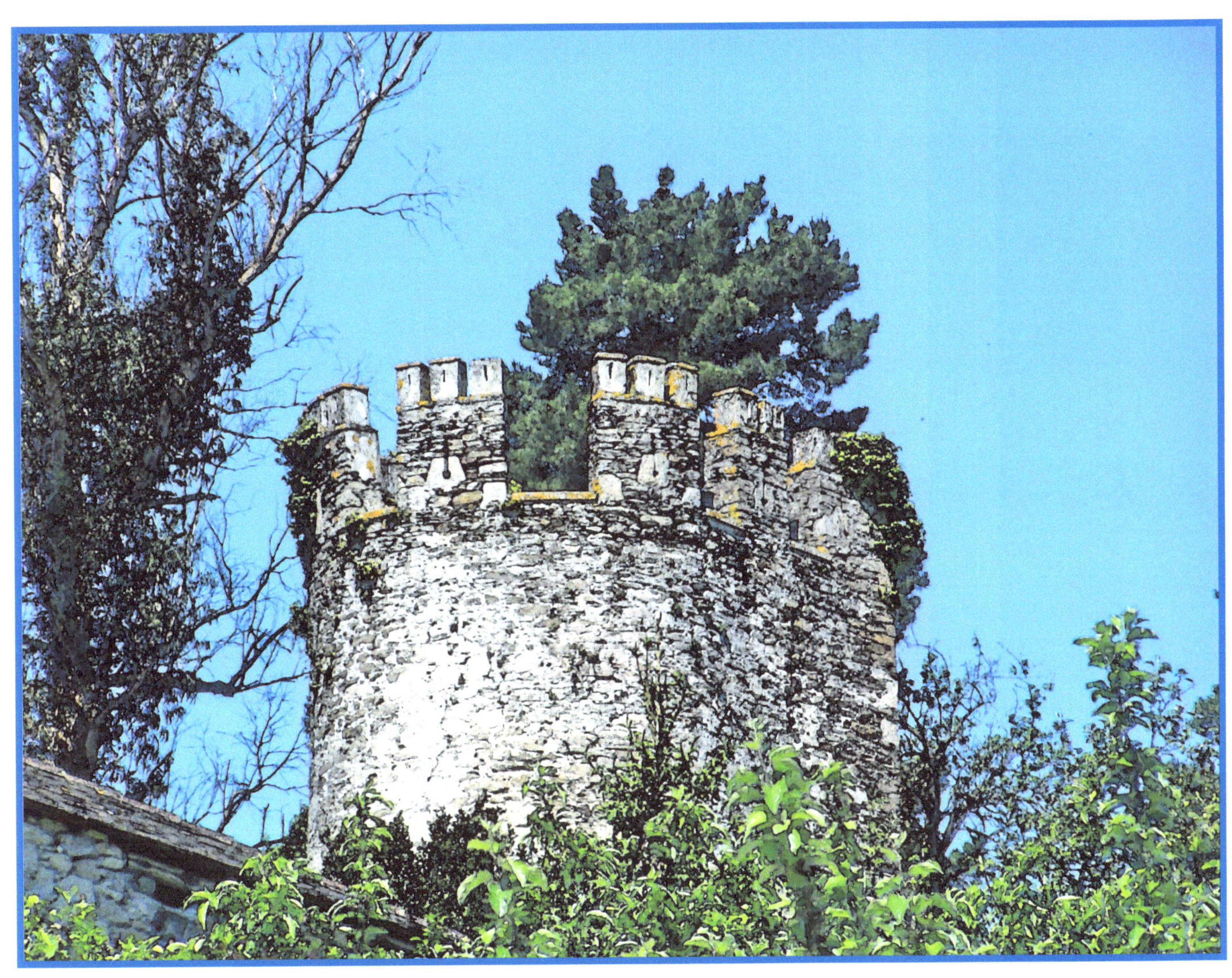

Remains of the Sarria Castle

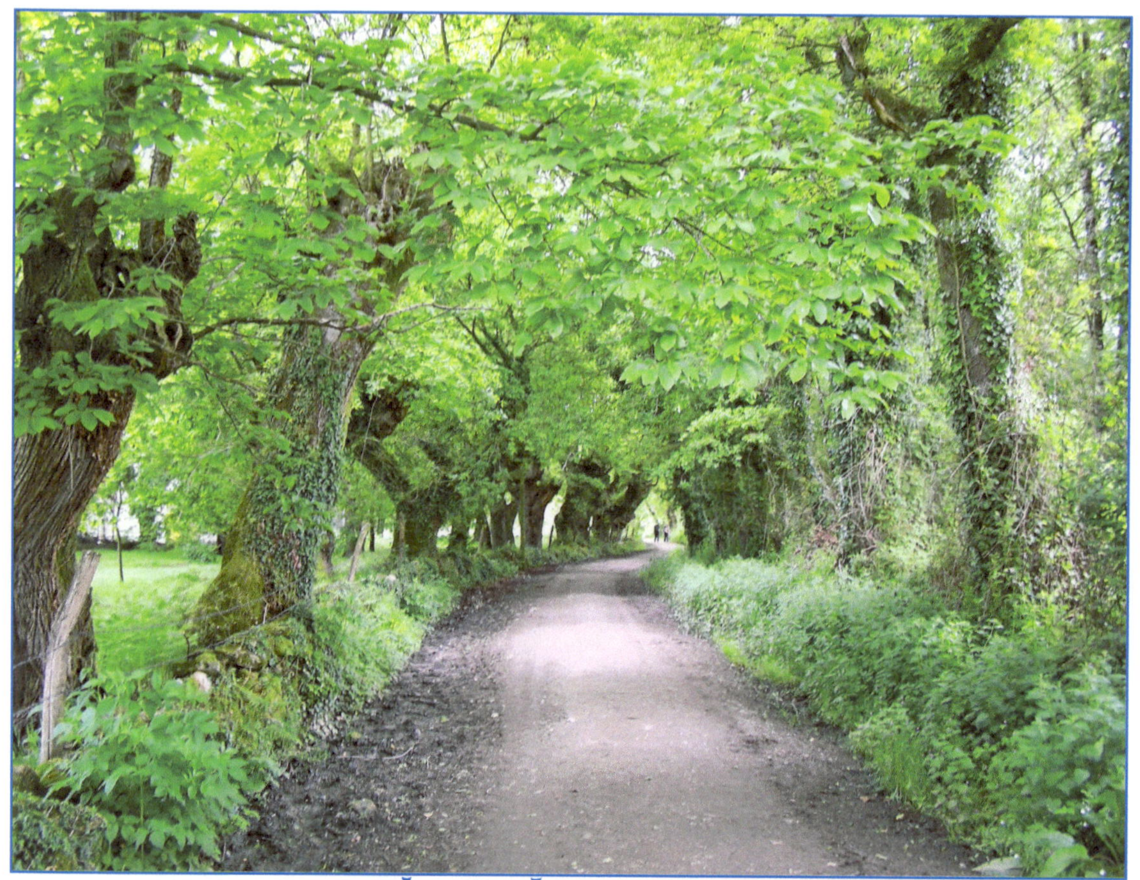

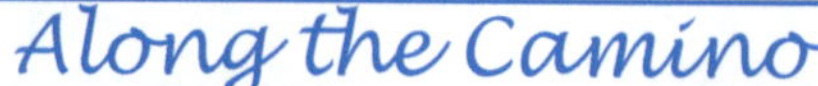
Along the Camino

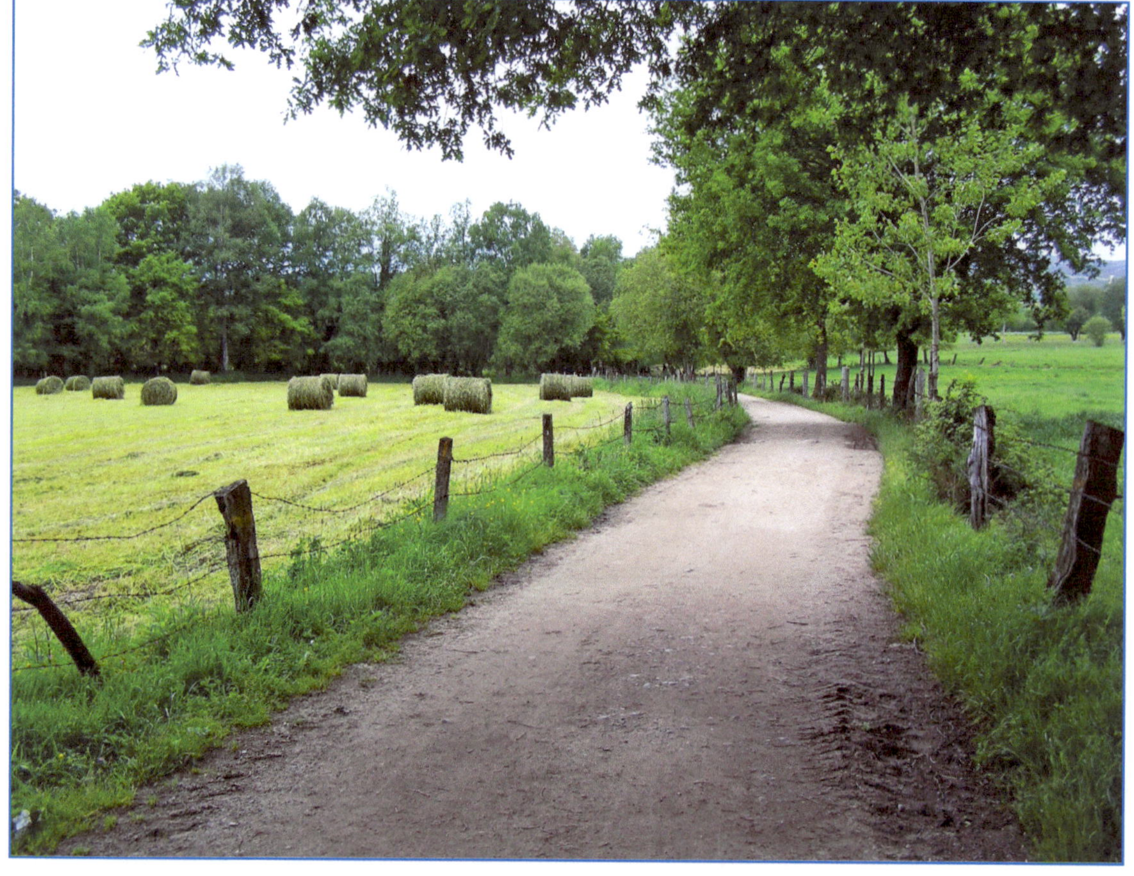

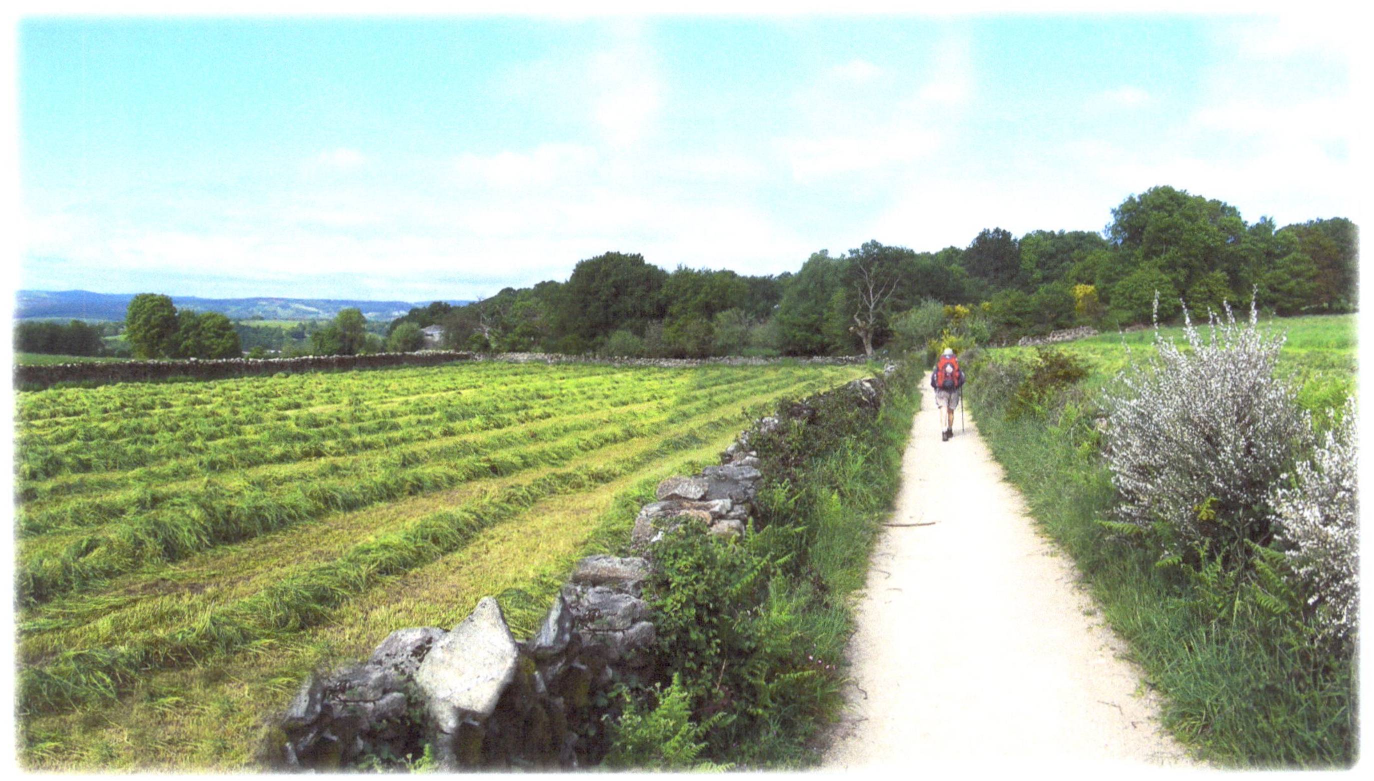

On the Camino just before Morgade

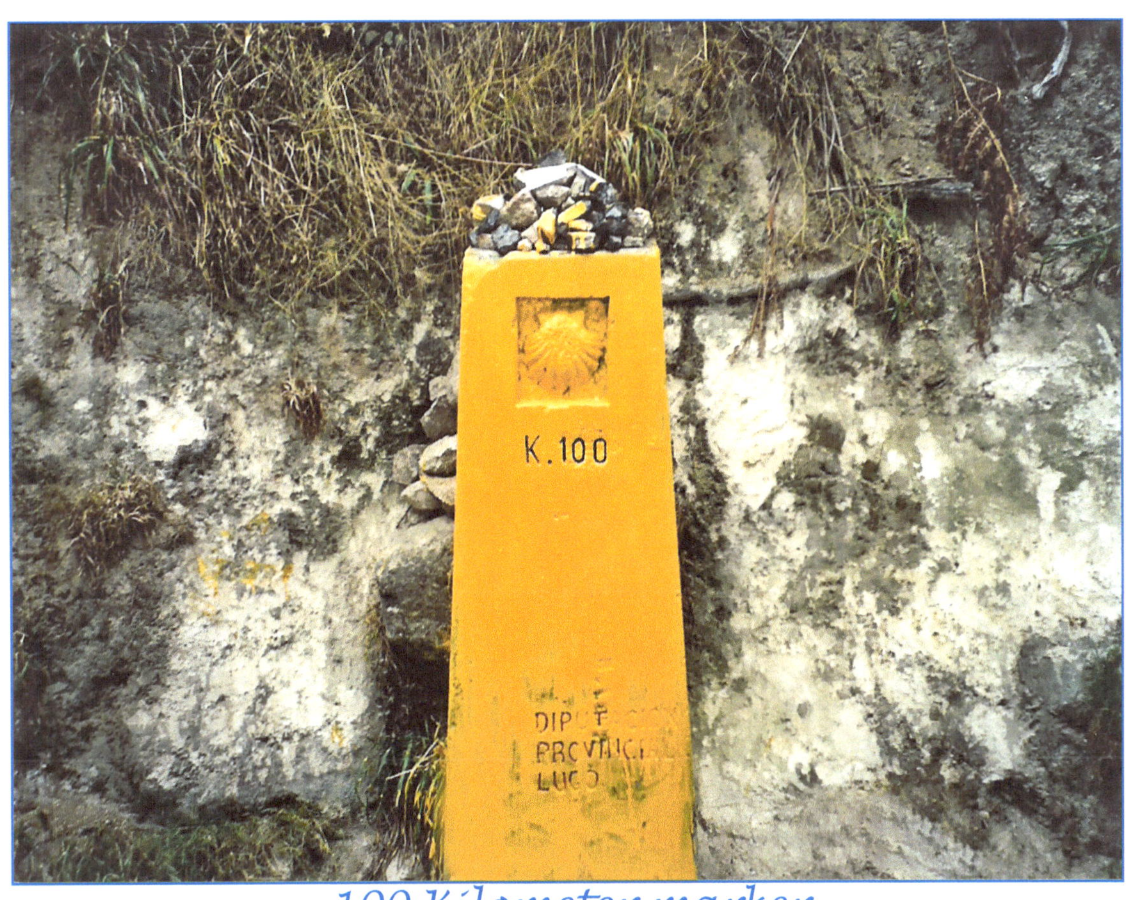

100 Kilometer marker

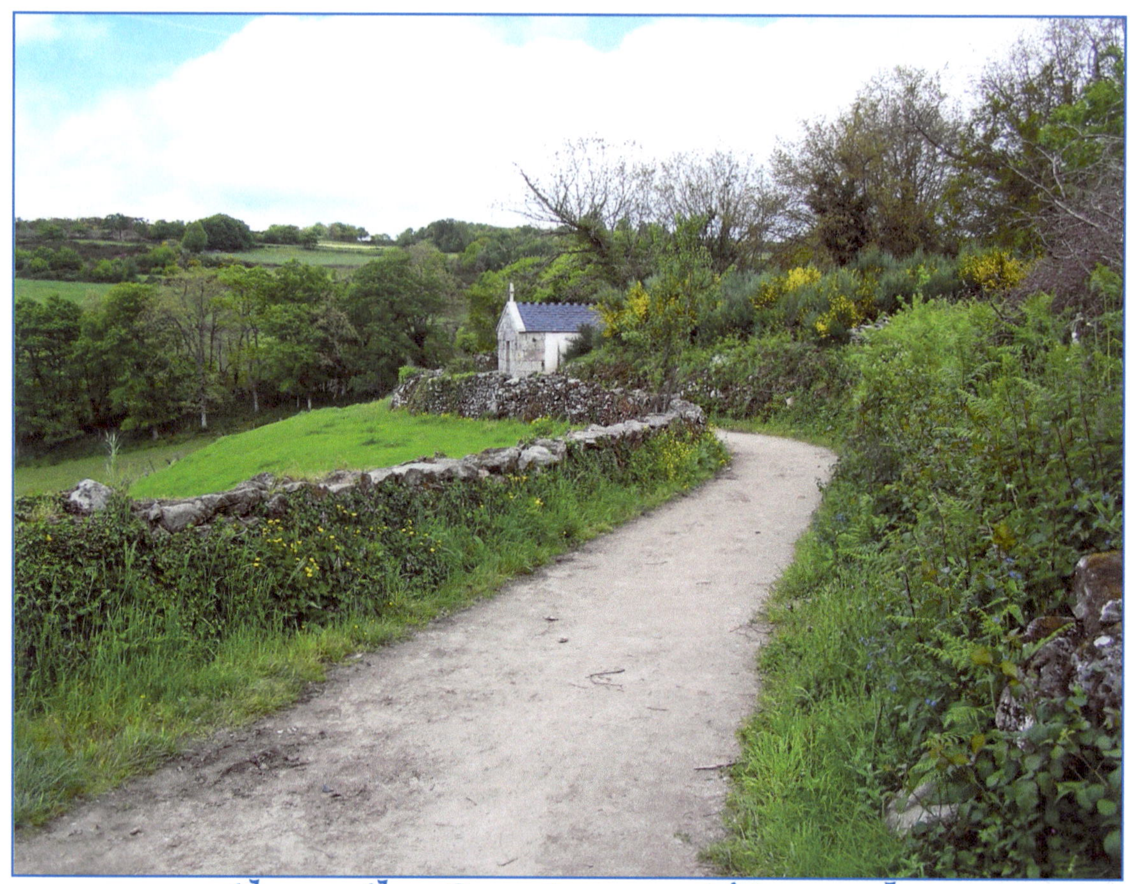

Along the Camino past Morgade

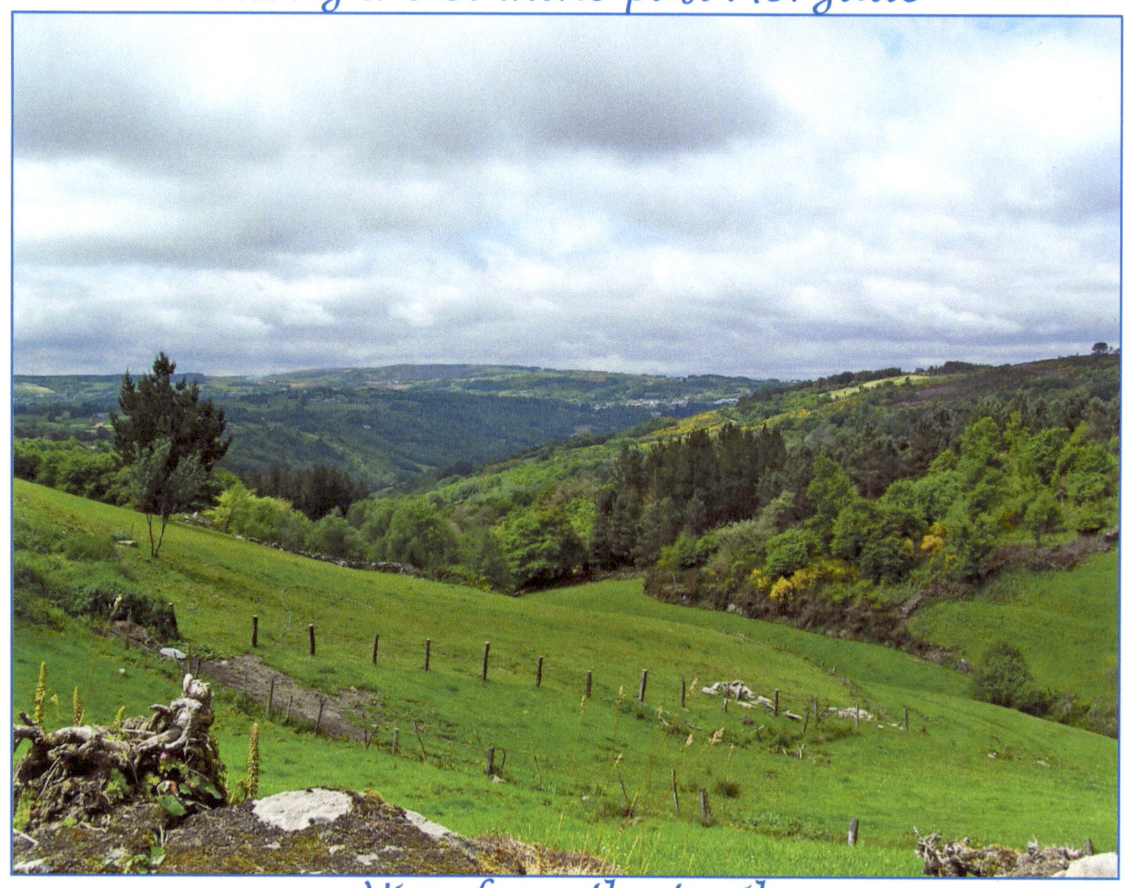

View from the trail

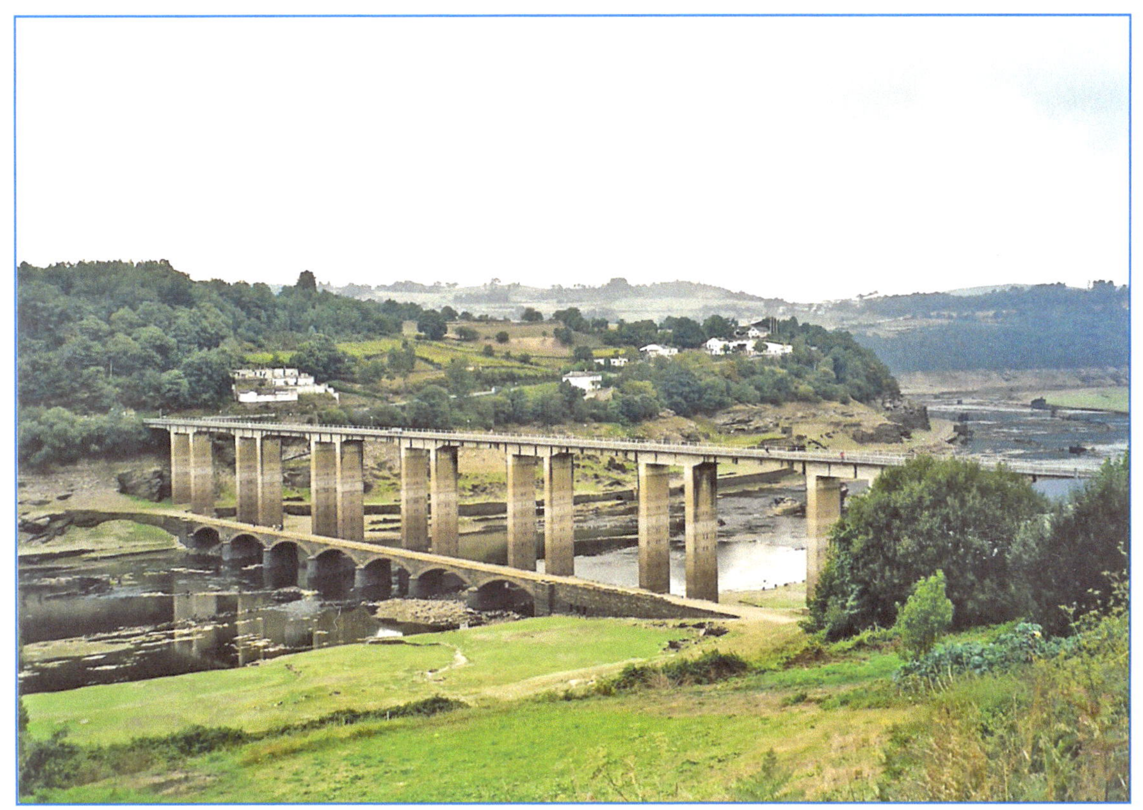

Portomarin bridges in 2003 - note old Roman bridge

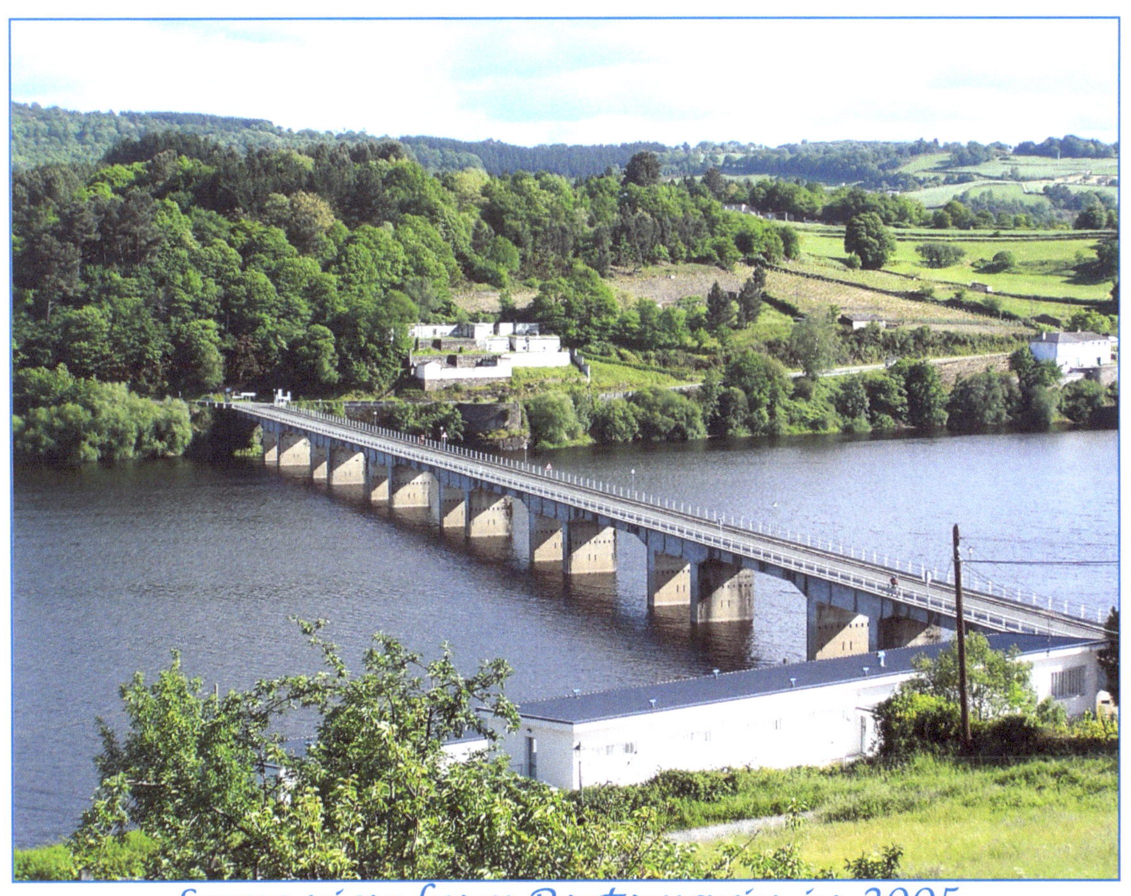

Same view from Portomarin in 2005

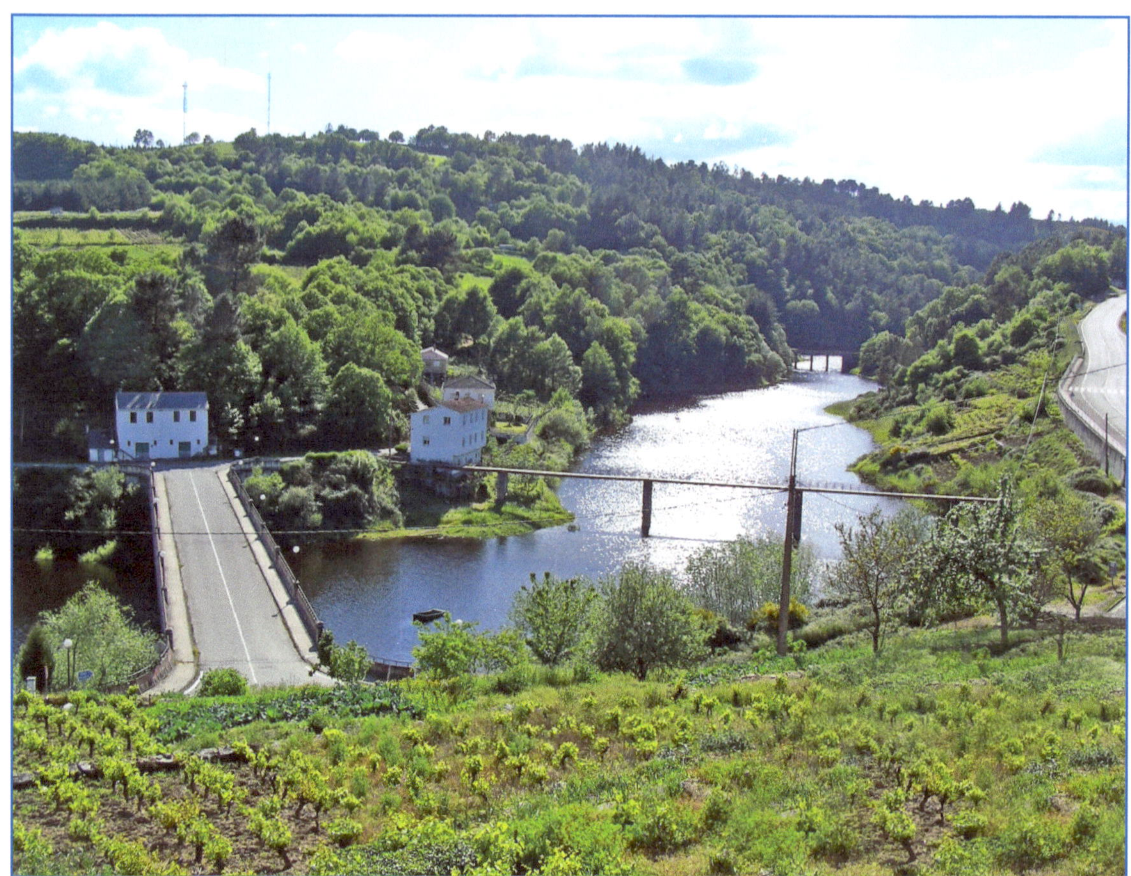

Foot bridge and road bridge leaving Portomarin

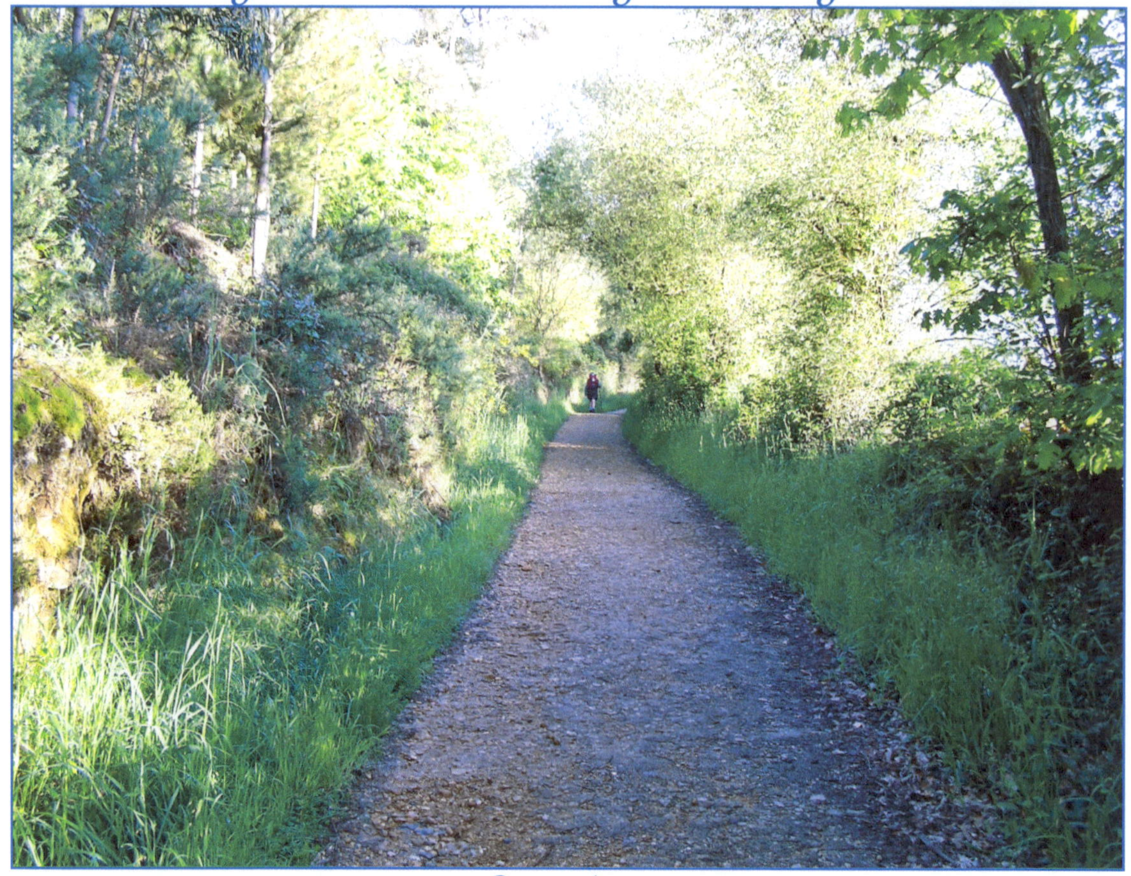

Camino

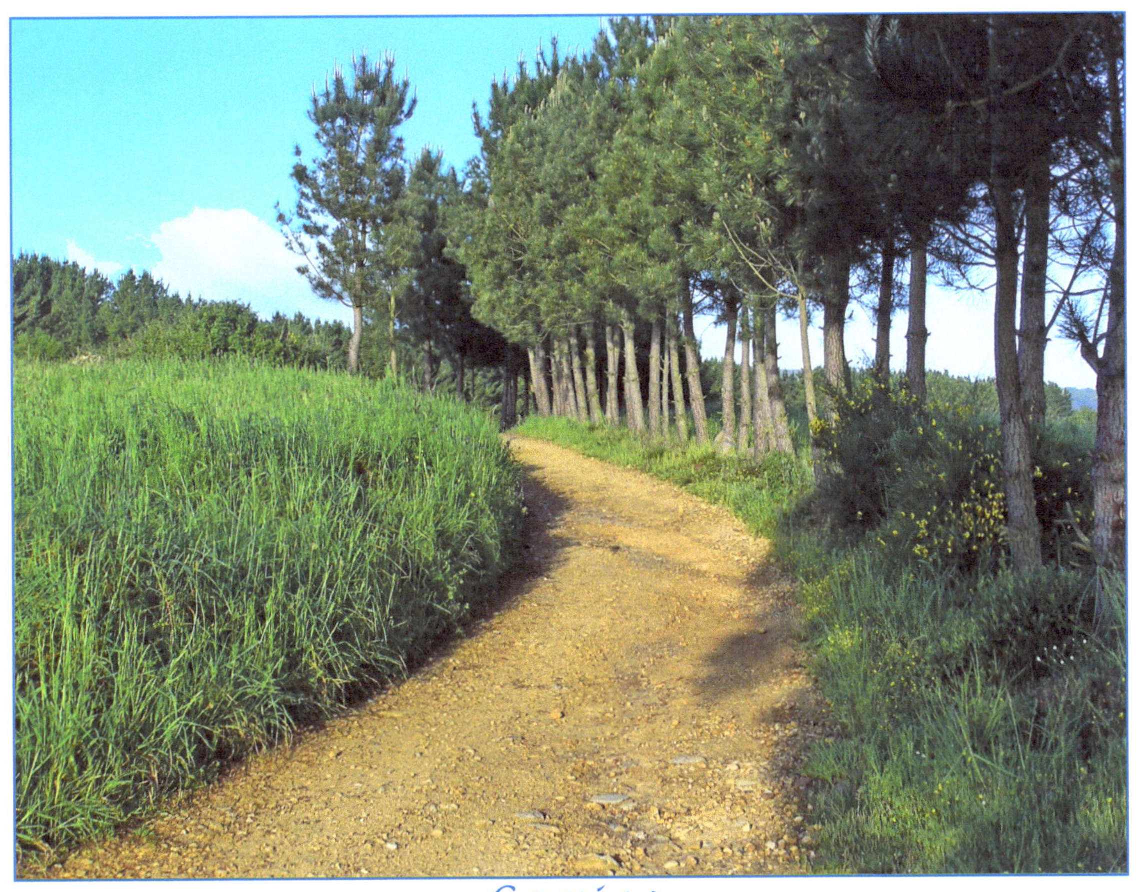

Camino

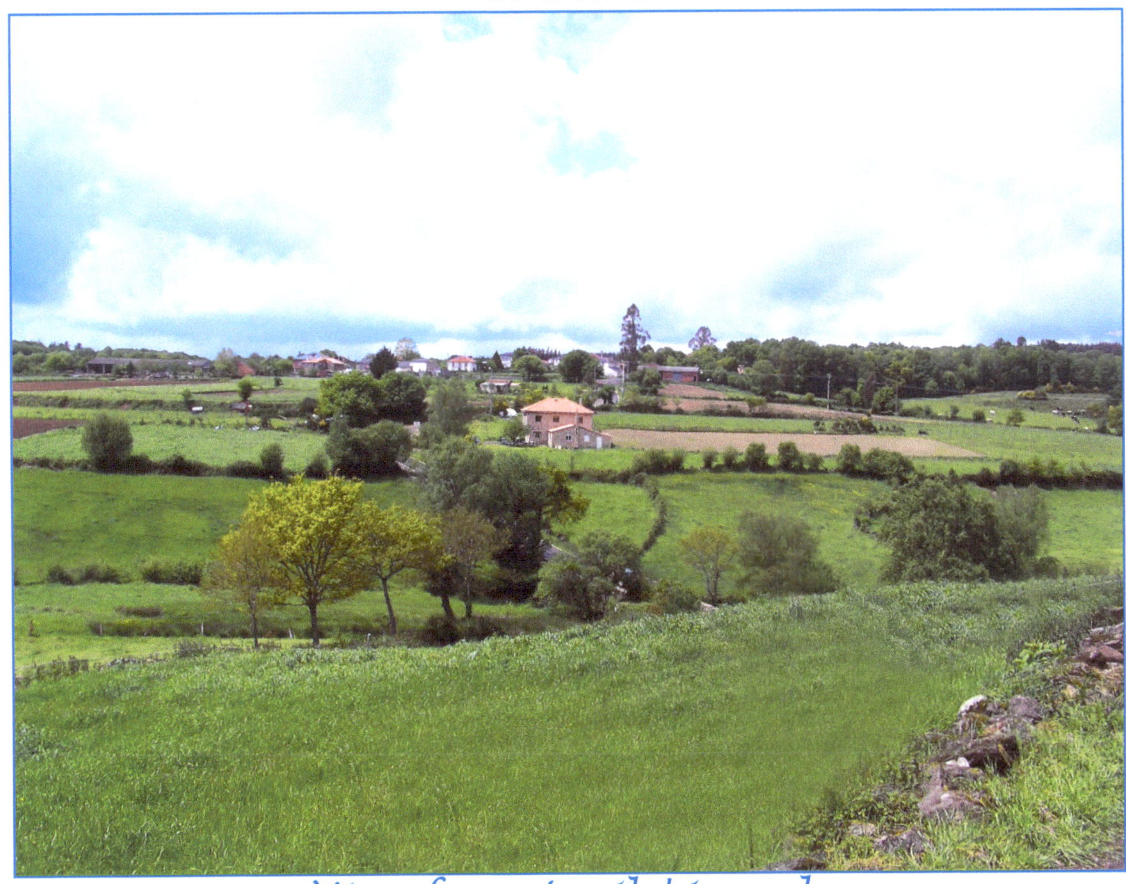

View from trail-Ligonde

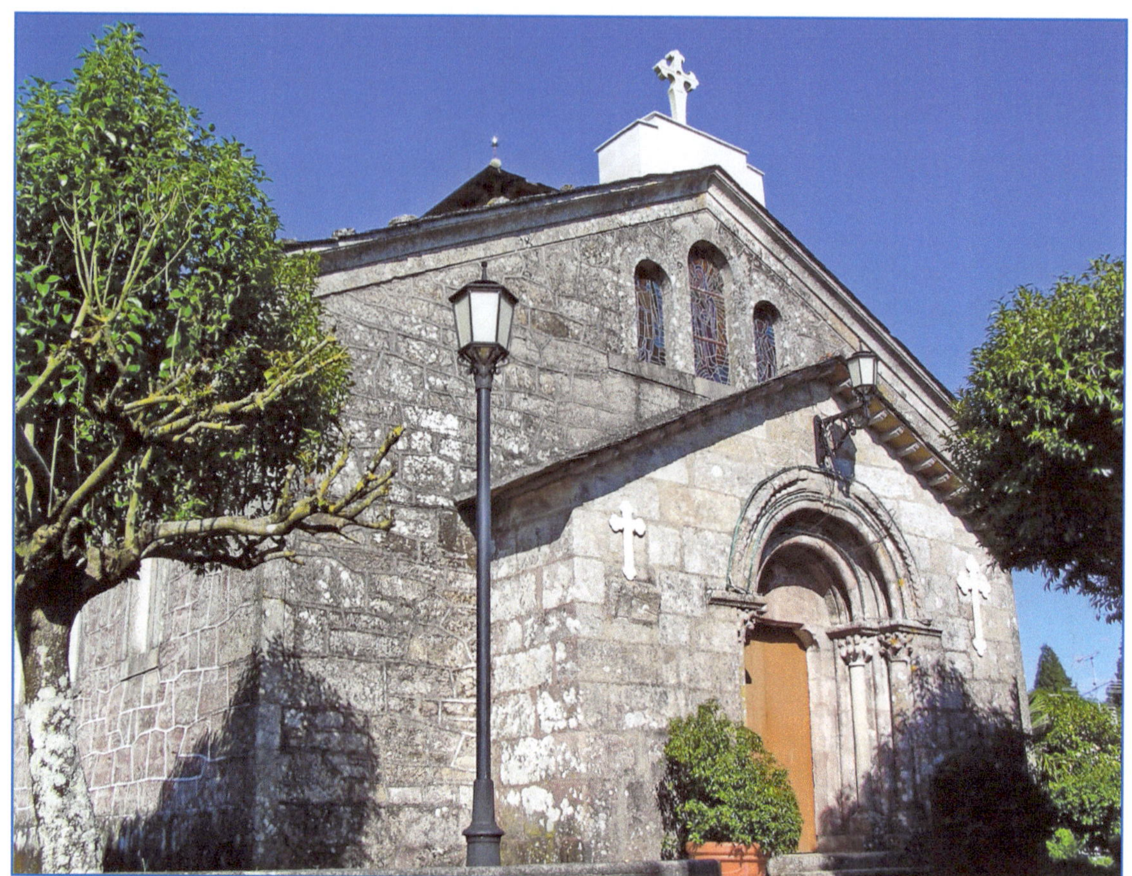

Church-Palas de Rei

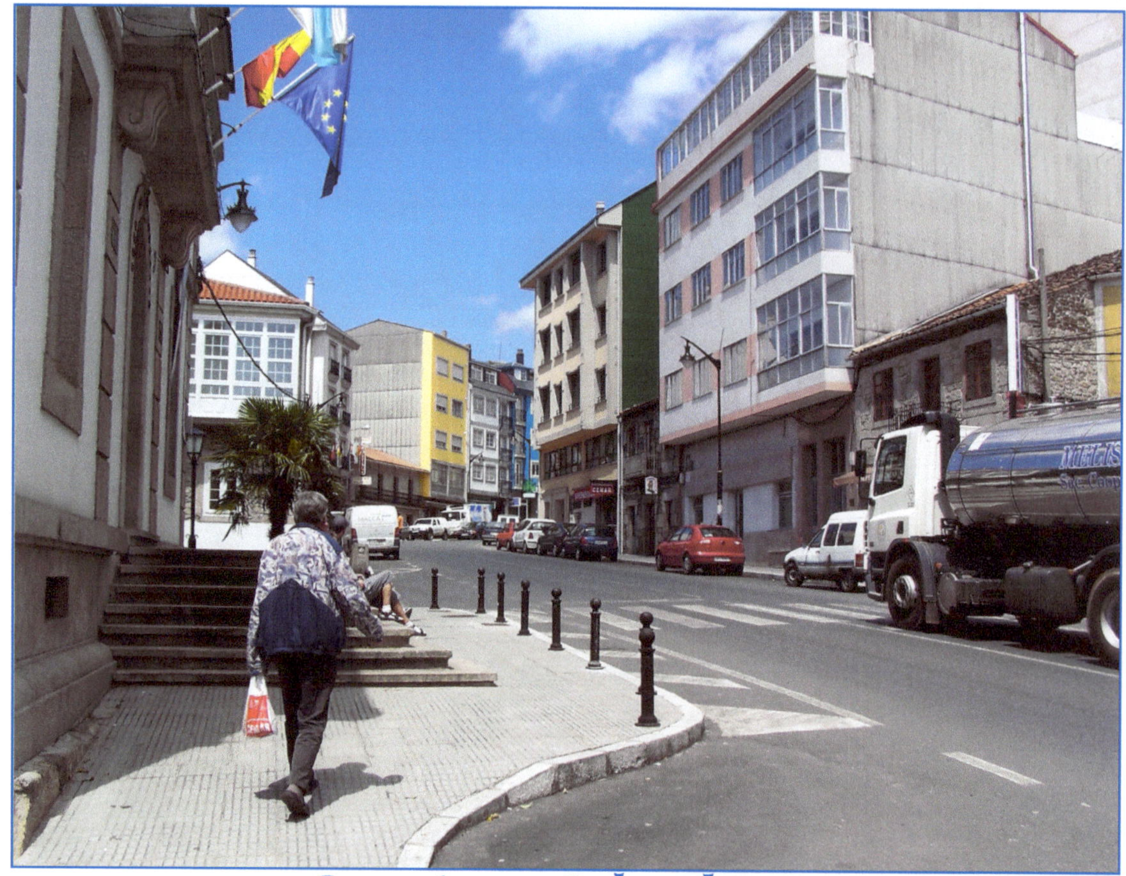

Downtown-Palas de Rei

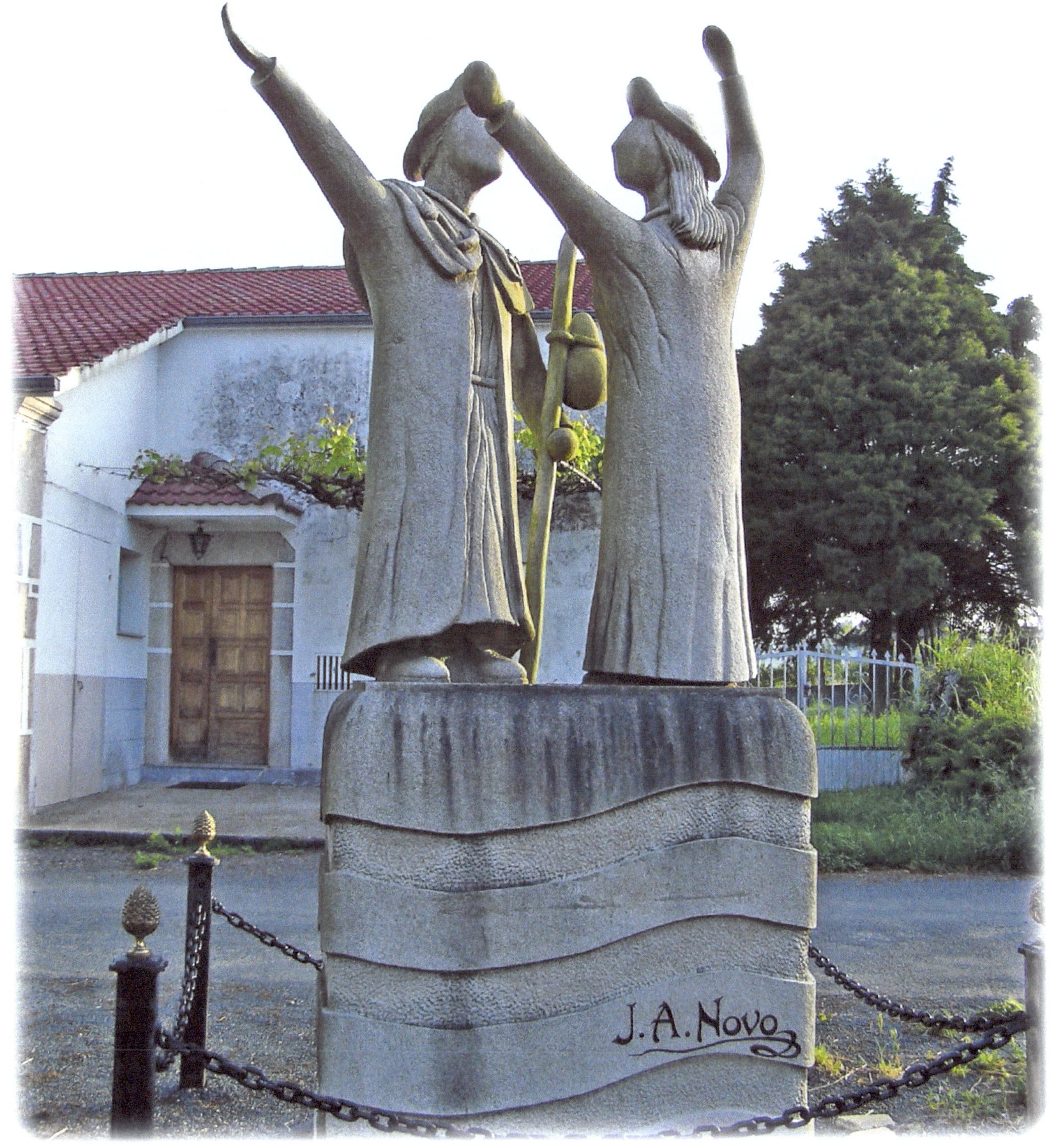

Pilgrim monument-Palas de Rei

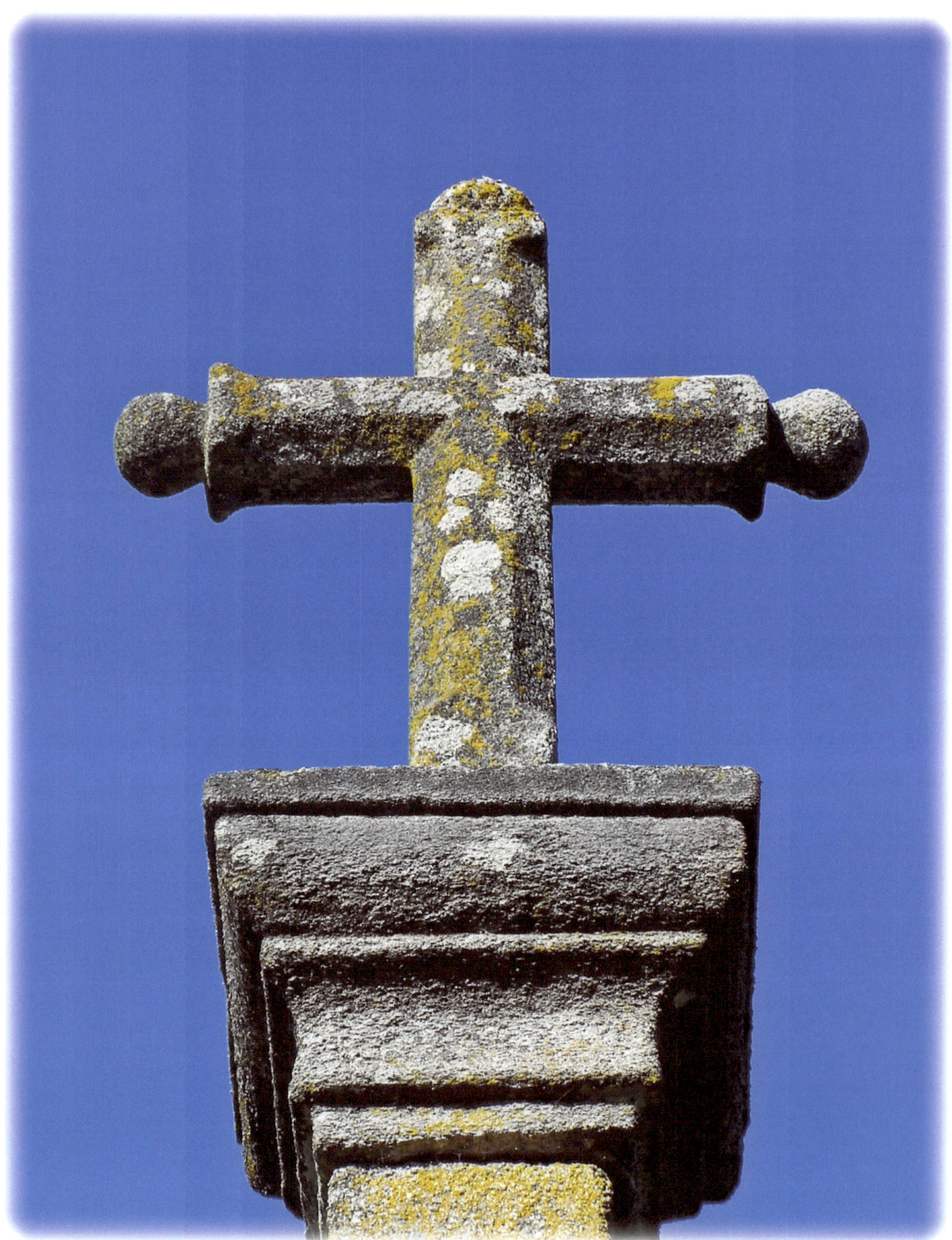

Cross-Palas de Rei

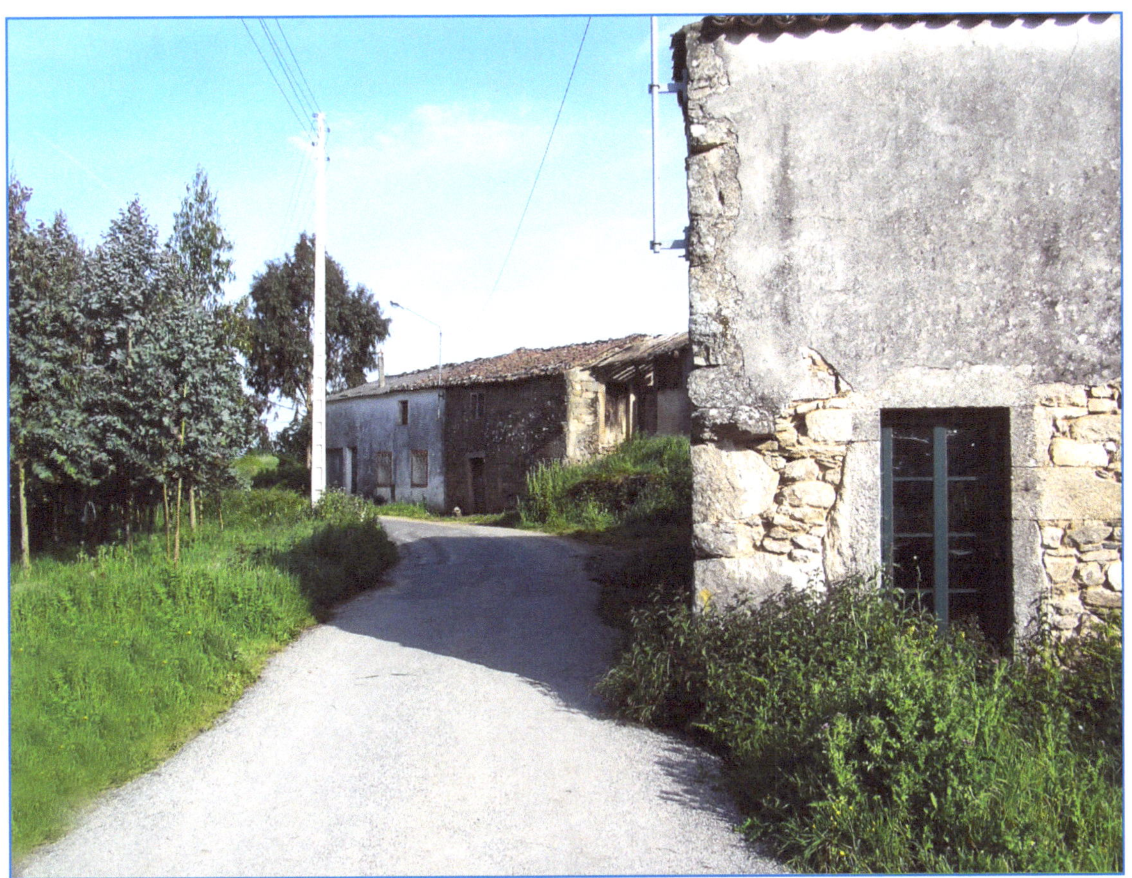

Along the Camino

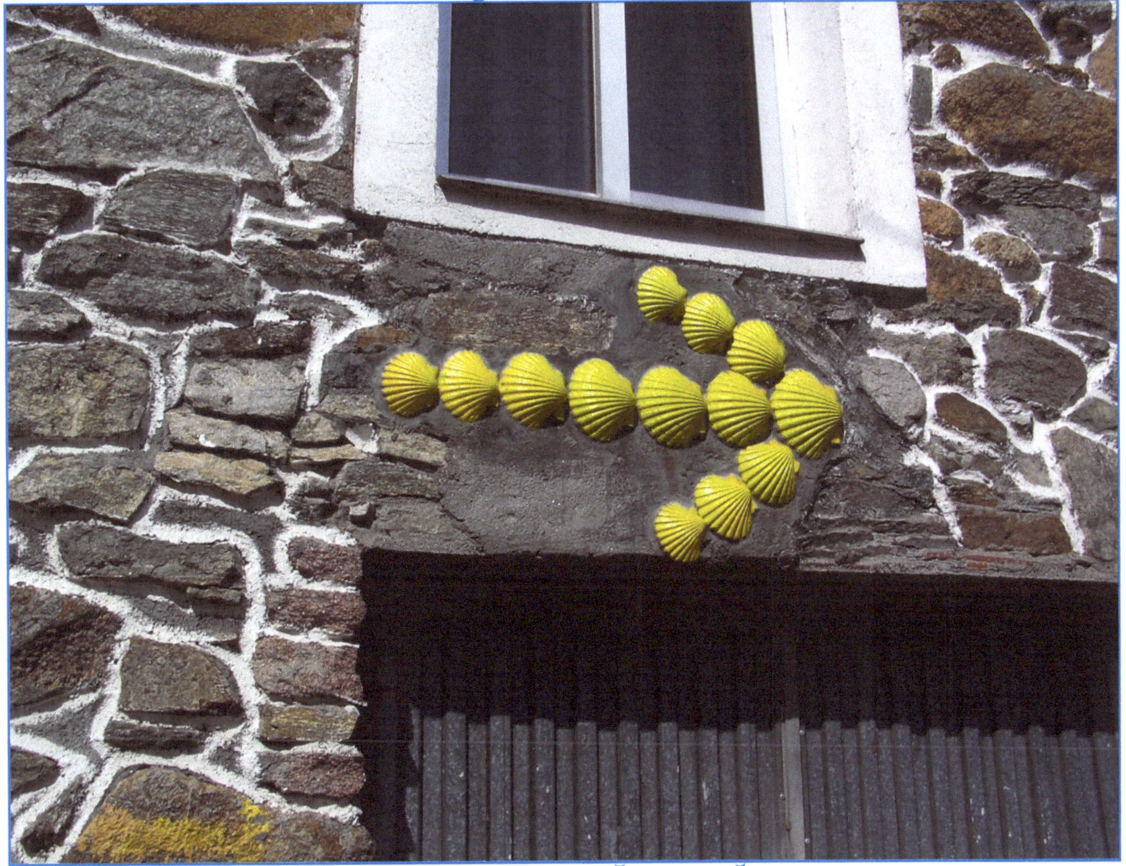

Camino trail marker

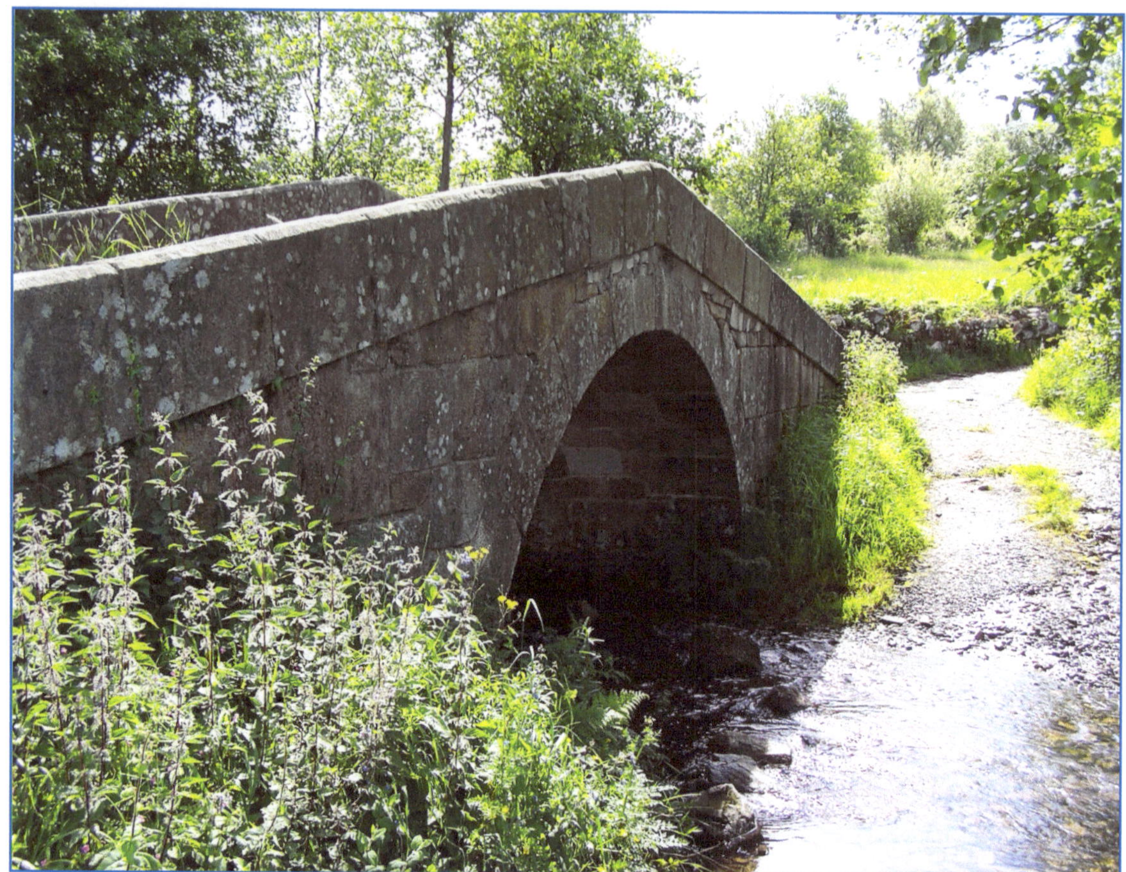

Medieval bridge-Maria Magdalena-Disicabo

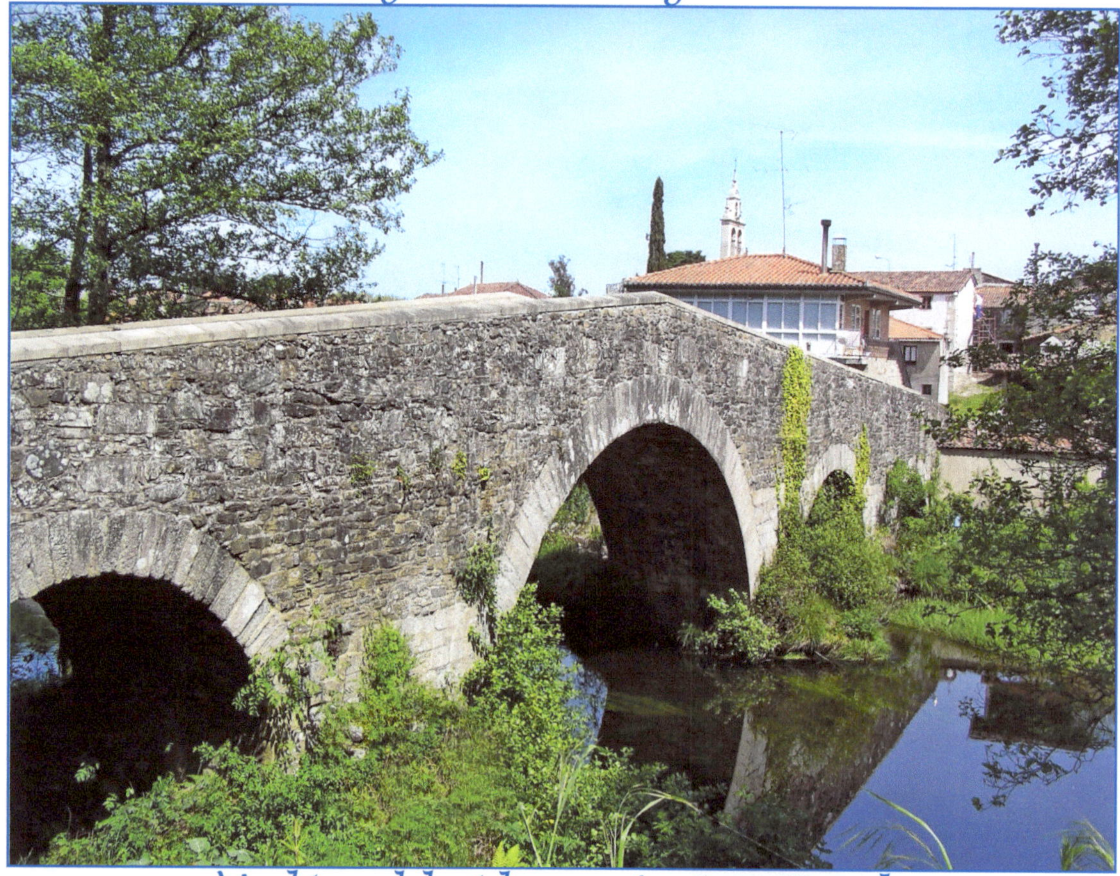

Medieval bridge entering Furelos

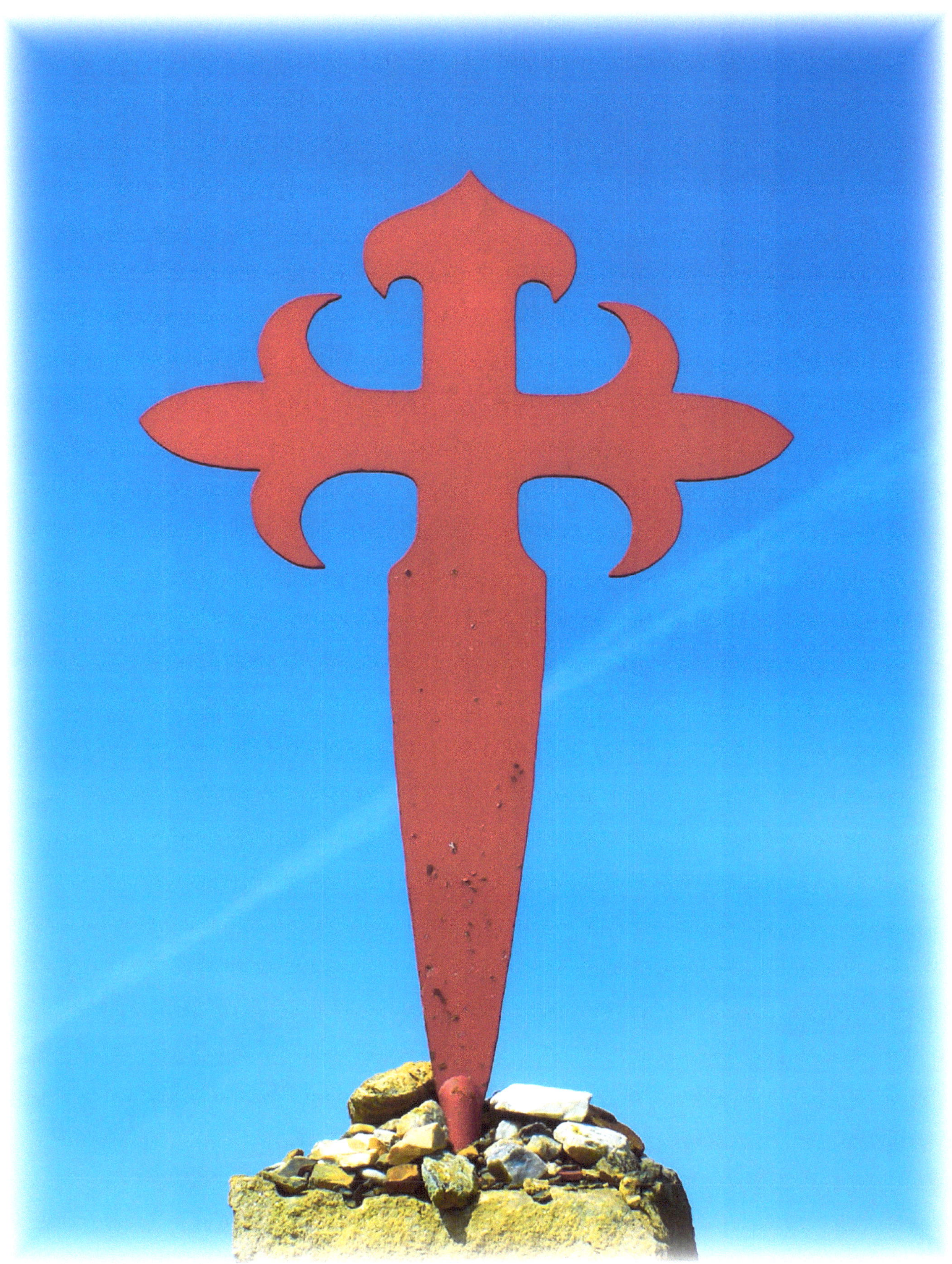

Metal cross on stone monument next to the Camino

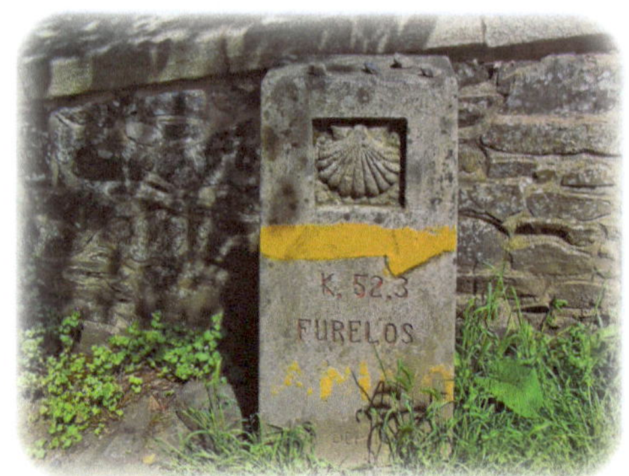

Camino marker

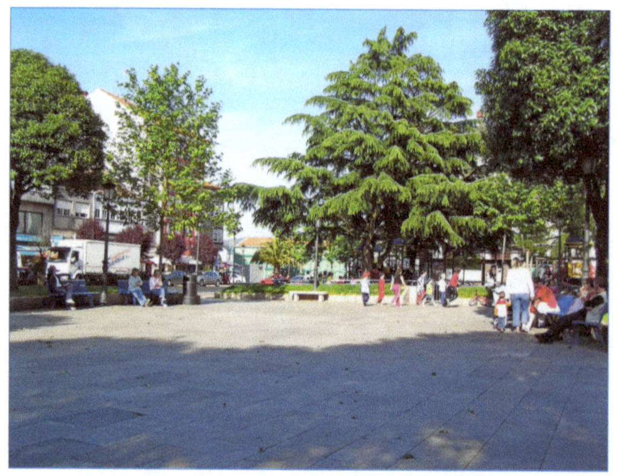

Main Plaza-in Melide

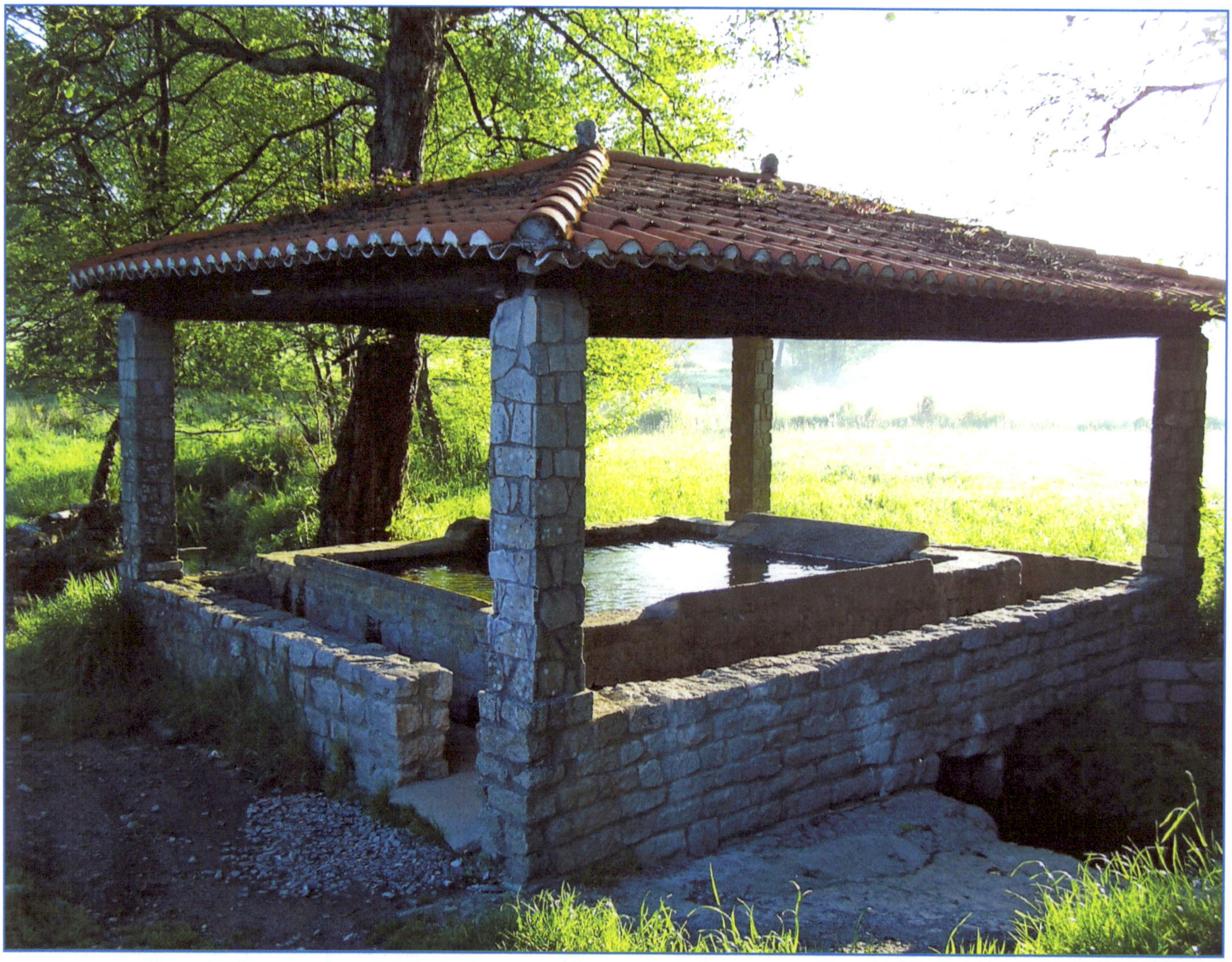

Communal clothes washing area outside of Melide

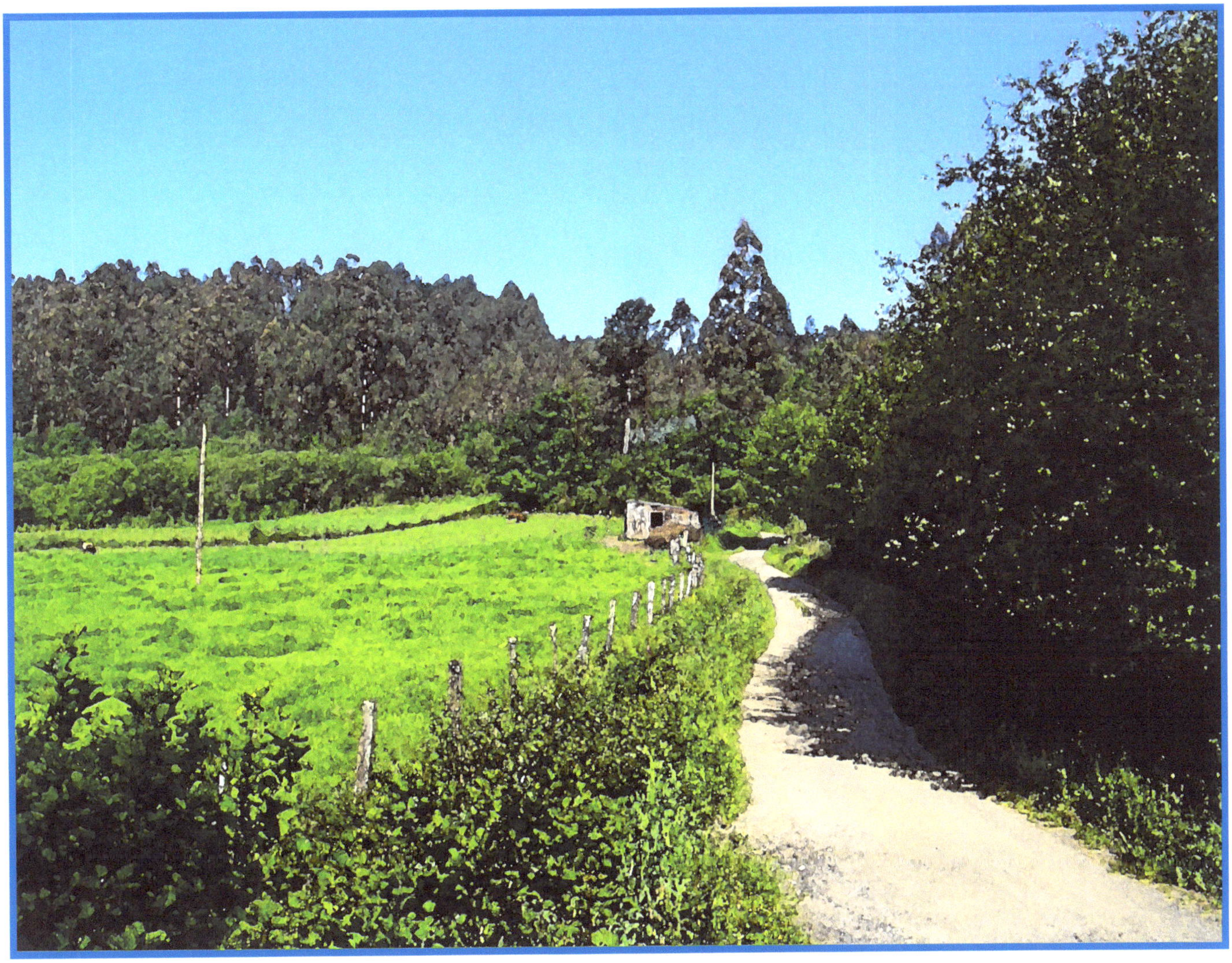

Along the Camino

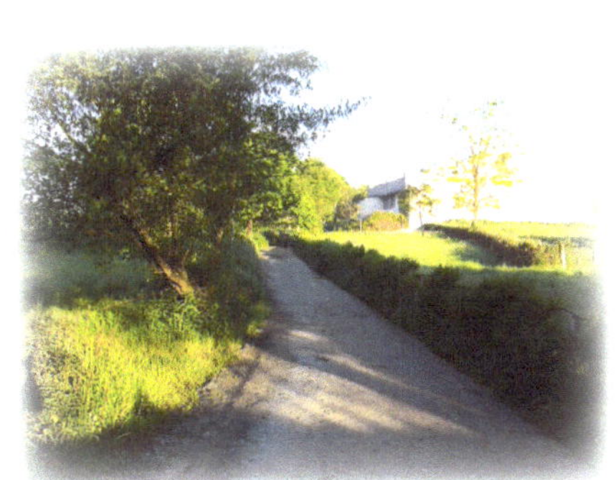

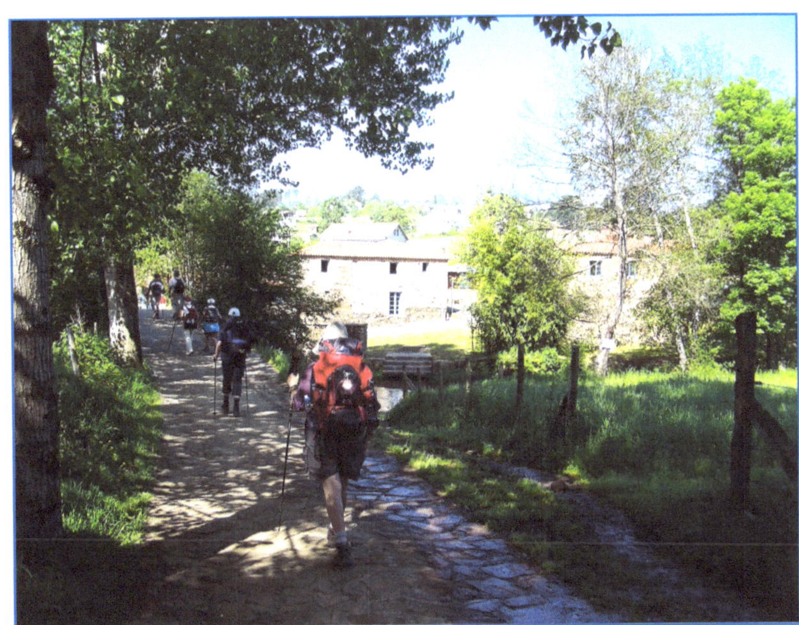

Pilgrims crossing the Rio Iso at Ribadiso

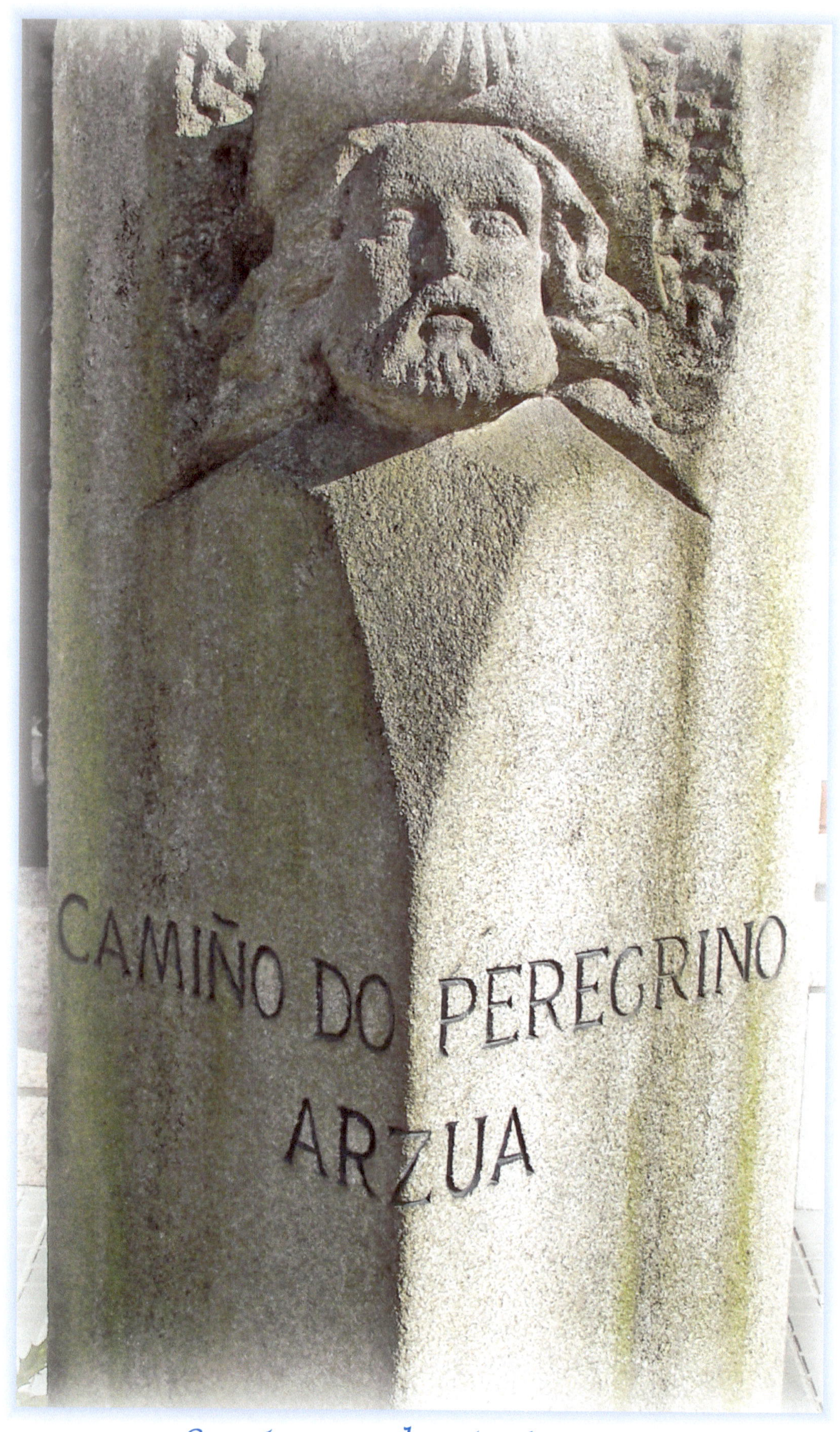

Camino marker in Arzua

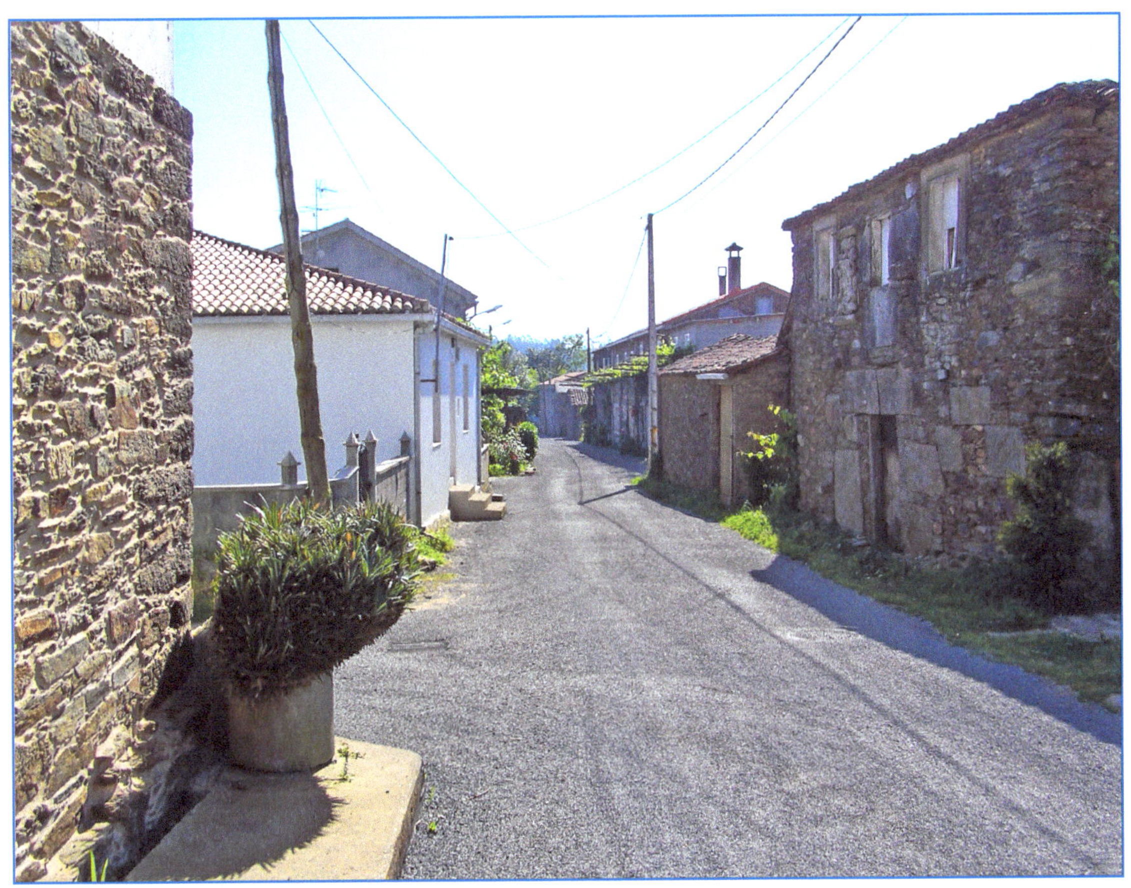

Camino through Arcu

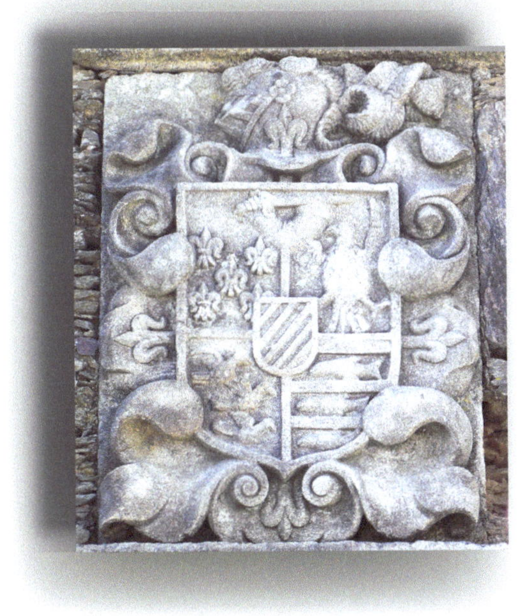

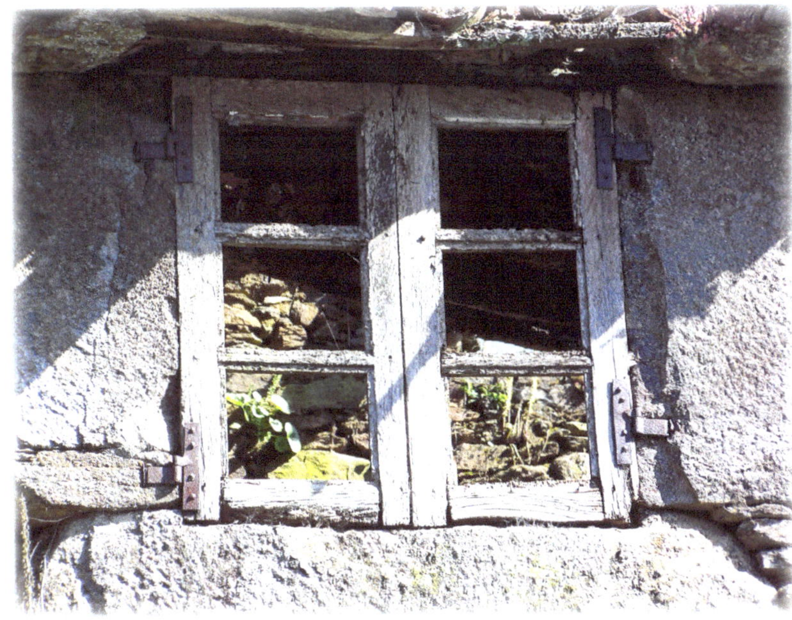

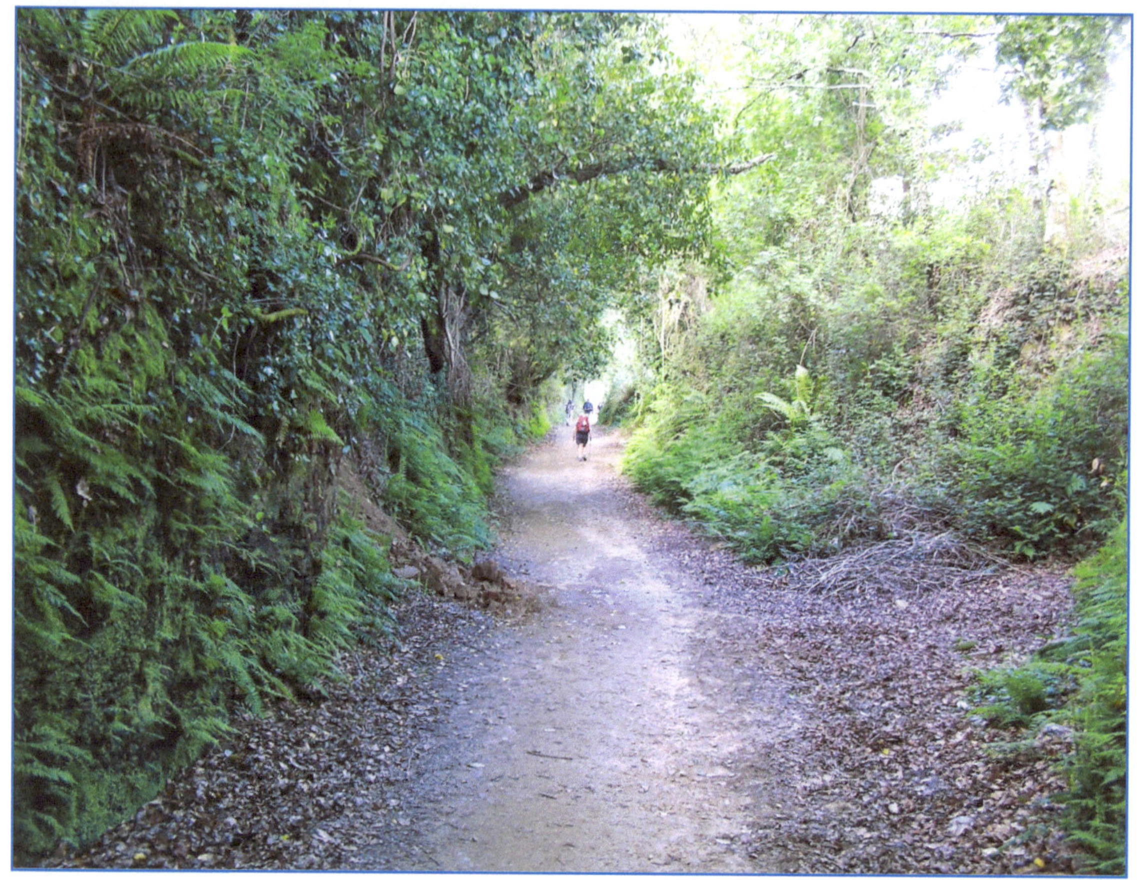

Camino

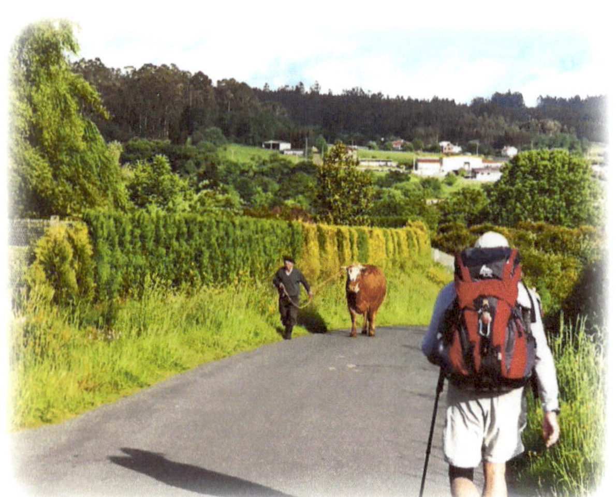

Lavacolla

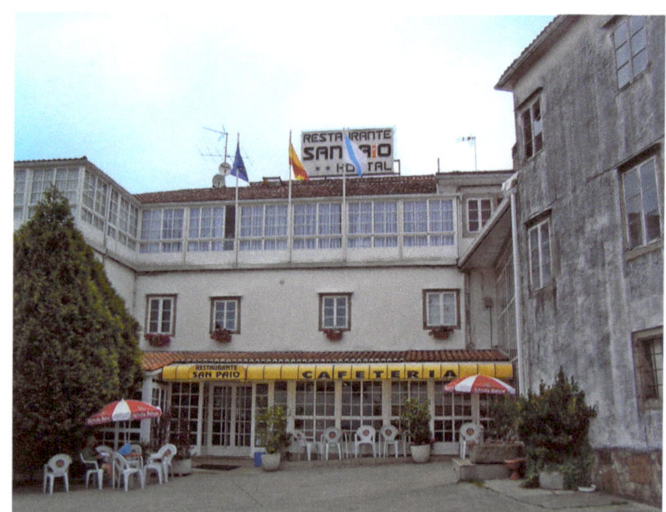

Hostal San Paio-Lavacolla

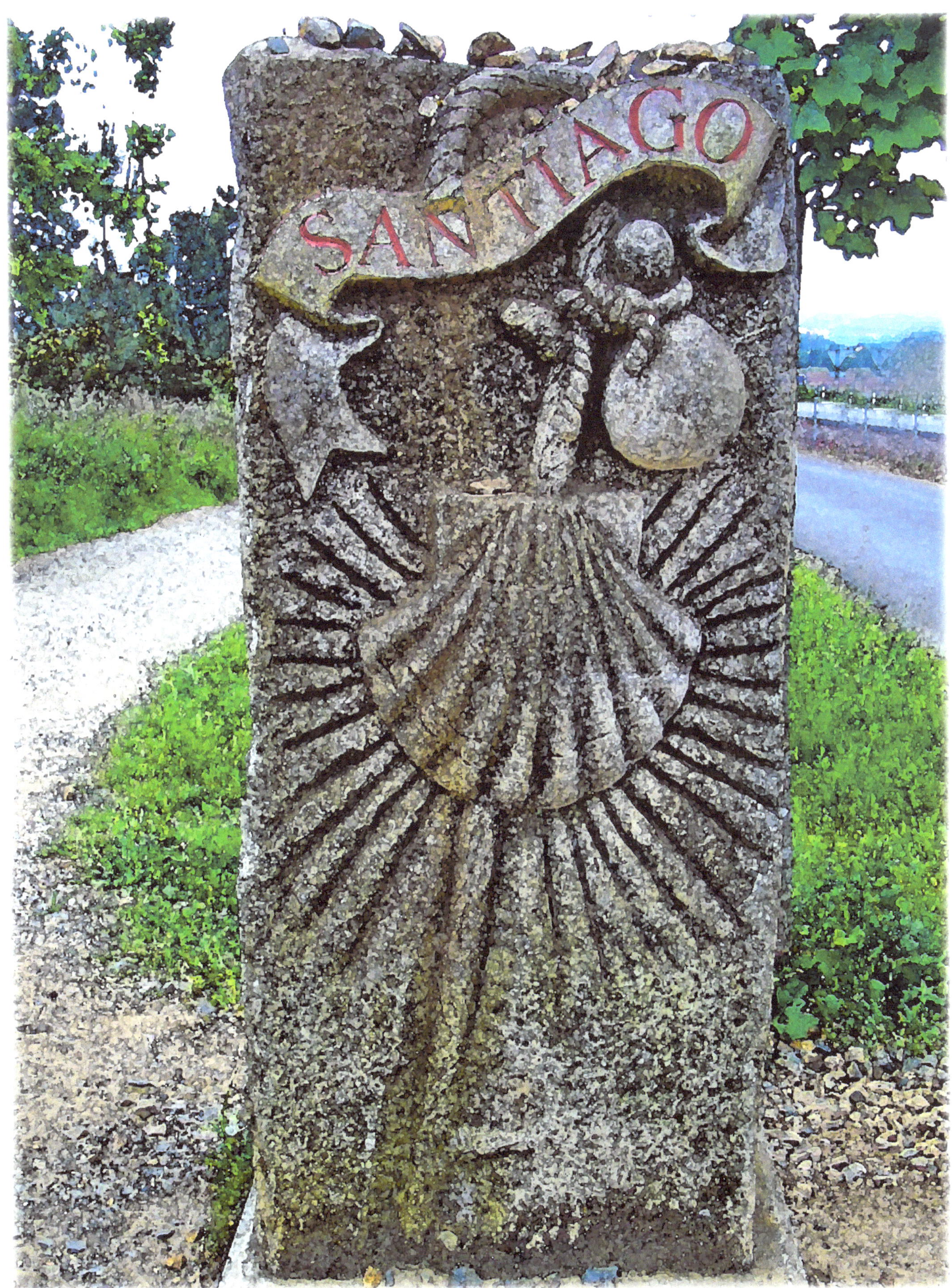
SANTIAGO

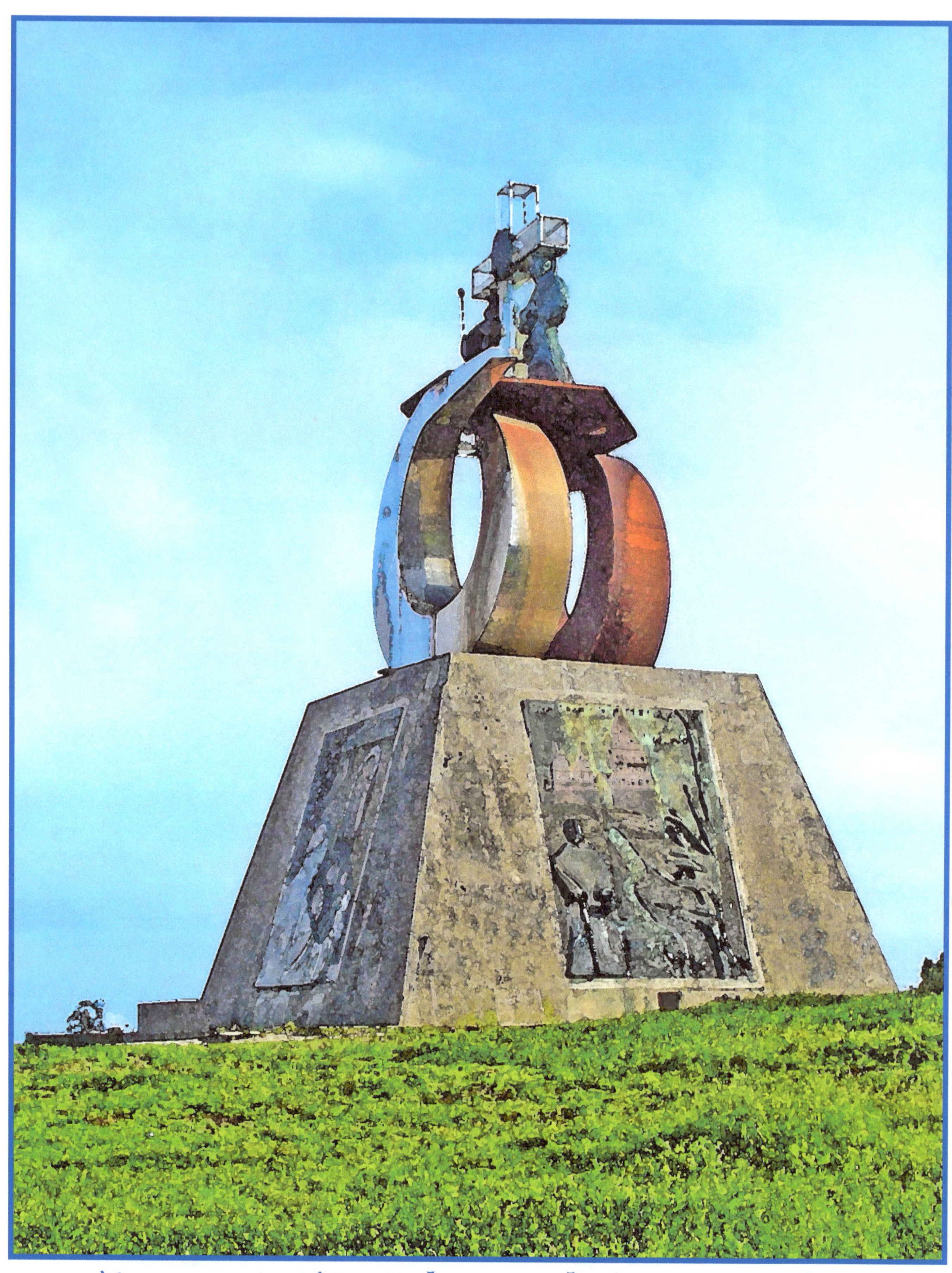

Monument at Monte de Gozo-The Mountain of Joy

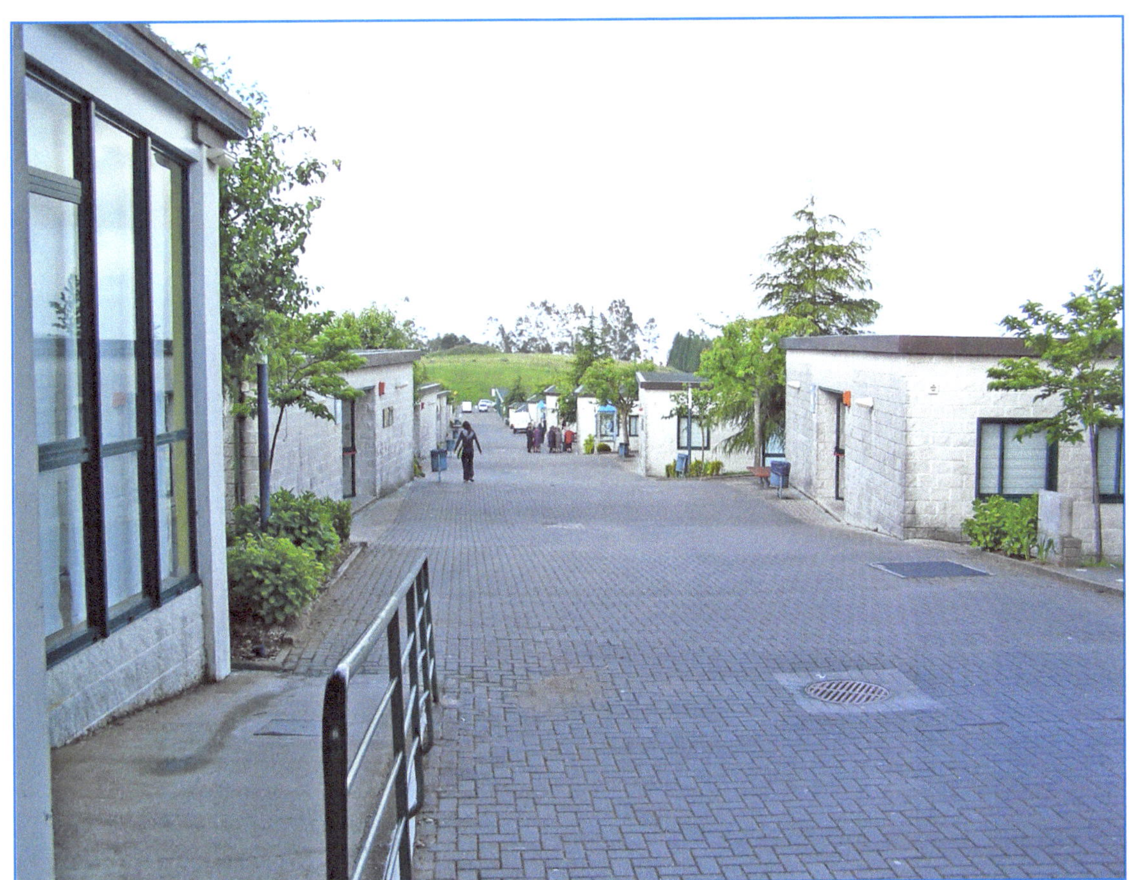

Very large Albergue-Hotel facility at Monte de Gozo

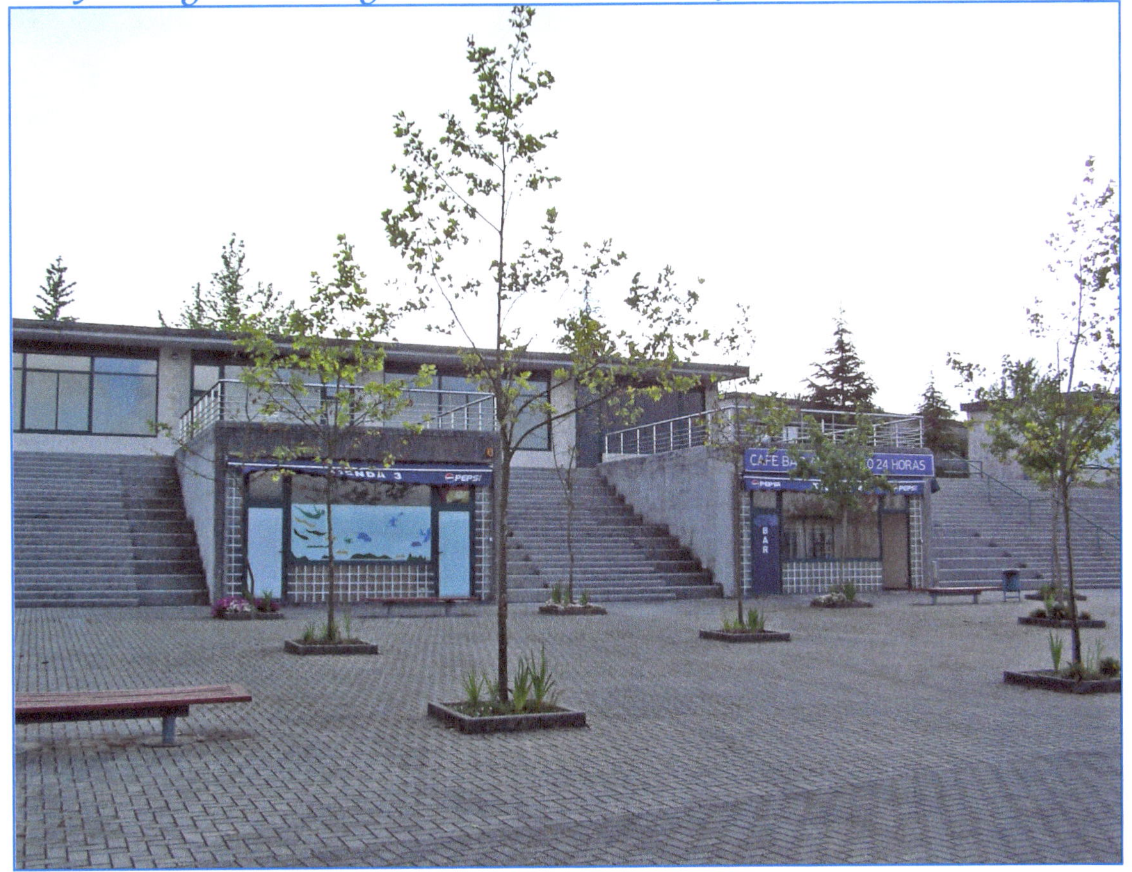

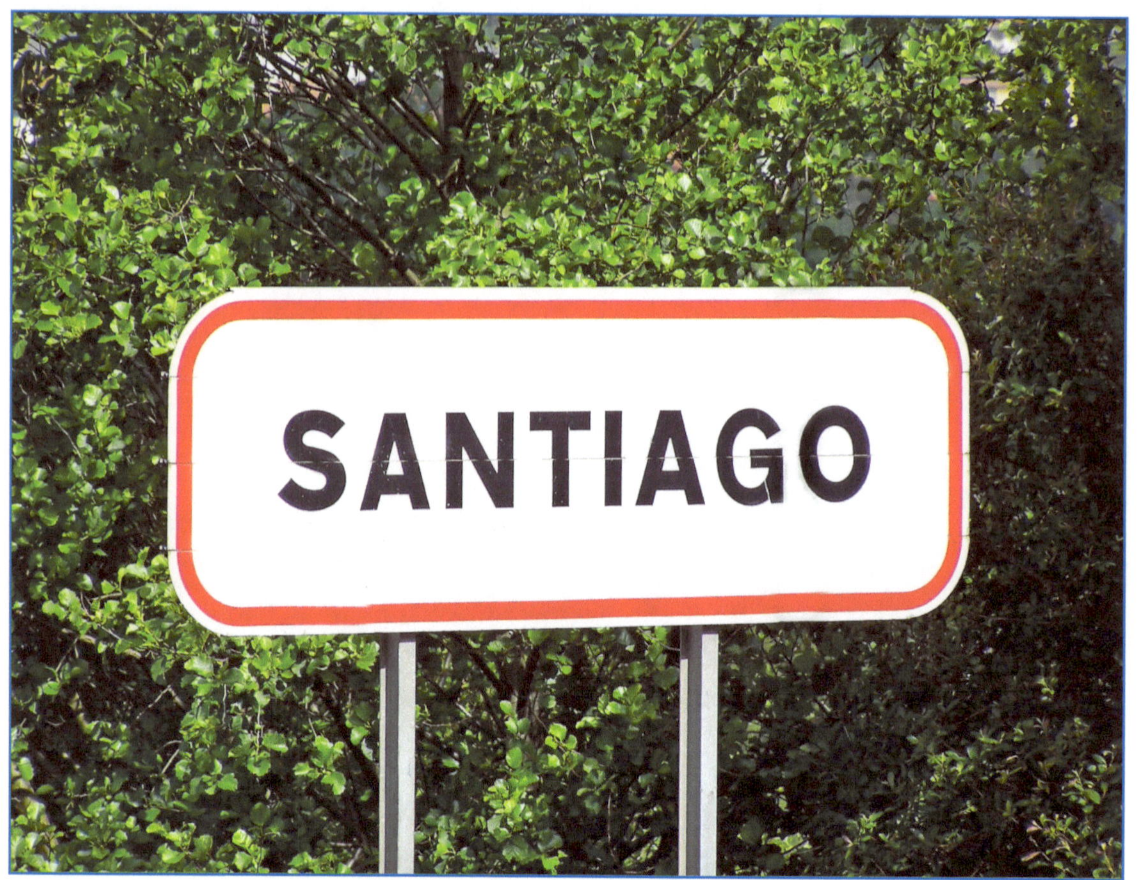

Entering Santiago

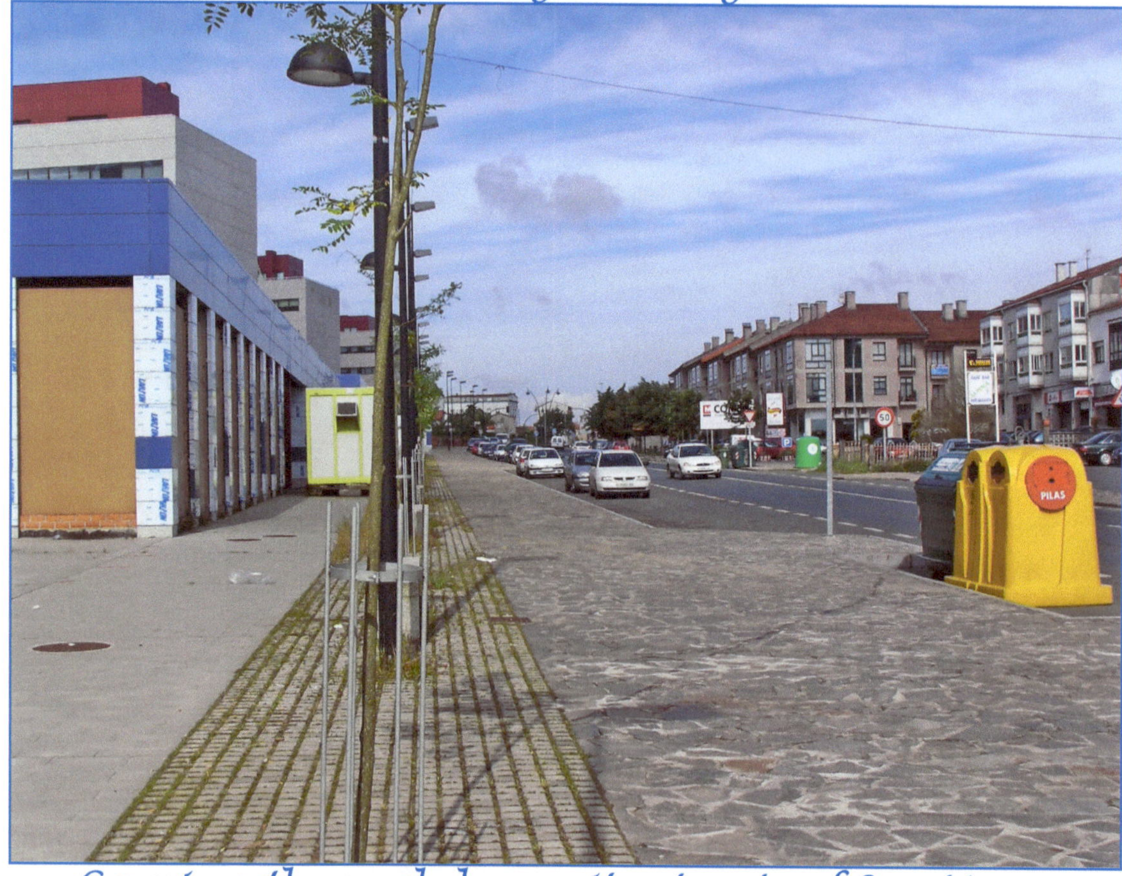

Camino through busy city streets of Santiago

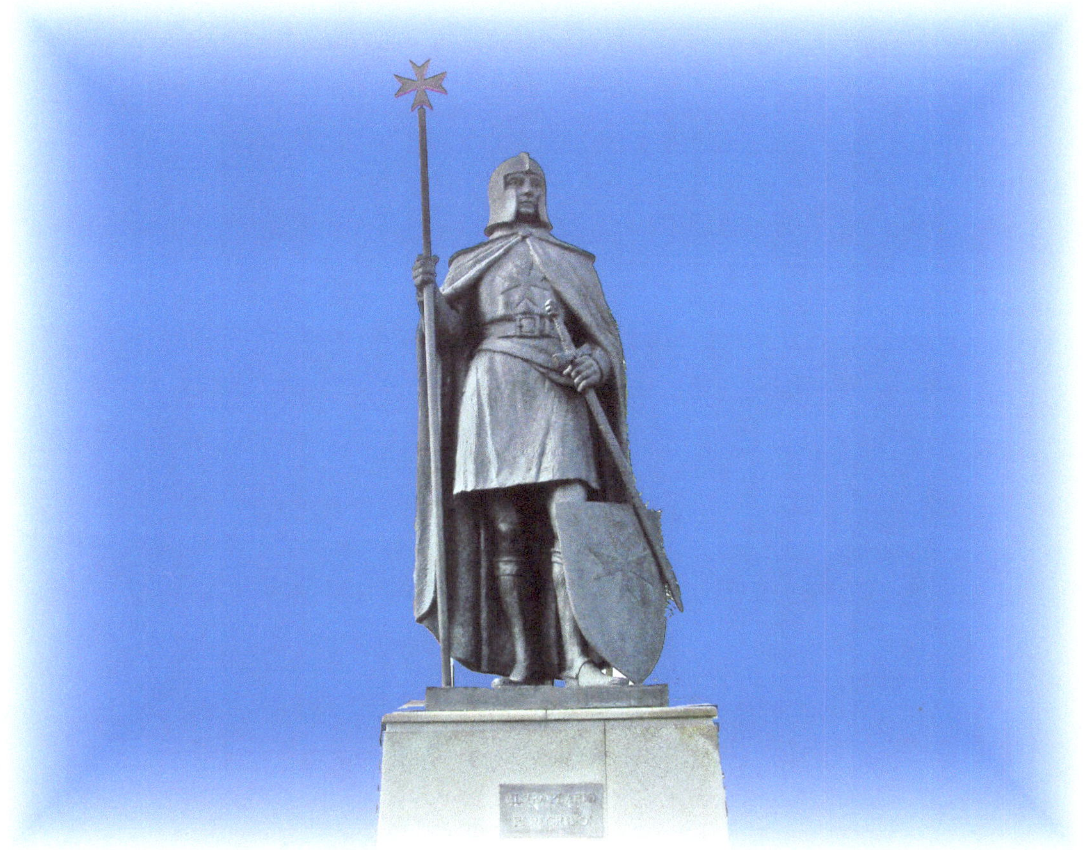

El Templario Peregrino

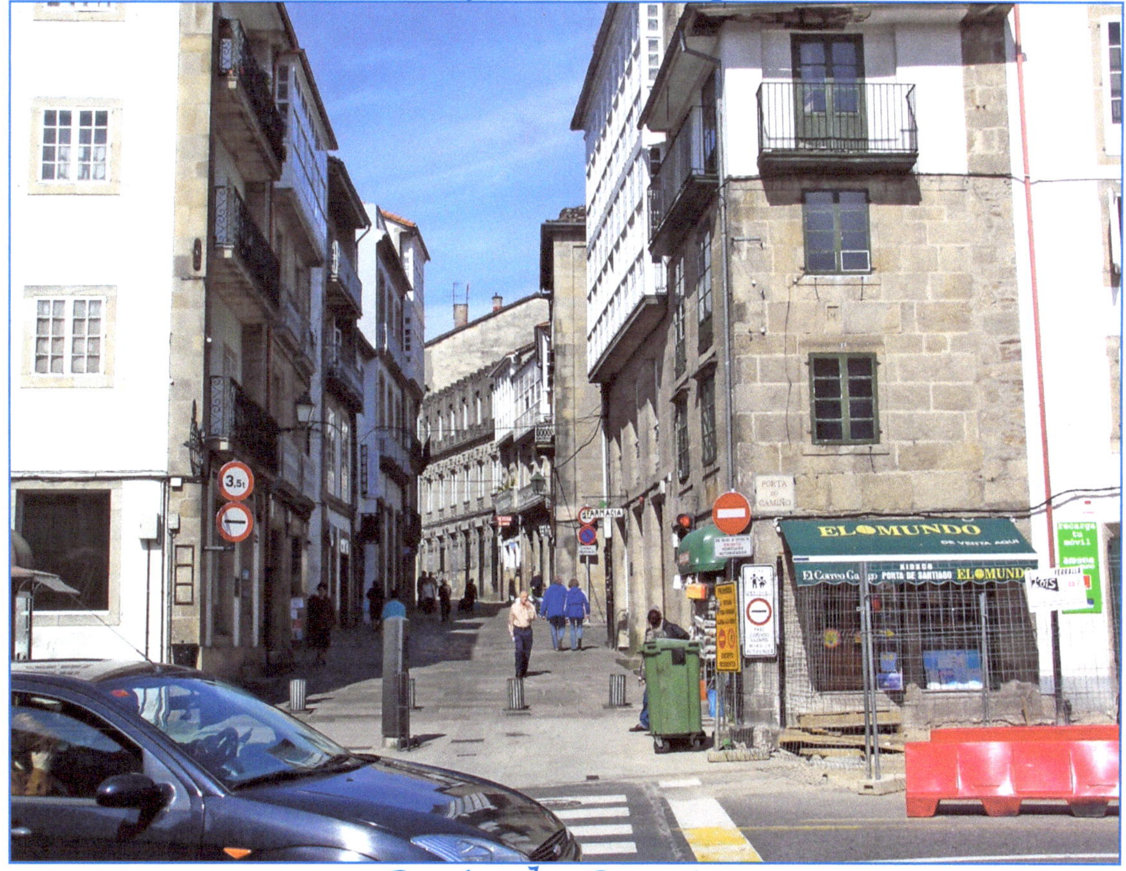

Porto do Camino

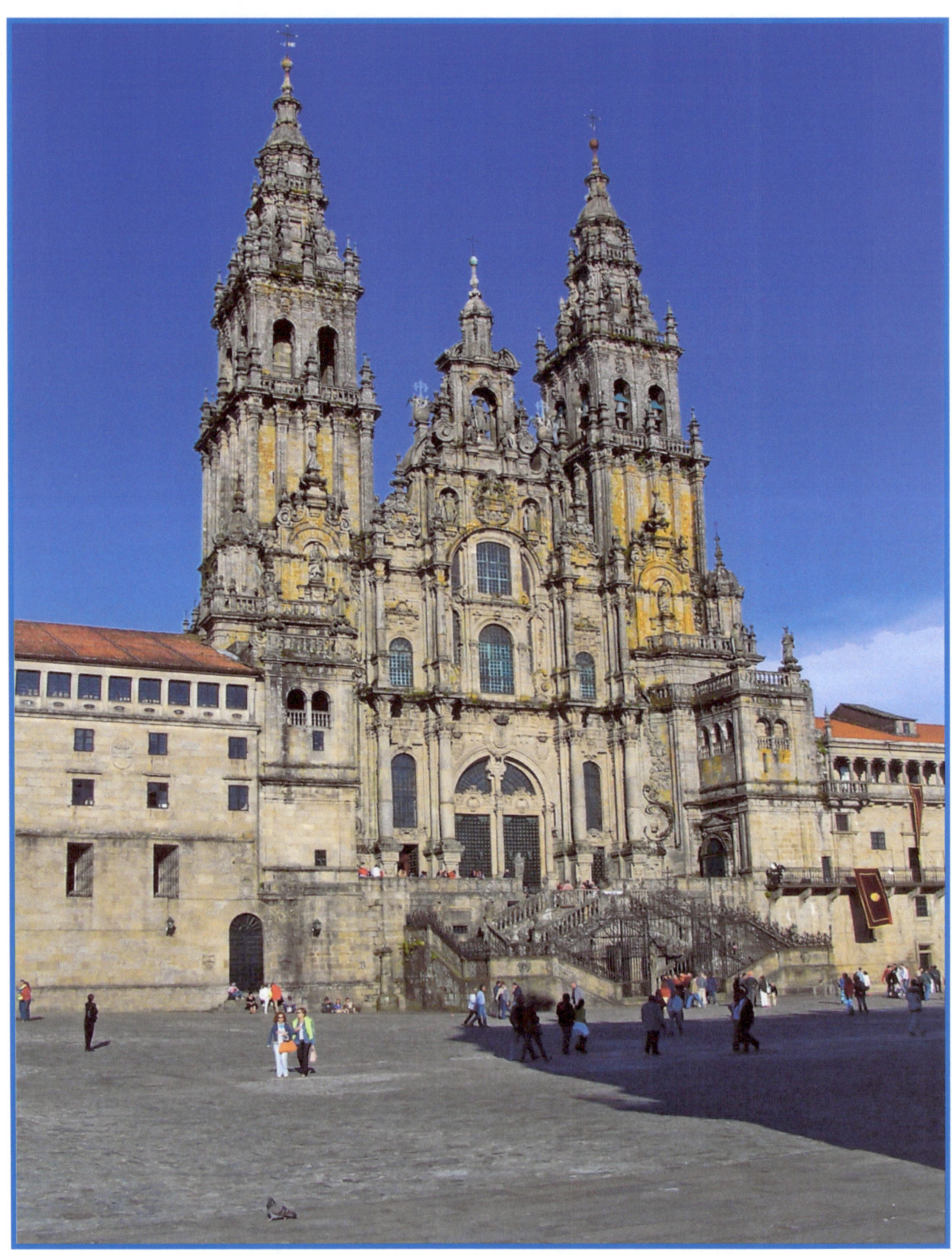

Cathedral Santiago de Compostela

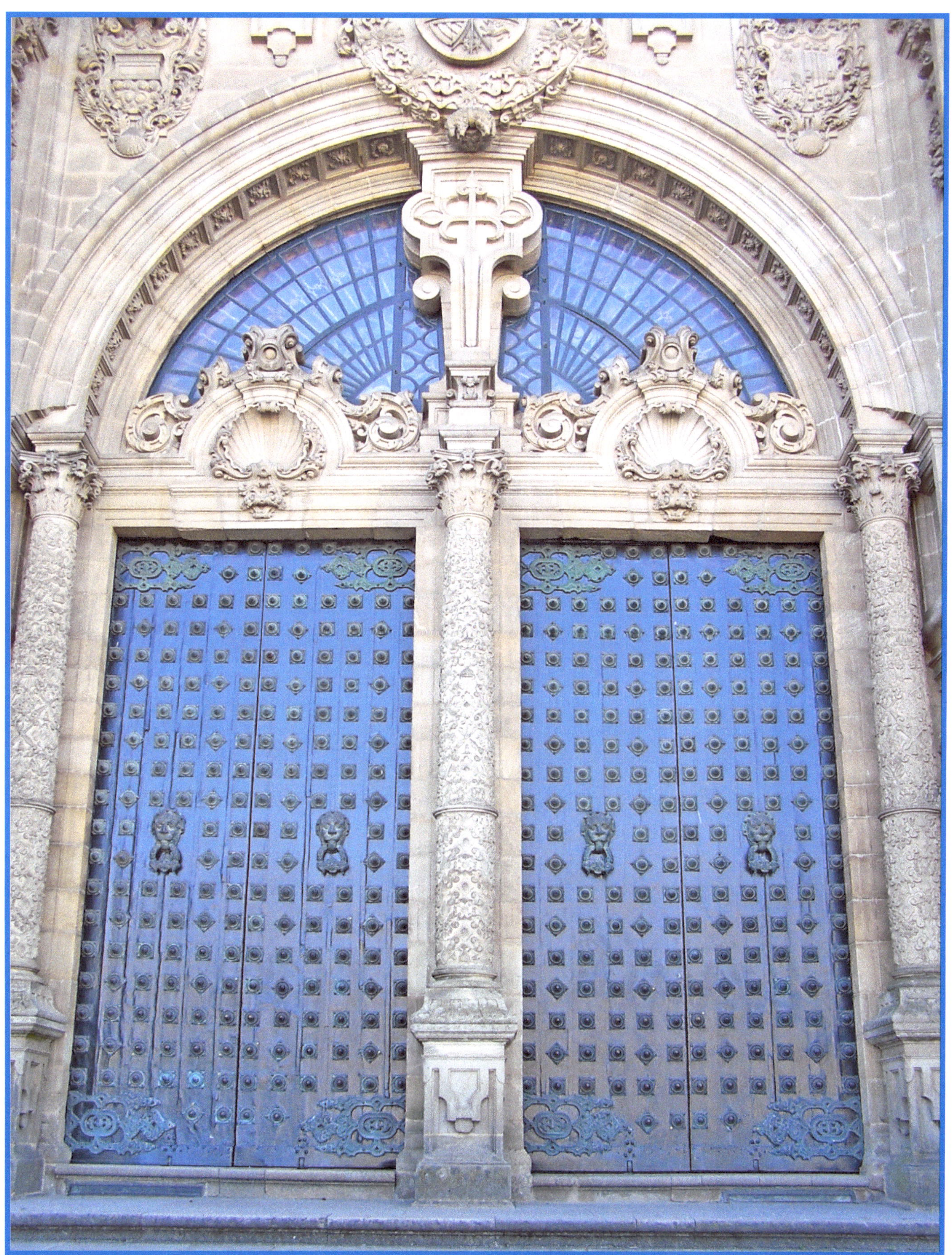

Cathedral doors

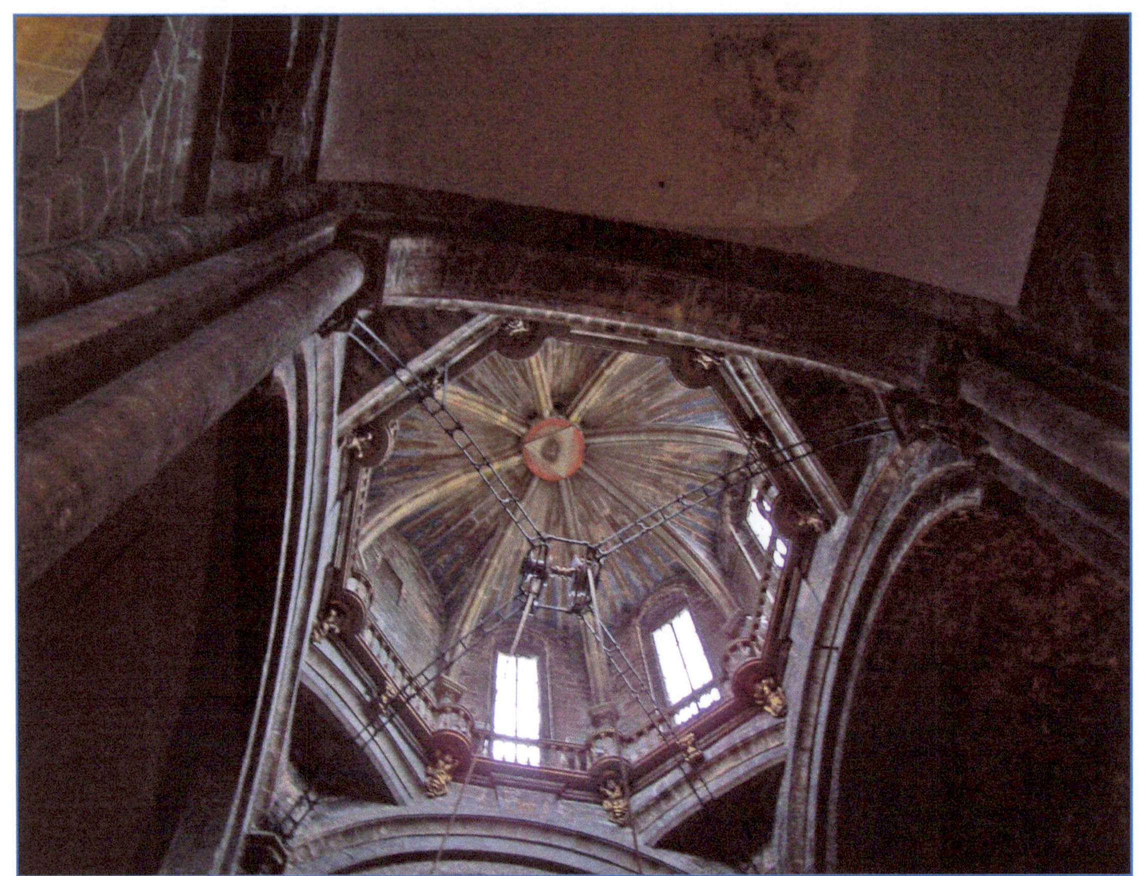

"All Seeing Eye" Main cathedral dome

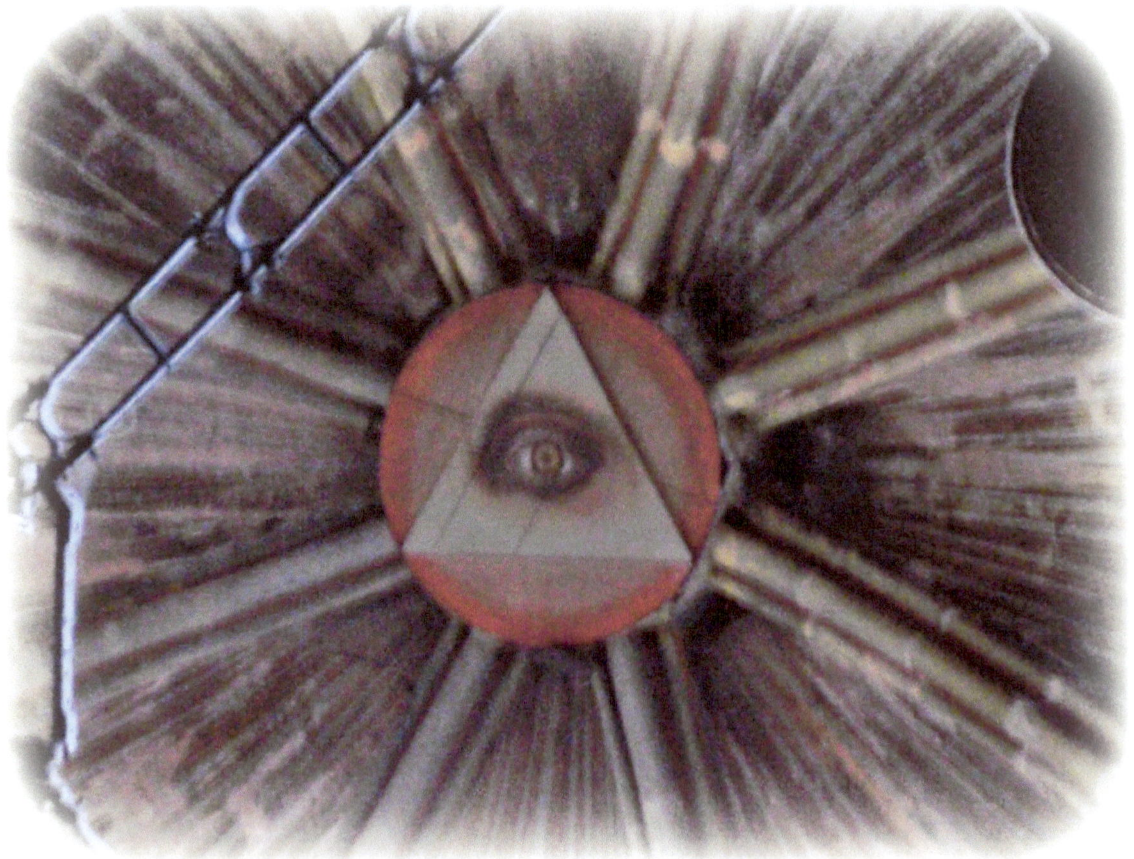

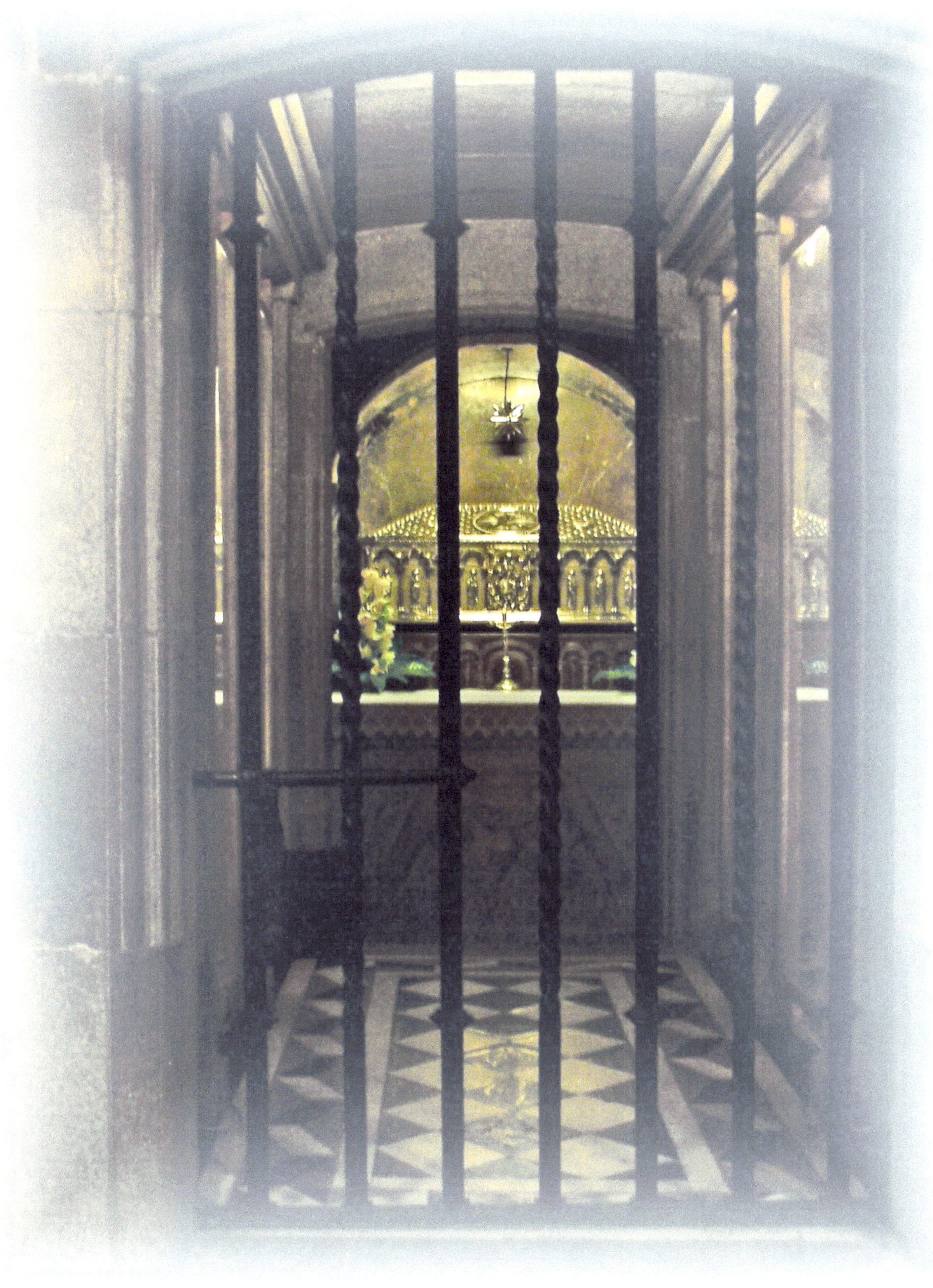

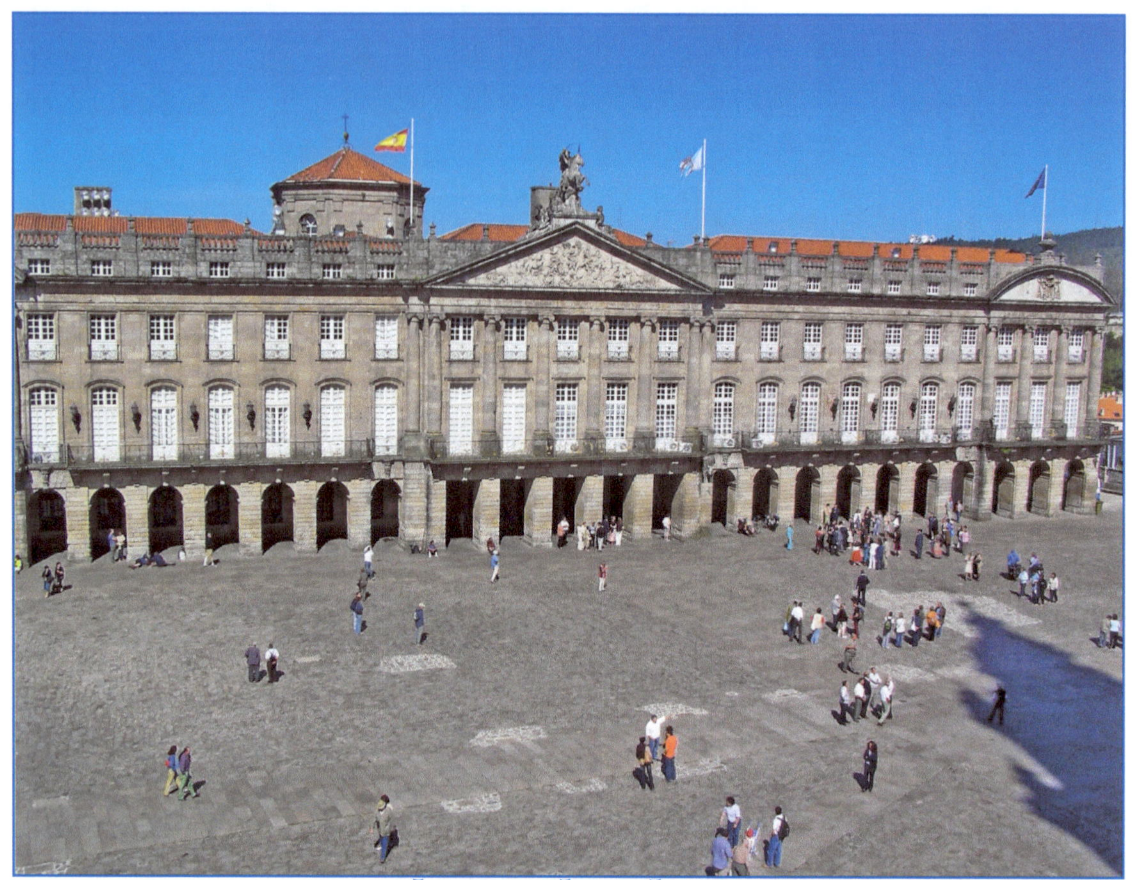

Plaza Obradoiro

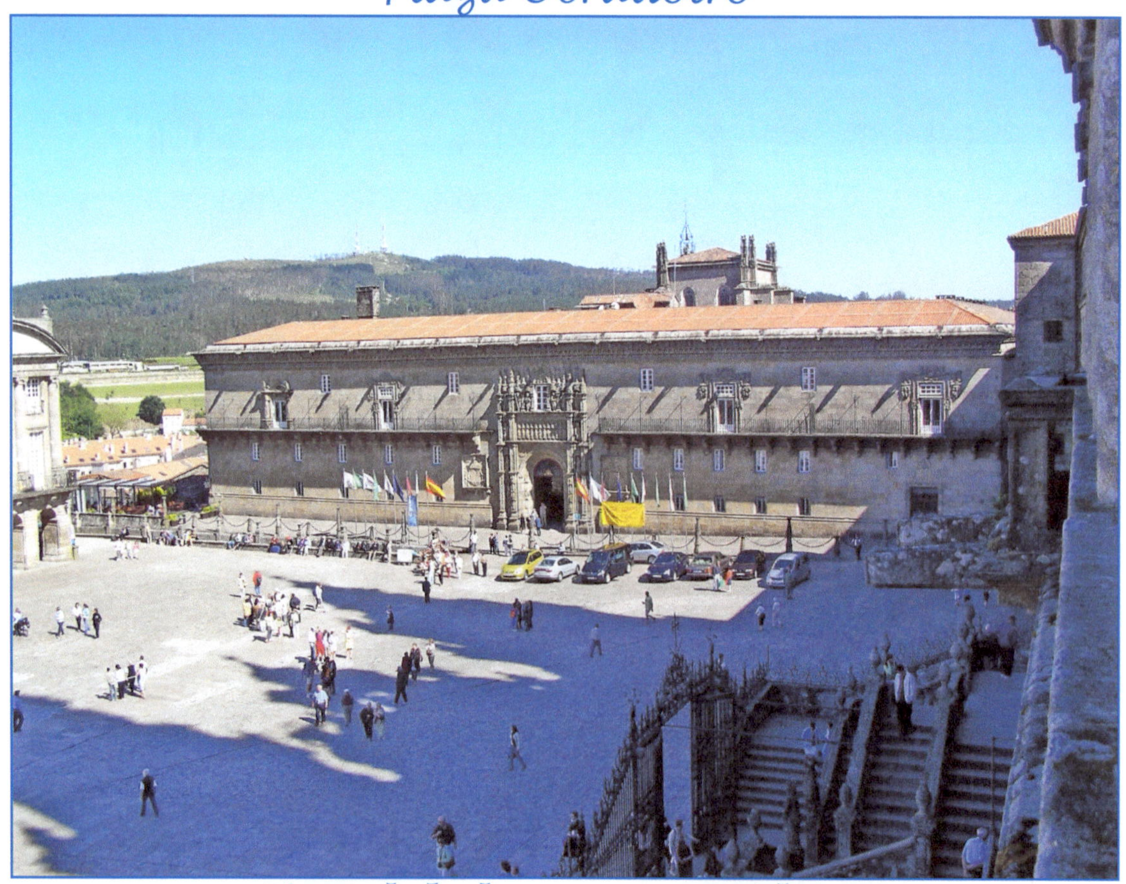

Hostal de los Reyes Catolicos

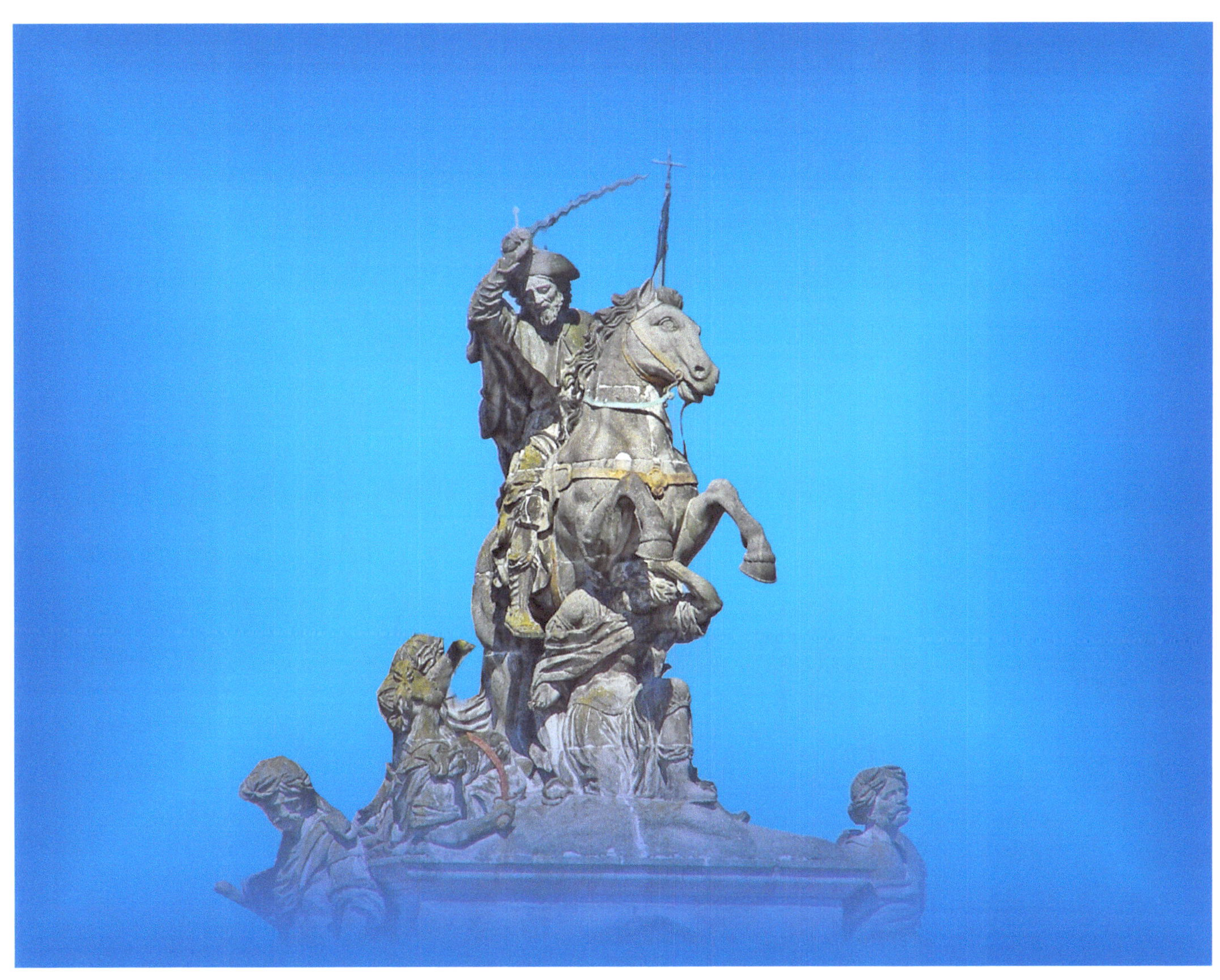

Santiago Matamoros

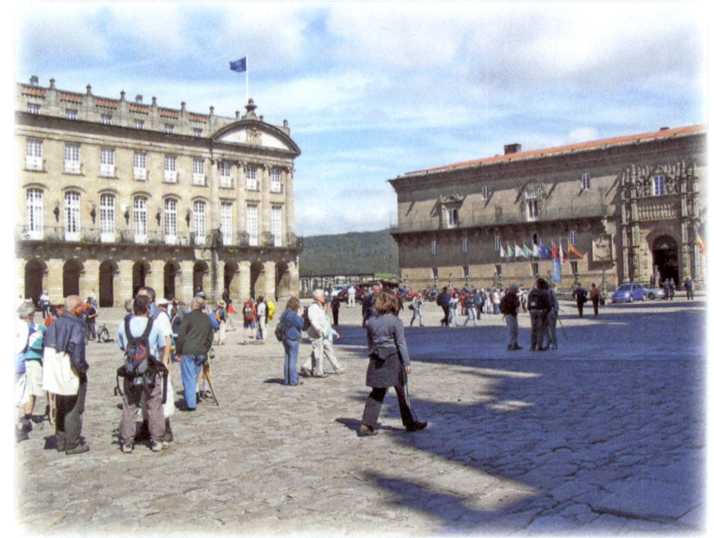

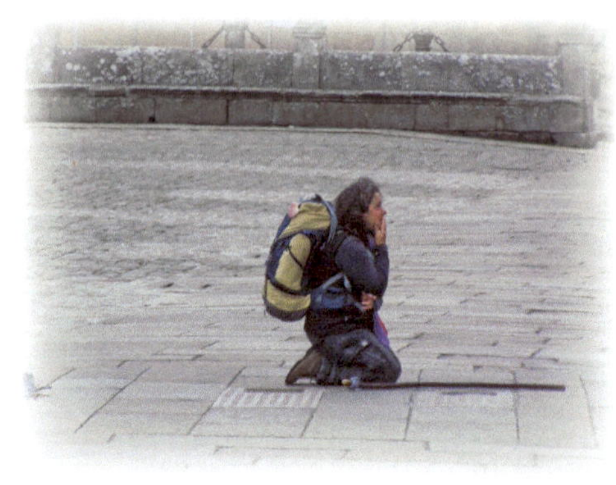

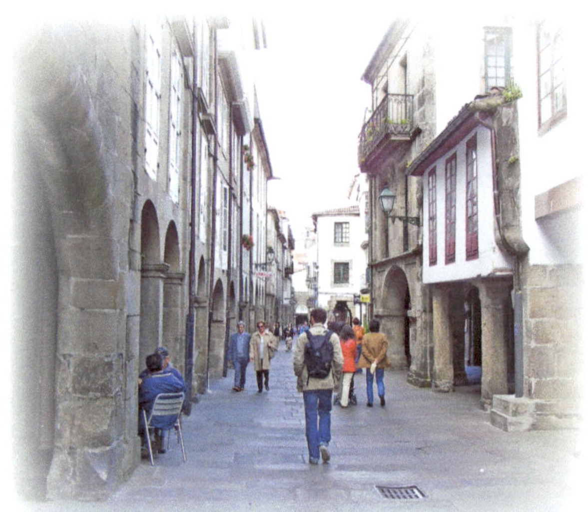

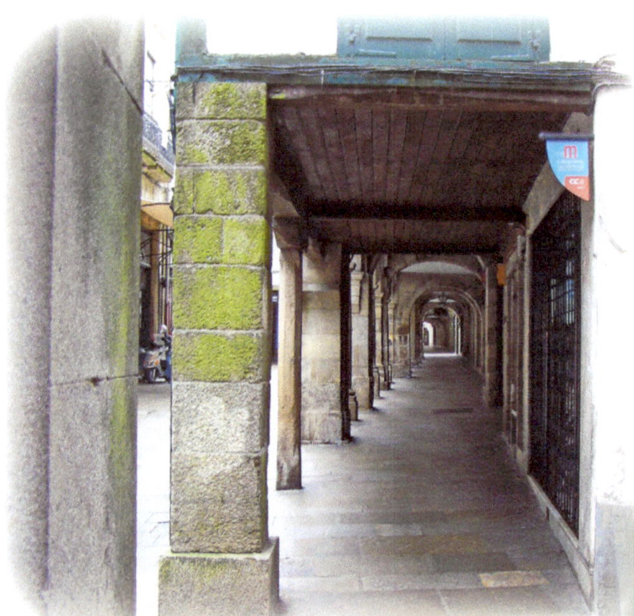

Old Town Santiago

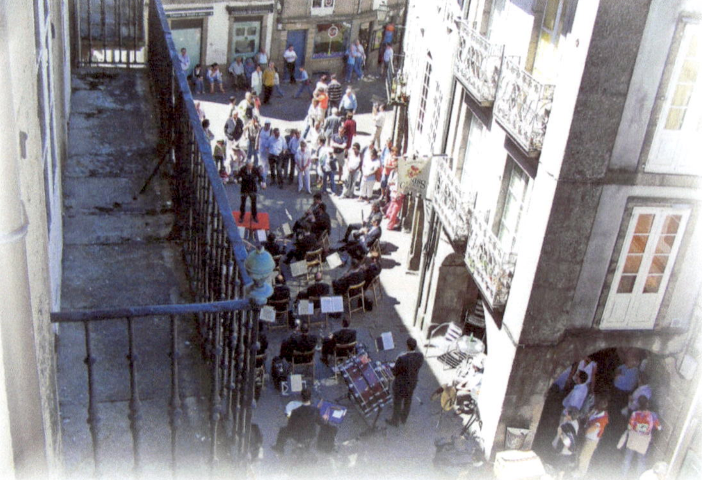

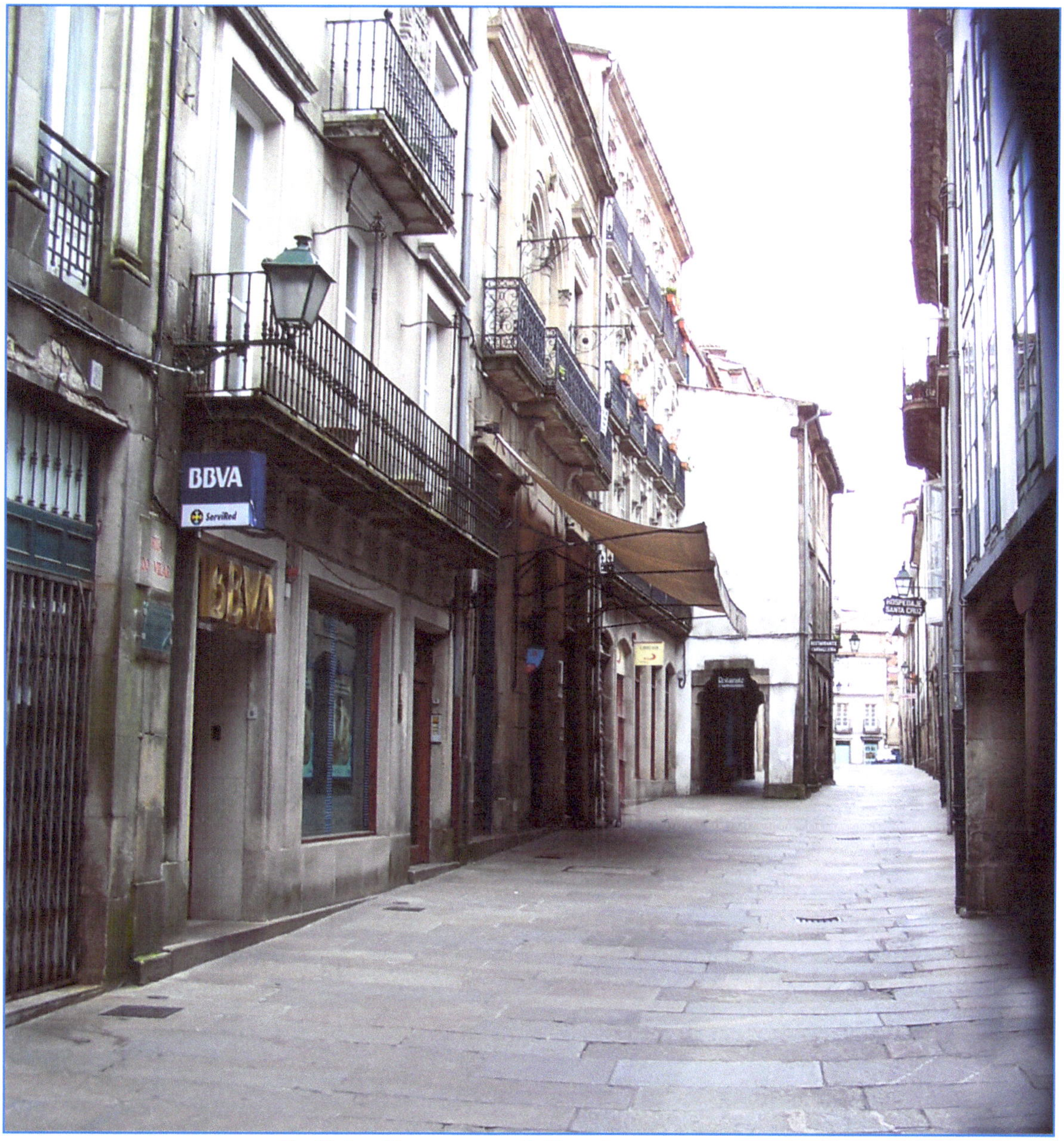

Rua del Vilar - Old Town Santiago

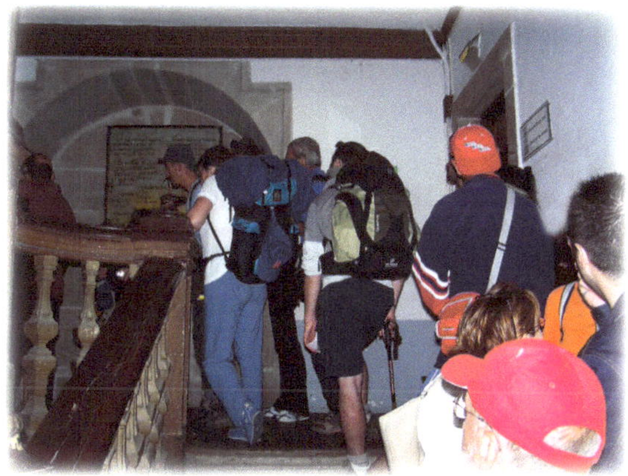

Pilgrim's Office

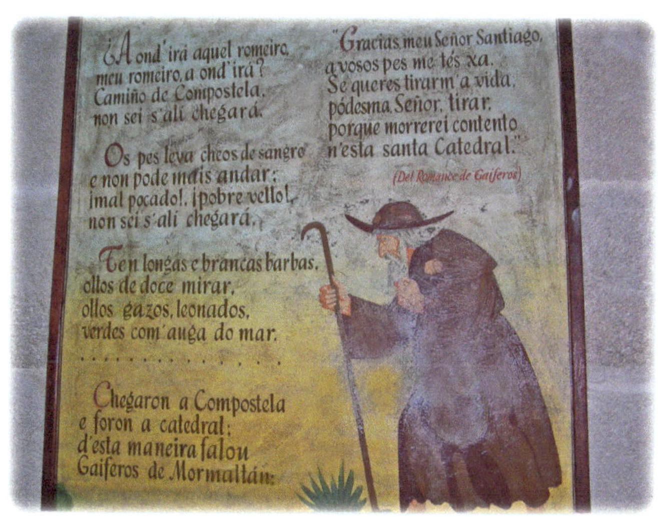

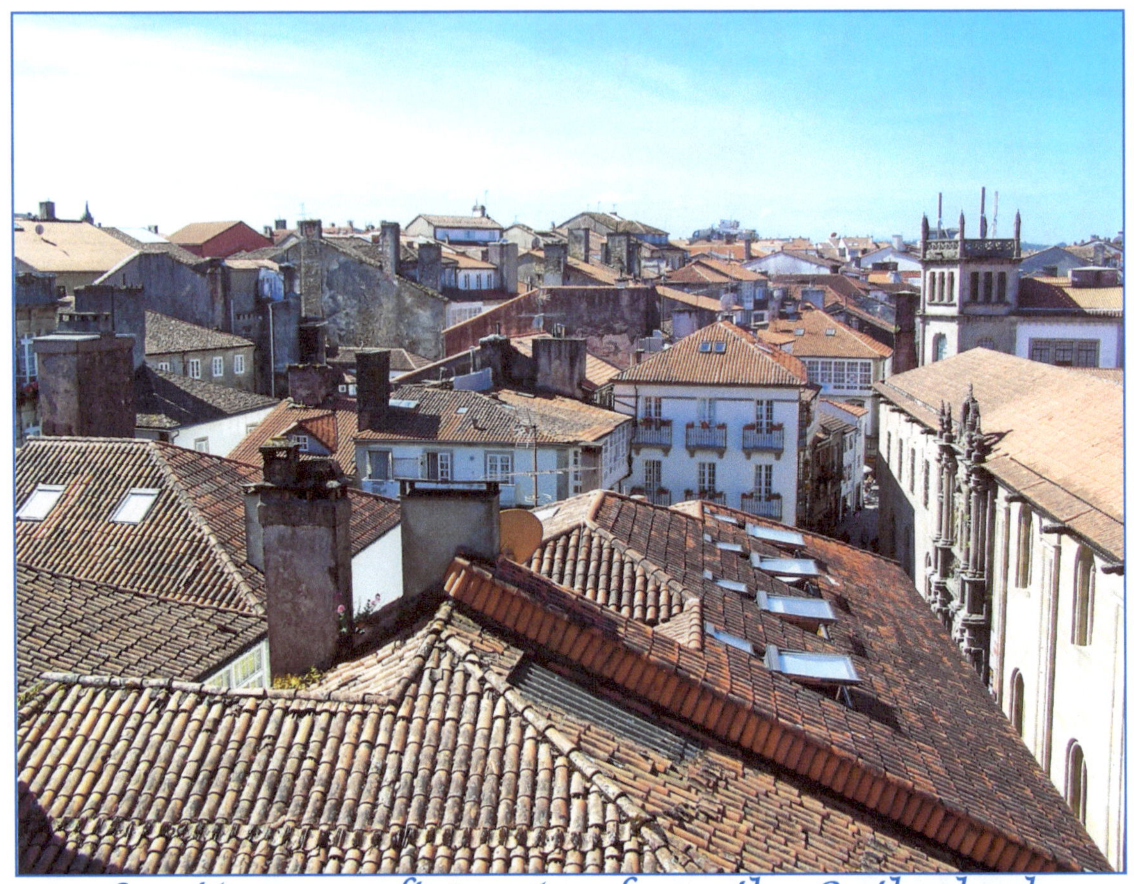

Santiago rooftops-view from the Cathedral

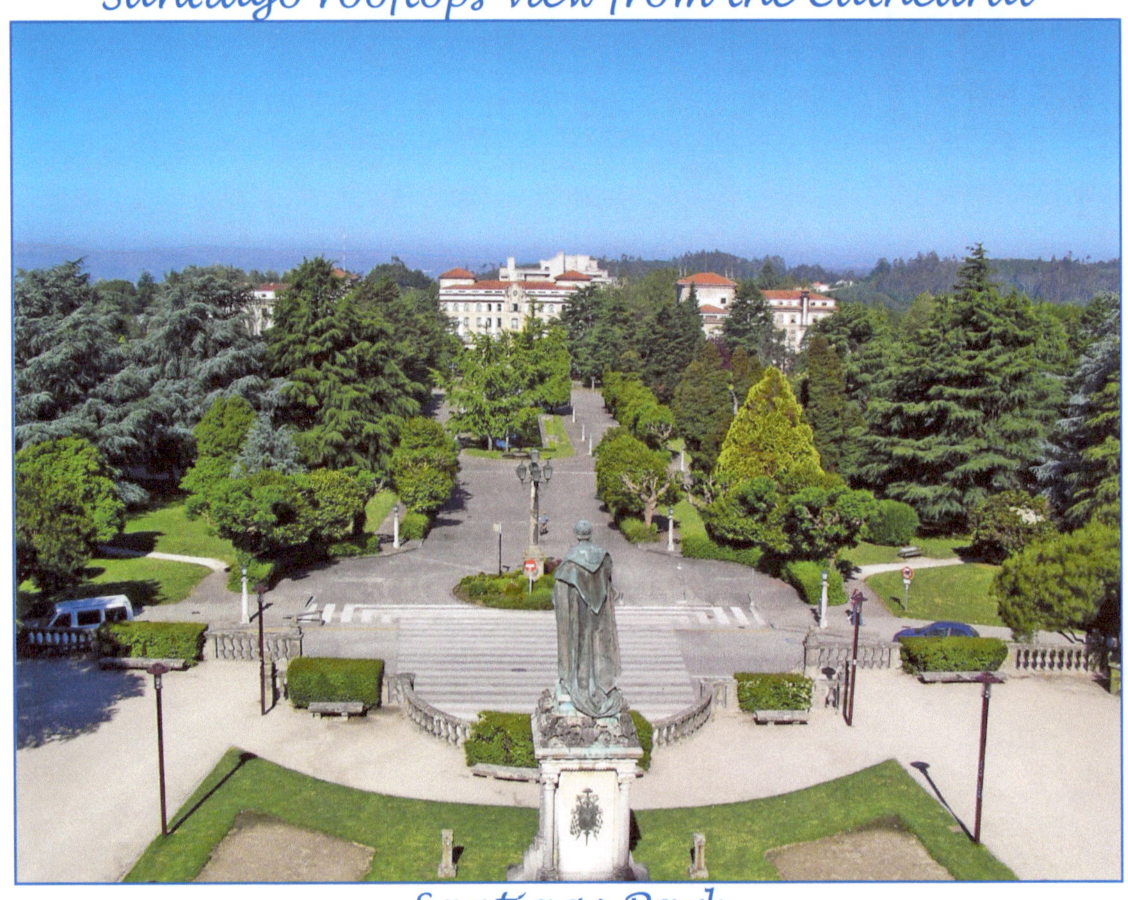

Santiago Park

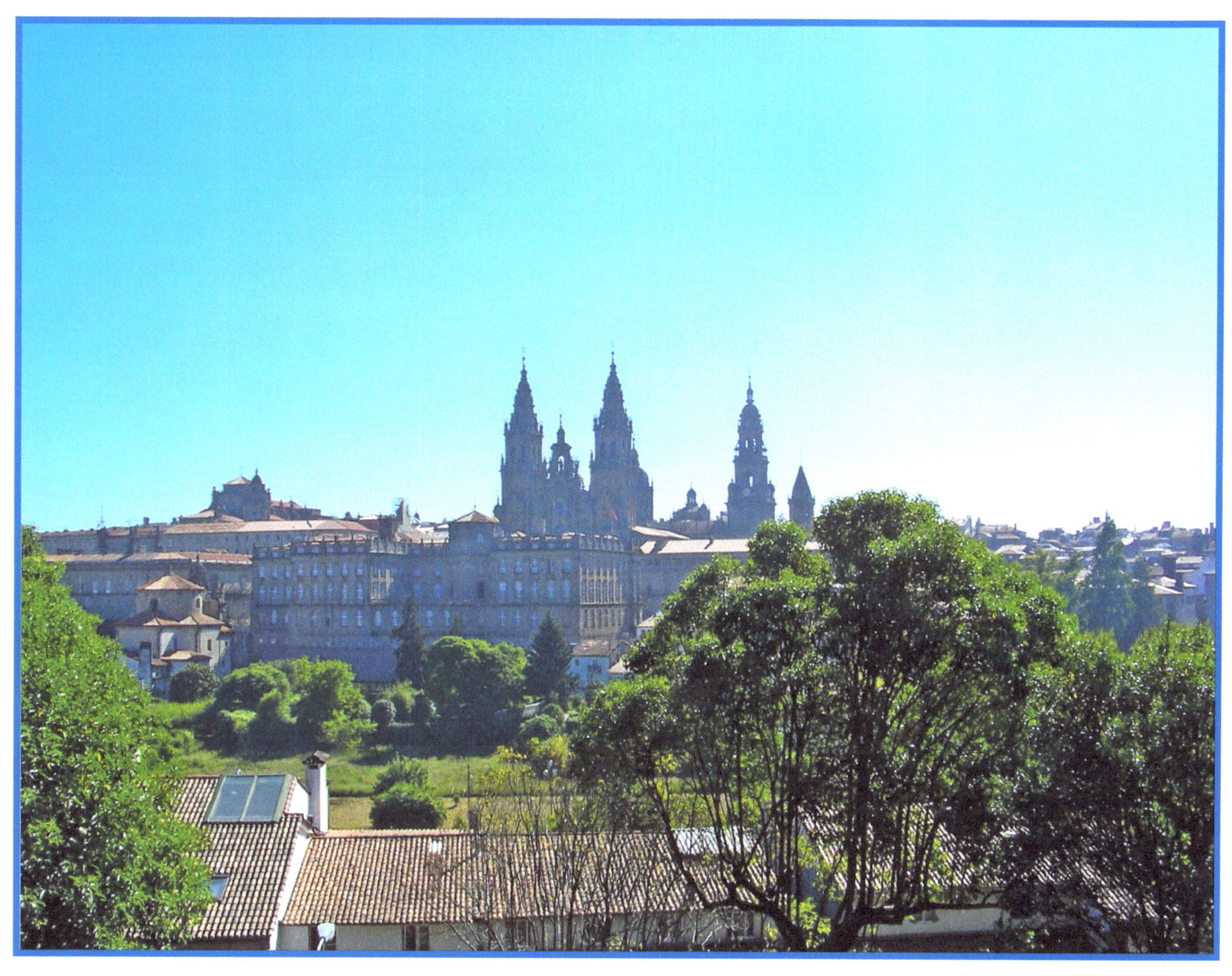

View of Santiago

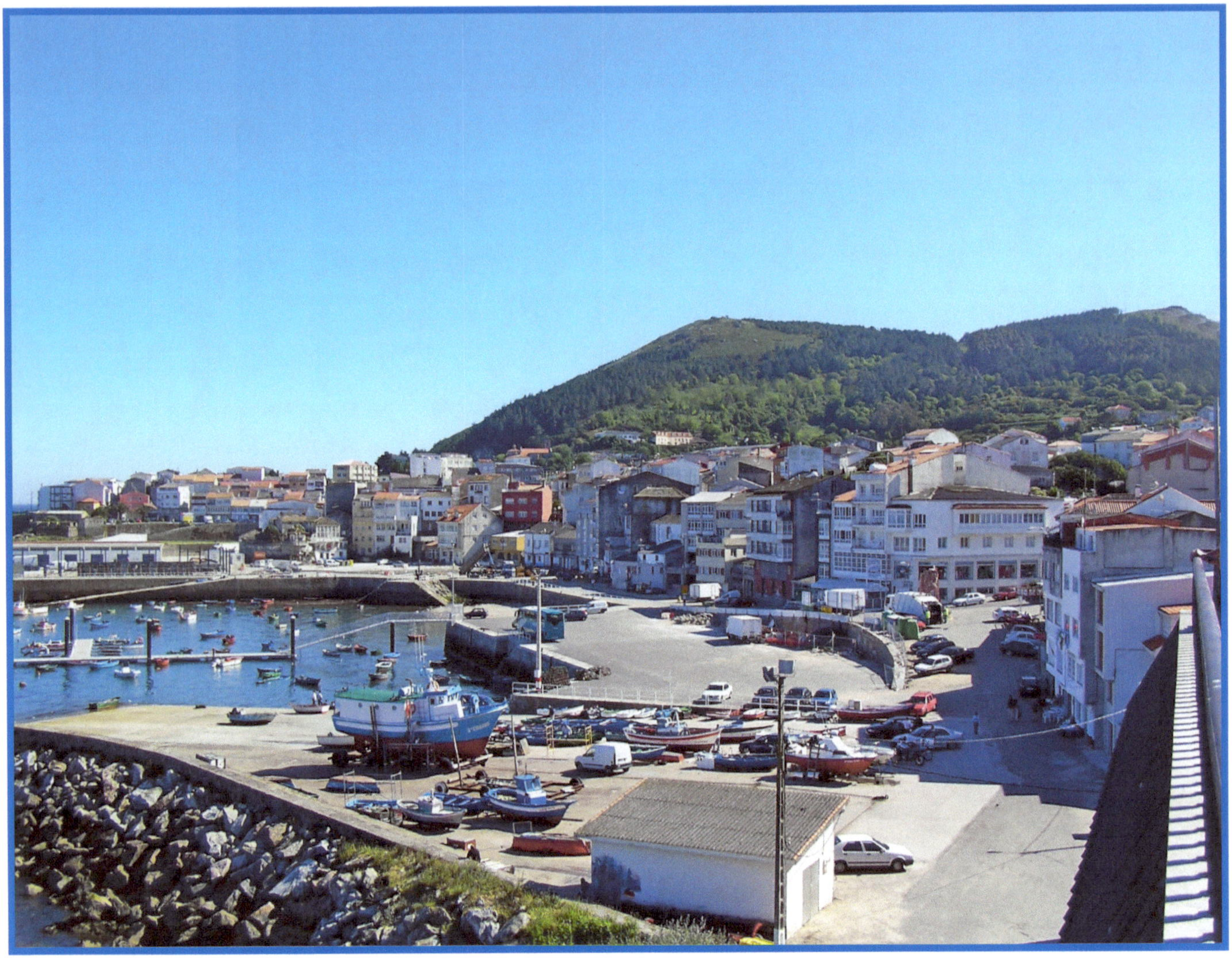

Finisterre

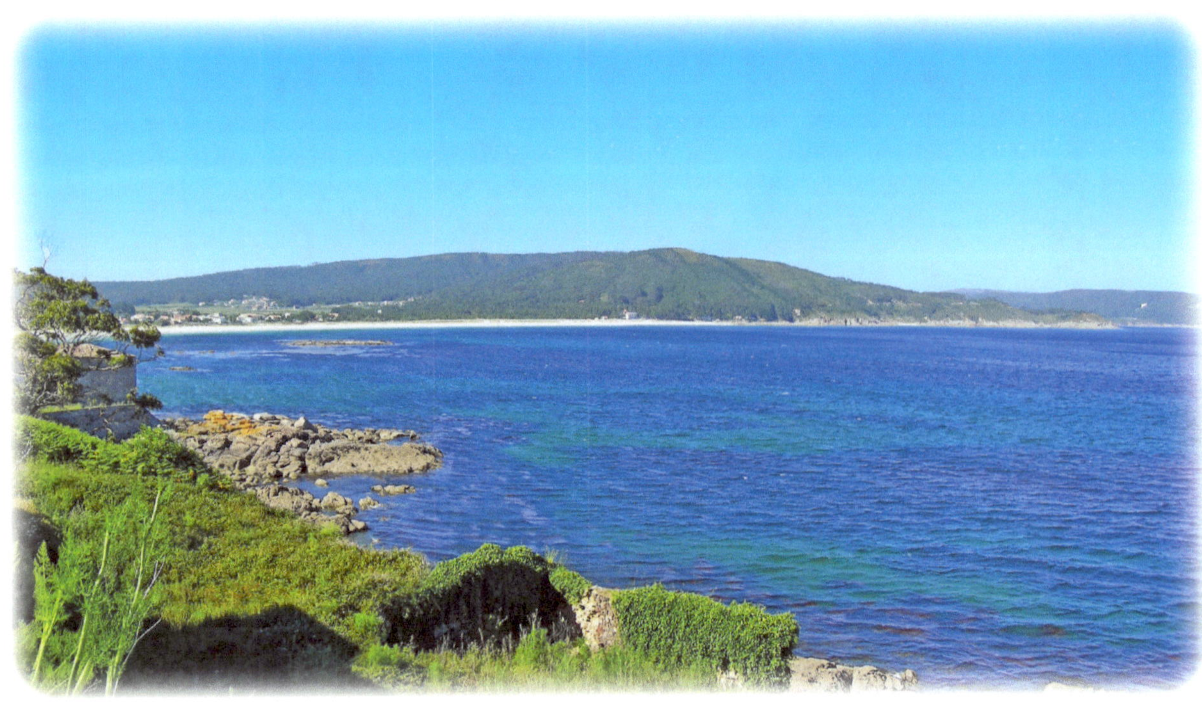

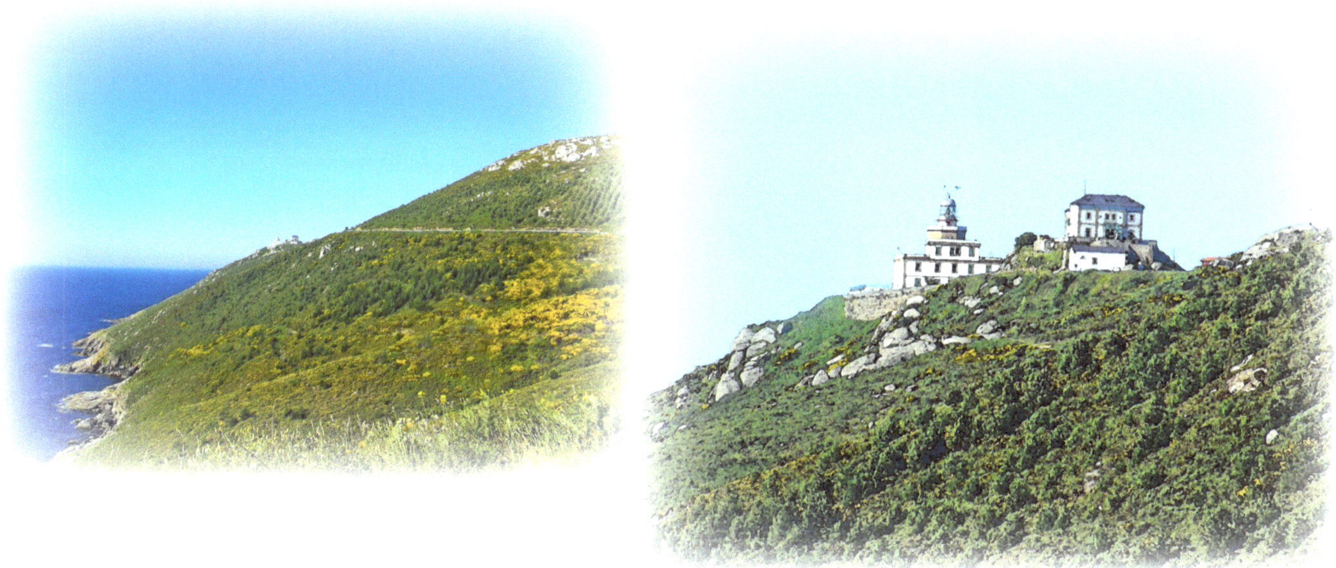

Cabo Finisterre-Lighthouse

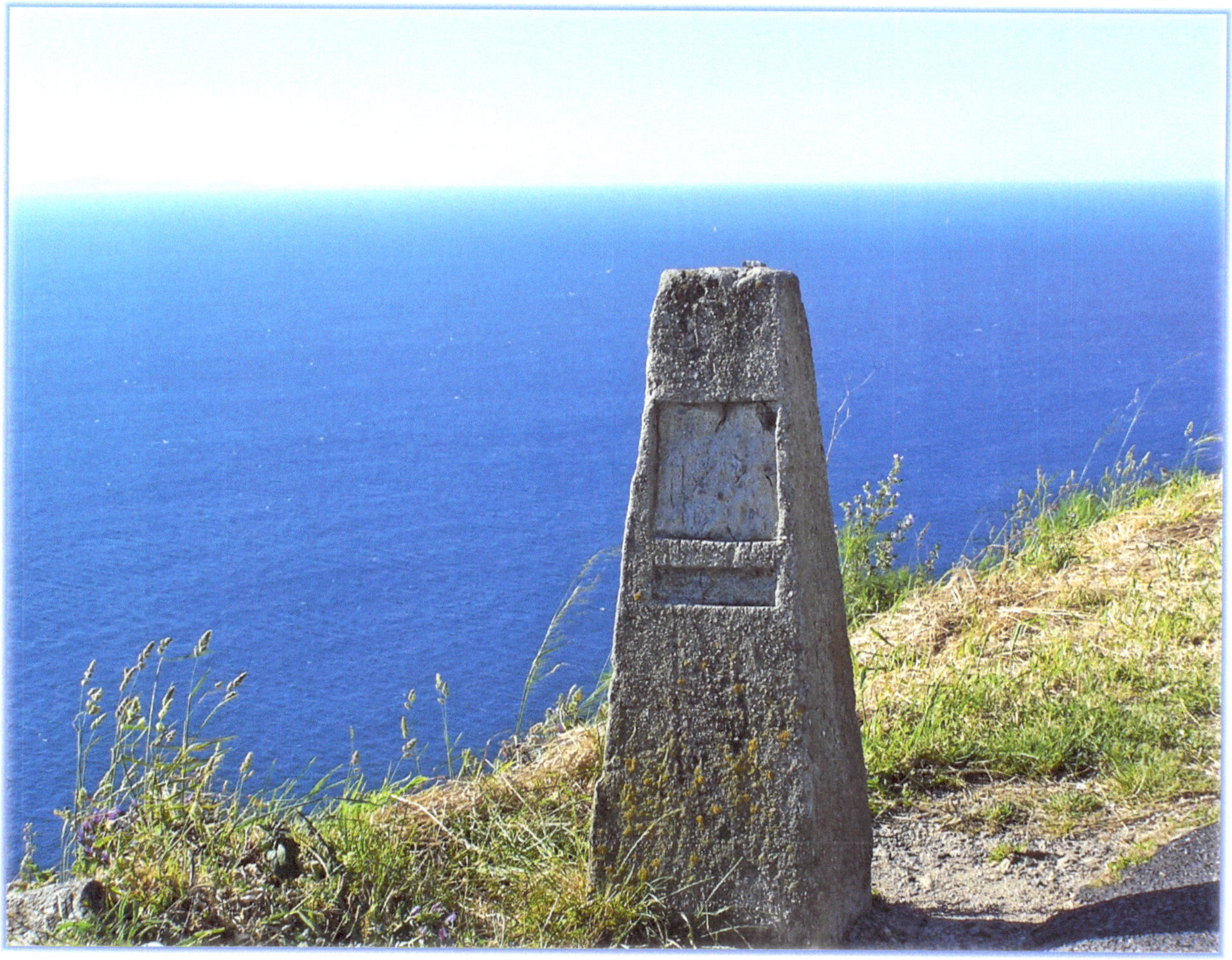

Last Camino marker

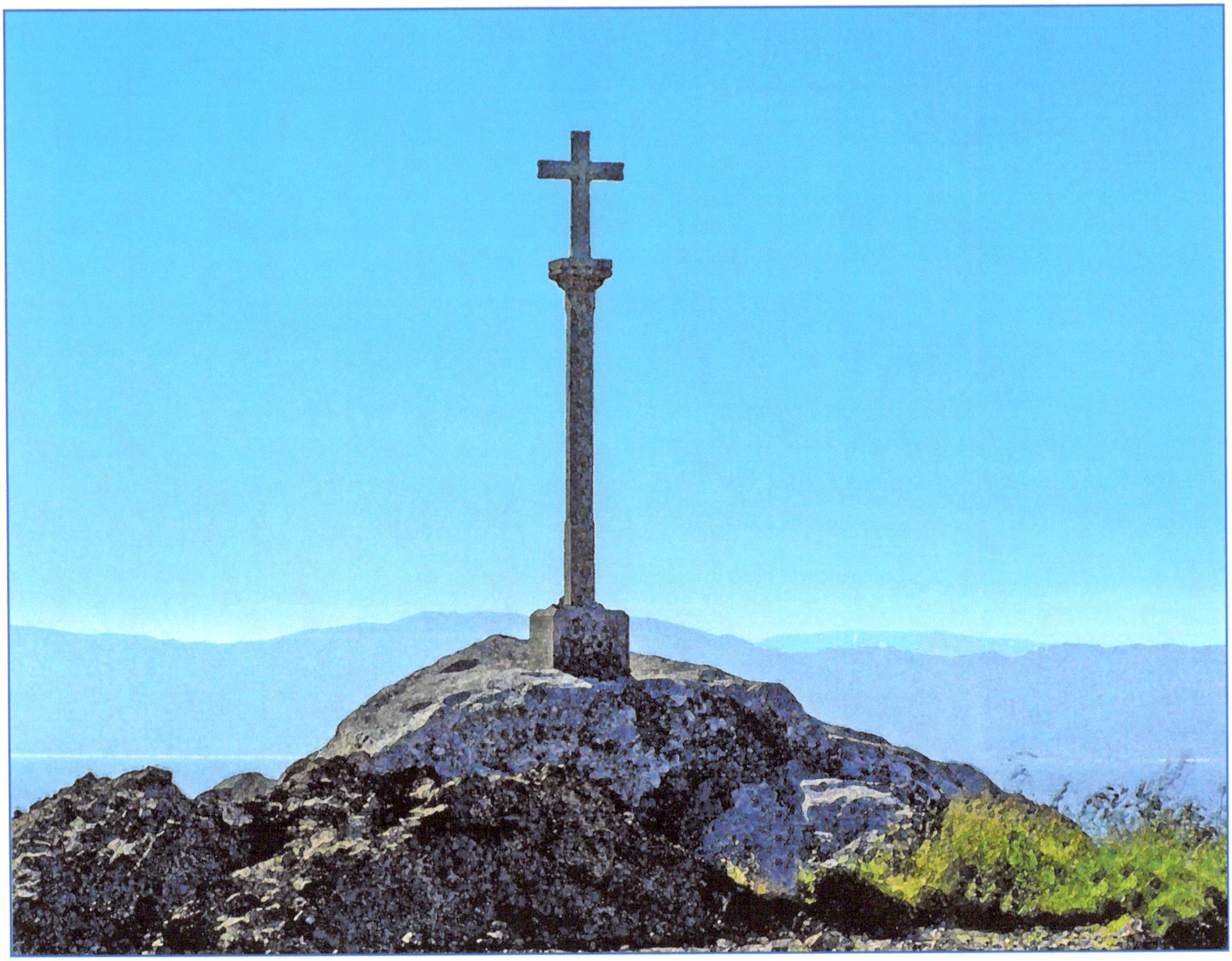

Cross-Cabo Finisterre

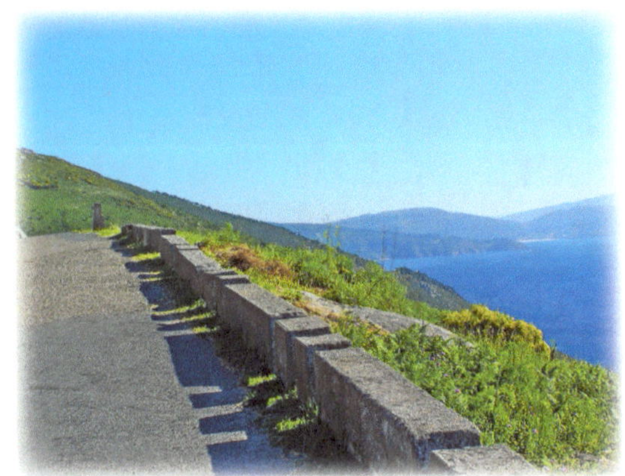

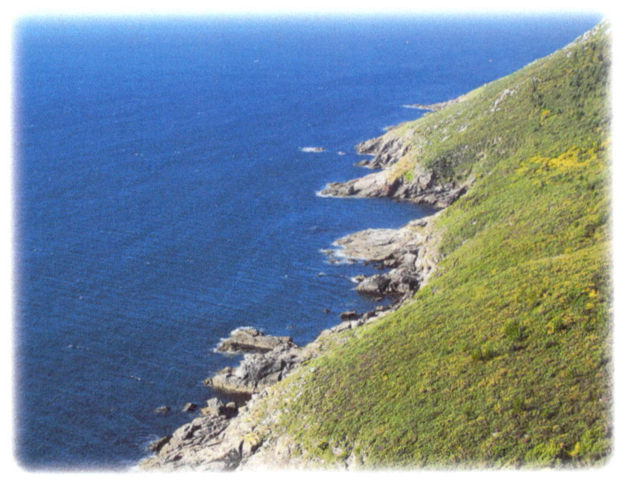

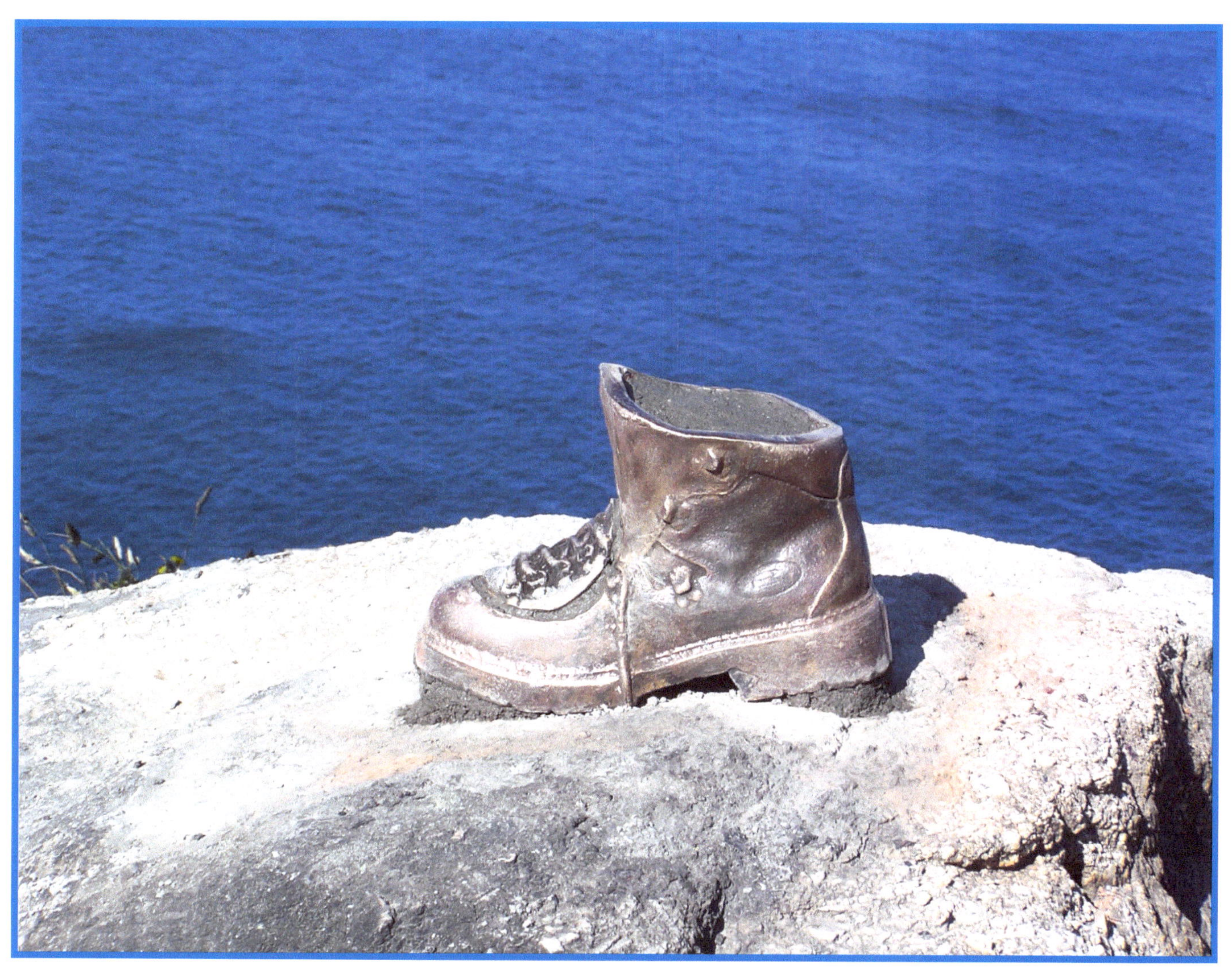

Bronze Pilgrim's boot-Cabo Finisterre

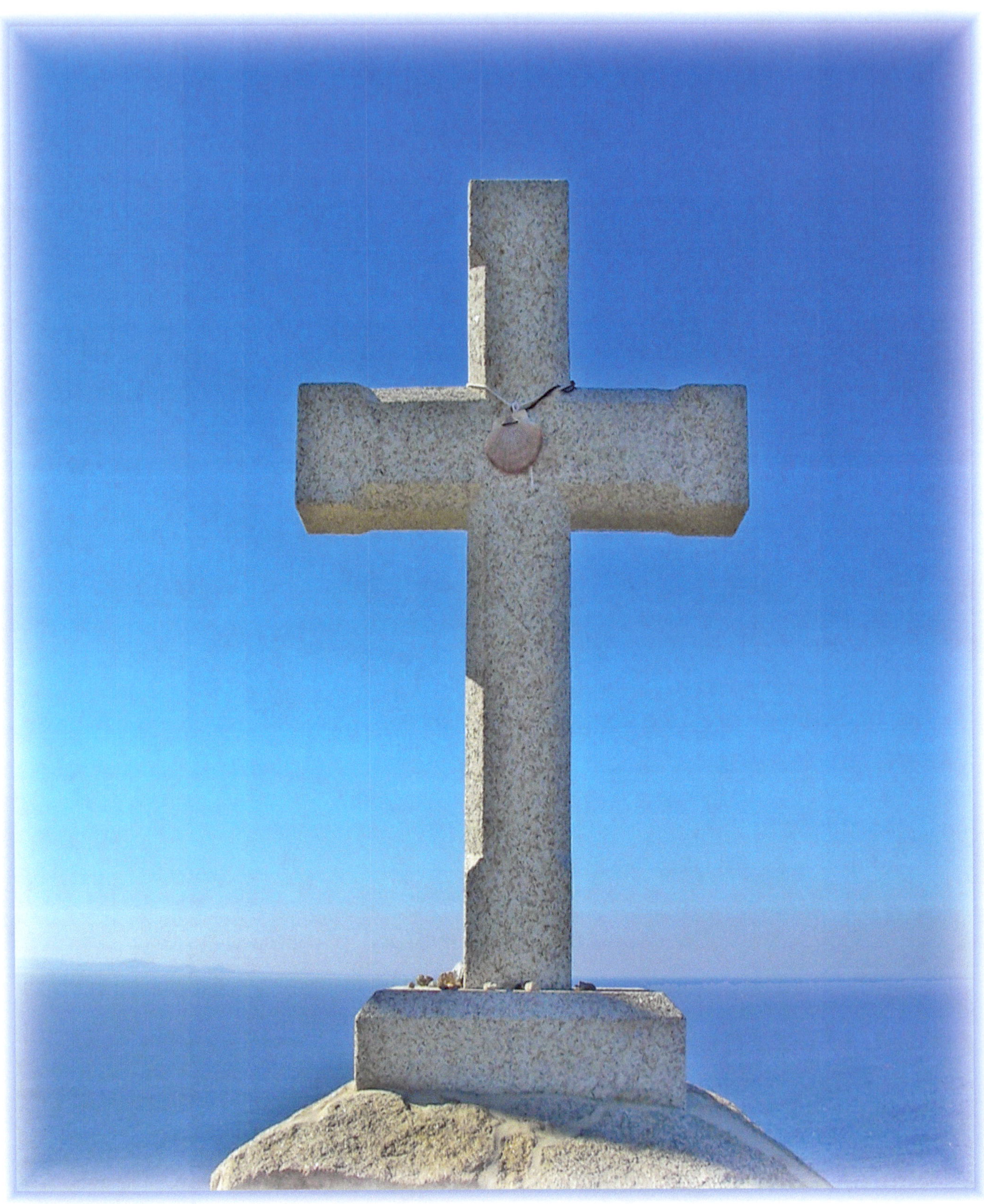

About the Authors

Jim Clem is a retired San Diego Police Detective. Eleanor is retired from America West Airlines. For several years they have been avid hikers and mountain climbers. They have hiked the Grand Canyon and Mt. Whitney (highest point in the lower 48 states) numerous times. In 1995 they climbed Mt. Kilimanjaro in Africa. The following year they hiked to the base camp of Mount Aconcagua in the Argentine Andes.

In 2003, they hiked 500 miles across Spain on the Camino de Santiago.

Their first book, Buen Camino-Hiking the Camino de Santiago is a day-to-day account of that adventure. They returned to the Camino in 2005. They live in Alpine, California.

Please visit their website at www.ourcamino.com

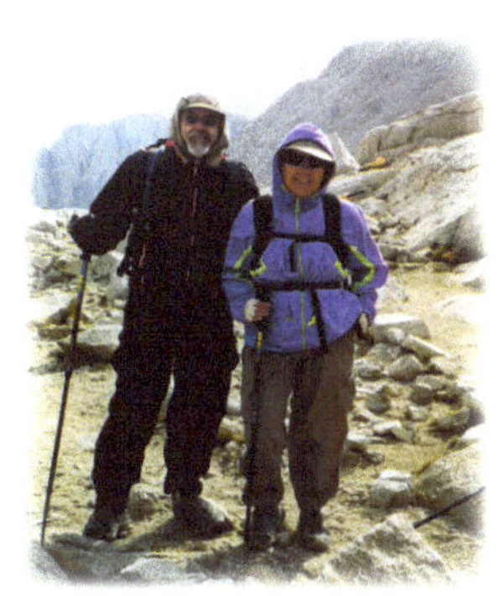

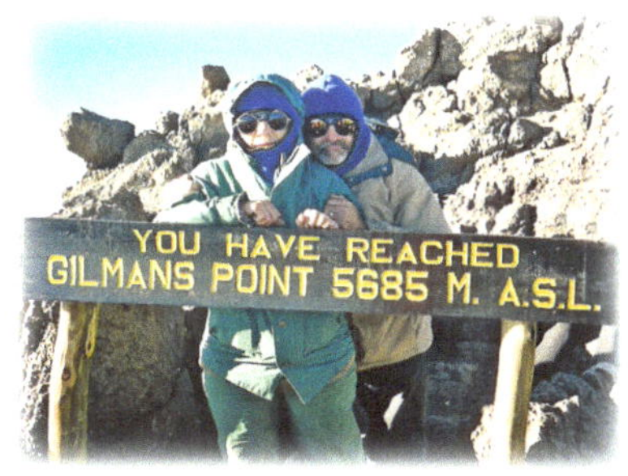

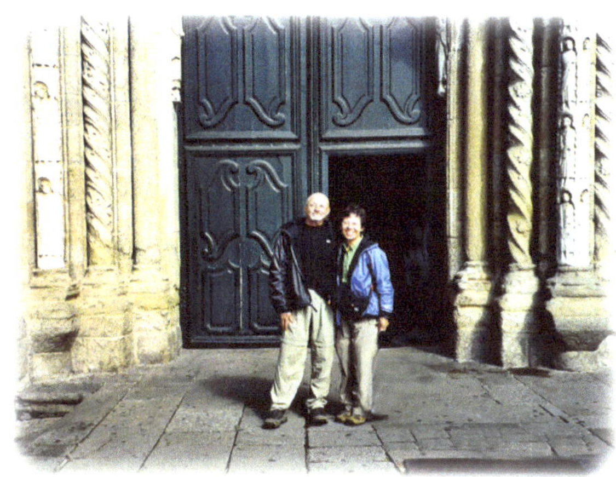

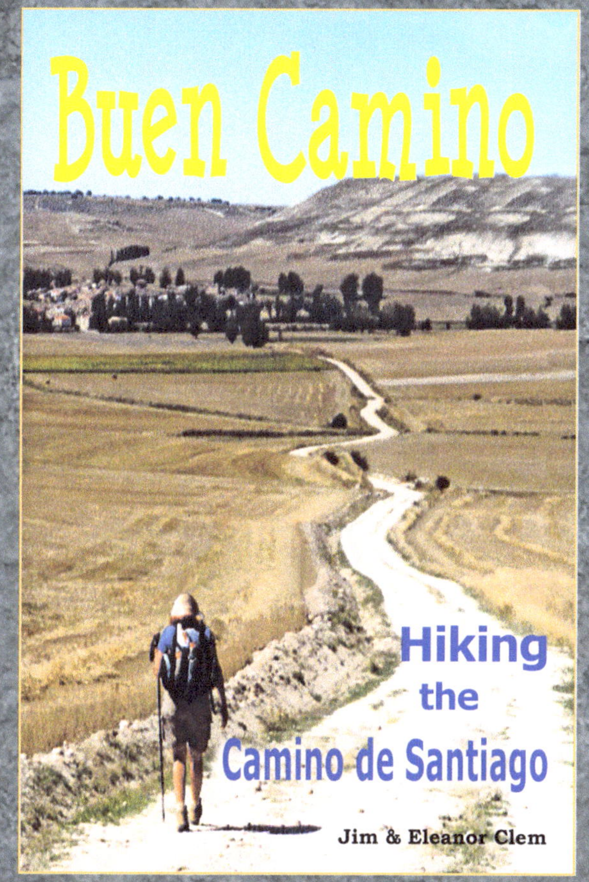

Buen Camino-Hiking the Camino de Santiago

by Jim & Eleanor Clem

ISBN # 978-0-9799628-0-6

Buen Camino-Hiking the Camino de Santiago is the day to day account of two modern day pilgrims, Jim and Eleanor Clem as they hike the Camino de Santiago. Over four mountain ranges, through big cities, rural areas, across the vast Meseta of central Spain, and through the green hills of Galicia, to their final destination, the Cathedral of Santiago de Compostela.

With over 160 photos, and a practical description of life on the trail, Buen Camino is a must read for anyone interested in the Camino de Santiago, long range hiking, or just a good adventure.

Buen Camino-Hiking the Camino de Santiago is available at amazon.com and most on-line book sellers. It can also be ordered from your local bookstore.

www.ingramcontent.com/pod-product-compliance
Lightning Source LLC
LaVergne TN
LVHW070126110826
845147LV00002B/194

* 9 7 8 0 9 7 9 9 6 2 8 1 3 *